Children of Alcoholics
CRITICAL PERSPECTIVES

The Guilford Substance Abuse Series
Howard T. Blane and Thomas R. Kosten, *Editors*

Children of Alcoholics
CRITICAL PERSPECTIVES

Edited by

MICHAEL WINDLE
Research Institute on Alcoholism
and State University of New York at Buffalo

JOHN S. SEARLES
University of Pennsylvania School of Medicine
and Veterans Administration Medical Center, Philadelphia

FOREWORD BY ROBERT A. ZUCKER

THE GUILFORD PRESS
New York   London

© 1990 The Guilford Press
A Division of Guilford Publications, Inc.
72 Spring Street, New York, NY 10012

Printed in the United States of America

This book is printed on acid-free paper.

Last digit is print number: 9 8 7 6 5 4 3 2 1

Library of Congress Cataloging-in-Publication Data

Children of alcoholics: critical perspectives / edited by Michael
   Windle and John S. Searles.
       p. cm.—(The Guilford substance abuse series)
   Includes bibliographical references.
   ISBN 0-89862-168-2
   1. Adult children of alcoholics—Mental health. 2. Adult children
of alcoholics—Psychology. 3. Alcoholism—Risk factors.
4. Psychotherapy. I. Windle, Michael T. II. Searles, John S.
(John Steven), 1946–   . III. Series.
[DNLM: 1. Alcoholism—psychology. 2. Child Development.
3. Family. 4. Parent–Child Relations. WM 274 C5364]
RC569.5.A29C45 1990
362.29'2—dc20
DNLM/DLC
for Library of Congress   89-23468
                                                          CIP

Contributors

Arthur W. K. Chan, Ph.D., Research Institute on Alcoholism, New York State Division of Alcoholism and Alcohol Abuse, Buffalo, New York

Theodore Jacob, Ph.D., Division of Child and Family Relations, University of Arizona, Tucson, Arizona

Susan B. Laird, B.S., Department of Psychiatry, University of Pittsburgh, School of Medicine, Pittsburgh, Pennsylvania

Howard B. Moss, M. D., Department of Psychiatry, University of Pittsburgh, School of Medicine, Pittsburgh, Pennsylvania

Marcia Russell, Ph.D., Research Institute on Alcoholism, New York State Division of Alcoholism and Alcohol Abuse, Buffalo, New York

John S. Searles, Ph.D., Department of Psychiatry, University of Pennsylvania School of Medicine, and Veterans Administration Medical Center, Philadelphia, Pennsylvania

Ruth Ann Seilhamer, Ph.D., Department of Psychiatry, Western Psychiatric Institute and Clinic, University of Pittsburgh, Pittsburgh, Pennsylvania

Ralph E. Tarter, Ph.D., Department of Psychiatry, University of Pittsburgh, School of Medicine, Pittsburgh, Pennsylvania

Carol N. Williams, Ph.D., Health and Addictions Research, Inc., and Alcohol & Drug Institute for Policy, Training and Research, Boston University, Boston, Massachusetts

Michael Windle, Ph.D., Research Institute on Alcoholism, New York State Division of Alcoholism and Alcohol Abuse, and Department of Psychology, State University of New York at Buffalo, Buffalo, New York

Acknowledgments

We would like to express our appreciation to Marguerite Saunders, Director of the New York State Division of Alcoholism and Alcohol Abuse, for her continued support of this project and others related to children of alcoholics. We are also indebted to Dr. Howard T. Blane, Director of the New York State Research Institute on Alcoholism, for stimulating the coeditors to embark upon this endeavor. Special thanks are extended to the contributors of this volume, who graciously accepted the difficult task of reviewing and evaluating a flourishing research literature. We believe that the fruits of their labor will contribute significantly to knowledge about children of alcoholics and provide a road map to future COA research. Cindy Russo and Carol Tixier were extremely helpful in typing carefully some of the chapters in this volume and in creating order out of chaos with regard to the correspondence associated with the book. Last, but not least, we are grateful to our wives, Rebecca and Maj, for their support and tolerance during this undertaking, and to Cody, who blessed us with his birth at the completion of the book—we have taken this as a good omen.

Michael Windle
John S. Searles

New Wave Interactionism: A Foreword

In 1972, Mark Keller, the dean of alcohololologists and long-time editor of the *Journal of Studies on Alcohol,* wrote a paper about alcoholism research in which he advanced the notion that whenever anyone isolated a characteristic that distinguished one group from another, further research with alcoholics would also show that they had more or less of it. In more recent times it has sometimes seemed as if the popular press and the children of alcoholics (COA) movement have taken Keller's Law to heart, and have noted a broad and indiscriminate array of COA characteristics, all of which, we are assured, are markers of this terrible scourge.

The scientific literature on the subject that has been available to counter these often ill-founded claims has been sparse in recent years, with a few exceptions. In an effort to keep this literature current, Windle and Searles originally set out to do an update review paper on the area. It is our good fortune that they came to the conclusion that the literature currently was too large and covered too many domains for the two of them to do adequate justice to it by themselves—hence the decision to move to this edited volume.

This book is of considerable practical significance. Its contributors review approximately a thousand papers, and the subject matter truly spans the biopsychosocial continuum. But the volume is especially important in another way. Both of the editors are seasoned alcohol researchers, but they are also comparatively junior members of the research establishment. Perhaps because of their being part of a younger scientific generational cohort, they bring to us a collection of perspectives that is clearly new wave interactionism at its best. The book's point of departure is biopsychosocial, but it is very fine-grained, and by being so it substantively expands this continuum. Virtually all of the contributors make significant efforts to synthesize across substantial portions of the biopsychosocial space in a way that earlier data would not allow, and that most earlier reviewers would have no awareness was important; and several of them have made significant efforts to embrace the entirety of this spectrum. What is especially noteworthy to me is the way these contributors have moved beyond simple notions of interactionism. There is here a genuine attempt, in a variety of different areas, to deal with the hierarchy of levels of alcohol problems, to begin to grapple with issues of across-domain salience and of integration of across-level data. There are other differences that I think also mark this new wave of synthesis. Rather than grouping studies by way of simplistic and ultimately etiologically irrelevant classifications, there is a conscious effort by all the authors to organize data by way of theory, albeit at different levels of specificity. And there is significant awareness that the entire COA field is one characterized by way of a developmental problem, *that of being a child of an alcoholic,* whether that be as child or as adult. The volume is exceptionally sensitive to developmental issues, and a life-span perspective clearly informs a number of the chapters.

At a broader level, in a workmanlike way this book addresses virtually all of the issues that have recently been identified in the Institute of Medicine's 1987 report on research needs in the alcohol field. To know that the volume's contributors reached this place substantially independently of the IOM project is both a mark of the work's sophistication as well as an indication that this field may be reaching a level of maturity it has not known before.

In closing this brief commentary, I want to repeat one of my favorite quotations from H. L. Mencken: "For every complex problem there is an easy answer . . . and it is wrong." The COA literature until now has more often than not been subject to easy answers. This volume sets the problem within the complex framework it deserves. In my view, it also is a reflection of a distinct and much-needed advance in level of conceptualization in the alcohol field about a topic of very central interest to so many of us, and to the public at large.

Robert A. Zucker
Michigan State University

Contents

Introduction and Overview: Salient Issues in the Children of Alcoholics Literature

JOHN S. SEARLES
MICHAEL WINDLE

The literature on children of alcoholics (COAs) can be conceptually divided into three distinct but somewhat complementary branches. First, there are the scientific reports that have wended their way through the standard publication process (submission, peer review, revision, resubmission) and appear in specialized professional journals such as the *Journal of Studies on Alcohol* and *Alcoholism: Clinical and Experimental Research.* This mechanism provides the opportunity for other scientists to judge methodological adequacy, scientific rigor, substantive significance, and practical application to the field the paper addresses. The system works to the extent that reports are evaluated scientifically, without personal bias. Examples of seemingly obtuse reviewers and editors who send papers to reviewers with diametrically opposite positions abound. Although the process is flawed, it functions as the enforcer of currently accepted scientific standards. This has the effect of maintaining rigor but occasionally impedes innovation. Perhaps the best known example of this is the difficulty that John Garcia had (and still has) in publishing his important work on conditioned toxicosis (bait shyness). Also, as we will demonstrate below, publication in a major journal does not automatically guarantee high-quality methodology and accurate interpretation of data.

Second, the scientific aspects have been loosely translated for lay consumption in the news media. Recently there has been a spate of popular press articles (major stories in *Time* and *Newsweek;* extended reports on network news programs) focusing on the difficulties encountered by children of alcoholic parents. These reports usually are highly selective and sometimes inadvertently slanted as a result of insufficient understanding of complex technical and methodological issues by the reporting staff. For example, at a recent professional conference Cloninger (1988) reported tentatively that alcoholics identified as Type 2 in his classification system may have difficulty with abstinence as a treatment goal. The newspaper account of the wide-ranging talk was headlined "Not all alco-

1

holics must abstain, professionals told" (Shealy, 1988). Often the press will focus on dramatic single case histories such as those reported by highly visible individuals (entertainers or politicians). While these accounts may evoke strong individual responses, they have scientific merit only to the extent that the circumstances are generalizable to other members of the population, a questionable assumption at best.

The third branch of the literature on children of alcoholic parents is derived from professionals in the clinical arena. Contributions from this group are often seen as the consensual scientific view because the authors frequently have advanced degrees that lend an aura of scientific respectability to the work. The books that result are typically based on a series of case reports as well as on the clinical impressions and professional expertise of the author. They are usually offered as adult self-help guides for persons who believe that their past or current psychological difficulties may be attributable, at least in part, to the psychic trauma of being reared by an alcoholic parent. This segment of the literature also suffers from generalizability problems as well as from a general lack of methodological rigor due to the often anecdotal and selective reporting techniques. A more serious deficiency is the overreliance on *post hoc* causal attributional analysis. That is, once the end state is identified (e.g., psychological distress or dysfunction) the articulation of a causal link between that end state and the parental alcoholism is accomplished. This strategy typically deemphasizes more proximal causal factors and stresses the primary significance of the effects of the alcohol-abusing parent. The immediate advantage of such an approach is an easily accessible, identifiable, and personally meaningful basis for the individual's difficulties, regardless of the validity of the causal relationship. It also has the effect of removing much of the responsibility from the individual for his or her own actions, feelings, and problems. Another problem in this area is the widely varying definition of what constitutes an alcohol-abusing parent. There are no standard criteria for a child of an alcoholic *or* for self-identifying one's parents as alcohol abusers. Again, such recognition and definition is often *post hoc* and may be dependent on the adult adjustment of the individual involved. Noncomparability of definitions of alcoholism across different reports is also a legitimate criticism and a vexing problem of the scientific literature.

Current clinical practice as exemplified by this third category has often been in conflict with the extant scientific literature over the interpretation of both theory and data. One reason for this is that good science requires experimental rigor at the expense of what sometimes appears to be ecological validity, while clinical data can be easily compromised with respect to empirical validity and reliability but retain substantial real-world meaning for specific individuals. Similarly, clinicians, and to some extent researchers, tend to ignore or reinterpret research findings that do not fit their theoretical orientation or personal world view, and researchers often dismiss clinical reports as uncontrolled or riddled with theoretical overinterpretation.

With respect to adult children of alcoholics (ACOAs), a cottage industry has evolved for counseling and "treatment" that has very limited scientific support. For example, there are few, if any, methodologically adequate studies evaluating the efficacy and/or durability of treatment for psychological problems as a consequence of being an ACOA.

There is the additional complication that no clinical syndrome has been identified that is distinct for ACOAs. Symptoms presumably linked to being an ACOA (such as low self-esteem, chronic depression, or difficulty in forming close personal relationships) are not uniquely associated with being a child of an alcohol-abusing parent. As Miller (1987) points out, however, contradictory data do not appear to be an obstacle for persons committed to the position that ACOAs exhibit a cohesive and distinctive clinical pattern. For example, some data have shown that adolescent sons of alcoholic fathers perform less well than controls on tests of cognitive and emotional functioning (e.g., Bennett, Wolin, & Reiss, 1988; Gabrielli & Mednick, 1983). However, both the target adolescents and controls consisting of adolescent sons of nonalcoholics typically score within the normal range for the test measures. That is, while there may be a nominal *relative* difference between groups, the *absolute* mean scores for each group are unremarkable, and sometimes both groups rank in the high normal range. This has also been found to be the case in neuropsychological and personality functioning (e.g., Tarter, Hegedus, Goldstein, Shelly, & Alterman, 1984). The etiological significance and behavioral implications of such findings, we believe, are at best unclear, although they are often interpreted as nascent indications of adult adjustment problems. Thus, despite the fact that children in both groups performed within the normal range of functioning, Bennett et al. (1988) state:

> On the basis of these analyses, we conclude that children from intact alcoholic families exhibit less successful functioning than children from nonalcoholic families, especially in the cognitive and emotional spheres. . . . We propose that alcoholic families are generally less successful in establishing a well-planned, stable, and meaningful family-ritual life than are nonalcoholic families and that lack of such a family environment is reflected in more problems among the children. (p. 189)

What this and similar studies fail to explicitly recognize is that *most individuals emerge from these environments relatively intact psychologically and emotionally,* and that there may be several complex factors independent of being a child of an alcoholic parent that could result in severe psychopathology. West and Prinz (1987) demonstrate that while a great deal of childhood psychopathology has been attributed to the stressful effects of parental alcoholism, a minority of children exposed to these effects actually exhibit clinically significant behaviors. Aldrich (1986) points out the hazards associated with predicting *any* future development and adjustment based on presumptive psychiatric diagnoses. He suggests that two factors combine to undermine the accuracy of prediction: accentuation of the functional significance of antecedent psychopathological states and minimization of individual capacity for personality change. We can add a third factor: underestimation of the importance of the conjoint effects of individual personality and associated idiosyncratic environmental pressures.

It should be clear that research reports and clinical evidence are often difficult to interpret and sometimes contradictory. Despite an intense research interest and obvious clinical importance of the COA area, there are few systematic reviews available to summarize past research results, guide future research planning, as well as to distill and clarify clinical findings. In fact, there are only two sources we have seen that are regularly cited: the review by Cotton (1979) and the report prepared for the Children of Alcoholics Foundation by Russell, Henderson, and Blume (1985) of the Research Institute on Alcoholism. The article by Cotton (1979) essentially established the fact that alcoholism runs in families and as such is the conceptual basis for almost every article that addresses the genetics of alcoholism.

The idea for this book evolved directly from the work of Russell et al. (1985). As originally planned, it was to be an update and expansion of the Russell et al. monograph. We felt that there had been an increase in the published literature since 1985 substantial enough to warrant another review, and more importantly, we thought that a critical assessment was necessary to organize and evaluate this conceptually and methodologically diverse literature. A systematic examination seemed particularly appropriate for the COA domain for several reasons. First, as mentioned above, research findings have sometimes been contradictory. For example, some studies have found that COAs exhibit increased body sway (static ataxia) compared with controls (e.g., Hill, Armstrong, Steinhauer, Baughman & Zubin, 1987) and others have found no difference between groups (e.g., Nagoshi & Wilson, 1987). Reconciliation of the results of these two studies may depend in part on a critical evaluation of their respective methodologies.

Second, there exists a considerable gap between research findings and clinical application. Clinical interventions have been developed and self-help groups have been formed to assist ACOAs despite the lack of research evidence supporting a clinical syndrome. Also, even though most research subjects have been men, most of the ACOAs seeking help are women. This is important because there may be different etiological pathways for male and female alcoholism as well as different subtypes within each sex (Bohman, Sigvardsson, & Cloninger, 1981; Cloninger, Bohman, & Sigvardsson, 1981). In addition, men and women may be differentially sensitive to the effects of living with an alcoholic parent.

Finally, the COA area is beginning to attract attention from social policy decision makers such as congressional committees, private employee assistance programs, and the judiciary. For example, the United States Supreme Court recently ruled that two veterans who said they were debilitated for several years by the "disease of alcoholism" did not qualify for an extension of their educational benefits; the Veterans Administration considers alcoholism a consequence of willful misbehavior. Although the Court explicitly did not rule on whether alcoholism is or is not a disease (as some thought it might), scientific reports on the genetics of alcoholism were used to support the veterans' claim that alcoholism is a medically definable disease. Given the dominant position that the disease model has in the United States, it quite likely came as a surprise to the general public that the alcoholism-as-a-disease paridigm is not the unanimous opinion of the scientific community. Many prominent scientists maintain that alcoholism is more of a behavioral than a medical problem. Fingarette (1988) has recently published a book that presents the nondisease position in easily understandable, nonscientific language. Because the nondisease position has consequences for COAs that are different from those of the disease model, it is important to reconcile their disparate implications. This is especially significant if there are distinct types of alcoholism, some that fit the disease model, some that are behaviorally induced, and still others that may be a hybrid of both. If government policy and corporate strategy are to be effective, they should be based on a rational evaluation of extant research.

We quickly realized that a pertinent and thorough critical review of this broad, multiperspective body of work was beyond the capabilities of one or two individuals. We also felt that the imposition of a single point of view in a comprehensive review of this important literature would be inappropriate. Therefore, we opted for an edited volume with contributions from professionals with expertise at different levels of analysis, thus capitalizing on their knowledge of salient research issues and prominent methodological approaches. We have identified seven substantive areas that provide a broad spectrum of methodological and analytical techniques as well as necessary and sufficient content for a comprehensive review: epidemiology, biochemical markers, neuropsychology and neurophysiology, behavior genetics, temperament and personality, family factors, and prevention and treatment of psychopathology (including alcoholism and substance abuse) associated with being COAs or ACOAs. Coverage extends from the molecular through the family level and includes information relevant to prevention and treatment. We asked each of the authors to be guided by the three major objectives of this book:

1. Assess critically substantive findings of the COA literature in relation to the quality of the methodologies employed.
2. Develop recommendations concerning scientific approaches and methodologies designed to improve research.
3. Identify issues concerning COAs that have been understudied and merit increased research attention.

It is anticipated that the range of literature reviewed will stimulate the interest of both researchers and clinicians and that it will contribute to a better understanding of how each group conceptualizes the COA field. The ultimate goal is to provide a clear, integrative representation of research findings, suggestions for future research, and an enhanced basis for the translation of research results into clinical applications.

Each chapter is intended to stand alone as an independent review of a substantive area. However, several of the content domains are not mutually exclusive, resulting in the interpretation of the same literature from slightly different perspectives. Since not all the authors come to the same conclusions, this emphasizes the controversial nature of several of the topics discussed.

Chapter 2, by Marcia Russell, reviews epidemiological studies pertinent to the prevalence of alcoholism and alcohol abuse among COAs. Several method-ological issues are presented that may influence our current estimates of preva-lence, including concerns about sample representativeness in extant studies and the strengths and limitations of alternative ways of assessing both alcoholism and family history of alcoholism. With respect to the assessment of alcoholism, the definition of alcohol abuse and dependence is a crucial issue in the alcoholism field in general and in the COA area in particular because rates of parental alcoholism (and thus the prevalence of COAs) vary as a function of the strictness of the criteria employed. Additional factors influencing estimates of alcoholism among COAs are also addressed, such as assortive mating, alcoholic subtypes, and secular trends. The prevalence of alcohol abuse and alcoholism among COAs is then provided for adoptee, clinical, and community sample studies. Finally, research relevant to fetal alcohol syndrome and its relation to COAs is reviewed.

In Chapter 3, Arthur W. K. Chan discusses biological markers for alcohol-ism. He presents a general introduction to the area and discusses conventional and potential biochemical markers. He then reviews biochemical studies involv-ing COAs, identifying markers such as prolactin, cortisol, and acetaldehyde that differ between COAs and nonCOAs in degree of responsivity following an ethanol challenge. The implications of this research for prevention, diagnosis, and treatment of alcoholism are elaborated and further research directions are proposed.

Ralph E. Tarter, Susan B. Laird, and Howard B. Moss in Chapter 4 review and critique the research literature associated with neuropsychological deficits among alcoholics in general and among COAs in particular. The authors exam-ine a broad range of research including studies of intellectual development, verbal information processing, planning and abstracting ability, and educational achievement. In addition, they review and critique neurophysiological studies such as event-related brain protentials in COAs—an area of intense current research interest. Tarter et al. also present a neuropsychological theory of alcoholism vulnerability that seeks to explain the neurobehavioral correlates of Cloninger's (1988) Type 2, male-limited alcoholics.

In Chapter 5, John S. Searles assesses research that converges on a genetic basis for the etiology of alcoholism. Substantial research resources are currently being channeled into this area, due in large part to the findings of the Swedish Adoption Study (Cloninger et al., 1981; Bohman et al., 1981) and further work by Cloninger (1988) on Type 1 and Type 2 alcoholics. The quantitative tech-niques used in these studies and more recent multivariate, structural equation modeling procedures are examined. Searles also relates theoretical notions in behavioral genetics such as gene × environment interaction and gene–environment correlation to current COA conceptualizations, and he discusses the implications of genetic and environmental factors, singly and in combination, in the development of alcohol abuse.

Michael Windle reviews and critiques the COA literature linking temperamental and personality factors with alcoholism in Chapter 6. The behavioral expression of early-developing temperamental traits such as hyperactivity, distractability, high activity level, and aggression in childhood have been to varying degrees associated with adolescent and adult manifestations of alcohol abuse. He discusses the research that suggests these temperamental features function as vulnerability factors that may predispose individuals toward alcoholism. In addition, he reviews the evidence that points to personality factors such as high sensation seeking, external locus of control, and low self-esteem as significant in the development of alcoholism. Finally, he examines the methodological issues (longitudinal research design and alternative methods of measurement, for instance) that need to be addressed to more fully delineate the functional role of temperament and personality traits with respect to alcoholism.

Chapter 7, by Ruth Ann Seilhamer and Theodore Jacob, focuses on the role of family context in the development of alcoholism. They review the literature pertinent to problematic outcomes (e.g., child abuse and neglect, neurological deficits, psychosomatic complaints) of COAs and familial moderators of such outcomes (e.g., number of family stressors, psychiatric disturbance in the nonalcoholic parent). Influenced by the "life history model" of Steinglass (1980), the authors use a family behavioral systems framework to discuss aspects of the family home environment that influence alternative interactional styles with regard to parent relations and parent–child relations. Several studies by Jacob and colleagues are reviewed that indicate drinking style (for instance, steady versus episodic) is influential in identifying alternative family interactional patterns, which are in turn influential in determining alcoholic risk among COAs.

Chapter 8, by Carol N. Williams, focuses on literature relevant to the prevention and treatment of alcohol abuse among COAs. With respect to prevention, numerous resources and programs have been utilized, including peer education, bibliotherapy, school instruction, and group psychotherapy. Treatment approaches have been largely influenced by family systems theory, and alternative techniques have emphasized the coherent functioning or dysfunctioning of the family as a unit. With regard to the relative effectiveness of alternative prevention methods, little empirical research has been conducted with COA samples. This chapter identifies some of the major issues to consider in designing evaluation research pertinent to the prevention and treatment of COA alcohol abuse.

Our final chapter provides an integrative summary of the previous chapters. Although each of the substantive chapters provides a review and an evaluation of research for particular domains, seven themes emerged across two or more of the chapters. These themes are identified and discussed with regard to their potential inclusion and significance in future COA research. A life-span developmental perspective was used to organize and blend the material presented in the separate chapters, providing a means of relating material from different substantive domains. This should serve both to clarify the interrelatedness of seemingly diverse areas of research and stimulate thought for subsequent investigations. Suggestions for future research directions are summarized, along with recommendations for the use of alternative methodological approaches.

REFERENCES

Aldrich, C. K. (1986). The clouded crystal ball: A 35 year follow-up of psychiatrists' predictions. *American Journal of Psychiatry, 143,* 45–49.

Bennett, L. A., Wolin, S. J., & Reiss, D. (1988). Cognitive, behavioral, and emotional problems among school-age children of alcoholic parents. *American Journal of Psychiatry, 145,* 185–190.

Bohman, M., Sigvardsson, S., & Cloninger, C. R. (1981). Maternal inheritance of alcohol abuse: Cross fostering analysis of adopted women. *Archives of General Psychiatry, 38,* 965–969.

Cloninger, C. R. (1988, June). *Types of alcoholism.* Paper presented at the annual meeting of the Research Society on Alcoholism, Wild Dunes, SC.

Cloninger, C. R., Bohman, M., & Sigvardsson, S. (1981). Inheritance of alcohol abuse: Cross fostering analysis of adopted men. *Archives of General Psychiatry, 38,* 861–868.

Cotton, N. S. (1979). The familial incidence of alcoholism. *Journal of Studies on Alcohol, 40,* 89–116.

Fingarette, H. (1988). *Heavy drinking: The myth of alcoholism as a disease.* Berkeley: University of California Press.

Gabrielli, W. F., Jr., Mednick, S. A. (1983). Intellectual performance in children of alcoholics. *Journal of Nervous and Mental Diseases, 171,* 444–447.

Hill, S. Y., Armstrong, J., Steinhauer, S. R., Baughman, T., & Zubin, J. (1987). Static ataxia as a psychobiological marker for alcoholism. *Alcoholism: Clinical and Experimental Research, 11,* 345–348.

Miller, W. R. (1987). Adult cousins of alcoholics. *Bulletin of Psychologists in Addictive Behaviors, 1,* 74–76.

Nagoshi, C. T., & Wilson, J. R. (1987). Influence of family alcoholism history on alcohol metabolism, sensitivity, and tolerance. *Alcoholism: Clinical and Experimental Research, 11,* 392–398.

Russell, M., Henderson, C., & Blume, S. B. (1985). *Children of alcoholics: A review of the literature.* New York: Children of Alcoholics Foundation, Inc.

Shealy, H. J. (1988, June 3). Not all alcoholics must abstain, professionals told. *The Charleston Evening Post,* p. 1b.

Steinglass, P. (1980). A life history model of the alcoholic family. *Family Process, 19,* 211–226.

Tarter, R. E., Hegedus, A. M., Goldstein, G., Shelly, C., & Alterman, A. I. (1984). Adolescent sons of alcoholics: Neuropsychological and personality characteristics. *Alcoholism: Clinical and Experimental Research, 8,* 216–222.

West, M. O., & Prinz, R. J. (1987). Parental alcoholism and childhood psychopathology. *Psychological Bulletin, 102,* 204–218.

CHAPTER TWO

Prevalence of Alcoholism among Children of Alcoholics

MARCIA RUSSELL

The tendency for alcoholism to occur more frequently in some families than in others has long been recognized. Such familial aggregation has been attributed to heredity, to environment, and more recently, to an interaction between the two. Currently, there is a great deal of interest in developing a better understanding of the magnitude of risk associated with familial alcoholism and how this risk is transmitted. Accurate estimates of the prevalence of alcoholism among children of alcoholics (cases) compared with that among children of nonalcoholics (controls) are central to both of these issues. The purpose of this chapter is to provide a critical review of the data on which such prevalence estimates have been based.

Prevalence estimates are influenced by methodological issues affecting reliability and validity, and also by factors other than parental alcoholism that may affect the incidence of alcoholism. The potential range of variability is illustrated by Mulford's (1982) finding that estimates of alcoholic prevalence for the United States range from approximately 2% to 50% or more of the drinkers. Before presenting data on alcoholism among children of alcoholics, the literature on factors that may influence prevalence estimates is reviewed. This will put the data on prevalence into perspective and provide a useful framework for evaluating individual studies as they are described.

In addition to reviewing findings from published data, new findings from a biracial community study are presented. Finally, the overlap between research on the children of alcoholics and the fetal alcohol syndrome is discussed.

FACTORS INFLUENCING PREVALENCE ESTIMATES

Generalizability and reliability are methodological issues of importance in evaluating alcoholism prevalence estimates. These concern the representativeness of samples studied and the definition of alcoholics. For example, many studies depend on clinical samples; however, the majority of alcoholics never enter treatment (Vaillant, 1983). Clinical samples are not only unrepresentative of untreated alcoholics, but differing admission policies and program characteristics produce clinical samples that vary markedly in sociodemographic makeup and in the type and stage of alcoholism seen. Furthermore, the diagnostic criteria and assessment techniques used to define alcoholism differ widely across studies. The potential influences of sample representativeness and diagnostic criteria are discussed below.

Representativeness of Samples

The severity of alcoholism in a study sample can affect generalizability. Alcoholic inpatients, often the source of subjects for studies on children of alcoholics, may represent the extreme end of a continuum reflecting the severity of the disorder (Cotton, 1979). Therefore, a major criticism of studies based on clinical populations is that they may severely overestimate risk of alcoholism in children of alcoholics (Heller, Sher, & Benson, 1982). The tendency to overestimate risk is related to ascertainment bias, confounding, and lack of healthy controls. The fact that either children or their parents are in treatment or have come to the attention of social service or correctional agencies probably biases sample selection toward more severe alcoholism. As will be demonstrated, severe paternal alcoholism is associated with a high prevalence of moderate alcoholism among sons and no excess of alcoholism among daughters (Cloninger, Bohman, & Sigvardsson, 1981). Accordingly, samples having large numbers of severely alcoholic fathers may overestimate alcoholism in their sons and underestimate it in their daughters. In addition, confounding may lead to prevalence overestimates if severe alcoholism is associated with other factors likely to increase alcoholism among offspring, such as poverty, unemployment, family conflict, divorce, and social alienation. Most studies focus on maladjustment in children and fail to follow up healthy offspring. For example, research based on samples of alcoholics who are questioned about alcoholism in their parents provides no information on offspring of alcoholics who do not become alcoholic.

Other mental disorders concomitant with alcoholism can also influence sample representativeness. Alcoholism among children of alcoholics is often compared with that among children of patients having other psychiatric disorders in order to control for the possibility that elevated rates of alcoholism in the offspring are produced by parental psychiatric disorders in general, rather than by parental alcoholism in particular. In making such comparisons, it is important to screen for alcoholism and other psychiatric disorders in both cases and controls.

Alcoholism is associated with a number of other psychiatric disorders, notably depression and sociopathy. These associations have been widely observed, both in clinical settings (e.g., Weissman & Myers, 1980; Schuckit,

1973) and in community surveys (Boyd et al., 1984). Having more than one mental illness tends to increase the likelihood that an individual will enter treatment. This suggests that a number of patients in psychiatric control groups may have concomitant alcoholism, secondary to their primary diagnosis. This would tend to be associated with higher than expected rates of alcoholism in their offspring based on their primary psychiatric diagnosis alone, and it would minimize the difference in alcoholism rates between their children and children of alcoholics. Similarly, if alcoholism rates were higher in children whose parents were alcoholic with a concomitant secondary psychiatric diagnosis, alcoholism rates in offspring could be exaggerated if the influence of the secondary psychiatric diagnosis is not taken into consideration. This illustrates the importance of screening psychiatric populations for alcoholism and screening alcoholics for associated psychiatric diagnoses before undertaking comparative studies.

Age at alcoholism diagnosis is another possible source of error. The period of vulnerability to alcoholism ranges from late adolescence through middle age, requiring lengthy observation for total ascertainment of all potential cases. The prevalence of alcoholism in children of alcoholics and their parents can be underestimated if it is based on data that do not cover the entire period during which they are vulnerable.

Race and sex must also be considered. Most of the data on alcoholism in children of alcoholics pertain to white males and may not apply equally well to females and other racial groups. In addition to the fact that females and minorities have been less studied than white males, there may be sex-related reporting biases that could influence the findings on alcoholism in children of alcoholics. In a review of data from studies on children of alcoholics in treatment, Cotton (1979) found a higher incidence of alcoholism among the relatives of female alcoholics than among the relatives of male alcoholics. In addition, data from the 1979 national survey on drinking in the United States indicated that females were more likely than males to report parental alcoholism, whether or not they themselves were problem drinkers (Midanik, 1983). Midanik (1983) suggested that alcoholic women may report more alcoholism in their relatives because the drinking behavior of women may be more influenced by the home environment, and/or it may be necessary to have a more severe family history of alcoholism for females to manifest alcohol problems. An alternative explanation, one consistent with the fact that nonalcoholic women also report more alcoholism among their relatives, is that women may use a less restrictive definition of "alcoholic" or "problem drinker" in classifying their parents, especially their fathers.

A meta-analysis of alcoholism in sons and daughters of alcoholics according to the sex of the alcoholic parent concluded that both male and female alcoholic patients more frequently come from homes in which the father, rather than the mother, is alcoholic, even when sex differences in alcoholism prevalence are taken into account (Pollock, Schneider, Gabrielli, & Goodwin, 1987). In addition, it was reported that female offspring of alcoholic mothers show alcoholism rates that are elevated relative to those expected in the general population, but that male offspring of alcoholic mothers do not. Although this meta-analysis considered sex differences in alcoholism prevalence, it is not clear that assortative mating (see below) was taken into account, even though it is likely to influence the prevalence of alcoholism among children from alcoholic families.

Diagnostic Criteria and Prevalence Estimates

Accurate prevalence estimates depend on accurate diagnosis of alcoholism in parents and their children. Accurate diagnosis is complicated by the fact that the majority of alcoholics never enter treatment for alcoholism (Weisner, 1987). Accordingly, diagnoses in studies of familial alcoholism are based on several types of data: records of alcoholism treatment, records of alcohol-related problems, reports of alcohol-related problems by relatives or some other person, and self-reports of alcohol-related problems or treatment for alcoholism. Confidence in the accuracy of diagnosis varies according to the source of the data on which it is based. For example, persons treated for alcoholism are more likely to be alcoholic than those having only a record of alcohol-related problems. Relatives are less likely to report sufficient information on respondents' alcohol-related problems to permit a diagnosis of alcoholism than respondents themselves (Thompson, Orvaschel, Prusoff, & Kidd, 1982).

Even when diagnoses are based on the same type of data, the data themselves may vary. Criteria for admission to alcoholism treatment programs and records of alcohol-related problems have varied over time, from country to country, and between types of facilities. Although there have been attempts in the United States to develop standardized diagnostic survey instruments for use with respondents (Robins, Helzer, Croughan, Williams, & Spitzer, 1981) and their relatives (Andreasen, Endicott, Spitzer, & Winokur, 1977), currently available studies vary considerably with respect to the survey instruments and interviewing techniques employed.

Thus, there are three ways in which diagnostic criteria used to define alcoholism may differ from study to study: The criteria themselves may differ, the source of the data used to determine whether the criteria are met may differ, and operationalization of criteria measurement may differ. Because of the long observation period necessary to diagnose alcoholism in two generations, diagnostic criteria used to define alcoholism in parents and offspring may differ within studies as well as between studies.

Problems in establishing reliable and thorough diagnostic procedures are compounded by the nature of the research question, dealing as it does with two generations. On the one hand, there is a tendency for parental alcoholism to be diagnosed retrospectively, which may be unreliable because of memory problems and/or incomplete or inaccurate records. On the other hand, although it may be more feasible to diagnose alcoholism in offspring prospectively, using a standard protocol, lengthy study periods are required to allow all offspring to pass completely through age of risk.

The accuracy of data regarding the presence or absence of alcoholism in relatives of cases and controls is crucial to the scientific value of family–genetic studies of alcoholism and to prevalence estimates of alcoholism in children of alcoholics. There are two interview methods available for obtaining information on alcoholism. One, the *family study method,* involves the direct interview of all available first-degree relatives (parents, siblings, and offspring) regarding their own status with respect to alcoholism. Data obtained directly from the concerned individual are considered more precise and accurate than data provided by others, and the family study method is the preferred technique in determining family prevalence of alcoholism. However, the *family history technique,* interviewing patients or relatives about alcoholism in any of their first-degree relatives, is faster, simpler, and less expensive. In the case of family members who cannot be interviewed, because of death, ill health, migration, or refusal to participate, for instance), family history data may be the only information available.

Studies comparing alcoholism diagnoses based on the family history method with those based on direct interview have found that subjects were much better at identifying relatives who were not alcoholic than they were at identifying those who were, producing few false positives, but rather more false negatives (Andreasen et al., 1977; Thompson et al., 1982; Rimmer & Chambers, 1969). However, Thompson et al. (1982) found that some relatives were better than others at correctly identifying alcoholism. Compared with alcoholism diagnoses based on direct interviews with subjects themselves, diagnoses of alcoholism based on family histories provided by offspring agreed 57% of the time ($n = 14$), whereas spouse data agreed only 45% of the time ($n = 20$), sibling data 30% of the time ($n = 47$), and parent data 24% of the time ($n = 43$). Having data from both a parent and a sibling boosted the proportions of alcoholics correctly identified from 25% and 28%, respectively, to 41% ($n = 32$). There was no increase in correct identification associated with having data from both spouse (45%) and offspring (55%), however, since only 55% of the alcoholics were diagnosed ($n = 11$). Although relatives failed to diagnose alcoholism in many subjects who were determined to be alcoholic by direct interview, almost all subjects who were diagnosed by their relatives were also found to be alcoholic on direct interview. All the latter comparisons were in the 95% to 99% range. A cautionary note is that some of these analyses are based on rather small numbers.

Thompson et al. (1982) note that although the family history method is likely to yield an underestimate of the risk of alcoholism in families, it may be useful in comparing the relative magnitude of risk for various subgroups (for instance, the risk of alcoholism in families of alcoholics compared with that in families of nonalcoholics), provided that the same proportion of affected relatives is misclassified in both of the groups being compared. To ensure that misclassification operates equally in the comparison groups, it is recommended that relatives be classified according to the source(s) from which diagnostic information was available and that this classification be treated as a covariate for inclusion in multivariate analyses of the study results.

Finally, Thompson et al. (1982) point out that the lack of sensitivity associated with the family history method dictates the use of less stringent criteria in making a diagnosis of alcoholism based on family history information than in making a similar diagnosis based on direct interview data. This is consistent with the approach taken by Andreasen et al. (1977). They developed an instrument, the Family History–Research Diagnostic Criteria (FH–RDC), that describes specific operational criteria for determining a diagnosis on the basis of information obtained by the family history method, with the goal of improving reliability. Since the family history method usually provides less specific descriptive data, less stringent criteria were required to make a diagnosis using the FH–RDC than would be required in a direct interview. Teams of psychiatrists and other professional raters in four major psychiatric centers evaluated 75 case vignettes for selected diagnoses based on the FH–RDC, achieving a high degree of interrater agreement, with κ coefficients greater than .90. An agreement coefficient of .96 was obtained for 76 diagnosed alcoholics among 1,020 subjects interviewed jointly by two interviewers (Andreasen et al., 1977).

A recent study by Sher and Descutner (1986) investigated multiple offspring reports of paternal drinking behavior via a short version of the Michigan Alcoholism Screening Test (MAST). Kappa coefficients ranged from .72 to .79 for 88 sibling pairs, which compared favorably with the κ value (.72) for a global judgment in response to the question, "Do you think your father is (was) an alcoholic?" This implies that this single-item measure is as reliable as the short MAST multiple-item measure. The intraclass correlation coefficient used to estimate intersibling reliability of the total score was .85. These measures of reliability are within the acceptable range, indicating that siblings tend to agree in their perception of their father's alcoholic status. However, at the highest value for κ (.79), 81 of the siblings agreed that their fathers were not alcoholic, four agreed that he was, and two disagreed. Thus, disagreements constitute a small proportion of the nonalcoholics, but a relatively large proportion of the alcoholics. This study did not include objective measures of parental alcoholism against which the perception of offspring could be evaluated. Mothers' alcoholism was investigated, but the prevalence rates were too low to warrant analysis.

A validity study using 49 parent–adult offspring pairs found that parent and offspring agreed on their assessment of a negative family history of alcoholism in 42 cases. However, they agreed on a positive family history in only two cases, and they disagreed in five cases, two in which the offspring, but not the parent, reported a positive history, and three in which the parent, but not the offspring, reported a positive history (O'Malley, Carey, & Maisto, 1986). The authors recommended that offspring who report a positive family history of alcoholism be considered at high risk, even if their parents deny alcohol problems. Although no data were presented to support this recommendation, it was reasoned that offspring have no motive to falsely report parental alcoholism, and that minimization of such problems was more to be expected, by both offspring and parents. This study demonstrates the importance of obtaining data from both parents and offspring whenever possible. If data from offspring only were available, only four of the seven would have been identified as being at high risk; whereas, if data from parents only were available, only five of the seven would have been identified. Failure to correctly identify alcoholic relatives would tend to minimize estimates of familial transmission in studies of the etiology of alcoholism.

In sum, there appears to be a general consensus that investigators should feel justified in relying on subjects' reports of drinking problems in family members. However, reports that parents do not have drinking problems warrant less confidence. It has also been suggested that maternal alcoholism may be underestimated more than paternal because women may be more likely to try to conceal their drinking than men (Sher & Descutner, 1986). It should be noted that these validity studies are based on small numbers of family history positive subjects and that the findings may not be stable.

Genetic Factors Influencing Prevalence Estimates

Recent research in adopted children of alcoholics indicates that the heritability of alcoholism varies according to *type of parental alcoholism* (Cloninger et al., 1981). This suggests that the prevalence of alcoholism among children in a given sample will be influenced by the distribution of alcoholic subtypes among their parents. To the extent that the distribution of alcoholic subtypes differs across studies, the prevalence of alcoholism among children of alcoholics may also be expected to differ. Few studies have taken this factor into account.

The tendency for women with alcoholic fathers to marry alcoholics has been observed repeatedly, as has the tendency for alcoholic women to marry alcoholic men (Hall, Hesselbrock, & Stabenau, 1983a, 1983b). Studies of alcoholism among children of alcoholics have not always taken into consideration alcohol abuse in both parents. However, such *assortative mating* is likely to increase the prevalence of alcoholism in children of alcoholics because they may inherit a predisposition toward alcoholism from the maternal side of the family in addition to the paternal, and because the alcohologenic nature of the rearing environment may also be increased. For example, children with two alcoholic parents were found to be more likely than children with one alcoholic parent (who were more likely than children with nonalcoholic parents) to be younger when first intoxicated, to have more pretreatment behavioral problems, and to proceed more rapidly from first intoxication to alcoholism treatment (McKenna & Pickens, 1981). However, measures of pretreatment drinking, the severity of drinking at the time of admission, and treatment outcome did not differ significantly according to number of alcoholic parents.

Environmental Factors

Alcoholism tends to be *more prevalent in lower than in higher socioeconomic classes*. This is a potential source of bias if one is trying to distinguish between genetic and environmental risk factors associated with being the child of an alcoholic. For example, many alcoholic treatment populations draw clients disproportionately from the lower socioeconomic classes. If, however, comparison groups of nonalcoholics contain more individuals with higher socioeconomic status, artificially inflated rates of alcoholism may be seen in children of alcoholics simply because they share their parents' lower socioeconomic status (nongenetic familial transmission).

Even in adoption studies, which are designed to minimize children's exposure to an alcoholic environment, selective placement, or matching of adoptive and biological families on ethnicity, religion, and socioeconomic status, may result in adopted children of alcoholic biological parents being exposed to an environment more conducive to the development of alcoholism than that experienced by controls (Murray, Clifford, & Gurling, 1983). Thus, studies must consider the extent to which alcoholism rates are influenced by these factors before observed differences in the prevalence of alcoholism among offspring are attributed to parental alcoholism.

Among the relatively few researchers who have addressed this issue, one group found that postnatal environment affected the severity of alcoholism experienced by sons of alcoholics (Cloninger et al., 1981) and another did not (Nylander & Rydelius, 1982). The latter utilized public records to conduct case control studies of juvenile asocial behavior, criminal behavior, and indications of addiction, among children of alcoholic fathers having high and low socioeconomic status (Nylander, 1960; Nylander & Rydelius, 1982; Rydelius, 1981). Data from a biracial community survey testing for an interaction between parental alcoholism and socioeconomic status will be presented later in this chapter.

Secular trends are another environmental factor affecting estimates of the prevalence of alcoholism. A landmark epidemiological study of mental disorders, the Epidemiological Catchment Area Study (ECA), which was conducted at five sites in the United States, found that the lifetime prevalence of alcohol abuse and dependence was higher at younger (less than 44 years) than at older ages (Robins et al., 1984). Similarly, studies of alcoholism among relatives of alcoholics found that recently born cohorts had increased expected lifetime prevalences of alcoholism and decreased ages of onset, when compared with older cohorts (Reich, Cloninger, VanEerdewegh, Rice, & Mullaney, 1988). Accordingly, methods were developed to take changing trends in the prevalence of alcoholism into consideration when analyzing the influence of parental alcoholism on alcoholism in offspring (Reich et al., 1988). It was found that "transmissibilities were greatest in the youngest cohorts . . . and the influence of parental transmissible factors was greater than that expected for polygenic transmission, strongly suggesting the presence of intrafamilial nongenetic familial transmission between generations" (Reich et al., 1988, p. 458).

Most other studies have not taken secular changes in the prevalence of alcoholism into account when examining the relationship between parental alcoholism and alcoholism in offspring. Clearly, current expansion of the alcoholism treatment system to include individuals in the earlier stages of alcoholism will change the nature of the treatment population, as well as its size, and may influence these relationships.

STUDIES OF ALCOHOLISM PREVALENCE

References to the prevalence of familial alcoholism most often state that there is a fourfold excess of alcoholism among children of alcoholics. Frequently cited in support of this statement are studies of alcoholism among children of alcoholics who were adopted in infancy by nonrelatives (Bohman, Sigvardsson, & Cloninger, 1981; Cloninger et al., 1981; Goodwin, Schulsinger, Hermansen, Guze, & Winokur, 1973). This methodology most successfully separates environmental from genetic influences on the etiology of alcoholism in children of alcoholics (Searles, 1988). Another approach has been to investigate the prevalence of alcoholism among the relatives of individuals in treatment for alcoholism or other psychiatric disorders (Cotton, 1979). Some longitudinal studies of alcohol etiology have taken parental alcoholism into consideration (Drake & Vaillant, 1988; Vaillant & Milofsky, 1982), and representative surveys of alcohol use and abuse in the community have included questions on parental alcoholism (Harford, Haack, & Spiegler, 1987; Midanik, 1983; Russell, Cooper, & Frone, 1989).

Data from studies representing these various approaches are presented now. Material presented so far has illustrated how sample characteristics and measurement of alcoholism influence the prevalence of alcoholism among children of alcoholics. Because sample characteristics and measurement techniques vary considerably across studies, brief descriptions of the methodology are given for each study reviewed. In many cases it is clear that findings are likely to be influenced by methodological issues and/or other factors that have been discussed above. To avoid repetition, this review does not comment on every example; however, readers should be aware that there is no single study that is not limited in one way or another. The information on sampling and measurement allows readers to evaluate the prevalence estimate from the perspective that is most relevant to them.

Because reported alcoholism rates vary greatly, it is difficult to compare them across studies. Although the previous discussion noted that methodological issues can affect the comparability of alcoholism rates even within studies, researchers in general try to hold constant all factors influencing alcoholism rates in cases and controls except parental alcoholism. In this research design, the ratio between alcoholism rates in children of alcoholics and children of nonalcoholics provides an estimate of the excess risk of alcoholism associated with being the child of an alcoholic. Thus, to the extent that comparable nonbiased methods are used to ascertain and define alcoholism for both cases and controls, within-study ratios control for between-study differences in prevalence rates, facilitating comparisons across studies. Accordingly, the ratio of alcoholism rates in cases compared with controls is provided for prevalence data presented here.

Adoptee Studies

Three adoption studies are reviewed. As indicated earlier, these studies investigated alcoholism in the biological and adoptive families of adoptees who were separated from their biological parents at an early age. They are designed to minimize the possible influence of exposure to biological parents' drinking behavior. If nongenetic familial transmission can be ruled out, it can be assumed that genetic familial transmission accounts for any excess risk of alcoholism seen in adopted children of alcoholic biological parents.

The first study to be reviewed was conducted in Denmark (Goodwin et al., 1973). Subjects came from a data base of 5,483 nonfamily adoptions between 1924 and 1947. Psychiatric records of adoptees and their biological and adoptive parents were screened. Cases were 55 males whose parents had been hospitalized primarily for alcoholism. There were two control groups, combined in the final analysis. One consisted of 27 males whose parents had a hospital record of a psychiatric condition other than alcoholism, mainly schizophrenia; and the other consisted of 50 males whose parents had no psychiatric hospital record. As indicated in Table 2.1, Goodwin et al. (1973) found that alcoholism was approximately four (3.6:1) times more prevalent among children whose biological parents were alcoholic than among those whose parents were not. Examination of the study design reveals both strengths and weaknesses:

1. *Diagnosis of alcoholism in offspring.* Offspring were personally interviewed by a psychiatrist using diagnostic criteria that presumably provided a reliable assessment of alcoholism, defined as heavy drinking plus alcohol problems in three of four areas, including social disapproval or marital problems; job trouble or legal difficulties; signs of tolerance; and loss of control. However, this classification has been criticized on the grounds that there were no significant differences in heavy drinking or problem drinking between cases and controls and that adoptees need not have had very severe symptoms to meet the criteria for a diagnosis of alcoholism (i.e., six or more drinks at least once a week, parental disapproval of drinking, having had a single traffic arrest for

TABLE 2.1. Alcoholism among Children of Alcoholics: Adoptee Studies

Adoptee study	Sample	Background	Environment	Alcoholism rates		
				N	%	Ratio
				Alcoholism		
Goodwin, Schulsinger, Hermansen, Guze, & Winokur (1973)	Copenhagen: 5,483 nonfamily adoption cases, 1924–1947	Alcoholic parents		10/55	18%	3.6:1
		Nonalcoholic parents		4/50	5%	
				Mild alcoholism		
Cloninger, Bohman, & Sigvardsson (1981)	Sweden: 862 men adopted in infancy by nonrelatives, 1930–1949	Type 1[a]	Environment			
		No	No	36/587	6.1%	4.4:1
		Yes	Yes	8/30	26.7%	
				Severe alcoholism		
		No	No	21/465	4.5%	2.3:1
		Yes	Yes	7/68	10.3%	
				Moderate alcoholism		
		Type 2[b]	Environment			
		No	No	5/28	17.9%	9.4:1
		Yes	Yes	11/567	1.9%	
				Alcoholism		
Bohman, Sigvardsson, & Cloninger (1981)	Sweden: 913 women adopted in infancy by nonrelatives, 1930–1949	Mother alcoholic ± father		5/51	9.8%	3.5:1
		Neither parent alcoholic		16/577	2.8%	
		Father only alcoholic		10/285	3.5%	

[a]Type 1 genetic background (milieu-limited): Mild parental alcoholism, mild parental criminality.

[b]Type 2 genetic background (male-limited): Early-onset severe alcoholism and serious criminality in father only.

drinking, and drinking in the morning.) Murray et al. (1983) suggest that the findings may be an artifact based on an arbitrary system of classifying alcoholism. However, cases were clearly more likely to have experienced severe alcoholism requiring treatment.

2. *Identification of alcoholic parents.* The fact that the sample was identified on the basis of parents having a hospital record of treatment suggests that parental alcoholism was severe. Therefore, the data are probably best interpreted in terms of alcoholism among the offspring of parents having severe alcoholism. Moreover, other, unknown factors, such as concomitant illness or lack of socioeconomic resources, may have contributed to parental hospitalization for alcoholism. These unknown factors may also influence the development of alcoholism in offspring, further limiting the extent to which alcoholism in offspring can be attributed to parental alcoholism.

3. *Age of offspring at time of alcoholism diagnosis.* Seventy-five percent of the sample was under the age of 34 years at the time of follow-up. This is a period during which there is a high prevalence of age-related alcohol problems followed by spontaneous remission. Fillmore (1987) noted the need to focus on chronic alcohol problems enduring over a number of years, most prevalent among people in their 30s and 40s. Also, the relatively young age of the offspring gives rise to the possibility that some may not have manifested their incipient alcoholism at the time of follow-up.

4. *Size of sample.* It is of major relevance to the reliability of the findings to note that, although the study began with 5,483 nonfamily adoption cases, the final prevalence estimates were based on only ten cases of alcoholism among cases and four among controls. Clearly, identification of only a few cases more or less in either group could greatly influence the results. The small sample size is especially relevant in view of the relatively young age of the offspring at follow-up noted above, which allows time for such changes in classification to take place as the sample ages.

5. *Environmental factors.* Schizophrenic patients tend to come from the higher socioeconomic classes, whereas alcoholics tend to come from the lower socioeconomic classes. Matching socioeconomic background of adoptive families with those of the biological parents may have produced differences in the environments of the cases and controls that could produce differences in alcoholism rates similar to those observed (Fillmore, 1987; Murray et al., 1983).

The second adoptee study, conducted in Sweden, used Temperance Board records to ascertain indications of alcohol abuse for all eligible adoptees and their parents, rather than selecting on the basis of parental hospital records (Bohman et al., 1981; Cloninger et al., 1981). Data on offspring were supplemented by reviewing records of psychiatric hospitals and clinics. Among men, alcohol abuse so identified was classified as mild (one Temperance Board registration), moderate (two or three registrations), or severe (four or more registrations and/or treatment). Cross-fostering analyses were conducted to investigate gene × environment interactions (Cloninger et al., 1981).

It was found that both genetic and environmental factors contributed significantly to the prediction of mild alcohol abuse, and that adoptees having both predisposing factors had an approximately fourfold greater prevalence of alcoholism than adoptees having neither (Table 2.1). Genetic, but not environmental, factors contributed significantly to the prediction of moderate alcoholism. Although both genetic and environmental factors were associated with slight increases in the prevalence of severe alcoholism, neither reached statistical significance.

Further analyses of these data led to the identification of two types of parental alcoholism with different patterns of heritability. The genetic background for Type 1 alcoholism consists of fathers with adult onset of mild alcohol abuse and no criminality requiring prolonged incarceration. Among sons of Type 1 alcoholics, the risk of alcoholism was doubled (data not presented). However, the severity of alcoholism depended on their environment. Thus, a severe environment, defined by adoptive fathers having an unskilled occupation, was associated with an increased risk of severe alcoholism; and a mild environment (adoptive fathers not having an unskilled occupation) was associated with higher rates of mild alcoholism. It is suggested that exposure to a pattern of heavy recreational drinking more often seen among unskilled than skilled workers precipitates severe alcoholism in genetically vulnerable males. This type of heredity is termed "milieu-limited" alcoholism.

The genetic background for Type 2 alcoholism consists of fathers who had extensive treatment for alcohol abuse and serious criminality beginning in their adolescence or early adulthood. In contrast to Type 1 alcoholism, environment did not make a significant contribution to alcoholism risk among adopted-away sons of Type 2, severely alcoholic fathers. Their risk of alcohol abuse was high, 9.4:1, but only for moderate alcohol abuse.

The third study is based on the same Swedish data as the previous study. It is one of the few studies to examine the heritability of alcoholism in women (Bohman et al., 1981). Daughters were found to be at increased risk of alcoholism only if their mothers were alcoholic, and risk seemed limited to mothers of low occupational status and mild criminality. Because alcoholic women tended to be married to mildly alcoholic men, alcoholism in daughters was associated with Type 1 alcoholism identified in the above study of sons. There was no increased risk of alcoholism in the adopted-away daughters of Type 2 severely alcoholic men; therefore, transmission of this type of alcoholism has been termed "male-limited."

These studies have been described in some detail because data are rarely available to conduct such research, and they make a unique contribution to the literature on the heritability of alcoholism. Moreover, results from these studies are widely quoted and have had a major impact on the field of alcohol research, despite the fact that they have been severely criticized (e.g., Fillmore, 1987; Murray et al., 1983; Searles, 1988), including criticisms provided here:

The use of Temperance Board registrations to define alcoholism has been questioned. Kaij (1972) found that alcohol abusers coming to the attention of the Temperance Board were more likely to be psychopathic than known alcohol abusers in the general population who had not come to the board's attention, suggesting that samples based on Temperance Board data are not representative of alcoholism in the general population (Murray et al., 1983).

Cloninger (1987) has responded by reporting that follow-up procedures employed in Sweden to determine alcoholism among biological and adoptive parents and their offspring depended on extensive record review, and that these sources are thought to identify 70% of alcoholics, with no appreciable bias toward Type 1 or Type 2 alcoholics. Lack of bias in follow-up is important to within-study rate comparisons; however, failure to identify all alcoholics suggests that absolute values of the prevalence may be underestimated by as much as 30%.

The basic difficulty of depending on Temperance Board data is compounded by analyses that use the number of such registrations to differentiate among mild, moderate, and severe alcoholism in offspring. These classifications were used in analyses to identify environmental factors associated with alcoholism, one of which was the occupational status of adoptive father. It seems likely that low occupational status might be related to the likelihood of Temperance Board registration, which would confound the findings.

The age of offspring at alcoholism diagnosis offers another basis for criticism. Adoptees ranged in age from 23 to 43 years at follow-up, and many would be expected to incur additional Temperance Board registrations and/or enter treatment before passing through the period of vulnerability. This has the potential to significantly change not only the number of alcoholic offspring in the study, but also their classification in terms of severity. Given that this classification scheme is the basis of elaborate cross-fostering analysis, the effect on the findings could be profound. Studies are currently under way to follow adoptees further to determine whether earlier findings still obtain.

The limitations mentioned above illustrate some of the difficulties inherent in estimating the prevalence of alcoholism in the offspring of alcoholics. It is especially problematic to replicate studies of adoptees because access to adoption records is often restricted. Prospective investigations of alcoholism in adoptees have not yet been reported, and retrospective investigations are, of necessity, highly dependent on hospital and other records for diagnostic information, despite well-recognized shortcomings in their completeness and reliability. Thus, findings from individual studies in this area are subject to systematic and unsystematic variability from many sources.

Indeed, if it is confirmed that alcoholism is influenced both by environment and by type of parental alcoholism, this will have an impact on estimates of alcoholism rates among children of alcoholics. Cloninger (1987) noted that while both types of alcoholism are common in men, Type 2 alcoholism is characteristic of most men in hospital treatment samples. Clearly, prevalence estimates based on hospital treatment samples (i.e., seven to nine times more alcoholism in sons) have the potential to overestimate alcoholism in sons of Type 1 alcoholics (only doubled). Such samples are likely to underestimate alcoholism in daughters. Although no excess alcoholism in daughters is associated with Type 2 alcoholism in fathers, alcoholism tends to be three times higher in daughters of alcoholic mothers, many of whom are married to Type 1 alcoholic men.

Clinical Studies

Many estimates of alcoholism in children of alcoholics are based on clinical samples. Cotton (1979) reviewed 39 studies of the familial incidence of alcoholism, most of which focused on inpatient and outpatient psychiatric samples. Although there was considerable variability between studies in the magnitude of the estimated risk ratios, she concluded, as had Goodwin (1971), that rates of alcoholism were higher among relatives of alcoholics than in the general population. Summarizing the results from studies providing sufficient data to permit the calculation of percentages, Cotton found that alcoholics were approximately four to five times more likely to have alcoholic parents than nonpsychiatric patients: 27.0% versus 5.2% for fathers and 4.9% versus 1.2% for mothers. Stated differently, on average, almost one third of any sample of alcoholics will have at least one alcoholic parent. A number of other observations from this review (Cotton, 1979) are significant in view of the earlier discussion of methodological issues likely to influence estimates of the prevalence of alcoholism in children of alcoholics. For example, based on the work of Schuckit, Pitts, Reich, King, and Winokur (1969), Winokur and Clayton (1967), Bleuler (1955), and Sherfey (1955), it was concluded that depression appeared to be the mental illness most frequently reported in relatives of alcoholics, other than alcoholism. Other findings include a higher incidence of alcoholism among the relatives of female than male alcoholics, and a tendency for women with alcoholic fathers to marry alcoholics. Familial alcoholism was also associated with younger age at first intoxication and younger age at onset of problem drinking. Alcoholic inpatients were more likely to be of lower social class and also to reflect a subset of the disorder that is at the extreme of the continuum.

    In her analysis of methods employed to ascertain alcoholism in relatives of alcoholics in treatment, Cotton (1979) found that 26 of the 39 studies relied on data from the patient only, and 13 interviewed relatives in addition to interviewing patients and/or reviewing their records. She concluded that: "Studies combining information from interviews of patients and relatives were most likely to reduce sources of error—by controlling for the possibility of patient denial or distortion of his own and his family's drinking behavior, by giving special attention to a family history of alcoholism and by using specific definitions of alcoholism and carefully designed questions" (Cotton, 1979, pp. 106–107).

A Longitudinal Study

Longitudinal studies of child development that have gathered information on parental alcoholism represent another source of data on the prevalence of alcoholism among children of alcoholics. One such study was based on nondelinquent, adolescent boys from Boston's inner city, recruited between 1940 and 1963 as a control group for a study of juvenile delinquency (Glueck & Glueck, 1950, 1968). The initial examination, conducted when the boys were 14 years old, included interviews with the boys, their parents, and their teachers, together with extensive reviews of public records for data on alcoholism, criminal behavior, and mental illness in all first-degree relatives. Alcohol abuse was assessed in interviews with more than 90% of surviving subjects at ages 25 and 31 (Glueck & Glueck, 1968), and with 87% of surviving subjects at age 47 (Vaillant, 1983). In contrast to clinical studies, these data come from a community sample that was relatively homogeneous with respect to social class and sex, and they have served as the basis of several studies (Vaillant, 1983; Vaillant & Milofsky, 1982; Zucker & Lisansky-Gomberg, 1986).

A recently published analysis of these data by Drake and Vaillant (1988) considers the role of paternal alcohol abuse and a number of other factors, including maternal alcoholism. A lifetime DSM-III (American Psychiatric Association, 1980) diagnosis of alcohol abuse/dependence was made using data relating to the period between ages 21 and 47. There was no significant difference between men with ($N = 149$) and without ($N = 250$) alcoholic fathers in the prevalence of alcohol abuse (14% versus 16%), but alcohol dependence was more than twice as prevalent among men with alcoholic fathers as it was among men without, 28% versus 12%, yielding a ratio of 2.3 to 1 (Drake & Vaillant, 1988).

Maternal alcoholism was more prevalent among men with alcoholic fathers than among those without (10% versus 6%), as were a number of other familial and adolescent characteristics associated with maladjustment, such as poor relationship with father, parental separation, and poor boyhood competence. However, among men with alcoholic fathers, alcohol dependence was significantly higher only among those having many alcoholic relatives, non-Mediterranean ethnicity, low socioeconomic status, and school problems (Drake & Valliant, 1988).

Representative Population Studies

Studies in representative household samples provide population-based estimates of risk attributable to parental alcoholism. The advantage of having a more representative sample of alcoholics is somewhat offset by the fact that few individuals who report alcohol problems in general populations have severe alcoholism. This limits the extent to which population-based data can provide information on types of alcoholism likely to predominate in clinical studies. However, having a representative sample permits the investigation of a broad range of drinking patterns, alcohol problem scales, and potentially confounding or moderating factors. Therefore, two population studies are reviewed in detail. First, data from the 1979 National Drinking Practices Survey were selected for review because they provide prevalence data for the United States as a whole (Harford et al., 1987; Midanik, 1983). Second, data from the 1986 Biracial Community Survey have been analyzed for inclusion here to provide more detailed information pertaining to sociodemographic factors that may moderate the relationship between alcoholism in parents and alcoholism in their offspring than is currently available (Russell et al., 1989). Prevalence data from these two sources are presented after a brief description of their methodologies.

1979 National Drinking Practices Survey

Familial alcoholism was defined in the 1979 National Survey by asking respondents, if, in their judgment, their father, mother, sister(s), or brother(s) had been alcoholics or problem drinkers *at any time in their lives*. Positive responses were recorded for each type of relative, but information regarding multiple siblings of the same sex was not obtained. This method of defining familial alcoholism is limited in that information on alcoholism was obtained in face-to-face interviews with respondents, and it was not validated by independent means (Midanik, 1983). Thus, the data reflect the perceptions of the respondents only. Also, no distinction was made between "alcoholic" and "problem drinker" in characterizing relatives, and no attempt was made to standardize these definitions for respondents. Despite these limitations, studies correlating global judgments regarding parental alcoholism with more detailed scales (O'Malley et al., 1986), sibling agreement (Sher & Descutner, 1986), and interviews with parents and children (Thompson et al., 1982), suggest that children may fail to identify alcoholism in a parent, but they are unlikely to incorrectly identify a nonalcoholic parent as having a drinking problem. Thus, although data on the reliability of measures of parental alcoholism used in this survey are lacking, the limited studies available on this issue seem to indicate that the measure is likely to yield relatively meaningful information.

The 1979 National Survey also included 21 questions on alcohol-related problems and 12 on dependence symptons (Williams, Stinson, Parker, Harford, & Noble, 1987). The latter were based in part on the conceptualization of alcohol dependence in the DSM-III. The list of alcohol-related problems included indicators of alcohol abuse used as criteria for DSM-III diagnoses of alcohol abuse in addition to less severe problems.

1986 Biracial Community Survey

Information on alcohol problems and alcoholism among parents and their offspring was gathered recently in representative samples of the black and white

TABLE 2.2. Parental Alcoholism Rates Reported by Male and Female Offspring: Community Studies

			Alcoholism in parents			
Community study			Neither parent	Father only	Mother only	Both parents
1979 National Drinking Practices Survey[a] (Harford, Haack, & Spiegler, 1987)	Men:	%	88.6	8.9	1.2	1.3
		(N)	(673)	(68)	(13)	(8)
	Women:	%	83.4	12.2	2.3	2.1
		(N)	(828)	(134)	(23)	(25)
1986 Biracial Community Survey[b] (Russell, Cooper, & Frone, 1989)	Men:	%	73.6	21.7	2.4	2.3
		(N)	(565)	(166)	(19)	(18)
	Women:	%	79.9	17.2	1.8	1.1
		(N)	(753)	(162)	(17)	(10)

[a]N's based on unweighted data; percentages based on weighted data.

[b]N's and percentages based on weighted data; data missing for 223 cases (11.5%).

household populations in Erie County, New York, as part of a study on stress, race, alcohol use, and blood pressure. Respondents were asked the following about their biological fathers: "Did his drinking ever cause problems with his (health/marriage/work around the house or on the job)?" If any of the three areas in question were answered positively, respondents were asked, "Was he ever treated for alcoholism or problem drinking?" These questions were then repeated for mothers. As in the 1979 National Drinking Practices Survey, this method of defining alcohol problems/alcoholism was limited to reports obtained in face-to-face interviews with respondents, and it was not validated by independent means. However, the inclusion of questions on specific problems provides greater definition of parental involvement with alcohol, and the question on having been treated for alcoholism defines a subsample of parents whose diagnosis can be considered well established.

Also included in the survey were seven questions on alcohol-related problems and ten on dependence symptoms from the National Institute of Mental Health Diagnostic Interview Schedule (Robins, Helzer, Croughan, Williams, & Spitzer, 1981), which approximates a psychiatric diagnosis of alcohol abuse or dependence according to DSM-III criteria (Robins, Helzer, Croughan, & Ratcliff, 1981).[1]

The prevalence of parental alcoholism reported by men and women participating in these two community surveys is summarized in Table 2.2 (Harford et al., 1987; Russell et al., 1989). It is of interest to note that the data from the 1979 National Drinking Practices Survey provide the basis for estimates of the number

[1]This method of diagnosing alcoholism was also used in the Epidemiology Catchment Area (ECA) surveys to study the prevalence of mental illness in five U.S. communities. See Robins et al. (1984) for a description of the overall study design.

of adult children of alcoholics in the United States. Applied to 1980 census data, these rates yield an estimate of approximately 22,000,000 offspring of alcoholics aged 18 years or older (Russell, Henderson, & Blume, 1984).

Rates of paternal alcoholism reported by men are more than twice as high in the Biracial Community Survey as in the 1979 National Survey. This may be related in part to secular increases in alcoholism that may have taken place during the time between the surveys rather than to sampling fluctuations. However, regional differences in the prevalence of parental alcoholism and differences in the questions used to measure parental alcoholism may also play a role in accounting for the discrepancy. It is of interest that differences in reporting paternal alcoholism were not as great for women as they were for men. Rates of maternal alcoholism and alcoholism in both parents are based on sample sizes too small to yield reliable estimates; however, they are of the same order of magnitude in both surveys and for both sexes.

Sex-specific prevalence data on alcohol-related problems and alcohol-dependence symptoms in the past year for the two surveys are summarized according to parental alcoholism in Table 2.3. In addition, Table 2.3 presents data on the prevalence of a lifetime DSM-III diagnosis of alcohol abuse/dependence from the Biracial Community Survey. Because of differences in how alcohol-related problems and dependence symptoms were measured, direct comparisons of prevalence between the two studies cannot be made. However, the within-study ratios comparing prevalence of alcohol-related outcomes, father only versus neither parent, are quite consistent, ranging from 1.4–1.7 to 1 in men and from 0.9–3.0 to 1 in women. As noted previously, alcoholism was rarely reported in mothers, and prevalence among offspring of alcoholic mothers or alcoholic mothers and fathers is based on numbers too small to support reliable interpretation.

In addition to the above prevalence estimates, data from the Biracial Community Survey were used to investigate the potential moderating influence of race and age on the relationship between parental alcoholism and alcoholism in the offspring. Hierarchical logistic regression was used to examine the main effects and potential interactions of family history, race, and age on alcoholism in respondents, controlling for sex and socioeconomic status. Analyses were conducted on weighted and unweighted data. Results were similar in both instances; therefore, findings based on unweighted data are presented here. Family history made a significant independent contribution to the prediction of lifetime alcoholism (relative odds ratio = 2.41, 95% confidence intervals = 1.76, 3.31). However, a significant three-way interaction was observed among parental alcoholism, race, and age. Relative odds ratios for the interaction are summarized in Table 2.4. Among whites, parental alcoholism was associated with a sevenfold increase in the risk of alcoholism among offspring over age 54. In contrast, among blacks, parental alcoholism was associated with a threefold increase in the risk of alcoholism among offspring age 54 or less.

Clearly findings such as these need to be replicated to determine whether

TABLE 2.3. Alcohol-Related Problems, Alcohol-Dependence Symptoms, and Alcoholism among Children of Alcoholics: Community Studies

Community study	Problems/symptoms			Neither parent	Father only	Mother only	Both only	Ratio[a]
				Alcoholism in parents				
1979 National Drinking Practices Survey[b] (Harford, Haack, & Spiegler, 1987)	One or more alcohol-related problems in past year	Men:	%	12.8	21.9	41.8	15.2	1.7:1
			(N)	(673)	(68)	(13)	(8)	
		Women:	%	4.5	9.6	12.3	20.3	2:1
			(N)	(828)	(134)	(23)	(25)	
	One or more alcohol-dependence symptoms in past year	Men:	%	10.5	15.2	16.3	15.2	1.4:1
			(N)	(673)	(68)	(13)	(8)	
		Women:	%	3.8	4.5	27.4	18.5	1.2:1
			(N)	(828)	(134)	(23)	(25)	
1986 Biracial Community Survey[c] (Russell, Cooper, & Frone, 1989)	One or more alcohol-related problems in past year	Men:	%	9.7	15.0	1.3	30.7	1.5:1
			(N)	(560)	(166)	(19)	(18)	
		Women:	%	2.2	1.9	1.8	32.4	0.9:1
			(N)	(748)	(160)	(17)	(10)	
	One or more alcohol-dependence symptoms in past year	Men:	%	11.6	17.9	1.3	18.5	1.5:1
			(N)	(560)	(163)	(19)	(16)	
		Women:	%	2.6	7.9	3.5	32.4	3:1
			(N)	(748)	(160)	(17)	(10)	
	Lifetime diagnosis of alcohol abuse/dependence according to DSM-III criteria	Men:	%	28.9	43.5	9.9	60.5	1.5:1
			(N)	(563)	(166)	(19)	(18)	
		Women:	%	3.4	9.3	8.8	43.6	2.7:1
			(N)	(749)	(160)	(17)	(10)	

[a] Prevalence in offspring with alcoholic fathers only:prevalence in those with neither parent alcoholic.

[b] N's based on unweighted data; percentages based on weighted data.

[c] N's and percentages based on weighted data; data missing for 223 cases (11.5%).

28

TABLE 2.4. Relative Odds Ratios for the Effect of Family History of Alcoholism on Alcoholism[a] in Respondents, by Race and Age[b]

Predictors	Whites (N = 787)		Blacks (N = 872)	
	Relative odds ratio	95% confidence intervals	Relative odds ratio	95% confidence intervals
Age 19–34				
Negative family history	1.00		1.00	
Positive family history	1.23	0.63, 2.38	3.48**	1.60, 7.57
Age 35–54				
Negative family history	1.00		1.00	
Positive family history	2.32*	1.04, 5.19	3.26**	1.48, 7.21
Age 55+				
Negative family history	1.00		1.00	
Positive family history	6.97**	2.00, 24.28	1.93	0.42, 8.85

[a]Lifetime diagnosis of alcohol abuse/dependence according to DSM-III criteria.

[b]Unweighted data.

*$p < .05$; ** $p < .01$.

they are reliable and if they hold for other populations; however, they illustrate the potential hazards involved in generalizing data on alcoholism prevalence among children of alcoholics across subgroups differing with respect to their sociodemographic characteristics.

FETAL ALCOHOL SYNDROME

Children of alcoholic women who drink heavily during pregnancy represent a special subgroup of children of alcoholics, in which the genetic aspects of having an alcoholic parent are combined with heavy *in utero* exposure to the toxic effects of alcohol and its metabolites. Although maternal drinking during pregnancy has long been suspected of harming the fetus (Warner & Rosett, 1975), it was not until 1968 that physicians in France described alcohol-related birth defects in the medical literature for the first time (Lemoine, Harousseau, Borteyru, & Menuet, 1968). This was followed by their independent rediscovery in the United States by Jones and Smith (1973), who coined the phrase "fetal alcohol syndrome" (FAS) to define a constellation of birth defects common to children whose mothers were chronic alcoholics who drank heavily throughout pregnancy. The diagnosis of FAS depends on signs of abnormality in each of the following three categories (Sokol & Clarren, 1989, p. 598):

1. Prenatal and/or postnatal growth retardation (weight and/or length or height below the tenth percentile when corrected for gestational age).

2. Central nervous system involvement, including neurological abnormality, developmental delay, behavioral dysfunction or deficit, intellectual impairment, and/or structural abnormalities such as microcephaly (head circumference below the third percentile) or brain malformations (found on imaging studies or autopsy).
3. A characteristic face, currently qualitatively described as including short palpebral fissures, an elongated midface, a long and flattened philtrum, thin upper lip, and flattened maxilla.

In addition, there is a broader spectrum of negative pregnancy outcomes associated with excessive maternal alcohol use, including spontaneous abortion (Harlap & Shiono, 1980), stillbirth (Kaminski, Rumeau, & Schwartz, 1978), and an increased incidence of anomalies similar to components of FAS in the absence of the full syndrome (Russell, 1982).

Animal studies in rodents, dogs, monkeys, and swine have confirmed that alcohol intake by a pregnant animal can lead to increased resorption of implanted fetuses, growth retardation, congenital malformations, and learning and behavioral changes (Abel, 1982). These have been demonstrated in the presence of adequate nutrition and in the absence of paternal alcohol exposure, preconception maternal alcohol exposure, or exposure of the offspring to alcohol-treated mothers after birth (cross-fostering).

Some of the features that have been reported in children with FAS (minor physical anomalies, hyperactivity, and central nervous system deficits, for example) have also been reported in children of alcoholics. In these cases, children were often identified because the father was alcoholic. Information as to whether the mother was alcoholic or whether she drank excessively during pregnancy was rarely ascertained. To the extent that FAS studies focus on maternal drinking during pregnancy and children of alcoholics studies focus on paternal alcoholism, overlapping symptoms in the children can be attributed to maternal alcoholism, excessive maternal drinking during pregnancy, or to paternal alcoholism. The tendency for alcoholics to marry alcoholics renders plausible the possibility of confounding the etiology of deficits in their offspring. A brief review follows of the evidence for genetic contributions to the fetal alcohol syndrome and for the influence of paternal drinking on pregnancy outcome.

Genetic Influences on the Effects of Alcohol

The causative factor in FAS is thought to be exposure to alcohol *in utero*, a prenatal environmental factor; however, it seems likely that heredity moderates the effect of maternal drinking during pregnancy on the fetus. Evidence for genetic influences in the etiology of FAS was reviewed by Riley and Lochry (1982). The most convincing demonstration of a genetic effect comes from studies using animal models of FAS, which have reported interspecies and strain differences in the effects of a given alcohol dose on the fetus (Chernoff, 1977). Twin studies of FAS provide a rare opportunity to investigate genetic influences on fetal response to alcohol. In comparing findings from a pair of dizygotic twins reported by Christoffel and Salafsky (1975) with those from a pair of monozygotic twins described by Palmer, Ouellette, Warner, and Leichtman (1974), Riley and Lochry (1982) noted that the effects of alcohol on the monozygotic twins were more concordant than they were for the dizygotic twins. This is consistent with the hypothesis that there is a genetic influence on fetal alcohol effects. However, the dizygotic pair was a dichorionic, diamniotic type, whereas the monozygotic twins shared a common placenta and a common umbilical cord, which may have produced a more homogeneous prenatal environment and therefore greater concordance in development. Finally, recent epidemiological studies of maternal alcohol use during pregnancy indicate that there may be racial differences in susceptibility to alcohol-related birth defects, with infants born to blacks affected more severely than those born to whites having similar alcohol exposures and similar sociodemographic characteristics (Sokol et al., 1986).

Thus, genetic characteristics of the mother and fetus, singly or in combination, seem to play a role in determining the extent of fetal damage associated with a given maternal drinking pattern. Differences in genetic susceptibility to the effects of *in utero* alcohol exposure complicate the issue of establishing safe limits for alcohol use during pregnancy. As further research provides a better understanding of the factors that determine fetal alcohol effects, it may be possible to predict which pregnancies are at greatest risk. Such knowledge could provide incentive for mothers whose fetuses are at high risk to abstain during pregnancy. Conversely, the ability to demonstrate low risk for bearing children with fetal alcohol effects might relieve anxiety in women who drank before they knew they were pregnant and alleviate guilt in light and moderate drinkers whose infants have birth defects.

Paternal Alcohol Consumption and Pregnancy Outcome

Evidence for the possible role of paternal alcohol consumption in the etiology of FAS was reviewed by Anderson (1982). Among men, alcoholism may result in loss of libido, lack of spermatozoa, or inability of spermatozoa to fertilize, all of which interfere with reproduction. However, a paternal influence on FAS can only occur if excessive alcohol consumption alters the genetic component of the male gametes so that birth defects are produced in the offspring.

Given the well-established tendency for assortative mating to occur among heavy drinkers, alcoholics, and children of alcoholics (Hall et al., 1983a, 1983b), it is likely that many children who are heavily exposed to alcohol *in utero* will also have fathers who drink excessively and whose sperm have been exposed to high alcohol concentrations. Such children may also inherit from their fathers, mothers, or both parents genotypes that predispose them to adverse consequences if exposed to alcohol.

The bulk of data relevant to the effect of paternal drinking on offspring comes from animal models. Studies conducted before the Prohibition era found adverse effects on the offspring of alcohol-treated male mice (Nice, 1917), guinea pigs (Stockard & Papanicolaou, 1918), and rabbits (Cole & Davis, 1914). More recent studies by Badr and Badr (1975), using a mouse model, found an increase in the number of dead implants per female, which they attributed to the induction of a dominant lethal mutation by alcohol, probably in epididymal spermatozoa and late spermatids. Klassen and Persaud (1976) noted higher prenatal mortality, smaller litter size, and an increased male to female sex ratio in offspring of male rats treated chronically with alcohol, compared with controls; however, malnutrition may have contributed to some of those effects. Anderson, Furby, Oswald, and Zaneveld (1981) and Pfeifer, Mackinnon, and Seiser (1977) confirmed the observations of Klassen and Persaud in mice and rats under conditions in which body weights of the males were maintained and controls were pair-fed. Both observed increased postnatal mortality among offspring sired by alcohol-treated males. Anderson et al. (1981) found an increased male to female ratio in litters sired by alcohol-treated males, and Pfeifer et al. (1977) concluded that behavioral testing of the offspring indicated that females were more sensitive to the effects of paternal alcohol consumption than males. These findings suggest that X-chromosome-bearing sperm may be more sensitive to alcohol than Y-chromosome-bearing sperm. Studies by Abel and Lee (1988) using mice demonstrated that chronic treatment of males affected the behavior of offspring in the absence of significant effects on litter size, birthweight, or weight at weaning. They also observed a dose-related decrease in serum testosterone levels at 55 days in male offspring sired by alcohol-consuming males.

There is much less information available in humans, and definitive work is lacking in this area. Most studies have not measured alcohol consumption in both mother and father, and few have adequately controlled for environmental factors associated with parental alcoholism that may also influence offspring. The offspring characteristics associated with both FAS and paternal alcoholism that have been most intensively studied are hyperactivity, with and without conduct disorder, and cognitive deficits. For reviews of this literature, see Russell et al. (1984), West and Prinz (1987), Johnson and Bennett (1988), and Tarter, Laird, and Moss (Chapter 4, this volume).

SUMMARY AND DISCUSSION

Children of alcoholics are consistently found to have higher rates of alcoholism and alcohol-related problems than are children whose parents are not alcoholic. However, the magnitide of the ratio between alcoholism rates varies from study to study. The highest ratio, reflecting a ninefold difference in rates, was observed among adopted sons of severely alcoholic (Type 2) fathers with early onset serious criminality (Cloninger et al., 1981). Intermediate ratios, around 4:1, were found in clinical studies of alcoholics who had not been selected for severity or criminality (Cotton, 1979; Goodwin et al., 1973). Rates only 1.5 to 3 times higher than those in children of nonalcoholics were observed in (1) adopted sons of mildly alcoholic parents and adopted daughters of alcoholic mothers (Bohman et al., 1981; Cloninger et al., 1981), (2) a longitudinal survey (Drake & Vaillant, 1988), and (3) community surveys (Harford et al., 1987; Midanik, 1983; Russell et al., 1989).

Risk ratios in the last range (1.5–3:1) could result if parental alcoholism is associated with sociodemographic or other alcoholism risk factors that were not adequately controlled in the study design or analysis, such as low socioeconomic status or cultural background.

A number of methodological, genetic, and environmental factors influencing the prevalence of alcoholism among children of alcoholics have already been discussed. In addition, it is informative to evaluate the significance of these prevalence data from the perspective of epidemiological studies of the natural history of alcoholism. Community surveys of alcoholism and alcohol-related problems have found that prevalence is highest among young men; however, alcoholics in treatment programs tend to be middle-aged (Mulford, 1982; Room, 1977). Longitudinal studies, in which alcohol-related behavior is observed at two points in time, have found that heavy drinking and alcohol-related problems at time 1 predict continued heavy drinking and problems at time 2 less well in young men than in older men (Fillmore & Midanik, 1984).

Observations such as these suggest that a portion of the younger individuals in community samples who drink alcoholically may simply be passing through a phase in their drinking careers that is tolerated by society (Edwards, 1984). As they mature and assume normative adult social roles such as worker, spouse, and parent, they tend to voluntarily moderate their drinking in response to these new societal demands. Such individuals may suffer acute consequences of alcohol abuse, such as accidental injury; however, they rarely receive treatment for alcoholism. Room (1977) coined the phrase "the two worlds of alcoholism" to dramatize the differences between community samples of untreated alcoholics and clinical samples.

Zucker (1987) attempted to integrate epidemiological data on alcoholism from clinical and community studies. In doing so, he identified four subtypes of alcoholism with different sequelae and different histories, and reflecting different developmental processes: (1) antisocial alcoholism, (2) developmentally cumulative alcoholism, (3) developmentally limited alcoholism, and (4) negative affect alcoholism. His typology takes into consideration the influence of genetic diathesis, sex, social class, time of onset, antisocial history, parental history of antisocial behavior or of unipolar affective disorder, ability to adapt successfully to life demands, whether or not treatment entry is likely, time of treatment entry, and prognosis.

Zucker's inclusion of the influence of genetic diathesis in his typology makes it particularly relevant to the present discussion. His descriptions of antisocial alcoholism and developmentally cumulative alcoholism correspond rather closely to the Type 2, male-limited, and Type 1, milieu-limited, alcoholisms described by Cloninger et al. (1981). One difference is that Cloninger et al. (1981) reported that sons of Type 2 (severe) alcoholics were only moderately alcoholic, and that severe alcoholism among offspring was associated with Type 1 (mild) alcoholism in parents with low socioeconomic status. These findings are not reflected in Zucker's typology.

Factors such as time of onset, likelihood of entry into treatment, and time of treatment entry determine the prevalence of a given subtype in samples of alcoholics and their children. Thus, genetic influence on the prevalence of alcoholism among children of alcoholics depends on the nature of the sample. For example, a sample of young men from an alcoholism treatment center would probably consist predominantly of antisocial alcoholics (Type 2), and given that this type of alcoholism may be highly heritable, one would expect a high rate of alcoholism among their offspring. In contrast, clinical samples of older alcoholic men and women might include a substantial number of developmentally cumulative and negative affect alcoholics, so the prevalence of alcoholism among their children might be higher than in community samples but lower than in clinical samples of alcoholic young men. Knowing the degree of genetic influence associated with the various subtypes and the prevalence of the subtypes in a given sample should improve the prediction of alcoholism in offspring for that sample or samples of that type. Factors such as prognosis, ability to adapt successfully to life demands, and likelihood of treatment would be useful in evaluating the clinical and socioeconomic significance of increased alcoholism related to parental alcoholism in a given sample.

Developmentally limited alcoholism corresponds to the subtype identified most often in community studies. It is noteworthy that no comment is made regarding the role of heredity in this subtype of alcoholism. This omission may stem from a lack of relevant information, or it may reflect an opinion that cultural and environmental factors are more important than genetic diathesis in its determination. It could be argued that ratios of alcoholism rates in children with and without alcoholic parents are lower in community than in clinical studies because family transmission does not play a major role in developmentally limited alcoholism. The early remission of problems associated with this subtype could influence family transmission of alcoholism, and/or its measurement. Because alcohol problems tend to be under control by the time alcoholics of this subtype establish their families, their children are likely to be spared exposure to the environmental stress often associated with active alcoholism and thought to have negative effects on offspring development that might contribute to their alcoholism as adults. Measurement could be affected because children are less likely to know that their parents had alcohol-related problems if these problems were resolved before their birth. Even in the absence of genetic influence or exposure to active parental alcoholism, low rates of family transmission could be produced if children were exposed to cultural influences similar to those that contributed to their parents' alcoholic phase.

These examples illustrate some of the ways in which greater precision in predicting alcoholism in offspring of alcoholics can be achieved. To date, prevalence studies of alcoholism in children of alcoholics have been used to develop alcoholism typologies, but few, if any, prevalence studies of alcoholism in children of alcoholics have taken alcoholism subtypes into account. Also, many studies of the familial transmission of alcoholism have failed to control for assortative mating or for the possibility that alcoholism in the offspring may have been influenced by exposure to alcohol *in utero*. Studies of alcoholism in children of alcoholics have much to contribute to our understanding of etiology. Future studies have the potential to benefit from greater attention to the methodological issues raised here and elsewhere, consideration of alcoholism subtypes in both parents and offspring, and careful measurement of alcohol exposure at conception and during pregnancy.

The increased rates of alcoholism among children of alcoholics have important implications for public health. However, this brief review suggests that the precise nature of those implications is not clear. Recent data from community surveys seem to indicate that past clinical studies may overestimate the prevalence of alcoholism among children of alcoholics in the general population. The very limited data on familial transmission of alcoholism associated with subtypes of alcoholism and in sociodemographically diverse subgroups of the population imply that a single estimate may underestimate risk in some subtypes and subgroups and overestimate it in others. Such variability in the magnitude of risk ratios suggests that it would be wise to take a conservative approach in developing public health messages regarding the prevalence of alcoholism among children of alcoholics. At the same time, the consistent finding of higher rates of alcoholism among children of alcoholics provides ample support for wide dissemination of this public health information, and for the funding of further research to better define the nature and extent of the risk and factors that influence its expression.

REFERENCES

Abel, E. L. (1982). Consumption of alcohol during pregnancy: A review of effects on growth and development of offspring. *Human Biology, 54*(3), 421–453.

Abel, E. L., & Lee, J. A. (1988). Paternal alcohol exposure affects offspring behavior but not body or organ weights in mice. *Alcoholism, 12,* 349–355.

American Psychiatric Association. (1980). *Diagnostic and statistical manual of mental disorders* (3rd ed.). Washington, DC: Author.

Anderson, R. A., Jr. (1982). The possible role of paternal alcohol consumption in the etiology of the fetal alcohol syndrome. In E. L. Abel (Ed.), *Fetal alcohol syndrome* (Vol. 3, pp. 83–112). Boca Raton, FL: CRC Press.

Anderson, R. A., Furby, J. E., Oswald, C., & Zaneveld, L. J. D. (1981). Teratological evaluation of mouse fetuses after paternal alcohol ingestion. *Neurobehavioral Toxicology and Teratology, 3*(2), 117–120.

Andreasen, N. C., Endicott, J., Spitzer, R. L., & Winokur, G. (1977). The family history method using diagnostic criteria. *Archives of General Psychiatry, 34,* 1229–1235.

Badr, F. M., & Badr, R. S. (1975). Induction of dominant lethal mutation in male mice by ethyl alcohol. *Nature, 253,* 134–136.

Bleuler, M. (1955). Familial and personal background of chronic alcoholics. In O. Diethelm (Ed.), *Etiology of chronic alcoholism* (pp. 110–166). Springfield, IL: Charles C. Thomas.

Bohman, M., Sigvardsson, S., & Cloninger, C. R. (1981). Maternal inheritance of alcohol abuse. Cross fostering analysis of adopted women. *Archives of General Psychiatry, 38,* 965–969.

Boyd, J. H., Burke, J. D., Jr., Gruenberg, E., Holzer, C. E. III., Rae, D. S., George, L. K., Karno, M., Stoltzman, R., McEvoy, L., & Nestadt, G. (1984). Exclusion criteria of DSM-III: A study of co-occurrence of hierarchy-free syndromes. *Archives of General Psychiatry, 41,* 983–989.

Chernoff, G. F. (1977). The fetal alcohol syndrome in mice: An animal model. *Teratology, 15,* 223–229.

Christoffel, K. K., & Salafsky, I. (1975). Fetal alcohol syndrome in dizygotic twins. *Journal of Pediatrics, 87* (6, Pt. 1), 963–967.

Cloninger, C. R. (1987). Recent advances in family studies of alcoholism. In H. W. Goedde & D. P. Agarwal (Eds.), *Genetics and alcoholism* (pp. 47–60). New York: Alan R. Liss.

Cloninger, C. R., Bohman, M., & Sigvardsson, S. (1981). Inheritance of alcohol abuse. *Archives of General Psychiatry, 38,* 861–868.

Cole, L. J., & Davis, C. L. (1914). The effect of alcohol on the male germ cells, studied by means of double matings. *Science, 39,* 476–477.

Cotton, N. S. (1979). The familial incidence of alcoholism. *Journal of Studies on Alcohol, 40,* 89–116.

Drake, D. E., & Vaillant, G. E. (1988). Predicting alcoholism and personality disorder in a 33-year longitudinal study of children of alcoholics. *British Journal of Addiction, 83,* 799–807.

Edwards, G. (1984). Drinking in longitudinal perspective: Career and natural history. *British Journal of Addiction, 79,* 175–183.

Fillmore, K. M. (1987). *Critical explanations—biological, psychological and social—of drinking patterns and problems from the alcohol-related longitudinal literature: Critiques and strategies for future analyses on behalf of the World Health Organization.* Unpublished manuscript.

Fillmore, K. M., & Midanik, L. (1984). Chronicity of drinking problems among men: A longitudinal study. *Journal of Studies on Alcohol, 45,* 228–236.

Glueck, S., & Glueck, E. (1950). *Unravelling juvenile delinquency.* New York: Commonwealth Fund.

Glueck, S., & Glueck, E. (1968). *Delinquents and nondelinquents in perspective.* Cambridge, MA: Harvard University Press.

Goodwin, D. W. (1971). Is alcoholism hereditary? *Archives of General Psychiatry, 25,* 545–549.

Goodwin, D. W., Schulsinger, F., Hermansen, L., Guze, S. B., & Winokur, G. (1973). Alcohol problems in adoptees raised apart from alcoholic biological parents. *Archives General Psychiatry, 28,* 238–243.

Hall, R. L., Hesselbrock, V. M., & Stabenau, J. R. (1983a). Familial distribution of alcohol use: II. Assortative mating of alcoholic probands. *Behavior Genetics, 13,* 373–382.

Hall, R. L., Hesselbrock, V. M., & Stabenau, J. R. (1983b). Familial distribution of alcohol use: I. Assortative mating in the parents of alcoholics. *Behavior Genetics, 13,* 361–372.

Harford, T. C., Haack, M. R., & Spiegler, D. L. (1987). Positive family history for alcoholism. *Alcohol Health and Research World, 12*(2), 138–143.

Harlap, S., & Shiono, P. H. (1980). Alcohol, smoking, and incidence of spontaneous abortions in the first and second trimester. *Lancet,* 173–176.

Heller, K., Sher, K. J., & Benson, C. S. (1982). Problems associated with risk overprediction in studies of offspring of alcoholics: Implications for prevention. *Clinical Psychology Review, 2,* 183–200.

Johnson, J. L., & Bennett, L. A. (1988). *School-aged children of alcoholics: Theory and research.* New Brunswick, NJ: Center of Alcohol Studies, Rutgers University.

Jones, K. L., & Smith, D. W. (1973). Recognition of the fetal alcohol syndrome in early infancy. *Lancet, 2,* 999–1001.

Kaij, L. (1972). Definitions of alcoholism and genetic research. *Annals of the New York Academy of Sciences, 197,* 110–119.

Kaminski, M., Rumeau, C., & Schwartz, D. (1978). Alcohol consumption in pregnant women and the outcome of pregnancy. *Alcoholism (NY), 2,* 155–163.

Klassen, R. W., & Persaud, T. V. N. (1976). Experimental studies on the influence of male alcoholism on pregnancy and progeny. *Experimental Pathology, 12,* 38–45.

Lemoine, P., Harousseau, H., Borteyru, J. P., & Menuet, J. (1968). Children of alcoholic parents; Abnormalities observed in 127 cases. In Department of Health, Education and Welfare (Ed.), *Selected translations of international alcoholism research* (pp. 476–482). Washington DC: National Clearinghouse for Alcohol Information.

McKenna, T., & Pickens, R. (1981). Alcoholic children of alcoholics. *Journal of Studies on Alcohol, 42,* 1021–1029.

Midanik, L. (1983). Familial alcoholism and problem drinking in a national drinking practices survey. *Addictive Behaviors, 8,* 133–141.

Mulford, H. A. (1982). The epidemiology of alcoholism and its implications. In E. M. Pattison & E. Kaufman (Eds.), *Encyclopedic handbook of alcoholism* (pp. 441–456). New York: Gardner Press.

Murray, R. M., Clifford, C. A., & Gurling, H. M. D. (1983). Twin and adoption studies: How good is the evidence for a genetic role? In M. Galanter (Ed.), *Recent developments in alcoholism* (Vol. 1, pp. 25–48). New York: Plenum Press.

Nice, L. B. (1917). Further observations on the effects of alcohol on white mice. *American Naturalist, 51,* 596–607.

Nylander, I. (1960). Children of alcoholic fathers. *Acta Paediatrica Scandinavica, 49,* 9–127.

Nylander, I., & Rydelius, P. A. (1982). A comparison between children of alcoholic fathers from excellent versus poor social conditions. *Acta Paediatrica Scandinavica, 71,* 809–813.

O'Malley, S. S., Carey, K. B., & Maisto, S. A. (1986). Validity of young adults' reports of parental drinking practices. *Journal of Studies on Alcohol, 47,* 433–435.

Palmer, R. H., Ouellette, E. M., Warner, L., & Leichtman, S. R. (1974). Congenital malformations in offspring of a chronic alcoholic mother. *Pediatrics, 53,* 490–494.

Pfeifer, W. D., Mackinnon, J. R., & Seiser, R. L. (1977). Adverse effects of paternal alcohol consumption on offspring in the rat. *Bulletin of the Psychonomic Society, 19,* 871–872.

Pollock, V. E., Schneider, L. S., Gabrielli, W. F., & Goodwin, D. W. (1987). Sex of parent and offspring in the transmission of alcoholism: A meta-analysis. *Journal of Nervous and Mental Disease, 175,* 668–673.

Reich, T., Cloninger, R., VanEerdewegh, P., Rice, J. P., & Mullaney, J. (1988). Secular trends in the familial transmission of alcoholism. *Alcoholism: Clinical and Experimental Research, 12*(4), 458–470.

Riley, E. P., & Lochry, E. A. (1982). Genetic influences in the etiology of fetal alcohol syndrome. In E. L. Abel (Ed.), *Fetal alcohol syndrome* (Vol. 3, pp. 113–130). Boca Raton, FL: CRC Press.

Rimmer, J., & Chambers, D. S. (1969). Alcoholism: Methodological considerations in the study of family illness. *American Journal of Orthopsychiatry, 39,* 760–768.

Robins, L. N., Helzer, J. E., Croughan, J., & Ratcliff, K. S. (1981). National Institute of Mental Health Diagnostic Interview Schedule: Its history, characteristics and validity. *Archives of General Psychiatry, 38,* 381–389.

Robins, L. N., Helzer, J. E., Croughan, J., Williams, J. B. W., & Spitzer, R. L. (1981). *NIMH Diagnostic Interview Schedule: Version III* (Contract No. MH 278-79-00). Rockville, MD: National Institute of Mental Health.

Robins, L. N., Helzer, J. E., Weissman, M. M., Orvaschel, H., Gruenberg, H., Burke, J. D. Jr., & Regier, D. A. (1984). Lifetime prevalence of specific psychiatric disorders in three sites. *Archives of General Psychiatry, 41,* 948–959.

Room, R. (1977). The measurement and distribution of drinking patterns and problems in general populations. In G. Edwards, M. M. Gross, M. Keller, J. Moser & R. Room (Eds.),

Alcohol-related disabilities (Offset Publication No. 32, pp. 2–154). Geneva: World Health Organization.

Russell, M. (1982). The epidemiology of alcohol-related birth defects. In E. L. Abel (Ed.), *Fetal alcohol syndrome* (Vol. 2, pp. 89–126). Boca Raton, FL: CRC Press.

Russell, M., Cooper, M. L., & Frone, M. F. (1989). *Age and race influences on the effects of parental alcoholism: Data from a community sample.* Unpublished manuscript.

Russell, M., Henderson, C., & Blume, S. B. (1984). *Children of alcoholics: A Review of the literature.* New York: Children of Alcoholics Foundation.

Rydelius, P. (1981). Children of alcoholic fathers: Their social adjustment and their health status over 20 years. *Acta Paediatrica Scandinavica (Suppl.), 286,* 1–89.

Schuckit, M. A. (1973). Alcoholism and sociopathy—Diagnostic confusion. *Quarterly Journal of Studies on Alcohol, 34,* 157–164.

Schuckit, M. A., Pitts, F. N., Jr., Reich, T., King, L. J., & Winokur, G. (1969). Alcoholism: I. Two types of alcoholism in women. *Archives of General Psychiatry, 20,* 301–306.

Searles, J. S. (1988). The role of genetics in the pathogensis of alcoholism. *Journal of Abnormal Psychology, 97,* 153–167.

Sher, K. J., & Descutner, C. (1986). Reports of paternal alcoholism: Reliability across siblings. *Addictive Behaviors, 11,* 25–30.

Sherfey, M. J. (1955). Psychopathology and character structure in chronic alcoholism. In O. Diethelm (Ed.), *Etiology of chronic alcoholism* (pp. 16–42). Springfield, IL: Charles C. Thomas.

Sokol, R. J., Ager, J., Martier, S., Debanne, S., Ernhart, C. B., Kuzma, J., & Miller, S. I. (1986). Significant determinants of susceptibility to alcohol teratogenicity. *Annals of the New York Academy of Sciences, 477,* 87–102.

Sokol, R. J., & Clarren, S. K. (1989). Guidelines for use of the terminology describing the impact of prenatal alcohol on the offspring. *Alcoholism (NY), 4,* 597–598.

Stockard, C. R., & Papanicolaou, G. (1918). Further studies of the modification of the germ-cells in mammals: The effect of alcohol on treated guinea pigs and their descendants. *Journal of Experimental Zoology, 26,* 119–126.

Thompson, W. D., Orvaschel, H., Prusoff, B. A., & Kidd, K. K. (1982). An evaluation of the family history method for ascertaining psychiatric disorders. *Archives of General Psychiatry, 39,* 53–58.

Vaillant, G. E. (1983). *The natural history of alcoholism.* Cambridge, MA: Harvard University Press.

Vaillant, G. E., & Milofsky, E. S. (1982). The etiology of alcoholism: A prospective viewpoint. *American Psychologist, 37,* 494–503.

Warner, R. H., & Rosett, H. L. (1975). The effects of drinking on offspring: An historical survey of the American and British literature. *Journal of Studies on Alcohol, 36,* 1395–1420.

Weisner, C. (1987). The social etiology of alcohol treatment in the U.S. In M. Galanter (Ed.), *Recent developments in alcoholism* (pp. 203–243). New York: Plenum Press.

Weissman, M. M., & Myers, J. K. (1980). Psychiatric disorders in a U.S. community: The application of Research Diagnostic Criteria to a resurveyed community sample. *Acta Psychiatrica Scandinavia, 62,* 99–111.

West, M. O., & Prinz, R. J. (1987). Parental alcoholism and childhood psychopathology. *Psychological Bulletin, 102,* 204–218.

Williams, G. D., Stinson, F. S., Parker, D. A., Harford, T. C., & Noble, J. (1987). Demographic trends, alcohol abuse and alcoholism: 1985–1995. *Alcohol Health and Research World, 11*(3), 80–83, 91.

Winokur, G., & Clayton, P. (1967). Family history studies: II. Sex differences and alcoholism in primary affective illness. *British Journal of Psychiatry, 113,* 973–979.

Zucker, R. A., & Lisansky-Gomberg, E. S. (1986). Etiology of alcoholism reconsidered. *American Psychologist, 41,* 783–793.

Zucker, R. A. (1987). The four alcoholisms: A developmental account of the etiologic process. In P. C. Rivers (Ed.), *Alcohol and addictive behaviors: Nebraska symposium on motivation, 1986* (pp. 27–84). Lincoln: University of Nebraska Press.

CHAPTER THREE

Biochemical Markers for Alcoholism

ARTHUR W. K. CHAN

The progression from excessive alcohol consumption to alcoholism is often accompanied by manifestations of social and medical problems. Therefore, physicians and health-care personnel have a sizable opportunity to encounter people with health problems associated with alcohol abuse or alcoholism. In fact, it has been estimated that at least 20% of the patients visiting physicians will qualify for an alcoholic label (Schuckit, 1984b, 1985, 1987b). Unfortunately, alcoholism or early stages of excessive drinking often remain unrecognized in general medical practice and in hospitals (Brown, Carter, & Gordon, 1987; Coulehan, Zettler-Segal, Block, McCelland, & Schulberg, 1987; Moore & Malitz, 1986; Reid, Webb, Hennrikus, Fahey, & Sanson-Fisher, 1986; Schuckit, 1987b; Skinner, Holt, Sheu, & Israel, 1986). Schuckit (1987b) has suggested several factors that could contribute to the underdiagnosis of alcoholism. These include inadequate training in diagnosing alcoholism, lack of understanding of the usual course of alcoholism, and erroneous stereotyping of the alcoholic by physicians. Many clinicians do not think that self-reported data can be used as a reliable tool in the detection of early alcohol abuse (Eckardt, Rawlings, & Martin, 1986). This may be because few physicians have received formal instruction on how to integrate historical information, laboratory data, and results of physical examinations specifically to arrive at a diagnosis of alcoholism (Schuckit, 1987b). Moreover, clinicians may be reluctant to spend time administering structured interviews and questionnaires. Some examples of simple screening tests are the CAGE (Ewing, 1984; Mayfield, McLeod, & Hall, 1974), the Michigan Alcoholism Screening Test (MAST; Selzer, 1971), the Reich interview (Reich et al., 1975), and the self-administered alcoholism screening test (SAAST; Davis, Hurt, Morse, & O'Brien, 1987). Several reviews have dealt with the detection of alcoholism by questionnaires or structured interviews (Babor & Kadden, 1985; Hays & Spickard, 1987; Jacobson, 1976; Miller, 1976; Skinner, Holt, & Israel, 1981; Wilkins, 1974). Since the usefulness of questionnaires for alcoholism screening in a medical setting may be limited because of vulnerability to deliberate falsification or unconscious denial (Babor & Kadden, 1985), objective methods such as biochemical indicators are generally preferred by clinicians.

Several recent reviews have summarized the pros and cons of old and new biological markers for alcoholism and heavy drinking (Cushman, Jacobson, Barboriak, & Anderson, 1984; Eckardt et al., 1986; Holt, Skinner, & Israel, 1981; Lumeng, 1986; Salaspuro, 1986; Schuckit, 1986, 1987b; Skinner & Holt, 1987; Watson, Mohs, Eskelson, Sampliner, & Hartmann, 1986). The primary objective of this paper is to review and evaluate research on biochemical markers for alcoholism, with emphasis on work involving children of alcoholics (COAs). The research literature concerning neuropsychological and neurophysiological factors associated with alcoholic risk is discussed by Tarter, Laird, and Moss (Chapter 4, this volume).

TYPES OF MARKERS

As Hill, Steinhauer, and Zubin (1987) have pointed out, the term "marker," as commonly used by alcohol researchers, carries the same meaning as "indicator," not the more restrictive meaning of "marker" used in genetic studies. In the latter studies, "marker" generally denotes an enduring heritable trait that usually has a known pattern of inheritance. For convenience of referring to published works, "marker" will be used synonymously with "indicator" in this chapter. However, it should be emphasized that at the present state of alcoholism research, a true genetic marker of alcoholism has not been detected.

Two major types of markers can be categorized: vulnerability (trait) markers and state markers. As the term implies, vulnerability markers identify people who may be vulnerable to developing alcoholism, even before they have consumed alcohol. State markers reflect the physiological, pathological, and biochemical changes in the body elicited by chronic and excessive alcohol intake. Ideally, both types of markers should be highly specific (few false positives) and sensitive (few false negatives). The predictive accuracy of these markers should not be affected by non-alcoholism-related factors such as age and sex differences, smoking, other drug use, and concomitant diseases. An ideal state marker would be capable of detecting regular drinkers as well as binge drinkers and would be sufficiently sensitive to distinguish light drinkers from heavy drinkers.

Since COAs, especially sons of alcoholic fathers, are known to have an increased risk of developing alcoholism (Goodwin, 1979; and see Searles, Chapter 5, this volume), a logical and frequently used approach to identify putative vulnerability markers is to compare people having a positive history of familial alcoholism (FHP) with those having a negative history of familial alcoholism (FHN). A vulnerability marker should be present in a significantly larger proportion of FHP subjects than in FHN subjects. Also, the same marker should be detectable in a sizable proportion of alcoholics. However, an indicator that appears to differentiate alcoholics from nonalcoholic controls may be either a state marker or a persistent characteristic of a vulnerability marker. It should be emphasized that persons who test positive for a vulnerability marker may not develop alcoholism throughout their lifetimes. Likewise, persons who test normal for a vulnerability marker are not immune to developing alcoholism. Not all (less than half) alcoholics have a positive history of familial alcoholism and most COAs will not develop alcoholism. A vulnerability marker should be detectable before a person is exposed to alcohol, and it should persist during the development of alcoholism as well as during abstinence. Hill, Steinhauer, and Zubin (1987) have speculated that it is theoretically possible to have a vulnerability marker that is detectable before a person is exposed to alcohol but not during the onset of alcoholism and that reappears after recovery from alcoholism. They have also speculated that a marker might be detectable before and during the onset of alcoholism, but that it might be normalized after the cessation of alcohol abuse. However, these different types of vulnerability markers have yet to be found. The use of prepubertal boys who have not yet been exposed to alcohol to identify putative vulnerability markers presents the risk of missing postpubertal markers and those markers that appear only after exposure to alcohol intake (Begleiter, Porjesz, Bihari, & Kissin, 1984; Behar et al., 1983).

State markers may or may not be reversible after long durations of abstinence from alcohol, and those that persist may be categorized erroneously as vulnerability markers. Residual state markers may or may not be detectable in persons undergoing the alcoholism phase of their lives (Hill, Steinhauer, & Zubin, 1987). Reversible state markers can be used to monitor treatment outcome and to detect relapses. Investigators have not determined whether those who are vulnerable to developing alcoholism are more susceptible to the damaging effects of alcohol. If this were the case, it would probably lead to an earlier appearance of state markers in vulnerable than in nonvulnerable persons having the same duration and quantity of alcohol intake. This is an empirical question not yet answered.

STATE MARKERS

Most investigations of proposed markers for excessive alcohol consumption involve comparisons between a group of known alcoholics, usually in a treatment center, and a group of nonalcoholics or abstainers matched on a number of relevant variables. This approach does not distinguish persistent state markers from vulnerability markers. Nevertheless, the knowledge gained from these studies can be applied by clinicians to improve their diagnostic accuracy. It also provides a basis to investigate whether persistent differences between alcoholics and controls are potential trait markers. Less often investigated is the use of single or multiple putative markers for the early identification of alcohol abuse in the general population or in special population groups such as young adults, pregnant women, drunk-driving offenders, and those needing medical attention. Similarly, not many putative markers have been tested for their correlations with self-reported alcohol intake within groups of individuals over a given period.

Conventional Markers

Table 3.1 summarizes the diagnostic values of the more conventional or older markers of excessive alcohol consumption. Part A of the table lists tests currently in general use; part B lists tests that have proved less sensitive and specific or too cumbersome for routine clinical use. Given the large numbers of publications dealing with these tests, the references cited are not meant to be comprehensive but are representative of either review articles or papers dealing directly with the particular test.

The only true indicator of alcohol intake is the detection of ethanol or one of its metabolites, namely, acetaldehyde and acetate, in a subject's body fluids. However, the relatively rapid elimination of these compounds renders them less useful as markers of alcohol abuse. Nevertheless, determinations of the level of alcohol in blood, urine, or breath have been found very effective in emergency hospital admissions, drunk-driving offenses, and in the follow-up of alcoholism treatment programs. Although the presence of alcohol does not distinguish acute from chronic alcohol intake, under certain circumstances it can be highly suggestive of abusive alcohol consumption. Thus, a blood alcohol level higher than 300 mg/dL recorded at any time, or a level higher than 100 mg/dL recorded during a routine medical examination, can be regarded as a strong indicator of alcoholism (National Council on Alcoholism, 1972). Likewise, a blood alcohol level exceeding 150 mg/dL in a patient without gross evidence of intoxication strongly suggests alcohol abuse and tolerance to alcohol. Using a sensitive method of detection involving gas chromatography–mass spectrometry, Tang (1987) found that ethanol concentrations in urine of 11 alcoholics after 14 days of abstention were at least seven times higher than those of social drinkers (excluding heavy drinkers) and ten times higher than those of control subjects who had not consumed alcohol during the 7 days before the test. In the morning following the day of admission, alcoholics had an average urine ethanol level nearly 160 times that found in light drinkers. The ability to detect ethanol in the urine even after two weeks abstinence greatly improves the reliability of the test as an indicator of heavy alcohol consumption. Tang speculated that the source of ethanol in urine might have been from ethanol conjugates. Because the number of heavy drinkers studied was very small, further investigations are needed to determine whether the measurement of ethanol in urine may be a specific marker for excessive alcohol intake. One possible limitation is the confounding effect of acute alcohol intake several hours before urine samples are taken.

None of the tests in Table 3.1, when used alone, has sufficient sensitivity and specificity to be a reliable marker of alcoholism or to be used as a screening test for heavy alcohol consumption. Nevertheless, clinicians can use an abnormal result as a reason for questioning a patient's drinking more closely. This applies especially to tests such as those for γ-glutamyltransferase (GGT) and mean corpuscular volume (MCV). These two tests, and especially the one for GGT, have been widely used with varying degrees of success as adjunctive instruments in the diagnosis of alcoholism and as screening tests for those arrested for

TABLE 3.1. Older, Conventional Markers of Excessive Alcohol Intake

Marker[a]	Diagnostic capability
Part A	
Ethanol (National Council on Alcoholism, 1972; Tang, 1987)	Low sensitivity because of rapid elimination; useful in cases of intoxication; urinary ethanol levels may be more sensitive.
Aspartate aminotransferase (ASAT) (Matloff, Seligran, & Kaplan, 1980; Nishimura & Teschke, 1983; Salaspuro, 1986)	Increased activity in 30%–75% of alcoholics; primarily an indicator of liver disease, but nonspecific for alcoholism; useful as an adjunct in diagnosis when combined with other tests.
Alanine aminotransferase (ALAT) (Cohen & Kaplan, 1979; Skude & Wadstein, 1977)	Same limitations as ASAT. A ratio of ASAT to ALAT greater than 2 is highly indicative of alcoholic etiology of liver disease.
γ-Glutamyltransferase (GGT) (Holt, Skinner, & Israel, 1981; Salaspuro, 1986)	Most commonly used test. Activity elevated in 35%–85% of alcoholics or heavy drinkers; nonspecific for alcoholism because it is also increased in liver diseases, other drug intake, and concomitant disease states. Useful as an adjunct in diagnosis when combined with other tests. Particularly useful in monitoring treatment results or in motivation of patients.
Mean corpuscular volume (MCV) (Holt et al., 1981; Salaspuro, 1986; Watson, Mohs, Eskelson, Sampliner, & Hartmann, 1986)	Elevated values in 31%–96% of alcoholics; low specificity because other diseases and drug intake can increase MCV values. Less sensitive but more specific than GGT. Very useful as an adjunctive test.
Part B	
α-Amino-n-butyric acid to leucine ratio (Chick, Longstaff, Kreitman, Thatcher & Waite, 1982; Herrington et al., 1981)	Increased in alcoholics but also in patients with either alcoholic or nonalcoholic liver disease; values dependent on nutritional status; low sensitivity and specificity.
Glutamate dehydrogenase (GDH) (Jenkins et al., 1982; Mills, Spooner, Russell, Boyle, & MacSween, 1981; Van Waes & Lieber, 1977)	Nonspecific for alcoholism; increased levels in patients with recent alcohol excess and in those with fatty liver or alcoholic hepatitis. Not very reliable as marker of liver cell necrosis in alcoholics.
Lactate dehydrogenase (LDH) (Konttinen, Hartel, & Louhija, 1970; Nygren & Sundblad, 1971; Watson et al., 1986)	Tendency to increase in some isoenzyme levels in intoxicated chronic alcohol abusers. Nonspecific.
Erythrocyte δ-aminolevulinic acid dehydrase (Flegar-Mestric, Tadej, & Subic-Albert, 1987; Hamlyn, Hopper, & Skillen, 1979)	Level reduced in more than 90% of recently drinking alcoholics; also reduced transiently following acute alcohol intake in nonalcoholic normal subjects. Low sensitivity.
High-density lipoprotein (HDL) cholesterol (Barboriak et al., 1980; Devenyi, Robinson, Kapur, & Roncari, 1981; Hartung et al., 1983)	Values increased in 50%–80% of alcoholics, and also in nonalcoholics drinking 75 g of ethanol daily for 5 weeks; alcoholics with liver diseases may show decreased levels. Low sensitivity and specificity. Most changes are within normal limits.
Uric acid (Drum, Goldman, & Jankowski, 1981; Holt et al., 1981; Watson et al., 1986)	Hyperuricemia is frequently associated with alcoholism and heavy alcohol intake. Low sensitivity and specificity.
Ferritin (Kristenson, Fex, & Trell, 1981; Valimaki, Harkonen, & Ylikahri, 1983)	Elevated levels in alcoholics and heavy drinkers; levels revert to normal with 2 weeks' abstinence. Primarily an indicator of hepatic dysfunction; nonspecific for alcoholism.

[a]Unless otherwise specified, tests are for serum or plasma samples.

drinking and driving (Dunbar et al., 1985; Gjerde, Sakshaug, & Morland, 1986), adolescent alcohol use (Westwood, Cohen, & McNamara, 1978), drinking in middle-aged men (Chick, Pikkarainen, & Plant, 1987; Peterson et al., 1983), and maternal alcohol abuse and fetal alcohol effects (Hollstedt & Dahlgren, 1987; Ylikorkala, Stenman, & Halmesmaki, 1987), as well as epidemiological indicators of alcohol consumption (Gjerde, Amundsen, Skog, Morland, & Aasland, 1987). However, neither test is an adequate substitute for a careful medical history and full clinical examination in the diagnosis of alcoholism or alcohol abuse (Barrison, Ruzek, & Murray-Lyon, 1987). Bernadt, Mumford, Taylor, Smith, and Murray (1982) have advocated the use of short questionnaires such as the brief MAST, the CAGE, and the Reich interview in favor of eight laboratory tests (including those for GGT and MCV) for the routine screening of alcoholism in hospital patients. These investigators tested only the efficacy of single laboratory tests and did not use combinations of tests and sophisticated statistical methods such as discriminant function analyses. Other investigators have reported less successful results with the short questionnaires (Babor & Kadden, 1985).

Not listed in Table 3.1 are a large number of laboratory tests that are routinely requested by physicians to aid them in general diagnoses. These include tests for glucose, urea nitrogen, creatinine, calcium, phosphorus, total protein, albumin, globulin, iron, sodium, potassium, magnesium, zinc, chloride, carbon dioxide, total bilirubin, alkaline phosphatase, creatine kinase, isocitrate dehydrogenase, ornithine carbamyl transferase, and hematological variables such as red and white cell counts, hematocrit, and hemoglobin levels. Each of these tests, used separately, is a poor marker of alcoholism or alcohol abuse. By using various combinations of these tests, however, or by combining them with those listed in Table 3.1, diagnostic efficiency can be greatly improved (Eckardt et al., 1986; Watson et al., 1986).

Combined Tests

In general, combinations of large numbers of tests have yielded better results than combinations of a few tests (e.g., Clark, Holder, Mullet, & Whitehead, 1983; Cushman et al., 1984; Korri, Nuutinen, & Salaspuro, 1985; Morgan, Colman, & Sherlock, 1981; Sanchez-Craig & Annis, 1981). The best results have been obtained by using statistical forms of pattern recognition, called discriminant function analyses, on laboratory test batteries. For example, using a quadratic discriminant function analysis (QDA) of 24 laboratory tests, Ryback, Eckardt, and Pautler (1980) and Ryback, Eckardt, Rawlings, and Rosenthal (1982) correctly identified 100% of medical ward alcoholics, 100% of nonalcoholic patients, and 94% of treatment-program alcoholics. The alcoholic subjects in these studies had many years of heavy drinking and most of them had severe symptoms of alcoholism. Therefore, it is not surprising that other studies involving different samples of alcoholics or heavy drinkers reported slightly less impressive results, yet still with high specificity and sensitivity. For example, Ryback and Rawlings (1985) used the same technique to study a much younger, less impaired group of alcoholics who had an average of less than 5 years of heavy drinking; most of the laboratory tests were within the normal range. They achieved correct identification of 75.5% and 73.8% of alcoholics, and 90.3% and 95.9% of nonalcoholics with rank QDA and rank linear discriminant analysis (LDA), respectively. Discriminant function analysis of a small number of tests in young adults did not achieve sufficient sensitivity in discriminatory power (Bliding, Bliding, Fex, & Tornqvist, 1982). In contrast, using a large number of tests, Stamm, Hansert, and Feuerlein (1984) reported a sensitivity of 86% and a specificity of 87% by optimizing decision limits for the discrimination of male alcoholics from other nonalcoholic patients. Using a stepwise LDA of 31 laboratory tests, Chan, Welte, and Whitney (1987) correctly classified 89% of young adult (age 18 to 28 years) alcoholics and 92% of nonalcoholics. Beresford, Low, Hall, Adduci, and Goggans (1982) reported a correct classification of 79% of alcoholic patients and 80% of nonalcoholic patients, using an LDA of 28 tests. However, the lower sensitivity and specificity might have resulted because their patient population had a wide age range (18 to 83 years), their definition of alcoholism was based solely on the CAGE interview, and the data were for a mixed population of men and women.

Other investigators have used discriminant function analysis of a panel of blood tests to identify heavy drinkers in selected population groups. Cowan, Massey, and Greenfield (1985) reported 96%–99% correct classification of young (18 to 23 years old) male heavy drinkers based on a measure of binge consumption for quantity/frequency of heavy drinking, and 90%–92% correct classification based on maximum number of drinks per occasion as an index of heavy drinking. Similarly, Hillers, Alldredge, and Massey (1986) correctly classified 91% of persons who reported consumption of less than or more than four drinks (48 g of ethanol) per day, using QDA of 15 blood tests. When the number of blood tests used was increased to 24 or 33, the correct classifications were 98% and 100%, respectively. The investigators cautioned that the percentage correctly classified may be inflated due to an excessive number of blood tests for the number of subjects. They recommended a minimum subject to variable ratio of 10:1. Other researchers have suggested smaller ratios, namely, 3:1 (Solberg, 1978) and 5:1 (Schnitt & Dove, 1986). Less successful results have been reported in two studies of health-screening subjects in which correct classifiations of heavy drinkers were less than 50% in one (Shaper, Pocock, Ashby, Walker, & Whitehead, 1985) and 92% in another (Whitfield, Allen, Adena, Gallagher, & Hensley, 1981). These may be due to the use of one set of discriminant functions for a diverse group of populations. As Ryback and Rawlings (1985) have pointed out, it is unlikely that one set of discriminant functions will correctly define all types of drinkers.

It should be stressed that the use of discriminant function analysis to develop a screening instrument for alcoholism is still in its infancy (Schnitt & Dove, 1986). There is a need for further research to be undertaken to optimize and refine this method before it can be effectively applied to early detection of heavy drinking. Perhaps different sets of discriminant functions are needed to correctly define heavy drinkers with different characteristics, such as history of other drug intake, health status, age range, sex, number of years of heavy drinking, frequency and quantity of alcohol consumption, and familial history of alcoholism. The sensitivity and specificity of discriminant analyses can possibly be improved by combining laboratory tests with data from rapid interviews such as CAGE or the brief MAST, as well as with one or more of the newer biochemical markers such as those discussed in the next section (Persson & Magnusson, 1988). Bernadt, Mumford, and Murray (1984) performed discriminant analysis of three rapid interviews (CAGE, brief MAST, and Reich) and nine laboratory tests. They found that a combination of Reich interview and GDH level achieved 100% sensitivity and about 80% specificity for excessive drinking and alcoholism.

The advantages of using discriminant function analysis of a large panel of laboratory tests are: (1) Nearly all the tests are those commonly ordered by physicians during regular physical examinations or hospital admissions. Most of them can be performed using automated procedures. The test results can complement the physician's diagnosis based on clinical symptoms and personal interview. (2) Abnormal test results can be used to advantage by the physician in counseling patients to overcome any denial response. (3) Classification accuracy is not changed by long abstinence (Eckardt, Rawlings, Ryback, Martin, & Gottschalk, 1984; Ryback, Rawlings, Faden, & Negron, 1985). (4) Good discrimination can be achieved even though values for the laboratory tests are within the normal range. (5) The automated test batteries are economically reasonable, being equivalent in cost to only two or three separate laboratory tests (Ryback et al., 1980). Limitations of the method are: (1) It cannot be used effectively in persons over 65 years of age because 50% would be classified as alcoholics even though they are not (Ryback et al., 1980; Ryback, Eckardt, Negron, & Rawlings, 1983). Fortunately, persons older than 65 constitute a relatively small proportion of chronic alcoholics. (2) Accuracy of classification is dependent on a precise separation of the groups under study; that is, precisely clear definitions are needed for alcoholics versus nonalcoholics and heavy drinkers versus light drinkers.

Another method that is potentially valuable for the early identification of heavy drinking involves a combination of clinical signs, medical history, laboratory tests, and alcohol questionnaires collectively called the Alcohol Clinical Index (Skinner et al., 1986; Skinner & Holt, 1987; Skinner, Holt, Schuller, Roy, & Israel, 1984). Widespread use of this relatively simple method by properly trained physicians or health-care professionals is very likely to result in substantial improvement in the ability of physicians to diagnose alcohol abuse or alcoholism. Whether the method is sufficiently sensitive to detect those who drink heavily but are without clinical signs of alcohol-related complications needs to be tested.

Newer Markers

Table 3.2 summarizes the more recent biochemical markers for alcoholism or alcohol abuse. These tests are not part of the automated blood test batteries. The two urine tests, for dolichol and alcohol-specific product, have the advantage of being noninvasive in sample collection, compared with blood tests. The disadvantages of the dolichol test are that moderate alcohol intake for 10 days does not cause an increase in urinary dolichol levels and that the half-life decay for increased urinary dolichol is about 3 days (Roine, 1988). Another disadvantage is its low specificity (see Table 3.2; Roine et al., 1988). Measurements of serum acetate and 2,3-butanediol have little value as screening instruments for early identification of alcoholism because their detection, especially that of acetate, is dependent on the presence of ethanol. Nevertheless, increased serum acetate could be used for the screening of problem drinking among drunken drivers (Roine et al., 1988). Tests in which abnormal values revert toward normal values within one or two weeks of abstinence may not be sufficiently sensitive and specific to identify binge drinkers or alcoholics in recent remission. Thus, nearly all of the tests in Table 3.2 fall into this category, except platelet adenylate cyclase, which may be a vulnerability marker. On the other hand, these tests may be good markers for monitoring abstinence in alcoholics under treatment. Because these tests are relatively new, investigations have been primarily confined

TABLE 3.2. Newer Markers of Excessive Alcohol Intake

Marker[a]	Diagnostic capability
Acetate Korri, Nuutinen, & Salaspuro, 1985; Nuutinen, Lindros, Hekali, & Salaspuro, 1985; Salaspuro, Korri, Nuutinen, & Roine, 1987; Roine et al., 1988)	Elevated level during ethanol oxidation is indicative of metabolic tolerance to alcohol. Specificity of increased acetate level is 92% and sensitivity is 65% for both alcoholism and heavy drinking. Requires presence of ethanol for analysis; therefore is useful only in intoxicated cases.
Urinary dolichol (Pullarkat & Raguthu, 1985; Roine, 1988; Roine, Turpeinen, Ylikahri, & Salaspuro, 1987; Roine et al., 1989b; Salaspuro et al., 1987)	Increased excretion in alcoholics and in other disease states. Values normalize within 1 week of abstinence. Low specificity because elevated levels are frequently seen in infections, malignancies, and during pregnancy.
Urinary alcohol-specific product (Tang, Devenyi, Teller, & Israel, 1986)	Presumably breakdown product of acetaldehyde-protein adduct. Levels very low in controls but increased 17 times in chronic alcoholics; values return to normal after 2 weeks' abstinence. In one study specificity was 100% and sensitivity was 79%.

(continued)

TABLE 3.2. (Continued)

Marker[a]	Diagnostic capability
Ratio of mitochondrial ASAT (m-ASAT) to total ASAT (Nalpas et al., 1984; Nalpas, Vassault, Charpin, Lacour, & Berthelot, 1986; Okuno et al., 1988)	Increased ratio in alcoholics with or without liver disease; 93%–100% sensitivity. After abstinence of 1 week, m-ASAT decreases by more than 50%.
Transferrin variant (Chapman, Sorrentino, & Morgan, 1985; Gjerde, Johnsen, Bjorneboe, Bjorneboe, & Morland, 1988; Stibler, Borg, & Allgulander, 1980; Stibler, Borg, & Joustra, 1986; Storey, Anderson, Mack, Powell, & Halliday, 1987; Vesterberg, Petran, & Schmidt, 1984)	Variant with isoelectric point 5.7 was elevated in alcholics and heavy drinkers (consumption of more than 60 g alcohol per day for 10 days). Levels decreased 50% after 14 days' abstinence. High sensitivity and specificity, but less successful results also have been reported.
Red cell morphology (Homaidan, Kricka, Bailey, & Whitehead, 1986)	Elevated number of triangulocytes in alcoholics (range 2.6%–18%) compared with healthy controls (0%–0.5%). Slow and laborious test.
Acetaldehyde-hemoglobin adduct (Hoberman & Chiodo, 1982; Homaidan, Kricka, Clark, Jones, & Whitehead, 1983; Lucas et al., 1988; Peterson et al., 1985)	Tends to be elevated in alcoholics compared with normal volunteers, but unreliable as marker of alcohol abuse. Sensitivity and specificity as marker of heavy drinking not studied in large samples.
Antibodies against acetaldehyde adducts (Hoerner et al., 1988; Israel, Harwitz, Niemela, & Arnon, 1986; Niemela et al., 1987)	Elevated antibody titers found in 73% of alcoholics; 39% of patients with nonalcoholic liver diseases also had elevated levels.
Erythrocyte aldehyde dehydrogenase (Agarwal, Volkens, Hafer, & Goedde, 1987; Fantozzi et al., 1987; Lin, Potter, & Mezey, 1984; Palmer & Jenkins, 1985; Towell, Barboriak, Townsend, Kolbfleisch, & Wang, 1986)	Activity generally decreased in chronic alcoholics, but increased activity has been reported. Low sensitivity and specificity. No correlation between daily alcohol intake or degree of liver injury and level of enzyme activity.
Apolipoprotein A-I and A-II (Malmendier & Delcroix, 1985; Puchois, Fontan, Gentilini, Gelez, & Fruchart, 1984; Puddey, Masarei, Vandongen, & Beilin, 1986)	Both increased in intemperate drinkers. Only A-II levels correlate significantly with self-reported alcohol intake. A-II may be more sensitive indicator of excessive alcohol intake than HDL cholesterol. Combination of GGT and A-II detected 72.9% of heavy drinkers; GGT alone detected only 59%.
2,3-Butanediol (Rutstein et al., 1983; Wolf et al., 1983)	Levels greater than 5 μM in severely alcoholic men after drinking distilled spirits, with sensitivity of 79%. Only 1 of 22 controls had level above 5 μM.
Platelet adenylate cyclase (Tabakoff et al., 1988; Tsuchiya et al., 1987)	Enzyme activity after stimulation with agents such as cesium fluoride significantly lower in alcoholics; long-lasting changes detectable in alcoholics abstinent for one to four years. Combined with another test, has sensitivity and specificity of approximately 75%.

[a]Unless otherwise specified, tests are for serum or plasma samples.

to comparisons between known alcoholics and nonalcoholics. It is to be expected that the sensitivity and specificity of each test will decrease when it is applied as a screening test in populations with drinkers having different intake levels. For example, Stibler, Borg, and Joustra (1986) reported that 89% of their alcoholic subjects had elevated serum levels of abnormal transferrin ($Tf_{5.7}$); but in another study (Gjerde, Johnsen, Bjorneboe, Bjorneboe, & Morland, 1988) only 68% of those who reported alcohol consumption above 40 g/day had elevated ($Tf_{5.7}$) values. The two tests, for m-ASAT and $Tf_{5.7}$, that were reported to have relatively high sensitivity and specificity in identifying alcoholics with a mean age of over 35, did not have sufficiently high sensitivity to identify young adult (mean age under 25) alcoholics (Chan et al., 1989). Although both tests showed significantly elevated levels compared with controls, there were many overlapping values between the alcoholics and controls. Depending on the cutoff limits, the sensitivity range for either test was only 15%–50%, while specificity ranged from 82%–96%. These authors speculated that the lower sensitivity and specificity could be due to a shorter duration of heavy drinking or to a greater resilience in young adults with regard to the damaging effects of alcohol. Another important factor is the number of days elapsed since a subject's last drink, because elevated levels might revert to normal values faster in young adults.

There have been no investigations using discriminant function analysis of combinations of these newer markers in conjunction with the more conventional markers, as well as with questionnaire data. This approach is very likely to improve the sensitivity and specificity of these tests as screening instruments for excessive alcohol intake.

Miscellaneous Tests

The following biochemical variables need to be further investigated for their potential usefulness as markers of alcoholism or heavy drinking.

Lysosomal Glycosidases

Increased β-hexosaminidase levels have been reported in 94.4% of chronic alcoholics with acute ethanol intoxication (Hultberg, Isaksson, & Tiderstrom, 1980). After 7 to 10 days of abstinence, about half of the alcoholic patients had normalized values of the enzyme (Isaksson, Blanche, Hultberg, & Joelsson, 1985). The same investigators reported that consumption of 60 g of alcohol daily for 10 days also significantly increased serum β-hexosaminidase activity.

Immunoglobulins (Ig)

Elevated serum IgA and IgE levels are often seen in chronic alcoholics (Hallgren & Lundin, 1983; Iturriaga, Pereda, Estevez, & Ugarte, 1977). Although IgA may also be increased in nonalcoholic liver diseases, the IgA/IgG ratio can be used to separate alcoholic from nonalcoholic origin of the liver damage (Iturriaga et al., 1977).

Serotonin Uptake

Platelet affinity for serotonin was significantly increased in alcoholics on admission for treatment and in alcoholics with short and long (up to 11 years) durations of abstinence (Boismare et al., 1987). Neiman, Beving, and Malmgren (1987) also reported an increased affinity for serotonin in recently admitted alcoholics, but found that this effect was transient and that normal affinity was restored during detoxification. Further investigations are needed to establish whether this test could be a marker for alcohol dependence.

Response to Thyrotropin-Releasing Hormone (TRH)

Alcoholics who had been abstinent for more than 20 days showed a blunted thyroid-stimulating hormone (TSH) response to TRH, compared with healthy controls (Casacchia, Rossi, & Stratta, 1985). A persistently blunted response was also reported in 31% of male alcoholics who were abstinent for 2 to 29 years (Loosen, Wilson, Dew, & Tipermas, 1983). The blunted response was postulated to be a trait marker for alcoholism. This possibility is discussed further in the section on vulnerability markers below.

Neurophysins

The polypeptide neurophysin II was elevated in the sera of alcoholics who also showed elevated levels of common blood markers for alcoholism such as GGT (Legros et al., 1983). These patients admitted to greater alcohol and less anxiolytic drug intake immediately before admission.

Alkaloid Condensation Products

The condensation of acetaldehyde with endogenous biogenic amines of the indolamine or catecholamine classes results in the formation of tetrahydroiso-quinolines or tetrahydro-β-carbolines. These products have been postulated to play a role in the development of alcoholism (Collins, 1985; Myers, 1985). Although some of these products, in particular salsolinol, have been detected in the urine of alcoholic subjects, the results might have been confounded by the presence of these alkaloids in foods and beverages, by methodological inconsistencies, or by possible artifactual condensations (Adachi et al., 1986; Collins, 1985; Hirst, Evans, & Gowdey, 1987; Matsubara, Fukushima, Akane, Hama, & Fukui, 1986; Rommelspacher & Schmidt, 1985).

Methanol

One of the congeners in alcoholic beverages is methanol. Because its metabolism by liver alcohol dehydrogenase can be inhibited by ethanol, high blood methanol levels could be present after prolonged drinking, especially in alcoholics whose liver function is compromised. Since methanol is oxidized rapidly after the disappearance of ethanol from blood, its clinical usefulness is limited to situations in which blood alcohol levels of 0.2 g/L or more are present (Roine et al., 1989a). It has been reported that some alcoholics have supplemented their regular intake with cleansing solutions containing up to 80% methanol (Martensson, Olofsson, & Heath, 1988), resulting in high blood methanol levels. Increased blood methanol levels are often detected in drunken drivers, and it has been suggested that a level exceeding 5 to 10 mg/L is indicative of alcohol-related problems (Bonte, Kuhnholz, & Ditt, 1985).

Age, Sex, and Race Differences

Ryback and Rawlings (1985) suggested that subpopulations of women including those who are menstruating, menopausal, and those taking estrogen supplements, can create problems for diagnostic instruments if men and women are grouped together. Sex differences in some blood variables have been documented (Vital and Health Statistics, 1982); for instance, men have significantly higher serum iron levels, hemoglobin, and hematocrit but lower MCV than women. It has been suggested that MCV is a better indicator of excessive alcohol consumption in women than in men, and that women are more susceptible to the hematological toxicity of ethanol (Chalmers, Chanarin, MacDermott, & Levi, 1980). Discriminant analysis of several blood chemistry items yielded better sensitivity and specificity for detecting female as opposed to male heavy drinkers (Chalmers, Rinsler, MacDermott, Spicer, & Levi, 1981). These findings are consistent with reports that women are more susceptible to the damaging effects of alcohol (e.g., Gavaler, 1982). Age and sex differences in the responses of alcoholic inpatients to a self-administered alcoholism screening test have been reported (Davis & Morse, 1987). Depending on the diagnostic instrument used, it may be necessary to have different criteria for the definition of alcoholism for subjects of different age groups and sex. This is an important issue because investigations of putative biochemical markers of excessive alcohol intake rely heavily on the accurate classifications of comparison groups by an independent method.

Some blood variables change with age; for instance, mean corpuscular hemoglobin levels and MCV increase with age regardless of sex and race (Vital and Health Statistics, 1982). Older heavy drinkers will generally have more years of exposure to alcohol than younger heavy drinkers, and such a difference may affect the discriminatory power of biochemical tests for alcoholism or heavy drinking. For example, the inappropriateness of several biochemical tests to screen young heavy drinkers has been reported (Bliding et al., 1982). Another related issue is, again, the possibility that young drinkers may be more resilient to the damaging effects of ethanol than older drinkers. During periods of abstinence, biochemical variables may revert to normal values much more quickly in young drinkers than in older drinkers. Therefore, it is important to elicit information from research subjects about the number of days that elapsed since they last drank alcohol. These issues have not been adequately examined.

No studies have systematically examined whether racial differences (e.g., between whites and blacks) exist in terms of the various biochemical markers for alcoholism or heavy drinking. Only one marker, cupro-zinc superoxide dismutase of erythrocyte lysates, has been reported to be increased in black alcoholics, compared with black or white controls (Del Villano, Tischfield, Schacter, Stilwil & Miller, 1979). There was too much overlap in enzyme activity between alcoholics and healthy controls to render the test a good marker for alcoholism in black patients. Nevertheless, it is possible that blacks and whites may show different blood chemistry profiles after chronic heavy alcohol intake, especially since blacks and whites show differences in some blood variables—for instance, whites of both sexes had consistently higher mean hematocrit and hemoglobin levels, higher MCV, and higher white blood cell counts. The mean serum iron levels of black females were lower than those of white females for all age groups (Vital and Health Statistics, 1982). Daily and dietary intake of thiamine and other vitamins was lower in blacks than in whites (Koplan et al., 1986; Vital and Health Statistics, 1982). Racial differences in alcohol dehydrogenase (ADH) and aldehyde dehydrogenase (ALDH) are discussed in the following section on vulnerability (trait) markers.

VULNERABILITY MARKERS

Methodological Issues

Several reviews have summarized the genetic aspects of alcoholism and research involving those presumed to be at high risk for the future development of alcoholism, namely COAs (e.g., Braude & Chao, 1986; Corder, McRee, & Rohrer, 1984; Deren, 1986; el-Guebaly, 1986; Goodwin, 1987; National Institute on Alcohol Abuse and Alcoholism [NIAAA], 1985; Russell, Henderson, & Blume, 1984; Schuckit, 1986). It should be emphasized that this high-risk group may not be homogenous in terms of risk for development of alcoholism because only about one third of the group will become alcoholics (Schuckit, Shaskan, Duby, Vega, & Moss, 1982; also see Russell, Chapter 2, this volume). Within the COA group there are those who are truly at risk and those who are not truly at risk because some FHP subjects may not have inherited a trait, or their relatives may have been misdiagnosed as alcoholics. Environmental factors also play important roles in the development of alcoholism. Likewise, the so-called low-risk group can loosely be considered as consisting of the same two subcategories because not all these people are immune to becoming alcoholics. Given these possible sources of error in comparing high-risk and low-risk groups (i.e., FHP versus FHN subjects), it is imperative that sample sizes be sufficiently large to enable adequate testing of the null hypothesis (Sher, 1983).

Other approaches to investigations of high-risk populations include studies involving COAs who were adopted and reared by nonalcoholic parents and studies of multiple generations of single families to search for markers that are unique in alcoholic relatives but are absent in nonalcoholic relatives (Schuckit, 1986, 1987a). Both methods are expensive and difficult to carry out. The former method is largely dependent on availability of adoption records (which may be hard to come by), while the latter method requires controlling for many factors such as age, lifestyle, and drinking history. The contribution of studies using these two methods and other behavior genetic approaches are presented in depth by Searles (Chapter 5, this volume). Investigations involving comparisons between cohorts of FHP and FHN subjects, however, remain more popular, practical, and economically feasible. Further, it should be stressed that the biochemical variables that are different in FHP and FHN subjects may not necessarily be genetically influenced. Thus, the term "genetic marker" has been inappropriately used for some of the putative trait markers, even though no evidence in support of genetic transmission of the marker is available. It is also essential to conduct follow-up studies of the same populations of FHP and FHN subjects. Reports of this kind of study have yet to appear because this research approach is so new.

Several approaches can be used in the search for putative trait markers in FHP subjects: (1) Individual and natural variations in the biochemical factor need to be ascertained. (2) The responses of the marker to acute ethanol administration can be studied, and these should be compared with data on the same variable in alcoholics. One main drawback of this approach is that it is difficult to differentiate primary drug effects from secondary effects caused by stress, anxiety, or other responses to drug intake. (3) When alcoholics are used in the investigation, confounding effects of alcohol withdrawal or acute intoxication need to be accounted for. Tests involving the administration of ethanol to abstinent alcoholics may be hindered by ethical concerns.

Markers in COAs and Alcoholics

Table 3.3 summarizes research on biochemical markers in which investigators compared alcoholics with nonalcoholics and FHP subjects with FHN subjects. Where the results on both cohorts are similar, they suggest that the biochemical variable involved may be a vulnerability marker. However, where the results are dissimilar, interpretation of the data becomes more difficult. It may mean either that the biochemical variable is not a vulnerability marker or that the putative trait marker might have been altered by chronic alcohol intake.

TABLE 3.3. Biochemical Variables in Alcoholics and COAs

Blood marker	Alcoholics[a]	COAs[b]
Acetaldehyde	Increased in nonabstinent subjects after alcohol intake. No difference after 2 weeks' abstinence.	Elevated levels after alcohol ingestion in one study, but no difference found in two other studies.
Prolactin	Resting level normal or slightly reduced in abstinent subjects. Increased after acute ethanol use in normal subjects and in drinking chronic alcoholics.	No difference in basal level. Initial (30 minute) increase after acute ethanol intake, followed by decline; significantly lower levels 150 minutes after ethanol use.
Cortisol	Basal level increased in nonabstinent alcoholics but appears normal during abstinence. Acute ethanol intake causes increase in normal subjects and in drinking alcoholics.	No difference in basal level. Transient (30 minute) increase after a high dose of ethanol followed by decline past basal level yielding significantly lower levels.
Transketolase	Decreased affinity (lower K_m) for thiamine pyrophosphatase in cultured fibroblasts of male subjects.	Decreased affinity (lower K_m) for thiamine pyrophosphate in males.
Response to TRH	Blunted response in abstinent alcoholics.	Higher basal and peak thyrotropin levels in males.
Monoamine oxidase (MAO)	Generally reduced activity even after long abstinence, but conflicting results have been reported.	Lower activity; also lower V_{max}.

[a]Compared with nonalcoholics.
[b]FHP versus FHN subjects.

Acetaldehyde

Several studies (reviewed by Di Padova, Worner, & Lieber, 1987) have shown that alcoholics have higher levels of blood acetaldehyde than normal controls after the ingestion of alcohol. However, this is not a consistent finding; some findings were confounded by problems with the analytical method (Eriksson & Peachey, 1980; Nuutinen, Lindros, & Salaspuro, 1983; Nuutinen, Salaspuro, Valle, & Lindros, 1984). Recently Di Padova et al. (1987) evaluated the blood levels of acetaldehyde after alcohol ingestion in abstinent and nonabstinent alcoholics. They found that the elevated acetaldehyde levels seen in nonabstinent alcoholics returned to normal values after 2 weeks of abstinence, suggesting that altered acetaldehyde metabolism in alcoholics is not a primary preexisting effect. Schuckit and Rayses (1979) reported that FHP subjects had higher acetaldehyde concentrations after alcohol ingestion than FHN subjects. However, this finding might have been confounded by artifactual acetaldehyde formation in the blood samples. The results of Schuckit and Rayses (1979) were not confirmed in two other studies (Behar et al., 1983; Eriksson, 1980). Therefore, there is not sufficient evidence to indicate that acetaldehyde is a vulnerability marker. However, there is strong evidence to suggest that increased acetaldehyde levels in Oriental subjects who show the flushing reaction after drinking alcohol may deter them from becoming heavy drinkers (reviewed by Chan, 1986); that is, acetaldehyde may be a negative vulnerability marker, or a protective marker. The higher levels of acetaldehyde in flushing subjects are caused by an unusually less active liver aldehyde dehydrogenase isozyme (ALDHI). Although not very likely, the possible contribution of an atypical alcohol dehydrogenase cannot be ruled out (Chan, 1986). Schuckit and Duby (1982) reported that FPH subjects showed higher levels of facial flushing in response to ethanol than did FHN subjects (10% versus 3%). The higher incidence of flushing in FHP subjects is still much less than that seen in Oriental populations (47%–85%). It is doubtful whether the increased flushing in FHP subjects is a vulnerability marker. As Chan (1986) has pointed out, the flushing phenomenon cannot be the sole explanation for differences in incidence of alcoholism among different racial groups.

Prolactin

Acute ethanol ingestion generally causes an increase in this anterior pituitary hormone within 30 minutes, with a return toward baseline by 90 minutes in normal volunteers and nonabstinent chronic alcoholics. This finding is not universally consistent (Cicero, 1983). In two studies of COAs, one with and the other without placebo controls, FHP subjects had lower prolactin levels at 150 minutes after a low (0.75 mL/kg) or high (1.1 mL/kg) dose of ethanol (Schuckit, Parker, & Rossman, 1983; Schuckit, Gold, & Risch, 1987b). These results seem to provide some basis for the previous findings that FHP subjects reported significantly less intense feelings of intoxication than FHN subjects, even though there were no differences in peak blood ethanol levels (Hill, Armstrong, Steinhauer, Baughman, & Zubin, 1987; Schuckit, 1980, 1981, 1984c, 1985; O'Malley & Maisto, 1985; Pollock, Teasdale, Gabrielli, & Knop, 1986). The use of a placebo control is essential, especially since Newlin (1985) clearly demonstrated that FHP subjects show a significantly enhanced antagonistic placebo response compared with FHN subjects; the former had a larger heart rate decrease than the latter after consuming what was believed to be malt liquor but was actually dealcoholized beer. The relationship between the group difference in postethanol prolactin levels and ethanol dose is not fully understood (Schuckit et al., 1987b).

Cortisol

Most human studies indicate that cortisol level increases in normal human volunteers and in nonabstinent alcoholics after drinking ethanol if the dose is high enough (Cicero, 1983; Schuckit, Gold, & Risch, 1987a). In abstinent alcoholics during acute withdrawal, cortisol levels after an ethanol challenge may be decreased or increased. The inconsistent findings are probably due to confounding effects of withdrawal reactions (Cicero, 1983). In two studies, one with and the other without placebo controls, FHP subjects demonstrated lower cortisol levels after alcohol ingestion (0.75 or 1.1 mL/kg) than FHN subjects (Schuckit, 1984a; Schuckit et al., 1987a). These data are consistent with previous reports showing family group differences in ethanol-induced decrements in performance and self-reported feelings of intoxication (O'Malley & Maisto, 1985; Pollock et al., 1986; Schuckit, 1980, 1984c, 1985). However, like the results for prolactin, these interesting and important findings do not provide any clue as to whether the group differences in ethanol response are genetically controlled or directly tied to an alcoholic predisposition (Schuckit et al., 1987a, 1987b). Follow-up studies of the same subjects will probably shed some light on the matter.

Schuckit reported at the 1988 annual meeting of the Research Society on Alcoholism that the adrenocorticotropic hormone (ACTH) response to a challenge dose of ethanol was significantly less in FHP than in FHN subjects. ACTH stimulates the human adrenal cortex to secrete cortisol and other steroids. Schuckit also found that the combination of cortisol and ACTH provided a better classification (83%) of FHP subjects than did cortisol alone (67%).

Transketolase

One of the neurological complications of severe alcoholism is the Wernicke–Korsakoff syndrome (Greenberg & Diamond, 1985). Both thiamine deficiency and neurotoxic effects of ethanol per se can contribute to the disorder. There may be a genetically determined abnormality in the thiamine-requiring enzyme, transketolase, which predisposes individuals to developing Wernicke–Korsakoff syndrome (Blass & Gibson, 1977, 1979). Thus, transketolase from skin fibroblasts of patients with alcoholism-related Wernicke–Korsakoff syndrome had a tenfold decrease in affinity (high K_m) for thiamine pyrophosphate compared with enzyme from the cells of normal subjects. Reproductibility of these results has been questioned (Greenberg & Diamond, 1985). Nevertheless, Mukherjee et al. (1987) recently confirmed the same K_m abnormality in cultured fibroblasts of patients with alcoholism-associated Wernicke–Korsakoff syndrome, familial chronic alcoholic males, and more importantly, male offspring of alcoholics without any history of alcoholism. The finding in the last group suggests a genetic predisposition to thiamine deficiency but does not necessarily allow the inference that such abnormality predisposes FHP subjects to developing alcoholism. Longitudinal studies are needed before further conclusions can be reached. Also, the results of Mukherjee et al. (1987) need to be replicated with a larger sample size.

Response to TRH

Moss, Guthrie, and Linnoila (1986) studied the responses of thyrotropin to TRH. They found that sons of familial alcoholics had significantly higher basal thyrotropin levels, peak thyrotropin levels and thyrotropin areas under the curve than did male controls. No differences were found between daughters of familial alcoholics and female controls. The findings are in contrast to the persistent blunting of thyrotropin response seen in some abstinent alcoholics. The neurochemical basis for the differential response has yet to be investigated.

Monoamine Oxidase (MAO)

This is a mitochondrial enzyme known to be under genetic control (Lykouras, Moussas, & Markianos, 1987). It catalyzes the oxidative deamination of biogenic amines and has an important role in regulating mood and behavior. Several studies have reported reduced platelet MAO activity in alcoholics (e.g., Alexopoulous, Lieberman, & Frances, 1983; Brown, 1977; Faraj et al., 1987; Fowler et al., 1981; Major & Murphy, 1978; Sullivan, Cavenar, Maltbie, Lister, & Zung, 1979), with some reporting that individuals with the lowest MAO activity also had the highest incidence of familial alcoholism (Alexopoulous et al., 1983; Lykouras et al., 1987; Major & Murphy, 1978; Sullivan et al., 1979). Because there was a great deal of overlap in activity of the enzyme in alcoholics and controls, some studies did not report lower MAO activity in alcoholics, but there was a trend toward lower activity in subgroups of individuals (Lykouras et al., 1987; von Knorring, Bohman, von Knorring, & Oreland, 1985; von Knorring, Oreland, & von Knorring, 1987). For example, A. L. von Knorring et al. (1985) and L. von Knorring et al. (1987) found that MAO activity was normal in Type 1 alcoholics (characterized by late-onset alcoholism and few social complications) but was clearly low in Type 2 alcoholics (characterized by early onset, use and abuse of other drugs, and several social complications). The latter finding was confirmed by Pandey, Fawcett, Gibbons, Clark, and Davis (1988). Likewise, Lykouras et al. (1987) reported that only those alcoholics with at least one alcoholic first-degree relative showed a trend toward lower MAO activity. If lower MAO activity is a vulnerability marker rather than a state marker of alcohol abuse, the enzyme activity should remain low after periods of abstinence. Data on recovering alcoholics appear to support the vulnerability concept, but the possibility of long-lasting effects of chronic alcohol intake cannot be ruled out (Faraj et al., 1987; Giller & Hall, 1983; Giller et al., 1984; Sullivan, Stanfield, Maltbie, Hammett, & Cavenar, 1978). Transient increases in MAO activity during the initial period of abstinence have also been reported (Agarwal, et al., 1983; Wiberg, 1979). Faraj et al. (1987) suggested that measurements of MAO function, including the kinetic parameter V_{max}, constitute a more reliable biochemical marker for alcoholism. This approach has not been used in studies of COAs, but lower MAO activity has been demonstrated in FHP subjects compared with FHN subjects (Alexopoulos et al., 1983; Schuckit, et al., 1982). Because abnormalities in platelet MAO activity are also common in patients with various psychiatric disorders (Major, Hawley, Saini, Garrick, & Murphy, 1985), the use of this enzyme alone may not definitively identify vulnerability to alcoholism. It needs to be combined with other trait markers if better separation of those genuinely at risk from those not at risk is desired.

Combination of Markers

Only one report has appeared in which several trait markers were used simultaneously to classify high-risk and low-risk subjects (Schuckit & Gold, 1988). The investigators compared a sample of 30 male FHP and 30 matched FHN subjects on the following measures: postethanol changes in subjective feelings, static ataxia, and plasma levels of prolactin and cortisol. Using a stepwise discriminant function analysis of these measures, they found that four items (subjective feelings after high ethanol dose, cortisol values at two time points after high dose, and prolactin results after low dose) combined to correctly classify 83% of FHN subjects and 70% of FHP subjects. It is hoped that future investigations will explore the potential usefulness of including additional variables, such as those discussed above, in the discriminant analysis of FHP–FHN pairs. Schuckit and Gold (1988) suggested that resting eye blink rate may be a good candidate. Other potentially useful variables that have been demonstrated to differ between FHP and FHN subjects are behavioral, cognitive, and neurophysiological parameters such as verbal IQs, auditory word span performance, reading comprehension, the P300 wave component of event-related potentials, and electroencephalographic patterns. These are reviewed by Tarter, Laird, and Moss (Chapter 4, this volume).

Miscellaneous Markers

A major metabolite of the neurotransmitter serotonin, 5-hydroxyindoleacetic acid (5-HIAA), has been reported to be low in the cerebrospinal fluid of alcoholics (Ballenger, Goodwin, Major, & Brown, 1979) and depressed relatives of alcoholics who themselves are not alcoholic (Rosenthal, Davenport, Cowdry, Webster, & Goodwin, 1980). Low levels of 5-HIAA have also been associated with several kinds of violent behavior (Virkkunen, Nuutila, Goodwin, & Linnoila, 1987). Most of the subjects have alcoholism problems. Thus, 5-HIAA may be a potential vulnerability marker, at least for a subgroup of FHP subjects, namely, those with Type 2 alcoholic personalities. Prospective studies with young FHP and FHN subjects who have not been exposed to alcohol need to be conducted to confirm this hypothesis. Since low levels of another monoamine metabolite, 3-methoxy-4-hydroxyphenylglycol, and a blood glucose nadir during glucose tolerance testing are found to coexist with low 5-HIAA levels in most arsonists (Virkkunen et al., 1987), these two may also be potential vulnerability markers that warrant further investigation.

Ledig et al. (1986) investigated eight enzymes, all known to be genetically determined, in alcoholics and controls with the aim of locating differences in phenotype distributions. Only one enzyme, glyoxalase-I in erythrocytes, showed a significant increase in frequency in phenotype 1 and a significant decrease in phenotype 2 in male alcoholics compared with controls. No differences were found between alcoholic and normal women. The investigators stated that the male-limited differences in glyoxalase phenotype 1 remain after alcohol withdrawal, but the duration of abstinence was not specified. Further studies of this enzyme in COAs and in families over several generations are needed to support the hypothesis that males with phenotype 1 of glyoxalase may be predisposed to alcoholism.

Hulyalkar, Nora, and Manowitz (1984) found a relatively high occurrence of the electrophoretic variant of arylsulfatase-A in mentally ill patients with alcoholism. Arylsulfatase-A is a lysosomal enzyme that catalyzes the conversion of sulfatides to cerebroside and sulfate. The abnormal enzyme is not primarily associated with mental illness. These investigators hypothesized that persons in whom the abnormal enzyme is expressed may be at risk for the neuropathological effects of alcohol. More research is needed to test this hypothesis.

A number of clinical reports have suggested the possibility that the development of alcoholic liver diseases might have a genetic basis. For example, HL-A antigens have been implicated as immunogenic markers of alcoholism and alcoholic liver disease (e.g., Saunders et al., 1982; Saunders & Williams, 1983; Shigeta et al., 1980). However, the findings are primarily confined to demonstrating a higher frequency of certain HL-A antigens in patients with alcoholic cirrhosis compared with healthy controls. Only the report by Hrubec and Omenn (1981) provides empirical support for the genetic basis of alcoholic cirrhosis. These investigators found a twin concordance rate for alcholic cirrhosis of 14.6% for monozygotic twins and 5.4% for dizygotic twins from a study of more than 15,000 male twin pairs.

ANIMAL STUDIES

Although there are no complete models of human alcoholism (Deitrich & Spuhler, 1984), the use of animal models to assess genetic influences on various aspects of alcoholism serves to provide guidance for human investigations by indicating promising leads out of the myriad possibilities. Animal studies on molecular and neurochemical mechanisms of actions of alcohol are indispensable because analogous studies in humans would be either impractical or unethical. These studies can lead to the design of better pharmacological interventions to prevent or treat alcoholism. Furthermore, the availability of genetically pure strains of mice and rats that differ in their responses to alcohol will greatly facilitate the search for vulnerability markers of alcoholism. These animal models will also enhance our understanding of the molecular and biochemical mechanisms underlying the development of tolerance to and physical dependence on alcohol, preference for alcohol, and differences in sensitivity to alcohol. The reader is referred to reviews summarizing the development of and research on the many animal models of alcoholism (e.g., Collins, 1986; Crabbe, Kosobud, Young, Tam, & McSwigan, 1985; Deitrich & Spuhler, 1984; Kosobud & Crabbe, 1986; Li, Lumeng, McBride, Waller, & Murphy, 1986; McClearn & Erwin, 1982).

CONCLUSIONS

There is compelling evidence to indicate that for some individuals genetic predisposition plays an important role in the development of alcoholism. However, environmental influences are equally important. Irrespective of whether individuals have the inherited risk of developing alcoholism, the early identification of those who drink heavily, preferably before any medical, economic, and social complications have set in, should remain a priority in our society. It follows that appropriate primary and secondary prevention strategies need to be developed to target the at-risk populations (Miller, Nirenberg, & McClure, 1983). Perhaps different intervention and prevention strategies are required for those who might develop milieu-limited alcoholism and those at risk for the male-limited form of hereditary alcoholism. In addition, prospective and retrospective investigations are needed to help identify the relevant environmental factors that also play important roles in the development of alcoholism. Some recommendations for future research pertaining to biochemical markers for alcoholism are listed below:

1. There is a need for further population studies to identify subcategories of genetic predisposition to alcoholism.

2. Studies of at-risk populations need to be continued to identify new trait markers. These should also include alcoholics and nonalcoholics with or without a family history of alcoholism. One unique approach is to compare those who have a multigenerational history of alcoholism with those who have a unigenerational history of alcoholism (Begleiter, presented at the 1988 meeting of the Research Society on Alcoholism). Follow-up investigations of young COAs previously tested for the presence of trait markers may reveal important information regarding the development of alcoholism, other drug abuse, or psychiatric problems. They should also provide useful data concerning environmental influence.

3. Multivariate analysis, such as discriminant analysis of several trait markers (Schuckit & Gold, 1988), is a very promising tool in the early identification of those who are genuinely at risk. The same battery of tests needs to be applied to alcoholics to determine whether they can be classified accurately and to test the hypothesis that chronic alcohol intake does not alter trait markers.

4. Currently available biochemical markers do not possess 100% sensitivity and specificity as screening devices in apparently healthy populations. Nevertheless, several promising methods, reviewed in this chapter, can be refined for routine clinical use to complement information on medical and drinking history and physical symptoms gathered by clinicians. Because of the inherent advantages of routine laboratory tests and the relatively high sensitivity and specificity that can be attained by using discriminant analyses of a battery of these tests, further investigations are needed to refine and optimize discriminant functions for various groups. As Ryback and Rawlings (1985) have suggested, it is unlikely that one set of discriminant functions will correctly define the universe of alcoholic versus nonalcoholic drinking patterns. It is necessary to define populations more precisely based on data such as quantity and frequency of alcohol intake, number of years of heavy drinking, whether ambulatory or nonambulatory, inpatient or outpatient, other drug intake, age, sex, smoking, and health status. Besides the standard laboratory tests, newer markers and responses to short diagnostic questionnaires such as the CAGE, MAST-10, or Reich interview, can also be included to improve overall diagnostic efficiency.

5. Although much emphasis has been placed on the identification of vulnerability markers, it may be equally fruitful to investigate the existence of negative vulnerability markers, which protect individuals from developing alcoholism. The use of longitudinal research designs to study FHP subjects who do not develop alcoholism represents one possible approach that may reveal important biological as well as environmental factors relevant to this issue.

6. There is an urgent need for physicians to be better educated about how to diagnose alcoholism (Barnes & O'Neill, 1984; Schuckit, 1987b).

7. Continued investigation with various animal models will sharpen foci in the search for specific behavioral, physiological, and biochemical traits associated with inherited risk for alcholism. These include factors underlying preference for alcohol, development of tolerance and dependence, neurochemical actions of acute and chronic alcohol intake, and initial sensitivity to ethanol.

ACKNOWLEDGMENTS

The expert review and comments of Dr. Mikko Salaspuro are gratefully acknowledged. I thank Carol Tixier for her skillful typing and Donna L. Schanley for proofreading.

REFERENCES

Adachi, J., Mizoi, Y., Fukunaga, T., Ueno, Y., Imamichi, H., Ninomiya, I., & Naito, T. (1986). Individual difference in urinary excretion of salsolinol in alcoholic patients. *Alcohol, 3,* 371–375.
Agarwal, D. P., Philippu, G., Milech, U., Ziemsen, B., Schrappe, O., & Goedde, H. W. (1983).

Platelet monoamine oxidase and erythrocyte catechol-*o*-methyltransferase activity in alcoholism and controlled abstinence. *Drug and Alcohol Dependence, 12,* 85–91.

Agarwal, D. P., Volkens, T., Hafer, G., & Goedde, H. W. (1987). Erythrocyte aldehyde dehydrogenase: Studies of properties and changes in acute and chronic alcohol intoxication. In H. Weiner & T. G. Flynn (Eds.), *Enzymology and molecular biology of carbonyl metabolism* (pp. 85–101). New York: Alan R. Liss.

Alexopoulos, G. S., Lieberman, K. W., & Frances, R. J. (1983). Platelet MAO activity in alcoholic patients and their first-degree relatives. *American Journal of Psychiatry, 140,* 1501–1504.

Babor, T. F., & Kadden, R. (1985). Screening for alcohol problems: Conceptual issues and practical considerations. In N. C. Chang & H. M. Chao (Eds.), *Early identification of alcohol abuse* (NIAAA Research Monograph No. 17, pp. 1–30). Washington, DC: U.S. Government Printing Office.

Ballenger, J. C., Goodwin, F. K., Major, L. F., & Brown, G. L. (1979). Alcohol and central serotonin metabolism in man. *Archives of General Psychiatry, 36,* 224–227.

Barboriak, J. J., Jacobson, G. R., Cushman, P., Herrington, R. E., Lipo, R. F., Daley, M. E., & Anderson, A. J. (1980). Chronic alcohol abuse and high density lipoprotein cholesterol. *Alcoholism, 4,* 346–349.

Barnes, H. N., & O'Neill, S. F. (1984). Early detection and outpatient management of alcoholism: A curriculum for medical residents. *Journal of Medical Education, 59,* 904–906.

Barrison, I. G., Ruzek, J., & Murray-Lyon, I. M. (1987). Drinkwatchers—description of subjects and evaluation of laboratory markers of heavy drinking. *Alcohol & Alcoholism, 22,* 147–154.

Begleiter, H., Porjesz, B., Bihari, B., & Kissin, B. (1984). Event-related brain potentials in boys at risk for alcoholism. *Science, 225,* 1493–1496.

Behar, D., Berg, C. J., Rapoport, J. L., Nelson, W., Linnoila, M., Cohen, M., Bozevich, C., & Marshall T. (1983). Behavioral and physiological effects of ethanol in high-risk and control children: A pilot study. *Alcoholism, 7,* 404–410.

Beresford, T., Low, D., Hall, R. C. W., Adduci, R., & Goggans, F. (1982). A computerized biochemical profile for detection of alcoholism. *Psychosomatics, 23,* 713–720.

Bernadt, M. W., Mumford, J., & Murray, R. M. (1984). A discriminant-function analysis of screening tests for excessive drinking and alcoholism. *Journal of Studies on Alcohol, 45,* 81–86.

Bernadt, M. W., Mumford, J., Taylor, C., Smith, B., & Murray, R. M. (1982). Comparison of questionnaire and laboratory tests in the detection of excessive drinking and alcoholism. *The Lancet, 1,* 325–328.

Blass, J. P., & Gibson, G. E. (1977). Abnormality of a thiamine-requiring enzyme in patients with Wernicke–Korsakoff syndrome. *New England Journal of Medicine, 297,* 1367–1370.

Blass, J. P., & Gibson, G. E. (1979). Genetic factors in Wernicke–Korsakoff syndrome. *Alcoholism, 3,* 126–134.

Bliding, G., Bliding, A., Fex, G., & Tornqvist, C. (1982). The appropriateness of laboratory tests in tracing young heavy drinkers. *Drug and Alcohol Dependence, 10,* 153–158.

Boismare, F., Lhuintre, J. P., Daoust, M., Moore, N., Saligaut, C., & Hillemand, B. (1987). Platelet affinity for serotonin is increased in alcoholics and former alcoholics: A biological marker for dependence? *Alcohol & Alcoholism, 22,* 155–159.

Bonte, W., Kuhnholz, B., & Ditt, J. (1985). Blood methanol levels and alcoholism. In M. Valverius (Ed.), *Punishment and/or treatment for driving under the influence of alcohol and other drugs* (pp. 255–259). Stockholm: International Committee on Alcohol, Drugs and Traffic Safety.

Braude, M. C., & Chao, H. M. (Eds.). (1986). *Genetic and biological markers in drug abuse and alcoholism* (NIDA Research Monograph No. 66). Washington, DC: U.S. Government Printing Office.

Brown, R. L., Carter, W. B., & Gordon, M. J. (1987). Diagnosis of alcoholism in a simulated patient encounter by primary care physicians. *Journal of Family Practice, 25,* 259–264.

Brown, S. A. (1977). Platelet MAO and alcoholism. *American Journal of Psychiatry, 134,* 206–207.

Casacchia, M., Rossi, A., & Stratta, P. (1985). Thyrotropin-releasing hormone test in recently abstinent alcoholics. *Psychiatry Research, 16*, 249–251.

Chalmers, D. M., Chanarin, I., MacDermott, S., & Levi, A. J. (1980). Sex-related differences in the haematological effects of excessive alcohol consumption. *Journal of Clinical Pathology, 33*, 3–7.

Chalmers, D. M., Rinsler, M. G., MacDermott, S., Spicer, C. C., & Levi, A. J. (1981). Biochemical and haematological indicators of excessive alcohol consumption. *Gut, 22*, 992–996.

Chan, A. W. K. (1986). Racial differences in alcohol sensitivity. *Alcohol & Alcoholism, 21*, 93–104.

Chan, A. W. K., Leong, F. W., Schanley, D. L., Welte, J. W., Wieczorek, W., Rej, R. O., & Whitney, R. B. (1989). Transferrin and mitochondrial aspartate aminotransferase in young adult alcoholics. *Drug and Alcohol Dependence, 23*, 13–18.

Chan, A. W. K., Welte, J. W., & Whitney, R. B. (1987). Identification of alcoholism in young adults by blood chemistries. *Alcohol, 4*, 175–179.

Chapman, R. W., Sorrentino, D., & Morgan, M. Y. (1985). Abnormal heterogeneity of serum transferrin in relation to alcohol consumption: A reappraisal. In N. C. Chang & H. M. Chao (Eds.), *Early identification of alcohol abuse* (NIAA Research Monograph No. 17, pp. 108–114). Washington, DC: U.S. Government Printing Office.

Chick, J., Longstaff, M., Kreitman, M. P., Thatcher, D., & White, J (1982). Plasma μ-amino-n-butyric acid leucine ratio and alcohol consumption in working men and in alcoholics. *Journal of Studies on Alcohol, 43*, 583–587

Chick, J., Pikkarainen, J., & Plant, M. (1987). Serum ferritin as a marker of alcohol consumption in working men. *Alcohol & Alcoholism, 22*, 75–77.

Cicero, T. J. (1983). Endocrine mechanisms in tolerance to and dependence on alcohol. In B. Kissin & H. Begleiter (Eds.), *The biology of alcoholism* (Vol. 7, pp. 285–357). New York: Plenum Press.

Clark, P. M., Holder, R., Mullet, M., & Whitehead, T. P. (1983). Sensitivity and specificity of laboratory tests for alcohol abuse. *Alcohol & Alcoholism, 18*, 261–269.

Cohen, J. A., & Kaplan, M. M. (1979). The SGOT/SGPT ratio—an indicator of alcoholic liver disease. *Digestive Diseases and Sciences, 24*, 835–838.

Collins, A. C. (1986). Genetics as a tool for identifying biological markers of drug abuse. In M. C. Braude & H. M. Chao (Eds.), *Genetic and biological markers in drug abuse and alcoholism* (NIDA Research Monograph No. 66, pp. 57–70). Washington, DC: U.S. Government Printing Office.

Collins, M. A. (1985). Alkaloid condensation products as biochemical indicators in alcoholism. In N. C. Chang & H. M. Chao (Eds.), *Early identification of alcohol abuse* (NIAAA Research Monograph No. 17, pp. 255–267). Washington, DC: U.S. Government Printing Office.

Corder, B. F., McRee, C., & Rohrer, H. (1984). A brief review of literature on daughters of alcoholic fathers. *North Carolina Journal of Mental Health, 10*, 37–43.

Coulehan, J. L., Zettler-Segal, M., Block, M., McClelland, M., & Schulberg, H. C. (1987). Recognition of alcoholism and substance abuse in primary care patients. *Archives of Internal Medicine, 147*, 349–352.

Cowan, R., Massey, L. K., & Greenfield, T. K. (1985). Average, binge and maximum alcohol intake in healthy young men: Discriminant function analysis. *Journal of Studies on Alcohol, 46*, 467–472.

Crabbe, J. C., Kosobud, A., Young, E. R., Tam, B. R., & McSwigan, J. D. (1985). Bidirectional selection for susceptibility to ethanol withdrawal seizures in *Mus musculus*. *Behavior Genetics, 15*, 521–536.

Cushman, P., Jacobson, G., Barboriak, J. J., & Anderson, A. J. (1984). Biochemical markers for alcoholism: Sensitivity problems. *Alcoholism, 8*, 253–257.

Davis, L. J., Hurt, R. D., Morse, R. M., & O'Brien, P. C. (1987). Discriminant analysis of the self-administered alcoholism screening test. *Alcoholism, 11*, 269–273.

Davis, L. J., & Morse, R. M. (1987). Age and sex differences in the responses of alcoholics to the self-administered alcoholism screening test. *Journal of Clinical Psychology, 43,* 423–430.

Deitrich, R. A., & Spuhler, K. (1984). Genetics of alcoholism and alcohol actions. In R. G. Smart, H. D. Cappell, F. B. Glaser, Y. Israel, H. Kalant, R. E. Popham, W. Schmidt, & E. M. Sellers (Eds.), *Research advances in alcohol and drug problems* (Vol. 8, pp. 47–98). New York: Plenum Press.

Del Villano, B. C., Tischfield, J. A., Schacter, L. P., Stilwil, D., & Miller, S. I. (1979). Cupro-zinc superoxide dismutase: A possible biologic marker for alcoholism (studies in black patients). *Alcoholism, 3,* 291–296.

Deren, S. (1986). Children of substance abusers: A review of the literature. *Journal of Substance Abuse Treatment, 3,* 77–94.

Devenyi, P., Robinson, G. M., Kapur, B. M., & Roncari, D. A. K. (1981). High-density lipoprotein cholesterol in male alcoholics with and without severe liver disease. *American Journal of Medicine, 71,* 589–594.

Di Padova, C., Worner, T. M., & Lieber, C. S. (1987). Effect of abstinence on the blood acetaldehyde response to a test dose of alcohol in alcoholics. *Alcoholism, 11,* 559–561.

Drum, D. E., Goldman, P. A., & Jankowski, C. B. (1981). Elevation of serum uric acid as a clue to alcohol abuse. *Archives of Internal Medicine, 141,* 477–479.

Dunbar, J. G., Ogston, S. A., Ritchie, A., Devgun, M. S., Hagart, J., & Martin, B. T. (1985). Are problem drinkers dangerous drivers? An investigation of arrest for drinking and driving, serum γ-glutamyltranspeptidase activities, blood alcohol concentrations, and road traffic accidents: The Tayside safe driving project. *British Medical Journal, 290,* 827–830.

Eckardt, M. J., Rawlings, R. R., & Martin, P. R. (1986). Biological correlates and detection of alcohol abuse and alcoholism. *Progress in Neuro-Psychopharmacology and Biological Psychiatry, 10,* 135–144.

Eckardt, M. J., Rawlings, R. R., Ryback, R. S., Martin, P. R., & Gottschalk, L. A. (1984). Effects of abstinence on the ability of clinical laboratory tests to identify male alcoholics. *American Journal of Clinical Pathology, 82,* 305–310.

el-Guebaly, N. (1986). Risk research in affective disorders and alcoholism: Epidemiological surveys and trait markers. *Canadian Journal of Psychiatry, 31,* 352–361.

Eriksson, C. J. P. (1980). Elevated blood acetaldehyde levels in alcoholics and their relatives: A reevaluation. *Science, 207,* 1383–1384.

Eriksson, C. J. P., & Peachey, J. E. (1980). Lack of difference in blood acetaldehyde of alcoholics and controls after ethanol ingestion. *Pharmacology Biochemistry & Behavior, 13,* 101–105.

Ewing, J. A. (1984). Detecting alcoholism. The CAGE questionnaire. *Journal of the American Medical Association, 252,* 1905–1907.

Fantozzi, R., Caramelli, L., Ledda, F., Moroni, F., Masini, E., Blandina, P., Botti, P., Peruzzi, S., Zorn, A. M., & Mannaioni, P. F. (1987). Biological markers and therapeutic outcome in alcoholic disease: A twelve-year survey. *Klinische Wochenshrift, 65,* 27–33.

Farej, B. A., Lenton, J. D., Kutner, M., Camp, V. M., Stammers, T. W., Lee, S. R., Lolies, P. A., & Chandora, D. (1987). Prevalence of low monoamine oxidase function in alcoholism. *Alcoholism, 11,* 464–467.

Flegar-Mestric, Z., Tadej, D., & Subic-Albert, N. (1987). Validity of 5-aminolevulinate dehydratase activity (5-ALAD) for the discrimination of alcoholics and nonalcoholics with chronic liver disease. *Clinical Biochemistry, 20,* 81–84.

Fowler, C. J., Wiberg, A., Oreland, L., Danielsson, A., Palm, U., & Winblad, B. (1981). Monoamine oxidase activity and kinetic properties in platelet-rich plasma from controls, chronic alcoholics, and patients with nonalcoholic liver disease. *Biochemical Medicine, 25,* 356–365.

Gavaler, J. S. (1982). Sex-related differences in ethanol-induced liver disease. Artifactual or real? *Alcoholism, 6,* 186–196.

Giller, E., Jr., & Hall, H. (1983). Platelet MAO activity in recovered alcoholics after long-term abstinence. *American Journal of Psychiatry, 140,* 114–115.

Giller, E., Jr., Nocks, J., Hall, H., Stewart, C., Schnitt, J., & Sherman, B. (1984). Platelet and fibroblast monoamine oxidase in alcoholism. *Psychiatry Research, 12,* 339–347.

Gjerde, H., Amundsen, A., Skog, O. J., Morland, J., & Aasland, O. G. (1987). Serum gamma-glutamyltransferase: An epidemiological indicator of alcohol consumption? *British Journal of Addiction, 82,* 1027–1031.

Gjerde, H., Johnsen, J., Bjorneboe, A., Bjornoboe, G.-E. A. A., & Morland, J. (1988). A comparison of serum carbohydrate-deficient transferrin with other biological markers of excessive drinking. *Scandinavian Journal of Clinical Laboratory Investigations, 48,* 1–6.

Gjerde, H., Sakshaug, J., & Morland, J. (1986). Heavy drinking among Norwegian male drunken drivers: A study of γ-glutamyltransferase. *Alcoholism, 10,* 209–212.

Goodwin, D. W. (1979). Alcoholism and heredity: A review and hypothesis. *Archives of General Psychiatry, 36,* 57–61.

Goodwin, D. W. (1987). Genetic influences in alcoholism. *Advances in Internal Medicine, 32,* 283–298.

Greenberg, D. A., & Diamond, I. (1985). Wernicke–Korsakoff syndrome. In R. E. Tarter & D. H. Van Thiel (Eds.), *Alcohol and the brain: Chronic effects* (pp. 295–314). New York: Plenum Press.

Hallgren, R., & Lundin, L. (1983). Increased total serum IgE in alcoholics. *Acta Medica Scandinavica, 213,* 99–103.

Hamlyn, A. N., Hopper, J. C., & Skillen, A. W. (1979). Assessment of δ-aminolevulinate dehydrase for outpatient detection of alcoholic liver disease: Comparison with γ-glutamyltransferase and causal blood ethanol. *Clinica Chimica Acta, 95,* 453–459.

Hartung, G.H., Foreyt, J. P., Mitchell, R. E., Mitchell, J. G. M., Reeves, R. S., & Gotto, A. M. (1983). Effect of alcohol intane on high-density cholesterol levels in runners and in inactive men. *Journal of the American Medical Association, 249,* 747–750.

Hays, J. T., & Spickard, W. A. (1987). Alcoholism: Early diagnosis and intervention. *Journal of General Internal Medicine, 2,* 420–427.

Herrington, R. E., Jacobsen, G. R., Daley, M. E., Lipo, R. F., Biller, H. B., & Weissgerber, C. (1981). Use of the plasma α-amino-n-butyric acid: leucine ratio to identify alcoholics. *Journal of Studies on Alcohol, 42,* 492–499.

Hill, S., Armstrong, J., Steinhauer, S. R., Baughman, T., & Zubin, J. (1987). Static ataxia as a psychobiological marker for alcholism. *Alcoholism, 11,* 345–348.

Hill, S. Y., Steinhauer, S. R., Zubin, J. (1987). Biological markers for alcoholism: A vulnerability model conceptualization. In P. C. Rivers (Ed.), *Alcohol and addictive behavior: Nebraska symposiun on motivation, 1986* (pp. 207–256). Lincoln: University of Nebraska Press.

Hillers, V. N., Alldredge, J. R., & Massey, L. K. (1986). Determination of habitual alcohol intake from a panel of blood chemistries. *Alcohol & Alcoholism, 21,* 199–205.

Hirst, M., Evans, D. R., & Gowdey, C. W. (1987). Salsolinol in urine following chocolate consumption by social drinkers. *Alcohol and Drug Research, 7,* 493–501.

Hoberman, H. D., & Chiodo, S. M. (1982). Elevation of the hemoglobin Al fraction in alcoholism. *Alcoholism, 6,* 260–266.

Hoerner, M., Behrens, U. J., Worner, T. M., Blacksberg, I., Braley, L. F., Schaffner, F., & Lieber, C. S. (1988). The role of alcoholism and liver disease in the appearance of serum antibodies against acetaldehyde adducts. *Hepatology, 8,* 569–574.

Hollstedt, C., & Dahlgren, L. (1987). Peripheral markers in the female "hidden alcoholic." *Acta Psychiatrica Scandinavica, 75,* 591–596.

Holt, S., Skinner, H. A., & Israel, Y. (1981). Early identification of alcohol abuse: 2. Clinical and laboratory indicators. *Canadian Medical Association Journal, 124,* 1279–1295.

Homaidan, F. R., Kricka, L. J., Bailey, A. R., & Whitehead, T. P. (1986). Red cell morphology in alcoholics: A new test for alcohol abuse. *Blood Cells, 11,* 375–385.

Homaidan, F. R., Kricka, L. J., Clark, P. M. S., Jones, S. R., & Whitehead, T. P. (1983). Acetaldehyde–hemoglobin adducts: An unreliable marker of alcohol abuse. *Clinical Chemistry, 30*, 480–482.

Hrubec, Z., & Omenn, G. S. (1981). Evidence of genetic predisposition to alcoholic cirrhosis and psychosis: Twin concordances for alcoholism and its biological end points by zygosity among male veterans. *Alcoholism, 5*, 207–215.

Hultberg, B., Isaksson, A., & Tiderstrom, G. (1980). β-Hexosaminidase, leucine aminopeptidase, cystidylaminopeptidase, hepatic enzymes and bilirubin in serum of chronic alcoholics with acute ethanol intoxication. *Clinica Chimica Acta, 105*, 317–323.

Hulyalkar, A. R., Nora, R., & Manowitz, P. (1984). Arylsulfatase A variants in patients with alcoholism. *Alcoholism, 8*, 337–341.

Isaksson, A., Blanche, C., Hultberg, B., & Joelsson, B. (1985). Influence of ethanol on the human serum level of β-hexosaminidase. *Enzyme, 33*, 162–166.

Israel, Y., Hurwitz, E., Niemela, O., & Arnon, R. (1986). Monoclonal and polyclonal antibodies against acetaldehyde-containing epitopes in acetaldehyde-protein adducts. *Proceedings of the National Academy of Sciences, 83*, 7923–7927.

Iturriaga, H., Pereda, T., Etevez, A., & Ugarte, G. (1977). Serum immunoglobulin A changes in alcoholic patients. *Annals of Clinical Research, 9*, 39–43.

Jacobson, G. (1976). *The alcoholisms: Detection, diagnosis and assessment.* New York: Human Sciences Press.

Jenkins, W. J., Rosalki, S. B., Foo, Y., Scheuer, P. J., Nemesanszky, E., & Sherlock, S. (1982). Serum glutamate dehydrogenase is not a reliable marker of liver cell necrosis in alcoholics. *Journal of Clinical Pathology, 35*, 207–210.

Konttinen, A., Hartel, G., & Louhija, A. (1970). Multiple serum enzyme analysis in chronic alcoholics. *Acta Medica Scandinavica, 188*, 257–264.

Koplan, J. P., Annest, J. L., Layde, P. M., & Rubin, G. L. (1986). Nutrient intake and supplementation in the United States (NHANES II). *American Journal of Public Health, 76*, 287–289.

Korri, U.-M., Nuutinen, H., & Salaspuro, M. (1985). Increased blood acetate: A new laboratory marker of alcoholism and heavy drinking. *Alcoholism, 9*, 468–471.

Kosobud, A., & Crabbe, J. C. (1986). Ethanol withdrawal in mice bred to be genetically prone or resistant to ethanol withdrawal seizures. *Journal of Pharmacology & Experimental Therapeutics, 238*, 170–177.

Kristenson, H., Fex, G., & Trell, E. (1981). Serum ferritin, gammaglutamyltransferase and alcohol consumption in healthy middle-aged man. *Drug and Alcohol Dependence, 8*, 43–50.

Ledig, M., Doffoel, M., Ziessel, M., Kopp, P., Charrault, A., Tongio, M. M., Mayer, S., Bockel, R., & Mandel, P. (1986). Frequencies of glyoxalase I phenotypes as biological markers in chronic alcoholism. *Alcohol, 3*, 11–14.

Legros, J. J., Deconinck, I., Willems, D., Roth, B., Pelc, I., Brauman, J., & Verbanck, M. (1983). Increase of neurophysin II serum levels in chronic alcoholic patients: Relationship with alcohol consumption and alcoholism blood markers during therapy. *Journal of Clinical Endocrinology and Metabolism, 56*, 871–875.

Li, T. K., Lumeng, L., McBride, W. J., Waller, M. B., & Murphy, J. M. (1986). Studies on an animal model of alcoholism. In M. C. Braude & H. M. Chao (Eds.), *Genetic and biological markers in drug abuse and alcoholism* (NIDA Research Monograph No. 66, pp. 41–49). Washington, DC: U.S. Government Printing Office.

Lin, C. C., Potter, J. J., & Mezey, E. (1984). Erythrocyte aldehyde dehydrogenase activity in alcoholism. *Alcoholism, 8*, 539–541.

Loosen, P. T., Wilson, I. C., Dew, B. W., & Tipermas, A. (1983). Thyrotropin-releasing hormone (TRH) in abstinent alcoholic men. *American Journal of Psychiatry, 140*, 1145–1149.

Lucas, D., Menez, J. F., Bodenez, P., Baccino, E., Bardou, L. G., & Floch, H. H. (1988).

Acetaldehyde adducts with haemoglobin: Determinations of acetaldehyde released from haemoglobin by acid hydrolysis. *Alcohol & Alcoholism, 23*, 23–31.

Lumeng, L. (1986). New diagnostic markers of alcohol abuse. *Hepatology, 6*, 742–745.

Lykouras, E., Moussas, G., & Markianos, M. (1987). Platelet monoamine oxidase and plasma dopamine-β-hydroxylase activities in non-abstinent chronic alcoholics. Relation to clinical parameters. *Drug and Alcohol Dependence, 19*, 363–368.

Major, L. F., Hawley, R. J., Saini, N., Garrick, N. A., & Murphy, D. L. (1985). Brain and liver monoamine oxidase type A and type B activity in alcoholics and controls. *Alcoholism, 9*, 6–9.

Major, L. F., & Murphy, D. L. (1978). Platelet and plasma amine oxidase activity in alcoholic individuals. *British Journal of Psychiatry, 132*, 548–554.

Malmendier, C. L., & Delcroix, C. (1985). Effect of alcohol intake on high and low density lipoprotein metabolism in healthy volunteers. *Clinica Chimica Acta, 152*, 281–288.

Martensson, E., Olofsson, U., & Heath, A. (1988). Clinical and metabolic features of ethanol–methanol poisoning in chronic alcoholics. *The Lancet, 1*, 327–328.

Matloff, D. S., Seligran, M. J., & Kaplan, M. M. (1980). Hepatic transaminase activity in alcoholic liver disease. *Gastroenterology, 78*, 1389–1392.

Matsubara, K., Fukushima, S., Akane, A., Hama, K., & Fukui, Y. (1986). Tetrahydro-β-carbolines in human urine and rat brain—no evidence of formation by alcohol drinking. *Alcohol & Alcoholism, 21*, 339–345.

Mayfield, D. G., McLeod, G., & Hall, P. (1974). The CAGE questionnaire: Validation of a new alcoholism screening instrument. *American Journal of Psychiatry, 131*, 1121–1123.

McClearn, G. E., & Erwin, V. G. (1982). Genetic influence in biological mechanisms in alcohol-related behaviors: Animal models. In *Alcohol consumption and related problems* (Alcohol and Health Monograph No. 1, pp. 271–285). Washington, DC: U.S. Department of Health and Human Services, Library of Congress.

Miller, P. M., Nirenberg, T. D., & McClure, G. (1983). Prevention of alcohol abuse. In B. Tabakoff, P. B. Sutker, & C. L. Randall (Eds.), *Medical and social aspects of alcohol abuse* (pp. 375–397). New York: Plenum Press.

Miller, W. R. (1976). Alcoholism scales and objective assessment methods: A review. *Psychological Bulletin, 83*, 649–674.

Mills, P. R., Spooner, R. J., Russell, R. I., Boyle, P., & MacSween, R. N. M. (1981). Serum glutamate dehydrogenase as a marker of hepatocyte necrosis in alcoholic liver disease. *British Medical Journal, 283*, 754–755.

Moore, R. D., & Malitz, F. E. (1986). Underdiagnosis of alcoholism by residents in an ambulatory medical practice. *Journal of Medical Education, 61*, 46–52.

Morgan, M. Y., Colman, J. C., & Sherlock, S. (1981). The use of a combination of peripheral markers for diagnosing alcoholism and monitoring for continued abuse. *British Journal of Alcohol and Alcoholism, 16*, 167–177.

Moss, H. B., Guthrie, S., & Linnoila, M. (1986). Enhanced thyrotropin response to thyrotropin releasing hormone in boys at risk for development of alcoholism. *Archives of General Psychiatry, 43*, 1137–1142.

Mukherjee, A. B., Svoronos, S., Ghazanfari, A., Martin, P. R., Fisher, A., Roecklein, B., Rodbard, D., Staton, R., Behar, D., Berg, C. J., & Manjunath, R. (1987). Transketolase abnormality in cultured fibroblasts from familial chronic alcoholic men and their male offspring. *Journal of Clinical Investigation, 79*, 1039–1043.

Myers, R. D. (1985). Alkaloid metabolites and addictive drinking of alcohol. In N. C. Chang & H. M. Chao (Eds.), *Early identification of alcohol abuse* (NIAAA Research Monograph No. 17, pp. 268–284). Washington, DC: U.S. Government Printing Office.

Nalpas, B., Vassault, A., Charpin, S., Lacour, B., & Berthelot, P. (1986). Serum mitochondrial aspartate aminotransferase as a marker of chronic alcoholism: Diagnostic value and interpretation in a liver unit. *Hepatology, 6*, 608–614.

Nalpas, B., Vassault, A., LeGuillou, A., Lesgourgues, B., Ferry, N., Lacour, B., & Berthelot, P.

(1984). Serum activity of mitochondrial aspartate aminotransferase: A sensitive marker of alcoholism with or without alcoholic hepatitis. *Hepatology, 4,* 893–896.

National Council on Alcoholism, Criteria Committee (1972). Criteria for the diagnosis of alcoholism. *American Journal of Psychiatry, 129,* 127–135.

National Institute on Alcohol Abuse and Alcoholism (NIAAA). (1985). *Alcoholism: An inherited disease.* Rockville, MD: U.S. Department of Health and Human Services.

Neiman, J., Beving, H., & Malmgren, R. (1987). Platelet uptake of serotonin (5-HT) during ethanol withdrawal in male alcoholics. *Thrombosis Research, 46,* 803–809.

Newlin, D. B. (1985). Offspring of alcoholics have enhanced antagonistic placebo response. *Journal of Studies on Alcohol, 46,* 490–494.

Niemela, O., Klajner, F., Orrego, H., Vidins, E., Blendis, L., & Israel, Y. (1987). Antibodies against acetaldehyde-modified protein epitopes in human alcoholics. *Hepatology, 7,* 1210–1214.

Nishimura, M., & Teschke, R. (1983). Alcohol and gamma-glutamyltransferase. *Klinische Wochenschrift, 61,* 265–275.

Nuutinen, H., Lindros, K., Hekali, P., & Salaspuro, M. (1985). Elevated blood acetate as an indicator of fast ethanol elimination in chronic alcoholics. *Alcohol, 2,* 623–626.

Nuutinen, H., Lindros, K. O., & Salaspuro, M. (1983). Determinants of blood acetaldehyde level during ethanol oxidation in chronic alcoholics. *Alcoholism, 7,* 163–168.

Nuutinen, H. U., Salaspuro, M. P., Valle, M., & Lindros, K. O. (1984). Blood acetaldehyde concentration gradient between hepatic and antecubital venous blood in ethanol-intoxicated alcoholics and controls. *European Journal of Clinical Investigation, 14,* 306–311.

Nygren, A., & Sundblad, L. (1971). Lactate dehydrogenase isoenzyme patterns in serum and skeletal muscle in intoxicated alcoholics. *Acta Medica Scandinavica, 189,* 303–307.

Okuno, F., Ishii, H., Kashiwazaki, K., Takagi, S., Shigeta, Y., Arai, M., Takagi, T., Ebihara, Y., & Tsuchiya, M. (1988). Increase in mitochondrial GOT (m-GOT) activity after chronic alcohol consumption: Clinical and experimental observations. *Alcohol, 5,* 49–53.

O'Malley, S. S., & Maisto, S. A. (1985). The effects of family drinking history on responses to alcohol: Expectations and reactions to intoxication. *Journal of Studies on Alcohol, 46,* 289–297.

Palmer, K. R., & Jenkins, W. J. (1985). Aldehyde dehydrogenase in alcoholic subjects. *Hepatology, 5,* 260–263.

Pandey, G. N., Fawcett, J., Gibbons, R., Clark, D. C., & Davis, J. M. (1988). Platelet monoamine oxidase in alcoholism. *Biological Psychiatry, 24,* 15–24.

Persson, J., & Magnusson, P. H. (1988). Comparison between different methods of detecting patients with excessive consumption of alcohol. *Acta Medica Scandinavica, 223,* 101–109.

Peterson, B., Trell, E., Kristensson, H., Fex, G., Yettra, M., & Hood, B. (1983). Comparison of gamma-glutamyltransferase and other health screening tests in average middle-aged males, heavy drinkers and alcohol nonusers. *Scandinavian Journal of Clinical & Laboratory Investigations, 43,* 141–149.

Peterson, C. M., Nguyen, L., Fantl, W., Stevens, V., Hawthorne, G., & Blackburn, P. (1985). Acetaldehyde adducts with hemoglobin. In N. C. Chang & H. M. Chao (Eds.), *Early identification of alcohol abuse* (NIAAA Research Monograph No. 17, pp. 68–77). Washington, DC: U.S. Government Printing Office.

Pollock, V. E., Teasdale, T. W., Gabrielli, W. F., & Knop, J. (1986). Subjective and objective measures of response to alcohol among men at risk for alcoholism. *Journal of Studies on Alcohol, 47,* 297–304.

Puchois, P., Fontan, M., Gentilini, J. L., Gelez, P., & Fruchart, J. C. (1984). Serum apolipoprotein A-II, A biochemical indicator of alcohol abuse. *Clinica Chimica Acta, 185,* 185–189.

Puddey, I. B., Masarei, J. R. L., Vandongen, R., & Beilin, L. J. (1986). Serum apolipoprotein A-II as a marker of change in alcohol intake in male drinkers. *Alcohol & Alcoholism, 21,* 375–383.

Pullarkat, R. K., & Raguthu, S. (1985). Elevated urinary dolichol levels in chronic alcoholics. *Alcoholism, 9,* 28–30.

Reich, T., Robins, L. N., Woodruff, R. A., Taibleson, M., Rich, C., & Cunningham, L. (1975). Computer-assisted derivation of a screening interview for alcoholism. *Archives of General Psychiatry, 32,* 847–852.

Reid, A. L. A., Webb, G. R., Hennrikus, D., Fahey, P. P., & Sanson-Fisher, R. W. (1986). General practitioners' detection of patients with high alcohol intake. *British Medical Journal, 293,* 735–737.

Roine, R. P. (1988). Effects of moderate drinking and alcohol abstinence on urinary dolichol levels. *Alcohol, 5,* 229–231.

Roine, R. P., Eriksson, C. J. P., Ylikahri, R., Penttila, A., & Salaspuro, M. (1989a). Methanol as a marker of alcohol abuse. *Alcoholism, 13,* 172–175.

Roine, R. P., Humaloja, K., Hamalainen, J., Nykanen, I., Ylikahri, R., & Salaspuro, M. (1989b). Significant increases in urinary dolichol levels in bacterial infections, malignancies and pregnancy but not in other clinical conditions. *Annals of Medicine, 21,* 13–16.

Roine, R. P., Korri, U. M., Ylikahri, R., Penttila, A., Pikkarainen, J., & Salaspuro, M. (1988). Increased serum acetate as a marker of problem drinking among drunken drivers. *Alcohol & Alcoholism, 23,* 123–126.

Roine, R. P., Turpeinen, U., Ylikahri, R., & Salaspuro, M. (1987). Urinary dolichol—a new marker of alcoholism. *Alcoholism, 11,* 525–527.

Rommelspacher, H., & Schmidt, L. (1985). Increased formation of β-carbolines in alcoholic patients following ingestion of ethanol. *Pharmacopsychiatry, 18,* 153–154.

Rosenthal, N. E., Davenport, Y., Cowdry, R. W., Webster, M. H., & Goodwin, F. K. (1980). Monoamine metabolites in cerebrospinal fluid of depressive subgroups. *Psychiatry Research, 2,* 113–119.

Russell, M., Henderson, C., & Blume, S. (1984). *Children of alcoholics: A review of the literature.* Buffalo: New York State Division of Alcoholism and Alcohol Abuse.

Rutstein, D. D., Veech, R. L., Nickerson, R. J., Felyer, M. E., Vernon, A. A., Needham, L. L., Kishore, P., & Thacker, S. B. (1983). 2, 3-Butanediol: An unusual metabolite in the serum of severely alcoholic men during acute intoxication. *The Lancet, 2,* 534–537.

Ryback, R. S., Eckardt, M. J., Negron, G. L., & Rawlings, R. R. (1983). The search for a biochemical marker in alcoholism. *Substance and Alcohol Actions/Misuse, 4,* 217–224.

Ryback, R. S., Eckardt, M. J., & Pautler, C. P. (1980). Biochemical and hematological correlates of alcoholism. *Research Communications in Chemical Pathology and Pharmacology, 27,* 533–550.

Ryback, R. S., Eckardt, M. J., Rawlings, R. R., & Rosenthal, R. S. (1982). Quadratic discriminant analysis as an aid to interpretive reporting of clinical laboratory tests. *Journal of the American Medical Association, 248,* 2342–2345.

Ryback, R. S., & Rawlings, R. R. (1985). Biochemical correlates of alcohol consumption. In N. C. Chang & H. M. Chao (Eds.), *Early identification of alcohol abuse* (NIAAA Research Monograph No. 17, pp. 31–48). Washington, DC: U.S. Government Printing Office.

Ryback, R. S., Rawlings, R. R., Faden, V., & Negron, G. L. (1985). Laboratory test changes in young abstinent male alcoholics. *American Journal of Clinical Pathology, 83,* 474–479.

Salaspuro, M. (1986). Conventional and coming laboratory markers of alcoholism and heavy drinking. *Alcoholism, 10,* 5S–12S.

Salaspuro, M. P., Korri, U.-M., Nuutinen, H., & Roine, R. (1987). Blood acetate and urinary dolichols—new markers of heavy drinking and alcoholism. *Progress in Clinical and Biological Research, 241,* 231–240.

Sanchez-Craig, M., & Annis, H. M. (1981). γ-Glutamyltranspeptidase and high density lipoprotein cholesterol in male problem drinkers: Advantages of a composite index for predicting alcohol consumption. *Alcoholism, 5,* 540–544.

Saunders, J. B., Haines, A., Portmann, B., Wodak, A. D., Powell-Jackson, P. R., Davis, M., & Williams, R. (1982). Accelerated development of alcoholic cirrhosis in patients with HLA-B8. *The Lancet, 1,* 1381–1384.

Saunders, J. B., & Williams, R. (1983). The genetics of alcoholism: Is there an inherited susceptibility to alcohol-related problems? *Alcohol & Alcoholism, 18,* 189–217.

Schnitt, J. M., & Dove, H. G. (1986). Issues in the development of alcoholism screening models using discriminant function analysis of blood profiles. *Substance Abuse, 7,* 38–51.

Schuckit, M. A. (1980). Self-rating of alcohol intoxication by young men with and without family histories of alcoholism. *Journal of Studies on Alcohol, 41,* 242–249.

Schuckit, M. A. (1981). Peak blood alcohol levels in men at high risk for the future development of alcoholism. *Alcoholism, 5,* 64–66.

Schuckit, M. A. (1984a). Differences in plasma cortisol after ingestion of ethanol in relatives of alcoholics and controls: Preliminary results. *Journal of Clinical Psychiatry, 45,* 374–376.

Schuckit, M. A. (1984b). *Drug and alcohol abuse: A clinical guide to diagnosis and treatment.* New York: Plenum Press.

Schuckit, M. A. (1984c). Subjective responses to alcohol in sons of alcoholics and controls. *Archives of General Psychiatry, 41,* 879–884.

Schuckit, M. A. (1985). Ethanol-induced changes in body sway in men at high alcoholism risk. *Archives of General Psychiatry, 42,* 375–379.

Schuckit, M. A. (1986). Biological markers in alcoholism. *Progress in Neuro-Psychopharmacology and Biological Psychiatry, 10,* 191–199.

Schuckit, M. A. (1987a). Biological vulnerability to alcoholism. *Journal of Consulting and Clinical Psychology, 55,* 301–309.

Schuckit, M. A. (1987b). Why don't we diagnose alcoholism in our patients. *The Journal of Family Practice, 25,* 225–226.

Schuckit, M. A., & Gold, E. O. (1988). A simultaneous evaluation of multiple markers of ethanol/placebo challenges in sons of alcoholics and controls. *Archives of General Psychiatry, 45,* 211–216.

Schuckit, M. A., & Duby, J. (1982). Alcohol-related flushing and the risk for alcoholism in sons of alcoholics. *Journal of Clinical Psychiatry, 43,* 415–418.

Schuckit, M. A., Gold, E., & Risch, C. (1987a). Plasma cortisol levels following ethanol in sons of alcoholics and controls. *Archives of General Psychiatry, 44,* 942–945.

Schuckit, M. A., Gold, E., & Risch, C. (1987b). Serum prolactin levels in sons of alcoholics and control subjects. *American Journal of Psychiatry, 144,* 854–859.

Schuckit, M. A., Parker, D. C., & Rossman, L. R. (1983). Ethanol-related prolactin responses and risk for alcoholism. *Biological Psychiatry, 18,* 1153–1159.

Schuckit, M. A., & Rayses, V. (1979). Ethanol ingestion: Differences in blood acetaldehyde concentrations in relatives of alcoholics and controls. *Science, 203,* 54–55.

Schuckit, M. A., Shaskan, E., Duby, J., Vega, R., & Moss, M. (1982). Platelet monoamine oxidase activity in relatives of alcoholics. Preliminary study with matched control subjects. *Archives of General Psychiatry, 39,* 137–140.

Selzer, M. (1971). The Michigan Alcoholism Screening Test: The quest for a new diagnostic instrument. *American Journal of Psychiatry, 127,* 1653–1658.

Shaper, A. G., Pocock, S. J., Ashby, D., Walker, M., & Whitehead, T. P. (1985). Biochemical and haematological response to alcohol intake. *Annals of Clinical Biochemistry, 22,* 50–61.

Sher, K. J. (1983). Platelet monoamine oxidase activity in relatives of alcoholics. *Archives of General Psychiatry, 40,* 466.

Shigeta, Y., Ishi, H., Takagi, S., Yoshitake, Y., Hirano, T., Takata, H., Kohno, H., & Tsuchiya, M. (1980). HLA antigens as immungenetic markers of alcoholism and alcoholic liver disease. *Pharmacology, Biochemistry & Behavior, 13,* Suppl. 1, 89–94.

Skinner, H. A., & Holt, S. (1987). *The alcohol clinical index: Strategies for identifying patients with alcohol problems.* Toronto: Alcoholism and Drug Addiction Research Foundation.

Skinner, H. A., Holt, S., & Israel, Y. (1981) Early identification of alcohol abuse: 1. Critical issues and psychosocial indicators for a composite index. *Canadian Medical Association Journal, 124,* 1141–1152.

Skinner, H. A., Holt, S., Schuller, R., Roy, J., & Israel, Y. (1984). Identification of alcohol abuse using laboratory tests and a history of trauma. *Annals of Internal Medicine, 101,* 847–851.

Skinner, H. A., Holt, S., Sheu, W. J., & Israel, Y. (1986). Clinical versus laboratory detection of alcohol abuse: The alcohol clinical index. *British Medical Journal, 292,* 1703–1708.

Skude, G., & Wadstein, J. (1977). Amylase, hepatic enzymes and bilirubin in serum of chronic alcoholics. *Acta Medica Scandinavica, 201,* 53–58.

Solberg, H. E. (1978). Discriminant analysis. *CRC Critical Reviews in Clinical Laboratory Science, 9,* 209–242.

Stamm, D., Hansert, E., & Feuerlein, W. (1984). Detection and exclusion of alcoholism in men on the basis of clinical laboratory findings. *Journal of Clinical Chemistry & Clinical Biochemistry, 22,* 79–96.

Stibler, H., Borg, S., & Allgulander, C. (1980). Abnormal microheterogeneity of transferrin—a new marker of alcoholism? *Substance and Alcohol Actions/Misuse, 1,* 247–252.

Stibler, H., Borg, S., & Joustra, M. (1986). Micro anion exchange chromatography of carbohydrate-deficient transferrin in serum in relation to alcohol consumption (Swedish Patent 8400587-5). *Alcoholism, 10,* 535–544.

Storey, E. L., Anderson, G. J., Mack, U., Powell, L. W., & Halliday, J. E. (1987). Desialylated transferrin as a serological marker of chronic excessive alcohol ingestion. *The Lancet, 1,* 1292–1294.

Sullivan, J. L., Cavenar, J. O., Maltbie, A. A., Lister, P., & Zung, W. W. K. (1979). Familial biochemical and clinical correlates of alcoholics with low platelet monoamine oxidase activity. *Biological Psychiatry, 14,* 385–394.

Sullivan, J. L., Stanfield, C. N., Maltbie, A. A., Hammett, E., & Cavenar, J. O. (1978). Stability of low blood platelet monoamine oxidase activity in human alcoholics. *Biological Psychiatry, 13,* 391–397.

Tabakoff, B., Hoffman, P. L., Lee, J. M., Saito, T., Willard, B., & De Leon-Jones, F. (1988). Differences in platelet enzyme activity between alcoholics and nonalcoholics. *New England Journal of Medicine, 318,* 134–139.

Tang, B. K. (1987). Detection of ethanol in urine of abstaining alcoholics. *Canadian Journal of Physiology and Pharmacology, 65,* 1225–1227.

Tang, B. K., Devenyi, P., Teller, D., & Israel, Y. (1986). Detection of an alcohol specific product in urine of alcoholics. *Biochemical and Biophysical Research Communications, 140,* 924–927.

Towell, J. F., Barboriak, J. J., Townsend, W. F., Kalbfleisch, J. H., & Wang, R. I. H. (1986). Erythrocyte aldehyde dehydrogenase: Assay of a potential biochemical marker of alcohol abuse. *Clinical Chemistry, 32,* 734–738.

Tsuchiya, F., Sirasaka, T., Ikeda, H., Hatta, Y., Watanabe, M., & Saito, T. (1987). Platelet adenylate cyclase activity in alcoholics. *Japanese Journal of Alcohol & Drug Dependence, 22,* 366–372.

Valimaki, M., Harkonen, M., & Ylikahri, R. (1983). Serum ferritin and iron levels in chronic male alcoholics before and after ethanol withdrawal. *Alcohol & Alcoholism, 18,* 255–260.

Van Waes, L., & Lieber, C. S. (1977). Glutamate dehydrogenase: A reliable marker of liver cell necrosis in the alcoholic. *British Medical Journal, 2,* 1508–1510.

Vesterberg, O., Petren, S., & Schmidt, D. (1984). Increased concentrations of a transferrin variant after alcohol abuse. *Clinica Chimica Acta, 141,* 33–39.

Virkkunen, M., Nuutila, A., Goodwin, F. K., & Linnoila, M. (1987). Cerebrospinal fluid monoamine metabolite levels in male arsonists. *Archives of General Psychiatry, 44,* 241–247.

Vital and Health Statistics (1982). Series II #232. Washington, DC: U.S. Department of Health and Human Services.

von Knorring, A. L., Bohman, M., von Knorring, L., & Oreland, L. (1985). Platelet MAO activity as a biological marker in subgroups of alcoholism. *Acta Psychiatrica Scandinavica, 72,* 51–58.

von Knorring, L., Oreland, L., & von Knorring, A. L. (1987). Personality traits and platelet MAO activity in alcohol and drug abusing teenage boys. *Acta Psychiatrica Scandinavica, 75,* 307–314.

Watson, R. R., Mohs, M. E., Eskelson, C., Sampliner, R. E., & Hartmann, B. (1986). Identification of alcohol abuse and alcoholism with biological parameters. *Alcoholism, 10,* 364–385.

Westwood, M., Cohen, M. I., & McNamara, H. (1978). Serum γ-glutamyl transpeptidase activity: A chemical determinant of alcohol consumption during adolescence. *Pediatrics, 62,* 560–562.

Whitfield, J. B., Allen, J. K., Adena, M., Gallagher, H. G., & Hensley, W. J. (1981). A multivariate assessment of alcohol consumption. *International Journal of Epidemiology, 10,* 281–288.

Wiberg, A. (1979). Increase in platelet monoamine oxidase activity during controlled abstinence after alcohol abuse. *Medical Biology, 57,* 133–134.

Wilkins, R. H. (1974). *The hidden alcoholic in general practice: a method of detection using a questionnaire.* London: Elek Science.

Wolf, S., Felver, M. E., Altschule, M. D., Werthessen, N. T., Gerner, R., & Veech, R. L. (1983). Abnormal metabolite in alcoholic subjects. *British Journal of Psychiatry, 142,* 388–390.

Ylikorkala, O., Stenman, U. H., & Halmesmaki, E. (1987). γ-Glutamyl transferase and mean cell volume reveal maternal alcohol abuse and fetal alcohol effects. *American Journal of Obstetrics & Gynecology, 157,* 344–348.

CHAPTER FOUR

Neuropsychological and Neurophysiological Characteristics of Children of Alcoholics

RALPH E. TARTER
SUSAN B. LAIRD
HOWARD B. MOSS

Based on the accumulating body of genetic evidence that alcoholism may have a largely heritable etiology (Goodwin, 1985, 1986), researchers have recently attempted to identify the biological pathways of gene expression. These studies have investigated children of alcoholics because such offspring are at up to sixfold greater risk of developing alcoholism than children of nonalcoholic parents (Cloninger, Bohman, & Sigvaardson, 1981). Most of the investigations have focused on biochemical and metabolic processes that are known to be under genetic control. These studies have examined such diverse processes as blood type (Korri, Nuutinen, & Salaspuro, 1985; Schuckit, Gold, & Risch, 1987), enzyme activity (Agarwal & Goeddle, 1980; Hulyalkar, Nora, & Manowitz, 1984; Ledig et al., 1986; Mukherjee et al., 1987), immune profiles (Rosler, Bellaire, Hengesch, Giannitsis, & Jarovici, 1983; Shigeta et al., 1980; von-Knorring, Bohman, von-Knorring, & Oreland, 1985) and peripheral markers of central neurotransmitter activity (Alexopoulos, Lieberman, & Frances, 1983; Borg, Krande, Mossberg, Valverius, & Sedwall, 1983; Swartz 1987; Nagoshi & Wilson, 1987).

Interest in neurological mechanisms, particularly physiological and psychological processes, was prompted by a number of important considerations. Although there is no *a priori* reason to assume that neurological processes must underlie alcoholism vulnerability, there are numerous reports of children who eventually become alcoholic, describing disturbed behavioral development (Goodwin, Schulsinger, Hermansen, Guze, & Winokur, 1975) and emotional disturbance (McCord & McCord, 1962; Robins, West, Ratcliff, & Herjanic, 1977). The question logically raised from the early studies concerned whether these disturbances could be related to a dysfunctional central nervous system. In effect, neurophysiological investigations addressed the possibility of a sensory information processing deficiency and an arousal regulation disorder by measuring event-related potentials and conducting spectral analysis of the electroencephalogram. Neuropsychological research, on the other hand, was inspired by a somewhat different, although related question. Namely, investigative efforts were directed to determining whether functional psychological capacities required for successful social adjustment were suboptimal in children of alcoholics, thereby predisposing them to coping failure and alcohol use.

Two additional reasons catalyzed a surge of research into the neurobehavioral correlates of alcoholism vulnerability. First, early as well as more recent research suggested an association between paternal alcoholism and a conduct disorder with accompanying hyperactivity features in male offspring (Stewart, de Blois, & Cummings, 1980). The disorder is commonly also associated with attentional deficits, but psychometric or performance measures documenting such impairment were not utilized. Thus, neurophysiological and neuropsychological studies were conducted in an attempt to determine whether a deficit could be directly elicited, if present, in an objective and quantitative fashion. And second, preliminary findings obtained from offspring of alcoholics (Drejer, Theilgaard, Teasdale, Schulsinger, & Goodwin, 1985; Goodwin, 1977; Knop, Teasdale, & Schulsinger, 1985) and from retrospective reports by alcoholics (Tarter, McBride, Buonpane, & Schneider, 1977) revealed a high prevalence of academic failure and maladjustment. Although researchers recognized the potential multifactorial basis of underachievement and maladjustment in school, one hypothesis entertained was the possibility of a specific learning disability as one manifestation of a developmental disorder. This working hypothesis was buttressed by the frequent observation linking a learning disability and conduct disorder; the latter, as previously mentioned, is a common antecedent to alcoholism in men. The above describes the historical context in which neurophysiological and neuropsychological investigations were implemented. This chapter reviews the methods and the findings obtained to date and integrates the available results in proposing a comprehensive neurobehavioral theory of alcoholism vulnerability.

CONSIDERATIONS FOR INVESTIGATING NEUROBEHAVIORAL PROCESSES

Rationale

Children of alcoholics are investigated for two different but overlapping reasons. First, based on the well-established observation that children of alcoholics are at heightened risk for developing an alcoholism disorder themselves, they comprise ideal subjects for elucidating vulnerability characteristics that may be present before drinking onset. To this end, research of this type is directed to identifying the etiologic determinants of alcoholism. And second, the disruptive home environment, parental psychopathology, conflict, and absenteeism of the parent caused by maternal or paternal drinking, as well as myriad other adverse circumstances such as economic deprivation, physical abuse, and neglect of health needs can all exert, singly and in combination, deleterious effects on the child's development and quality of psychosocial adjustment. Much attention has been given recently to the supposedly unique and disruptive effects of growing up in an alcoholic household; however, apart from anecdotal accounts, little empirically based information is available. Nonetheless, despite the paucity of investigations, the study of children of alcoholics has important practical ramifications with respect to prevention and early intervention from a public health standpoint.

Population Sampling

Characterizing children of alcoholics is difficult for a variety of reasons. First, it should be emphasized that alcoholism is a heterogeneous condition. Individuals labeled as alcoholic differ sharply according to drinking pattern, comorbid psychopathology, medical sequelae of chronic alcohol abuse, and natural history of drinking behavior. Therefore, generalizations about the characteristics of children of alcoholics must be tempered by an awareness of the variability among individuals in this population. Doubtless, a substantial proportion of children of alcoholics do not exhibit a clinically significant or profound psychological disorder. Among those who do manifest cognitive and behavioral disturbances, the etiologic basis is most probably multiply determined, thereby militating against the derivation of simple characterizations or univariate causal models of disturbance in children of alcoholics. Indeed, in the absence of intensive empirical analysis, conclusions are likely to be distorted and hence invalid. To highlight this important point, a recently completed study by Bremer, Tarter, Jacob, and Carra (in press) demonstrated that male offspring of early-age-onset alcoholic fathers were more cognitively deficient and behaviorally disturbed than sons of later-age-onset alcoholic fathers. However, controlling for the severity of home environment disruption, it was found that the behavioral differences initially observed dissipated. These results underscore the multifactorial basis of psychological deficit in children of alcoholics and the need to comprehensively characterize parental status.

Related to the above issue, it is essential also to recognize the importance of differential effects of paternal and maternal alcoholism on the psychological development of the offspring. The father's alcoholism is commonly associated with violent physical abuse resulting in neurologic trauma, absenteeism from the home, and role modeling featuring antisocial behavior (Tarter, Hegedus, & Alterman, 1984). Maternal alcoholism, on the other hand, is more likely to transmit psychological disorder to the offspring via ethanol teratogenicity, neglect of health care, nutritional and affectional deprivation, and role modeling featuring predominantly withdrawal and depression. Thus, the psychological development of the child must be considered in the context of parental status, including potential additional exacerbating or (alternatively) protective effects that a parent may have where one or both biological parents are not raising the child. To date, the influence of these factors on children of alcoholics has not been submitted to empirical scrutiny.

In attempting to characterize the offspring of alcoholics, careful attention must thus be given to the recruitment and ascertainment criteria of the parents and offspring. This is especially important for extrapolations beyond the particular sample studied. For example, the characteristics of children whose fathers are recruited from drug rehabilitation facilities, prisons, or the at-large community are likely to differ greatly. The criteria used for diagnosis, either objectively evaluated or self-professed, correlate with severity and other features associated with alcohol use that could have an impact on the child's development. The socially nonnormative behavioral disposition of many alcoholic men and women may unwittingly lead researchers to naively and incorrectly assume that paternity necessarily implies the spouse of the child's mother. Furthermore, characteristics revealed in children of alcoholics can be influenced by whether the proband is the child or the parent, and whether recruitment is voluntary and self-initiated or based on experimenter solicitation of random or consecutive cases. Significantly, in one study of college students who were compared according to the presence or absence of an alcoholic father, it was found that the alcoholics' children reported *less* alcohol consumption, although they experienced greater deleterious consequences from drinking (Alterman, Bridges, & Tarter, 1986).

To date, none of the above factors has been systematically studied with respect to identifying differences between children of nonalcoholics and alcoholics. Moreover, apart from a few studies, no systematic research has attempted to delineate *specific* differences between children of alcoholics and psychiatrically disturbed parents. Hence, it is currently not known which of the neuropsychological and neurophysiological characteristics of children of alcoholics are particular to alcoholism alone. Without such research, inferences are likely to be mistakenly advanced that purportedly characterize children of alcoholics. For example, long latency and voltage attenuation in the P300 component of event-related potentials have been observed in a variety of psychiatric and behavioral conditions apart from alcoholism and children of alcoholics.

In view of the complexity of variables and the paucity of available research findings, conclusions about the psychological and neurological status of children of alcoholics should be considered tentative and heuristic. Most investigations have studied relatively small samples and have not attempted to bring under experimental control the type of variables described above, which could enable investigators to derive generalizable conclusions about the specific characteristics of children of alcoholics. Bearing the preliminary nature of the research in mind, the following review summarizes the existing literature.

NEUROPHYSIOLOGICAL CHARACTERISTICS

Resting or spontaneous electroencephalographic (EEG) recordings have revealed neurophysiological differences between children of alcoholics and nonalcoholics. Although EEG activity is nonspecific with respect to underlying neuronal mechanisms and reflects the summation of interacting cortical and subcortical activity, the demonstration of differences between children of alcoholics and nonalcoholics is important because it could implicate central nervous system (CNS) abnormality. EEG wave form and activity is, however, largely under genetic control (Propping, 1983), suggesting that observed deviations may reflect an inherited vulnerability.

Male children of alcoholics have been observed to have an excess of high-frequency EEG activity (Gabrielli et al., 1982). It also has been shown that following an alcohol challenge, offspring of alcoholics reveal relatively greater augmentation of alpha energy (Pollock et al., 1983). These interesting but as yet unreplicated findings indicate that the response of children of alcoholics to alcohol is suggestive of a combined calming and arousing effect; if confirmed, this could implicate a differentially more reinforcing effect of ethanol in such individuals. Interestingly, a similar physiological hypothesis has been advanced based on observations of autonomic reactivity (Finn & Pihl, 1987).

Evoked-potential (EP) measurements enable more specific analyses of neurophysiological phenomena. Following exteroceptive stimulation (e.g., mild electric shock, tones, visual signals or displays), the neural pathways involved in processing the stimulus can be measured directly. This is accomplished using computer averaging techniques whereby the time-locked sensory signals are extrapolated from the generalized background of the EEG.

The first EP study, performed by Elmasian, Neville, Woods, Schuckit, and Bloom (1982), studied young adult children of alcoholics and nonalcoholics after placebo and low- and high-dose ethanol challenge. The subjects were presented with a series of tones of which the last one (the target tone) had a shorter duration. The most significant finding was that subjects with a familial alcoholism history exhibited reduction of the P300 wave amplitude (voltage) component. This wave form appears to be a neurophysiological substrate of attentional processes, particularly where there is concomitant uncertainty regarding stimulus predictability. It is also interesting to note that the children of alcoholics demonstrated the P300 attenuation under the placebo condition, although initial group baseline differences were not observed. Significantly, offspring of alcoholics have been reported in a number of studies using different experimental procedures to have a differential response to placebo, possibly reflecting idiosyncratic attentional or expectancy regulations relative to children of nonalcoholics (Newlin, 1985).

The P300 is a positive wave form occurring approximately 300 milliseconds after a stimulus presentation. It is a relatively late-appearing component, but one

78   R. E. Tarter, S. B. Laird, and H. B. Moss

which has received much attention because of its potential psychological significance. Not surprisingly, therefore, other researchers have also focussed on this
particular wave component. The next EP study, conducted by Schmidt and
Neville (1984) on a small group ($N = 10$) of sons of alcoholic and nonalcoholic
men, yielded somewhat different findings. Significantly, this study controlled
for maternal drinking and did not administer alcohol to the subjects, thereby
eliminating the possible confounding affects of expectancy on the results. Using
auditory stimuli requiring paired stimulus discrimination, the investigators found
no P300 wave differences between sons of alcoholics and nonalcoholics. However, when drinks per occasion were considered, there was lower amplitude and
longer latency in the P300 in the family history positive (FHP) group, compared
with control subjects. These findings are open to at least two competing in-
terpretations, namely, that this CNS characteristic may predispose a person to
drink, or alternatively, that FHP subjects may for unknown reasons be more
sensitive to the CNS consequences of alcohol consumption.

The ambiguity regarding causation was addressed directly by Begleiter,
Porjesz, Bihari, and Kissin (1984), who investigated adolescent subjects with no
alcohol consumption experience. Using a complex visual stimulus, sons of
alcoholic men were found to have an attenuation of the P300 wave, compared
with controls. These data unequivocally reflect CNS functioning that is unrelated
to alcohol's acute or chronic effects.

Since Begleiter et al.'s (1984) important findings, several other studies have
been performed with primarily positive results. Schuckit (1985a), Whipple,
Parker, and Noble (1988), O'Connor, Hesselbrock, and Tasman (1986), and
O'Connor, Hesselbrock, Tasman, and De Palma (1987) have for the most part
replicated the EP findings, whereas Polich, Haier, Buchsbaum, and Bloom
(1988) observed neither latency nor voltage differences between sons of alcoholics and nonalcoholics. The reasons for the failure to replicate results are likely
quite numerous; however, one particular important factor may be that this last
study sampled college students, who by definition have made a successful
adjustment. Offspring of alcoholics with abnormal CNS functioning are less
likely to enroll in a university because of cognitive disabilities involving attentional and memory processes.

In a study of alcoholics having a parent who was either alcoholic or
nonalcoholic, Patterson, Williams, McLean, Smith, and Schaeffer (1987)
observed a lower P300 amplitude in the FHP subjects, although latency was
indistinguishable between the groups.

In an interesting study of the association between language processing and
EP patterns, Schmidt and Neville (1985) found that the amplitide of an N430
wave was smaller in sons of alcoholics than in those of nonalcoholics. The
latency of the N430 wave was also negatively correlated with drinking history in
the family history positive subjects. Moreover, the differences between groups
were most pronounced from recordings over the right hemisphere. Although the

sample size was small ($N = 5$ in each group), the results suggest that a language processing deficiency may be associated with alcoholism vulnerability.

In summary, EP studies have yielded intriguing findings. The value of the methodology lies in its promise to link physiological processes to the neuroanatomical substrate as well as to overt behavioral disturbance and cognitive incapacity. The P300, for example, appears to be generated from the hippocampus. Although other as yet unidentified generator sources may underlie the P300, the hippocampus is an especially integral structure for subserving attention, short-term memory, and visuospatial capacities. Also, because of its connection to other limbic system structures, CNS dysfunction may underlie certain of the emotional and motivational disturbances commonly demonstrated by children of alcoholics. Formal research studies have, however, not been conducted. Nonetheless, the EP investigations have inspired investigators to pursue the biological basis of alcoholism vulnerability using techniques that can precisely measure the sensory information processing capacity that relates to the underlying neural substrate. Furthermore, such research has been of heuristic value by suggesting a possible etiologic basis for the attentional and learning disabilities that have been reported in children of alcoholics.

NEUROPSYCHOLOGICAL CHARACTERISTICS

For all of the reasons previously discussed (e.g., heterogeneity of the disorder), the neuropsychological research conducted to date has yielded an array of conflicting and confusing findings. The general thrust of the results suggests cognitive impairment in a significant percentage of children of alcoholics. However, the etiology of the manifest deficits, their pattern or configuration into a syndrome, and the underlying dysfunctional neuroanatomical substrate remain unknown.

Standard batteries of clinical neuropsychological tests have not revealed consistent or robust deficits in children of alcoholics. Initial findings by Tarter, Hegedus, and Alterman (1984) and Hegedus, Alterman, and Tarter (1984) reported that delinquent sons of alcoholic men exhibited decrements on tests of memory, verbal information processing, and educational achievement level, compared with delinquent sons of nonalcoholic men. It is significant to note that the disrupted home environment of these children, often marked by physical and sexual abuse (Tarter, Hegedus, & Alterman, 1984), could have contributed to the observed deficits. Thus, while delinquent boys who have an alcoholic father are the highest risk in the population to develop alcoholism, clarification of the unique contributory role of paternal alcoholism on neuropsychological deficits is difficult in view of the multiple potential contributing factors bearing on cognitive development.

Conflicting results have been revealed by investigations of whether alcoholics' offspring who are not specifically selected for study have the putative behavioral disposition (i.e. conduct disorder) associated with high risk. Workman-Daniels and Hesselbrock (1987), and Hesselbrock, Stabenau, and Hesselbrock (1985) found no systematic differences between adult children of alcoholics and nonalcoholics on the Halstead–Reitan Battery and related tests.

Other investigators have noted that children of alcoholics perform within the normal ranges on standardized neuropsychological tests although at a statistically significant lower level than control children of nonalcoholics (Bennett, Wolin, & Reiss, 1988). Such findings suggest either that there is a subset of outliers in samples studied, thereby depressing the overall sample mean, or that it is only at the most demanding tasks that children of alcoholics are deficient. Neither of these alternative explanations has yet been submitted to empirical study.

Whipple et al. (1988), comparing offspring with strong genetic loading (alcoholic father plus at least one additional alcoholic second-degree relative) and low genetic loading (no first- or second-degree alcoholic relatives), found that the former subjects obtained lower performance IQ scores and lower scores on tests of digit span memory, verbal learning and memory, perceptual closure, and visuospatial organization. Bennett et al. (1988) reported significant differences between children of alcoholics and nonalcoholics in emotional functioning and cognitive abilities and performance. Children of alcoholics performed deficiently on four different measures of intelligence and cognitive performance compared with those of nonalcoholics. Ervin, Little, Streissguth, and Beck (1984) observed that offspring raised with an alcoholic father in the home had IQ scores approximately 7 points lower than controls. More recently, Tarter, Jacob, and Bremer (1989) found only a trend for deficits on several tests of planning and perceptual efficiency in a sample of boys whose fathers met criteria for alcoholism but had no treatment exposure. Extending these findings, Bremer et al. (in press) observed that deficits, where manifest, were greatest in boys whose fathers had an early age of onset of alcoholism, although the impairments were mild and inconsistent across subjects.

The results of studies of children living in intact families are thus highly inconsistent, although they generally implicate neurocognitive deficits in a substantial percentage of children of alcoholics. Considering the heterogeneity of samples with respect to recruitment criteria, gender, age, and ascertainment procedure combined with variability in types of tests administered, it is not surprising that the findings are erratic. In addition, the manner in which the data are analyzed and reported bears greatly on the interpretation of the results. For example, most studies have reported mean group differences between samples of children of alcoholics and nonalcoholics, even though from a clinical standpoint, performance is within the normal ranges for both groups. Thus, significant group differences may reflect sampling error; however, it is also possible that a subtle or low-grade deficit is tapped only weakly by standard psychometric tests and that more sensitive measures may yield more distinct group differences. At this stage in the research enterprise, it may be heuristic to shift from a psychometric to an information processing strategy so that efficiency as well as capacity in cognitive functioning can be measured with precision. Furthermore, there is no reason to assume that all children of alcoholics in any given sample will manifest a cognitive deficit—that is, have the underlying vulnerability. In addition to examining mean group differences, it may also be worthwhile to attempt first to identify subgroups of persons who have impairment and from there to clarify the severity and pattern of deficit.

One procedure for controlling for a substantial amount of variance on test performance is to examine children who are not living with their alcoholic parents. This paradigm affords the opportunity to circumvent major confounding effects pertaining to home environment and rearing practices, which are more likely to be disturbed in alcoholic families. The Danish Adoption Study (see Searles, Chapter 5, this volume) is ideal in this regard and has been the impetus behind much of the current research delineating the nature of the vulnerability in children of alcoholics. Although adopted children and their adoptive parents are arguably not totally representative of the population at large, the heuristic value of investigating children of alcoholics who have been raised by nonalcoholic adoptive parents cannot be overemphasized. Indeed, it is one of the most powerful methods for separating genetic and environmental influences.

Several interrelated studies of cognitive performance in children of alcoholics who have been raised by nonalcoholic foster parents have been conducted. Reports by Knop et al. (1985) described academic achievement deficiency, problems in verbal information processing, and impairment in planning and abstracting ability in school-age children of alcoholics. Drejer et al. (1985) documented deficits in categorizing ability and planning capacity. These studies provide the strongest evidence that children of alcoholics may have neuropsychological deficits that cannot be attributed to being reared in the adverse environment of their alcoholic parents. Unfortunately, numerous cognitive processes were not sampled in these investigations. Nonetheless, the available findings suggest that alcoholism vulnerability may be associated with neurologically mediated cognitive deficits. How such impairments affect the risk for developing alcoholism remains unknown, however. One hypothesis that can be entertained, based on the data accumulated to date, is that deficient planning and abstracting ability and deficiency in verbal information processing, in combination with poor self-control or the impulsivity often found in prealcoholics (Tarter, Alterman, & Edwards, 1985), may predispose persons to alcohol selection as a coping style in lieu of cognitive focused coping. As will be discussed later, considering all the available evidence, it is plausible to advance a teleological hypothesis of alcoholism etiology in which neurological factors underlying the childhood developmental process prominently influence the ultimate outcome of alcohol abuse in adulthood.

In addition to the above studies of children and adolescents, several investigations have evaluated alcoholic men and women who have alcoholic parents. The results of these studies must be interpreted cautiously because the effects of chronic alcohol abuse on neuropsychological test performance in such persons could obscure or interact in unknown ways with the effects of family history. Bearing this caveat in mind, several interesting studies comparing the neuropsychological test performance of alcoholics and nonalcoholics having either a positive or a negative history of parental alcoholism have been reported. In the first such study, Schaeffer, Parsons, Yohman, Yohman, and Robert (1984) found a main effect for family history of alcoholism on the test performance of alcoholics. The poorest level of capacity was found on tests of abstracting and learning and memory ability in alcoholic men with a positive family history. Using a more clinically oriented battery, Reed, Grant, and Adams (1987) found that family history was not a factor in the neuropsychological test performance of alcoholics. Verbal and nonverbal abstracting deficits have also been observed in female alcoholics who have a positive family history, compared with alcoholic women without a family alcoholism history (Turner & Parsons, 1988).

In conclusion, the findings derived from alcoholics are consistent with respect to the contribution of family history on neurocognitive test performance. Where deficits are observed, they are similar in type to those found in adopted nonalcoholic offspring of alcoholics (Drejer et al., 1985; Knop et al., 1985) and children raised by their alcoholic parents (Tarter, Hill, Jacob, Hegedus, & Winsten, 1984). The negative findings on adult subjects obtained by Reed et al. (1987) are, however, consistent with other research (Workman-Daniels & Hesselbrock, 1987; Hesselbrock et al., 1985) in which the Halstead–Reitan Neuropsychological Test Battery was employed. This battery consists of rather nonspecific cognitive tests that are geared toward patients with neurological disease. It is possible that the sensitivity of these tests are too low to detect specific and subtle impairment in persons found to be vulnerable to alcoholism.

NEUROLOGICAL DISTURBANCE

Neurological disturbances may be overpresented in children of alcoholics. The prevalence of such disturbance is, however, unknown. Recent findings suggest that this issue should be explored more intensively. For example, male offspring of alcoholic men have been found in several studies to be more ataxic than children of nonalcoholics (Hegedus, Tarter, Hill, Jacob, & Winsten, 1984; Lester & Carpenter, 1985; Lipscomb, Carpenter, & Nathan, 1979). On a quantified Romberg test, subjects tested while sober demonstrate more upper body sway if there is paternal alcoholism. One study (Schuckit, 1985b) found no baseline differences between children of alcoholics and nonalcoholics but did find body sway to be less pronounced in the former group after an acute alcohol challenge. The reasons for the discrepancy in findings among studies is unknown; however, one plausible explanation is that Schuckit investigated college students who by definition are showing a high level of adaptive functioning and are thus less likely to have neurological impairments. In effect, the sample may have already selected out the less functionally adaptive children of alcoholics, hence no impairments were detected when tested while sober.

Investigations of handedness also suggest that the organization of neurological processes may be deviant in children of alcoholics. An overrepresentation of sinistrality has been documented in alcoholics, which undoubtedly presaged the onset of drinking (London, Kibbee, & Holt, 1985). Moreover, a recent study by London (1987) observed that approximately 50% of left-handed alcoholic men or a first-degree relative had an alcoholic father, in contrast to 26% of right-handed men. Although these findings are in need of replication and confirmation, they suggest that the pattern of functional cerebral organization may be different in a high percentage of offspring who subsequently develop alcoholism. The high prevalence of sinistrality may also contribute to the manifest behavioral and cognitive disturbances observed in samples of alcoholics' offspring where group mean scores are obtained. In this regard, it is important to recognize that learning disability, conduct disorder, and associated cognitive and academic problems are more prevalent in left-handed persons.

The mechanisms underlying the possible anomalous cerebral dominance have not been addressed. Genetic, congenital prenatal, and postnatal factors all influence the development of handedness. Controlled studies of possible teratogenic factors due to prenatal alcohol exposure especially need to be considered. Nonetheless, at the descriptive level, the findings indicate that cognitive development and information processing style and capacity may be related to an idiosyncratic functional cerebral organization in a subset of vulnerable persons.

BEHAVIORAL DYSREGULATION

Children of alcoholics have been reported to manifest behavioral disturbances that could potentially reflect abnormal CNS functioning. Most attention has been directed to determining whether childhood hyperactivity is a predisposing factor in alcoholism (Alterman & Tarter, 1983). Early findings by Cantwell (1975) and Morrison and Stewart (1971) suggested that hyperactive children reared by nonalcoholic adoptive parents had an elevated prevalence of alcoholism in the biological father. Subsequent research revealed that alcoholic men who reported retrospectively a large number of childhood hyperactivity characteristics had more alcoholic relatives and an earlier age of onset of alcoholism than alcoholics who reported few hyperactivity features (Tarter et al., 1977; Wood, Wender, & Reimherr, 1983). A prospective follow-up study of sons of alcoholics who subsequently became alcoholic themselves revealed a hyperactivity disorder in more than half of the cases (Goodwin et al., 1975). The observation that almost 50% of the variance of alcoholism severity could be predicted by childhood hyperactivity and premorbid social adjustment underscores the prognostic importance of hyperactivity (Tarter, 1982).

Since the demonstration that hyperactivity may be a component of alcoholism vulnerability, much has been learned regarding its presence and significance as a risk factor. First, where present, hyperactivity is typically embedded in a more generalized conduct disorder. Comparing adolescent delinquent sons of alcoholic and nonalcoholic men revealed no statistically significant differences on 50 characteristics related to hyperactivity and minimal brain dysfunction (Tarter et al., 1985).

Second, the presence of hyperactivity symptoms is significantly related to neuropsychological functioning. Severity of hyperactivity correlates with magnitude of neuropsychological deficit in young adult offspring of alcoholics (Workman-Daniels & Hesselbrock, 1987; Hesselbrock et al., 1985). These findings suggest that the disturbances in behavioral regulation may have a direct neurological basis. Conceptualizing hyperactivity from a neuropsychological framework, Barkley (1981) concluded that the disorder stems from a failure to self-monitor goal-directed behavior. This aspect of motivation is subserved by the so-called executive regulatory processes (Luria, 1966) of which the anatomical substrate is in the anterior cerebral regions.

Third, hyperactivity, as used clinically, refers to a constellation of state- and trait-specific behaviors that include impulsivity, disinhibition, overreactivity to minimally provocative stimuli, distractibility, and high energy level. Investigations of prealcoholics, heavy drinkers prodromal to alcoholism, young alcoholics, and unaffected offspring of alcoholics reveal a high prevalence of these behavior, which are often, but not always, also found in conjunction with a conduct disorder or antisocial personality disorder (McCord & McCord, 1962; Jones, 1968; Robins et al., 1977).

And fourth, it is of more than passing interest that amphetamines are the second most preferred drug by many alcoholics (Cadoret, Troughton, & Widmer, 1984). The implication of this finding is that amphetamines are reinforcing for such persons in perhaps the same way that they are therapeutic for hyperactive children. Elucidating the neurochemical mechanisms underlying hyperactivity may, therefore, also help clarify the biological basis of alcoholism vulnerability for a subset of the population.

NEUROPSYCHOLOGICAL THEORY OF ALCOHOLISM VULNERABILITY

The proposed neuropsychological theory of alcoholism vulnerability applies only to a subset of individuals in the population. Because alcoholism is a very heterogeneous disorder, varying greatly between individuals with respect to etiology and clinical characteristics, it is unreasonable to expect that any one theory could be both comprehensive and specific enough to define the nature of the vulnerability for all alcoholic individuals. Consequently, the theory advanced herein pertains to persons who meet the following criteria: an early age of onset of heavy drinking without an identifiable precipitating cause, severe manifestations of alcoholism symptomatology, and antisocial propensities. The proposed theory does not claim to apply to cases of alcoholism that are secondary to another psychopathological condition, where alcohol dependence arises from habit or in response to stress. In effect, the proposed theory attempts to marshal the available evidence to explain the neurobehavioral correlated of what Cloninger (1987) refers to as Type 2 alcoholism.

A neuropsychological theory addresses only organismic characteristics. Hence, it does not claim to account for all aspects of alcoholism etiology. For alcoholism to develop, alcoholic beverages must be accessible in society. Facilitative influences such as ambivalence about drinking by family and peers, as well as the socioeconomic and cultural macrosystems, also affect drinking behavior and ultimately the risk for becoming an alcoholic. Thus, alcoholism can be viewed as the end point in a chain of events involving the interaction between numerous environmental factors and a vulnerable organism. Conceptualizing alcoholism etiology in this manner (that is, from a diathesis–stress perspective) affords the opportunity to investigate etiology as a multifactorial phenomenon, and to quantify the interaction and impact of the plethora of variables that could either exacerbate or attenuate the risk. Neuropsychological impairment, considered in this context, is thus but one of a number of etiologically relevant factors.

The proposed neuropsychological theory encompasses the domain of psychobiological processes and capacities mediated by the neural systems coursing along the prefrontal–midbrain axis. As such, the theory accommodates a variety of behavioral phenomena that, although superficially disparate (e.g., cognition, affect, arousal, etc.), are united by the fact that they are functionally integrated within this neuroanatomical system.

The theory that an anterior–basal dysfunction underlies the vulnerability to alcoholism has at least three major research ramifications. First, it raises the possibility that the dysfunction, hypothesized to be neurochemical in nature, renders the person highly susceptible to the adverse neurological effects of alcohol consumption. In one preliminary investigation, Begleiter, Porjesz, and Kissin (1982) found that familial alcoholics, those presumably possessing a greater genetic loading for this disorder, exhibited more brain atrophy than nonfamilial alcoholics, even when age and duration of drinking history were controlled. It is also interesting to note that Wilkinson and Carlen (1980a, 1980b) have identified two neuropsychological subtypes; these being a premature aging profile and an amnesic profile. The fact that the brain atrophy appeared to occur relatively early in the drinking career in the amnesic type points to a particular vulnerability to alcohol's deleterious effects in these persons. Unfortunately, no information about family history or genetic predisposition was obtained. However, alcoholics with a familial history of alcoholism perform more poorly on neuropsychologic tests than alcoholics without a family alcoholism history (Schaeffer et al., 1984).

A second and somewhat related ramification is that alcoholic persons with the anterior–basal dysfunction may be more susceptible than others to the acute physiological effects of alcohol. It is conjectured that alcoholics with such brain dysfunction are more inclined than other alcoholics to experience blackouts, delirium tremens, and withdrawal; disturbances that appear to be the consequence of a disruption of limbic and diencephalic mechanisms (Segal, Kushnarev, Urakov, & Misionzhnik, 1970). The finding that these symptoms of alcoholism are not highly correlated with duration of alcoholism and are very often found in young alcoholics (Bergman & Agren, 1974) suggests that there may be a differential vulnerability to experience these symptoms in some alcoholics.

Third, a dysfunctional anterior–basal system may result in a differentially greater reinforcing response to the acute effects of alcohol, since the brain mechanisms subserving reward are contained within this neural system. Hence, it is speculated that the reinforcement consequences of alcohol consumption, and the associated emotional and motivational changes from intoxication, are different for persons at high risk for alcoholism than for the rest of the population. Significantly, three reports have described greater reinforcing effects, *vis-à-vis* stress dampening in young adults at high risk for alcoholism (Finn & Phil, 1987; Levenson, Oyama, & Meek, 1987; Sher & Levenson, 1982). Moreover, the finding by Tarter et al. (1977) of a euphoric response to alcohol in primary alcoholics also suggests that drinking may be particularly reinforcing for persons who develop early-onset alcoholism and typically have a family history of this disorder.

Before reviewing the research evidence, it is necessary to consider whether the anterior–basal brain region, consisting of a substantial proportion of cerebral mass, is a functionally integrated system. Two lines of evidence suggest that this is indeed the case. First, it has been convincingly argued that the prefrontal region of the cortex is the association area for the limbic system (Fulton, 1952; Pribram, 1960). Consequently, it is not surprising that limbic and prefrontal lesions produce similar behavioral changes (Pribram, 1960, 1969). Second, tissue degenerative techniques have revealed the organization of the fiber tracts that emanate from the prefrontal cortex. Fibers from the dorsolateral area project to the superior temporal gyrus, while those from the orbital area project to the middle and inferior temporal gyrus; both tracts project to the temporal lobe via the fasciculus uncinatus (Nauta, 1964).

A hypothalamic–frontal tract also has been identified (Clark & Meyer, 1950), which synapses first in the dorsomedial nucleus of the thalamus before projecting to the prefrontal areas. Three important tracts emanating from the dorsomedial nucleus of the thalamus also project to the prefrontal regions, the pars paramellaris to the dorsolateral convexity, the pars parvocellularis to the dorsolateral frontal region, and the pars magnocellularis to the orbital region. It is also of particular interest that the frontal eye fields and midbrain structures, particularly the reticular activating system and the superior colliculus, are connected and conjointly subserve and integrate such complex functions as arousal, attention, visual search, and spatial analysis (Crowne, 1983).

Thus, there are specific reciprocally innervated connections between prefrontal, diencephalic, and midbrain structures. From a functional standpoint, it is apparent that these systems are integrally involved in mediating cognitive processes via the neocortex, emotional and motivational processes via the prefrontal and limbic regions, and organismic arousal via the diencephalon and the midbrain. Therefore, in advancing this substrate as being dysfunctional in persons vulnerable to alcoholism, it is essential that a neuropsychological analysis embrace the above diverse aspects of psychological functioning.

The following review of the evidence, implicating anterior–basal systems as the underlying substrate, is organized into three sections: prefrontal dysfunction, limbic and diencephalic dysfunction, and midbrain dysfunction. This is done for convenience and clarity of exposition only, since these brain regions, as emphasized above, comprise an integrated functional system.

Neurobehavioral Correlates of the Prefrontal Region

Over a century ago, Sir Hughlings Jackson postulated that the anterior brain region exerted a regulatory role over behavior by modulating the activity of lower brain structures. Through primarily inhibitory mechanisms innervating diencephalic, midbrain, and spinal structures, the prefrontal cortex was hypothesized to mediate choice behavior and self-regulation (Jackson, 1958). Extensive research conducted on both humans and animals has since confirmed Jackson's position. In the syntax of contemporary neuropsychology, the prefrontal region subserves the "executive" functions of the brain; that is, planning or goal formulation, initiating and sustaining behavior programs, self-monitoring, and self-evaluation of behavior (Lezak, 1982). Luria (1966) emphasizes the importance of language mediation as integral to behavioral self-regulation and goal persistence. Of particular interest is Luria's assertion that the maturation of the anterior–frontal brain region does not take place until the fifth or last stage of development, during early to midadolescence. This has especially salient ramifications for the present theory, since it suggests that the cerebral dysfunction evidenced behaviorally in high-risk individuals would first be detected in adolescence, at which time age-appropriate capacities have not been acquired.

In light of the above, it is interesting to note that the neuropsychological impairments observed by Schaeffer et al. (1984) in nonalcoholics who had a family history of alcoholism were found in the "higher" cognitive functions and were primarily circumscribed to a cluster of tests that are sensitive to anterior brain dysfunction. These tests included the Category Test of the Halstead–Reitan Battery, the Conceptual Level Analogy Test, the Abstraction Test of the Shipley Institute of Living Scale, Levine's Hypothesis Test, the Wechsler Adult In-

88   R. E. Tarter, S. B. Laird, and H. B. Moss

telligence Scale (WAIS) Block Design, and a word-finding test. It was further
observed that there was no significant interaction between the effects of alcoholism in the subject and the familiality (family history) variable, suggesting that the
neuropsychological deficits are independently and additively determined by
these two factors.

Pathology or dysfunction of the anterior–frontal brain region results in
behavioral and cognitive disturbances that are similar to those found in persons at
risk for alcoholism. One frequent sequela of prefrontal pathology is hyperactivity. Hyperactive adolescents are more likely to abuse alcohol than other teenagers (Blouin, Bornstein, & Trites, 1978; Mendelson, Johnson, & Stewart, 1971).
Childhood hyperactivity also appears to be a risk factor for the development of
alcoholism (Goodwin et al., 1975; Jones, 1968). In addition, hyperactive male
children have a relatively high prevalence of alcoholism in their biological
fathers, but not their adoptive fathers (Cantwell, 1972; Morrison & Stewart,
1973). While the etiological mechanisms underlying hyperactivity are not completely understood, it appears to be associated with a disruption of arousal
mechanisms (Douglas, 1980) and a deficiency in rule-governed behavior (Barkley, 1981). On the basis of the above findings it is, therefore, reasonable to
conjecture that hyperactivity, implicated as one of the risk factors for alcoholism,
may involve an anterior brain dysfunction.

Evidence obtained from two other lines of research also points to a dysfunction in the anterior brain region. First, the pattern of neuropsychological deficits
found in psychopathy, a disorder that is often associated with alcoholism,
predates alcoholism, and is frequently present in the families of alcoholics,
implicates an anterior brain dysfunction (Yeudall, 1980). And second, two
recent neuropsychological studies of delinquent offspring of alcoholic fathers
have revealed impairments consistent with an interpretation of an anterior
dysfunction (Tarter, Hill, Jacob, Hegedus, & Winsten, 1984; Hegedus, Alterman, & Tarter, 1984). In these studies, the sons of alcoholics and nonalcoholics
were very similar in performance on Wechsler Intelligence Scale for Children
(WISC) or WAIS measures of intelligence. However, the subjects with alcoholic
fathers performed significantly more poorly on several subtests of the Peabody
Individual Achievement Test (PIAT), a standardized measure of educational
achievement. Deficits were also detected on tests of attention, short-term memory, and language expression. While these results should be viewed as preliminary, they are intriguing in that they provide the first direct evidence for
neuropsychological impairments in persons at heightened risk to become
alcoholic.

Behavioral disinhibition, restlessness, attentional disturbances, and impulsivity have been reported in prealcoholics (Jones, 1968; Loper, Kammeier, &
Hoffman, 1973; McCord & McCord, 1960) as well as in persons who are at
elevated risk for alcoholism (Goodwin et al., 1975). Such behavioral disturbances are often sequelae of anterior brain pathology, raising the possibility

that the same neuroanatomical system is disrupted in persons vulnerable to alcoholism. In an important theoretical integration, Gorrenstein and Newman (1980) argue that behavioral disinhibition, characteristic of alcoholics and psychopaths, is associated with a frontal–septal lesion or dysfunction. A more recent overview of the neurochemical research also suggests a disruption in the frontal–basal systems underlying the vulnerability to alcoholism as well as other addictions (Barnes, 1988).

Neurobehavioral Correlates of the Limbic and Diencephalic Regions

These brain regions are primarily responsible for mediating emotional and motivational processes (Heilman, Bowers, & Valenstein, 1979). Anterior to the hypothalamus there is a neural circuit possessing primitive executive functions that are conditionable to both homeostatic states of the organism and environmental incentives (Panksepp, 1982). The primary function of this translimbic system is to initiate motor activity in preparation for consummatory behavior. In effect, this neural substrate provides the anatomical basis for the psychological process of expectancy.

The "expectancy" neural system has been shown to play a major role in addiction (Panksepp, 1981). Indeed, expectancy variables are at least as influential as demographic variables in predicting adolescent drinking (Christiansen & Goldman, 1983) and appear also to play a major role in alcoholism (Higgins & Marlatt, 1973). At low doses, expectancy is probably more important than alcohol's pharmacological properties in determining an individual's emotional and motivational reactions (Wilson & Abrams, 1977).

Limbic and diencephalic mechanisms also regulate organismic arousal. Evidence for a dysfunction of arousal regulation mechanisms in persons at risk for alcoholism is derived from at least four sources. First, Mawson and Mawson (1977), in a comprehensive theoretical and empirical review, concluded that a neurotransmitter disequilibrium constitutes the neurobiological basis for psychopathy. Considering the similarities and associations between psychopathy and the type of alcoholism here under discussion, it is reasonable to suspect that a similar neurochemical disorder underlies alcoholism. Studies of persons at high risk for alcoholism implicate disturbances in serotonergic and monoaminergic neurotransmitter mechanisms (Barnes, 1988).

Second, evidence for a disorder in arousal regulation has been derived from psychophysiological research, Kissin and Hankoff (1959) reported that alcohol exerted a "normalizing" effect in alcoholics, suggesting that drinking may initially be prompted by arousal instability. The observation that alcoholics sustained a heart rate increment after the consumption of alcohol longer than nonalcoholics also points to a homeostatic disorder (Rosenberg & Buttsworth,

1969). In addition, Rubin, Gottheil, Roberts, Alterman, and Holstine (1980) found evidence for arousal disturbances using pupillometric measures. While possibly confounded somewhat by the effects of chronic drinking, the evidence nonetheless suggests the possibility of disrupted arousal mechanisms.

Third, alcoholics frequently abuse stimulants (including nicotine and caffeine) as well as tranquilizers and hypnotics (Kaufman, 1982). The motivation to use drugs may thus not be merely to achieve a desired pharmacological effect of either a high or low level of arousal, but rather may be aimed at attenuating arousal lability. This is perhaps the most parsimonious explanation of the finding that amphetamines are the second most preferred drug among many alcoholic men, particularly where there is an accompanying antisocial personality (Cadoret, O'Gorman, Troughton, & Heywood, 1985).

And fourth, behavioral investigations also implicate an impairment in arousal homeostasis. Prealcoholics have been found to be restless, unpredictable, and disinhibited—behaviors that suggest unstable and rapidly oscillating arousal states. Impulsivity, which is associated with emotional excitability and anxiety (Gray, Owen, Davis, & Tsaltas, 1983), has also been reported to antedate alcoholism. Sensation seeking, reflecting a need to augment as well as optimize arousal states, is also correlated with alcohol use (Schwarz, Burkhart, & Green, 1978; Zuckerman, Bone, Neary, Mangelsdorff, & Brustman, 1972). Emotional immaturity and moodiness, observed in preadolescent sons of alcoholics (Aronson & Gilbert, 1963), additionally suggest that there is dispositional lability in persons at high-risk, although the possibility remains that these disturbances may be due, in part, to the stress of living in a disrupted home environment. Furthermore, the demonstration that emotional excitability and neuroticism are predictive of subsequent drug abuse (Sieber & Bentler, 1982) and that alcoholics under 30 years of age are characterized by abnormally high levels of anxiety (Rosenberg & Buttsworth, 1969) is congruent with the notion of a disruption of arousal-regulating mechanisms. And finally, neuroticism has been found to be characteristic of both alcoholics (Barnes, 1983) and sons of alcoholics (Barnes, 1983; Tarter, Hegedus, Goldstein, Shelly, & Alterman, 1984), a personality trait that Eysenck (1983) has argued develops from innate lability of the limbic system. Furthermore, body sway is positively correlated with measures of neuroticism (Eysenck, 1947). Persons at elevated risk for alcoholism, as previously discussed, have been found to be more ataxic. Considered collectively, the available evidence indicates that arousal instability characterizes prealcoholics, children at risk for alcoholism, and already affected alcoholics.

Limbic system involvement is also suggested by the particularly strong reinforcing effects that alcohol has in certain persons. The medial forebrain bundle is integrally involved in mediating positive reinforcement. A differential positive reinforcing response to alcohol has been reported in young men at elevated risk for alcoholism (Sher & Levenson, 1982), suggesting that alcohol exerts particularly strong effects on the neuronal substrate subserving reinforcement in vulnerable individuals.

Neurobehavioral Correlates of the Midbrain Region

Among the functions primarily subserved by the midbrain region are consciousness, attention, and arousal. To date, there have been no neurobehavioral studies specifically directed to elucidating midbrain functioning in prealcoholics or in persons at risk for developing alcoholism. However, deficient attention and concentration processes appear to characterize persons at risk for alcoholism (Wender, Reimherr, & Wood, 1981; Wood, Reimherr, Wender, & Johnson, 1976; Wood et al., 1983), which by inference implicates the midbrain reticular activating system. Approximately one out of three alcoholic individuals meets the criteria for an attention deficit disorder–residual type, suggesting that the attention problems persist into adulthood and augment the risk for becoming alcoholic (Wood et al., 1983). Pupillometric studies of alcoholics also point to a disturbance in midbrain mechanisms (Rubin, Gottheil, Roberts, Alterman, & Holstine, 1977, 1978, 1980).

Alcoholics enhance or magnify sensory input. Results of the kinesthetic aftereffect test (Petrie, 1967) and measurement of brain evoked potentials (Buchsbaum & Ludwig, 1980; Coger, Dymond, Serafitinedes, Lowenstam, & Pearson, 1976), reveals that alcoholics are "stimulus augmenters." Inasmuch as the reticular formation is integrally involved in modulating and controlling stimulus input (Hernandez-Peon, 1961), it can be concluded that the risk for alcoholism is, to some extent, related to the neurophysiological activity of this neural substrate.

PRACTICAL IMPLICATIONS

If subsequent research confirms the theory that neuropsychological characteristics are associated with the risk for alcoholism, it would substantially increase our capacity not only to identify potential alcoholics, but also to apply specific prophylactic interventions. For instance, the capacities subserved by the anterior–frontal region could be targeted by developmental monitoring. If intervention at some point is deemed desirable, the child could then be taught rule-learning strategies to enhance cognitive skills or be placed in a behavioral modification program to reduce behavioral problems stemming from a dysfunction of this brain region. The fact that the anterior brain regions do not functionally mature until adolescence (Luria, 1961, 1966; Vygotsky, 1962), suggests that deficits in high-risk children may not be observed until then. In other words, preadolescent high-risk children may not be distinguishable from other children. The prodromal signs of a negative outcome are, nonetheless, still expressed at a young enough age to be treated before the onset of problematic drinking in most cases. Thus, primary prevention strategies with circumscribed and well-defined cognitive and behavior change objectives could be applied to high-risk individuals.

Other practical ramifications of the theory pertain to the affective components of vulnerability. For example, the hypothesized disruption of homeostasis mechanisms, resulting in emotional lability and anxiety, may be amendable to interventions like biofeedback, which emphasizes self-regulation of physiological activity.

The hypothesis that a neurochemical disturbance is responsible for difficulties in arousal regulation also suggests the possible value of pharmacological interventions. The demonstration that certain drugs such as lithium (Merry, Reynolds, Bailey, & Copper, 1976), Ritalin (Wood et al., 1976), and Cylert (Wood et al., 1976) are therapeutically beneficial for some alcoholics is in agreement with the theory advanced herein that arousal dysregulation is associated with vulnerability to alcoholism.

SUMMARY

Little doubt can be harbored regarding the genetic predisposition to alcoholism. The phenotypic expression of the genetic diathesis has not, however, been systematically studied in humans. Previous reviews by the authors have argued for the heritability of certain behavioral characteristics that, if present, increase the risk for alcoholism (Alterman & Tarter, 1983; Tarter et al., 1985). The present discussion extends this line of reasoning by demonstrating that the psychological evidence can be organized into a neurobehavioral framework. The inheritance of cognitive capacities is well documented, and hence the thesis contained herein, by addressing the question of *what* is inherited, can be considered to comprise a neurobehavioral–genetic theory.

The proposed neuropsychological theory is compatible with social learning and conditioning perspectives of alcoholism etiology. While this chapter addressed the interrelationship between the anatomical substrate and cognitive, emotional, and motivational processes associated with alcoholism vulnerability, the importance of learned patterns of behavior and cognition was also considered in the context of the neural system mediating expectancy. These learned patterns of behavior are, however, theorized to be predisposed in vulnerable individuals. Carving for alcohol and impaired control over drinking involves the interaction between cognitive and physiological processes (Ludwig, 1983). Clarifying the role and functions of the "expectancy" neural system may, therefore, contribute to a better understanding of the factors underlying symptomatic problems with alcohol, especially since expectancy in psychological research has been shown to influence the occurrence of these symptoms in alcoholics. Moreover, the range of psychological processes subserved by the anterior–basal system raises other important questions pertinent to social learning and conditioning theories of alcoholism. For example, how does the implicated disturbance in arousal affect conditionability? And, how does the hypothesized inability to self-monitor behavior relate to the capacity to acquire social skills? Thus, the present theory affords the opportunity to investigate a variety of manifest behavioral characteristics associated with the propensity for alcohol abuse and alcoholism from the perspective of a dysfunctional brain system.

ACKNOWLEDGMENTS

This work was supported by Grant No. R01 AA06936-01A1 from the National Institute on Alcohol Abuse and Alcoholism.

REFERENCES

Agarwal, D. P., & Goedde, H. W. (1987). Human aldehyde dehydrogenase isozymes and alcohol sensitivity. *Isozymes: Current Topics in Biological Medical Research, 16,* 21–48.

Alexopoulos, G. S., Lieberman, K. W., & Frances, R. (1983). Platelet MAO activity in alcoholic patients and their first-degree relatives. *American Journal of Psychiatry, 140*(11), 1501–1504.

Alterman, A., & Tarter, R. (1983). The transmission of psychological vulnerability. Implications for alcoholism etiology. *Journal of Nervous and Mental Disease, 171,* 147–154.

Alterman, A. I., Bridges, R., & Tarter, R. E. (1986). Drinking behavior of high risk college men: Contradictory preliminary findings. *Alcoholism: Clinical and Experimental Research, 10*(3), 305–309.

Aronson, H., & Gilbert, A. (1963). Preadolescent sons of male alcoholics. *Archives of General Psychiatry, 8,* 47–53.

Barkley, R. (1981). *Hyperactive children: A handbook for diagnosis and treatment.* New York: Guilford Press.

Barnes, G. (1983). Clinical and prealcoholic personality characteristics. In B. Kissin & H. Begleiter (Eds.), *The pathogenesis of alcoholism* (Vol. 6, pp. 113–183). New York: Plenum Press.

Barnes, D. M. (1988). The biological tangle of drug addiction. *Science, 241,* 415–417.

Begleiter, H., Porjesz, B., Bihari, B., & Kissin, B. (1984). Event-related brain potentials in boys at risk for alcoholism. *Science, 225*(4669), 1493–1496.

Begleiter, H., Porjesz, B., & Kissin, B. (1982). Brain dysfunction in alcoholics with and without a family history of alcoholism. *Alcoholism: Clinical and Experimental Research, 6*(1), 136.

Bennett, L. A., Wolin, S. J., & Reiss, D. (1988). Cognitive, behavioral, and emotional problems among school-age children of alcoholic parents. *American Journal of Psychiatry, 145*(2), 185–190.

Bergman, H., & Agren, G. (1974). Cognitive style and intellectual performance in relation to the progress of alcoholism. *Quarterly Journal of Studies on Alcoholism, 35,* 1242–1255.

Blouin, A., Bornstein, R., & Trites, R. (1978). Teenage alcohol use among hyperactive children: A five year follow-up study. *Journal of Pediatric Psychology, 3*(4), 188–194.

Borg, S., Krande, H., Mossberg, D., Valverius, P., & Sedwall, G. (1983). Central nervous system noradrenaline metabolism and alcohol consumption in man. *Pharmacology, Biochemistry and Behavior, 18,* 375–378.

Bremer, D., Tarter, R., Jacob, T., & Carra, J. (in press). Behavioral and cognitive characteristics of sons of early and late onset alcoholics. *Alcoholism: Clinical and Experimental Research.*

Buchsbaum, M., & Ludwig, A. (1980). Effects of sensory input and alcohol administration on visual evoked potentials in normal subjects and alcoholics. In H. Begleiter (Ed.), *Biological effects of alcohol.* New York: Plenum Press.

Cadoret, R., O'Gorman, T., Troughton, E., & Heywood, E. (1985). Alcoholism and antisocial personality. Interrelationships, genetic and environmental factors. *Archives of General Psychiatry, 42,* 161–167.

Cadoret, R., Troughton, E., & Widmer, R. (1984). Clinical differences between antisocial and primary alcoholism. *Comprehensive Psychiatry, 25,* 108.

Cantwell, D. P. (1975). Familial-genetic research with hyperactive children. In D. W. Cantwell (Ed.), *The hyperactive child: Diagnosis, management and current research* (pp. 93–105). New York: Halstead Press.

Christiansen, B., & Goldman, M. (1983). Alcohol-related expectancies versus demographic/ background variables in the prediction of adolescent drinking. *Journal of Consulting and Clinical Psychology, 51,* 249–257.

Clark, W., & Meyer, M. (1950). Anatomical relationships between the cerebral cortex and the hypothalamus. *British Medical Bulletin, 6,* 341–345.

Cloninger, C. R. (1987). Neurogenetic adaptive mechanisms in alcoholism. *Science, 236,* 410–416.

Cloninger, C. R., Bohman, M., & Sigvaardson, S. (1981). Inheritance of alcohol abuse: Cross-fostering analyses of adopted men. *Archives of General Psychiatry, 38,* 861–867.

Coger, R., Dymond, A., Serafitinedes, E., Lowenstam, I., & Pearson, D. 1976). Alcoholism: Average visual evoked response amplitude-intensity slap and symmetry in withdrawal. *Biological Psychiatry, 1,* 435–443.

Crowne, D. (1983). The frontal eye field and attention. *Psychological Bulletin, 93,* 232–260.

Douglas, V. (1980). Treatment and training approaches to hyperactivity: Establishing internal or external control. In C. Whalen & B. Henker (Eds.), *Hyperactive children: The social ecology of identification and treatment* (pp. 283–316). New York: Academic Press.

Drejer, K., Theilgaard, A., Teasdale, T. W., Schulsinger, F, & Goodwin, D. W. (1985). A prospective study of young men at risk for alcoholism: Neuropsychological Assessment. *Alcoholism: Clinical and Experimental Research, 9*(6), 498–502.

Elmasian, R., Neville, H., Woods, D., Schuckit, M., & Bloom, F. (1982). Event-related brain potentials are different in individuals at high risk and low risk for developing alcoholism. *Proceedings of the National Academy of Science, U.S.A., 79,* 7900–7903.

Ervin, C., Little, R., Streissguth, A., & Beck, D. (1984). Alcoholic fathering and its relation to child's intellectual development: A pilot investigation. *Alcoholism: Clinical and Experimental Research, 8,* 362–365.

Eysenck, H. (1947). *Dimensions of personality.* London: Routledge & Kegan Paul.

Eysenck, H. (1983). Neurotic conditions. In R. Tarter (Ed.), *The child at psychiatric risk* (pp. 245–286). New York: Oxford University Press.

Finn, P. R., & Pihl, R. O. (1987). Men at high risk for alcoholism: The effect of alcohol on cardiovascular response to unavoidable shock. *Journal of Abnormal Psychology, 96,*(3), 230–236.

Fulton, J. (1952). *The frontal lobes and human behavior: The Sherrington lectures.* Liverpool, England: Liverpool University Press.

Gabrielli, W. F., Mednick, S. A., Volavka, J., Pollack, V. E., Schulsinger, F., Itil, T. M. (1982). Electroencephalograms in children of alcoholic fathers. *Psychophysiology, 19,* 404–407.

Goodwin, D. W. (1977). Genetic and experimental antecedents of alcoholism: A prospective study. *Alcoholism: Clinical and Experimental Research, 1*(3), 259–265.

Goodwin D. W. (1985). Alcoholism and genetics: The sins of the fathers. *Archives of General Psychiatry, 42*(2), 171–174.

Goodwin, D. W. (1986). Heredity and alcoholism. *Annals of Behavioral Medicine, 8*(2–3), 3–6.

Goodwin, D. W., Schulsinger, F., Hermansen, L., Guze, S. B., & Winokur, G. (1975). Alcoholism and the hyperactive child syndrome. *Journal of Nervous and Mental Disease, 160*(5), 349–353.

Gorrenstein, E., & Newman, J. (1980). Disinhibitory psychopathology: A new perspective and a model for research. *Psychological Bulletin, 87,* 301–315.

Gray, J., Owen, S., Davis, N., & Tsaltas, E. (1983). Psychological and physiological relations between anxiety and impulsivity. In M. Zuckerman (Ed.), *Biological basis of sensation seeking, impulsivity and anxiety* (pp. 181–227). Hillsdale, NJ: Erlbaum.

Hegedus, A. M., Alterman, A. I., & Tarter, R. E. (1984). Learning achievement in sons of alcoholics. *Alcoholism: Clinical and Experimental Research, 8*(3), 330–333.

Hegedus, A. M., Tarter, R., Hill, S., Jacob, T., & Winsten, N (1984). Static ataxia: A biological marker for alcoholism? *Alcoholism: Clinical and Experimental Research, 8,* 580–582.

Heilman, K., Bowers, D., & Valenstein, E. (1979). Emotional disorders associated with neurological diseases. In K. Heilman & E. Valenstein (Eds.), *Clinical neuropsychology* (pp. 377–396). New York: Oxford University Press.

Hernandez-Peon, R. (1961). Reticular mechanisms of sensory control. In W. Rosenblith (Ed.), *Sensory communication* (pp. 497–520). Cambridge, MA: M.I.T. Press

Hesselbrock, V. M., Stabenau, J. R., & Hesselbrock, M. N. (1985). Minimal brain dysfunction and neuropsychological test performance in offspring of alcoholics. In M. Galanter (Ed.), *Recent developments in alcoholism* (pp. 65–82). New York: Plenum Press.

Higgins, R., & Marlatt, G. (1973). The effects of anxiety arousal on the consumption of alcohol by alcoholics and social drinkers. *Journal of Consulting and Clinical Psychology, 41,* 426–433.

Hulyalkar, A. R., Nora, R., & Manowitz, P. (1984). Arylsulfatase A variants in patients with alcoholism. *Alcoholism, 8*(3), 337–341.

Jackson, J. (1958). *Selected writings of John Hughlings Jackson* (Vols. 1–2) (J. Taylor, Ed.). New York: Basic Books.

Jones, M. (1968). Personality correlates and antecedents of drinking patterns in adult males. *Journal of Consulting and Clinical Psychology, 32,* 2–12.

Kaufman, E. (1982). The relationship of alcoholism and alcohol abuse to the abuse of other drugs. *American Journal of Drug and Alcohol Abuse, 9,* 1–17.

Kissin, B., & Hankoff,. L. (1959). The acute effects of ethyl alcohol on the Funkenstein mecholyl response in male alcoholics. *Quarterly Journal of Studies on Alcohol, 20,* 696–703.

Knop, J., Teasdale, T. W., & Schulsinger, F. (1985). Prospective study of young men at high risk for alcoholism: School behavior and achievement. *Journal of Studies on Alcohol, 46*(4), 273–278.

Korri, U. M., Nuutinen, H., & Salaspuro, M. (1985). Increased blood acetate: A new laboratory marker of alcoholism and heavy drinking. *Alcoholism: Clinical and Experimental Research, 9,* 468.

Ledig, M., Diffuel, M., Ziessel, M., et al. (1986). Frequencies of Glyoxalase I phenotypes as biological markers in chronic alcoholism. *Alcohol, 3*(1), 11–14.

Lester, D., & Carpenter, J. A. (1985). Static ataxia in adolescents and their parentage. *Alcoholism: Clinical and Experimental Research, 9*(2), 212.

Levenson, D., Oyama, O., & Meek, P. (1987). Greater reinforcement from alcohol for those at risk: Parental risk, personality risk, and sex. *Journal of Abnormal Psychiatry, 96,* 242–253.

Lezak, M. (1982). The problem of assessing executive functions. *International Journal of Psychology, 17,* 281–297.

Lipscomb, T. R., Carpenter, J. A., & Nathan, P. E. (1979). Static ataxia: A predictor of alocoholism? *Journal of Addiction, 74,* 289–294.

London, W. P. (1987). Cerebral laterality and the study of alcoholism. *Alcohol, 4*(3), 207–208.

London, W. P., Kibbee, P., & Holt, L. (1985). Handedness and alcoholism. *Journal of Nervous and Mental Disorders, 173*(9), 570–572

Loper, R., Kammeier, M., & Hoffman, H. (1973). MMPI characteristics of college freshman males who later became alcoholics. *Journal of Abnormal Psychology, 82*(1), 159–162.

Ludwig, A. (1983). Why do alcoholics drink? In B. Kissin & H. Begleiter (Eds.), *The pathogenesis of alcoholism* (Vol. 6, pp.197–214). New York: Plenum Press.

Luria, A. (1961). *The role of speech in the regulation of normal and abnormal behavior.* London: Pergamon.

Luria, A. (1966). *Higher cortical functions in man.* New York: Basic Books.

Mawson, A., & Mawson, C. (1977). Psychopathy and arousal: A new interpretation of the psychophysiological literature. *Biological Psychiatry, 12,* 49–74,

McCord, W., & McCord, J. (1960). *Origins of alcoholism.* Stanford, CA: Stanford University Press.

McCord, W., & McCord, J. (1962). A longitudinal study of the personality of alcoholics. *Society, Culture and Drinking Practices, 36,* 413–430.

Mendelson, W., Johnson, N., & Stewart. M. A. (1971). Hyperactive children as teenagers: A follow-up study. *Journal of Nervous and Mental Disease, 153*(4), 273–279.

Merry, J., Reynolds, C., Bailey, J., & Coppen, A. (1976). Prophylactic treatment of alcoholism by lithium carbonate. *Lancet, 2,* 481–482.

Morrison, J., & Stewart, M. (1971). A family study of the hyperactive child syndrome. *Biological Psychiatry, 3,* 189–195.

Morrison, J., & Stewart, M. (1973). The psychiatric status of the legal families of adopted hyperactive children. *Archives of General Psychiatry, 28,* 888–891.

Mukherjee, A. B., Svoronos, S., Ghazanfari, A., et al. (1987). Transketolase abnormality in cultured fibroblasts from familial chronic alcoholic men and their male offspring. *Journal of Clinical Investigation, 79*(4), 1039–1043.

Nagoshi, C. T., & Wilson, J. R. (1987). Influence of family alcoholism history on alcohol metabolism sensitivity and tolerance. *Alcoholism, 11*(4), 392–398.

Nauta, W. (1964). Unpublished communications to S. Ackerly, 1962. Cited by S. Ackerly in J. Warren & K. Akert (Eds.), *The frontal granular cortex and behavior.* New York: McGraw-Hill.

Newlin, D. B. (1985), Offspring of alcoholics have enhanced antagonistic placebo response. *Alcoholism: Clinical and Experimental Research, 9*(2), 210.

O'Connor, S., Hesselbrock, V., & Tasman, A. (1986). Correlates of increased risk for alcoholism in young men. *Progress in Neuro-Psychopharmacology and Biological Psychiatry, 10*(2), 211–218.

O'Connor, S., Hesselbrock, V., Tasman, A., & DePalma, N. (1987). P3 amplitudes in two distinct tasks are decreased in young men with a history of paternal alcoholism. *Alcohol, 4*(4), 323–330.

Panksepp, J. (1981). Brain opiads–A neurochemical substrate for narcotic and social dependence. In S. Cooper (Ed.), *Theory in psychopharmacology* (pp. 149–176). New York: Academic Press.

Panksepp, J. (1982). Toward a general psychobiological theory of emotions. *Behavioral and Brain Sciences, 5,* 407–467.

Patterson, B. W., Williams, H. L., McLean, G. A., Smith, L. T., & Schaeffer, K. W. (1987). Alcoholism and family history of alcoholism: effects on visual and auditory event-related potentials. *Alcohol, 4*(4), 265–274.

Petrie, A. (1967). *Individuality in pain and suffering.* Chicago: University of Chicago Press.

Polich, J., Haier, R. J., Buchsbaum, M., & Bloom, F. E. (1988). Assessment of young men at risk for alcoholism with P300 from a visual discrimination task. *Journal of Studies on Alcohol, 49*(2), 186–190.

Pollock, V. E., Volavka, J., Goodwin, D. W., Mednick, S. A., Gabrielli, W. F., Knop, J., & Schulsinger, F. (1983). The EEG after alcohol administration in men at risk for alcoholism. *Archives of General Psychiatry, 40*(8), 857–861.

Pribram, K. (1960). A review of theory in physiological psychology. *Annual Review of Psychology, 11,* 1–40.

Pribram, K. (1969). The primate frontal cortex. *Neuropsychologia, 7,* 259–266.

Propping, P. (1983). Pharmacogenetics of alcohol's CNS effect: implications for the etiology of alcoholism. *Pharmacology, Biochemistry and Behavior, 18*(1), 549–553.

Reed, R., Grant, I., & Adams, K. (1987). Family history of alcoholism does not predict neuropsychological performance in alcoholics. *Alcoholism, 11*(4), 340–344.

Robins, L. N., West, P. A., Ratcliff, K. S., & Herjanic, B. M. (1977). Father's alcoholism and children's outcomes. *Currents in Alcoholism, 4,* 313–327.

Rosenberg, C., & Buttsworth, F. (1969). Anxiety in alcoholics. *Quarterly Journal of Studies on Alcohol, 30,* 729–732.

Rosler, M., Bellaire, W., Hengesch, G., Giannitsis, D., & Jarovici, A. (1983). Genetic markers in alcoholism: no association with HLA. *Archives für Psychiatrie und Nervenkrankheiten, 233*(4), 327–331.

Rubin, L., Gottheil, E., Roberts, A., Alterman, A., & Holstine, J. (1977). Effects of stress on autonomic reactivity in alcoholics. Pupillometric studies I. *Journal of Studies on Alcohol, 38,* 2036–2048.

Rubin, L., Gottheil, E., Roberts, A., Alterman, A, & Holstine, J. (1978). Autonomic nervous system concomitants of short-term abstinence in alcoholics. Pupillometric studies II. *Journal of Studies on Alcohol, 39,* 1895–1907.

Rubin, L., Gottheil, E., Roberts, A., Alterman A., & Holstine, J. (1980). Effects of alcohol on autonomic reactivity in alcoholics. Pupillometric studies III. *Journal of Studies on Alcohol, 41,* 611–622.

Schaeffer, K., Parsons, O., & Yohman, R., Yohman, A., & Robert, J. (1984). Neuropsychological differences between male familial and nonfamilial alcoholics and nonalcoholics. *Alcoholism: Clinical and Experimental Research, 8*(4), 347–351.

Schmidt, A., & Neville, H. (1985). Language processing in men at risk for alcoholism: An event-related potential study. *Alcohol, 2*(3), 529–533.

Schmidt, A. L., & Neville, H. J. (1984). Event related potentials in sons of alcoholic fathers. *Alcoholism: Clinical and Experimental Research, 8*(1), 117.

Schuckit, M. A. (1985a). Behavioral effects of alcohol in sons of alcoholics. In M. Galanter (Ed.), *Recent developments in alcohol* (Vol. 3, pp. 11–19). New York: Plenum Press.

Schuckit, M. A. (1985b). Ethanol-induced changes in body sway in men at high alcoholism risk. *Archives of General Psychiatry, 42*(4), 375–379.

Schuckit, M. A., Gold, E., & Risch, C. (1987). Serum prolactin levels in sons of alcoholics and control subjects. *American Journal of Psychiatry, 144*(7), 854–859.

Schwarz, R., Burkhart, B., & Green, B. (1978). Turning on or turning off: Sensation seeking or tension reduction as motivational determinants of alcohol use. *Journal of Consulting and Clinical Psychology, 46,* 1144–1145.

Segal, B., Kushnarev, V., Urakov, I., & Misionzhnik, E. (1970). Alcoholism and disruption of the activity of deep cerebral structures: Clinical laboratory research. *Quarterly Journal of Studies on Alcohol, 31,* 587–601.

Sher, K., & Levenson, R. (1982). Risk for alcoholism and individual differences in the stess-response-dampening effect of alcohol. *Journal of Abnormal Psychology, 91,* 350–367.

Shigeta, Y., Ishii, H., Takagi, S., et al. (1980). HLA antigens as immunogenetic markers of alcoholism and alcoholic liver disease. *Pharmacological, Biochemical Behavior,13*(1), 89–94.

Sieber, M., & Bentler, P. (1982). Kausalmodelle zu persönlichkeit und dem späteren dosum legaler und illegaler drogew. *Separatabzug, 41,* 1–15.

Stewart, M. A., deBlois, C. S., & Cummings, C. (1980). Psychiatric disorder in the parents of hyperactive boys and those with conduct disorders. *Journal of Child Psychology and Psychiatry and Allied Disciplines, 21,* 268–273.

Swartz, C. M. (1987). Decreased epinephrine in familial alcoholism. Initial findings. *Archives of General Psychiatry, 44*(11), 938–941.

Tarter, R. (1982). Psychosocial history, minimal brain dysfunction and differential drinking patterns of male alcoholics. *Journal of Clinical Psychology, 38*(4), 867–873.

Tarter, R., Alterman, A., & Edwards, K. (1985). Vulnerability to alcoholism in men: A behavior-genetic perspective. *Journal of Studies on Alcohol, 46,* 329–356.

Tarter, R., Hegedus, A., & Alterman, A. (1984). Neuropsychological personality and familial characteristics of physically abused juvenile delinquents. *Journal of the Academy of Child Psychiatry, 23,* 668–674.

Tarter, R., Hill, S., Jacob, T., Hegedus, A., & Winsten, N. (1984). Neuropsychological comparison of sons of alcoholic, depressed, and normal fathers. *Alcoholism: Clinical and Experimental Research, 8*(1), 123.

Tarter, R., Jacob, T., & Bremer, D. (1989). Cognitive status of sons of alcoholic men. *Alcoholism: Clinical and Experimental Research, 13*(2), 232–235.

Tarter, R. E., Hegedus, A. M., Goldstein, G., Shelly, C., & Alterman, A. I. (1984). Adolescent sons of alcoholics: Neuropsychological and personality characteristics. *Alcoholism: Clinical and Experimental Research, 8*(2), 216–222.

Tarter, R. E., McBride, H., Buonpane, N. & Schneider, D. U. (1977). Differentiation of alcoholics. *Archives of General Psychiatry, 34*, 761–768.

Turner, J., & Parsons, O. (1988). Verbal and nonverbal abstracting—problem solving abilities and familial alcoholism in female alcoholics. *Journal of Studies on Alcohol, 49*(3), 281–287.

von-Knorring, A. L., Bohman, M., von-Knorring, L., & Oreland, L. (1985). Platelet MAO activity as a biological marker in subgroups of alcoholism. *Acta Psychiatrica Scandinavica, 72*(1), 51–58.

Vygotsky, L. (1962). *Thought and language.* Cambridge, MA: M.I.T. Press.

Wender, P., Reimherr, F., & Wood, D. (1981). Attention deficit disorder ("Minimal brain dysfunction") in adults: A replication study of diagnosis and drug treatment. *Archives of General Psychiatry, 38*, 449–455.

Whipple, S. C., Parker, E. S., & Noble, E. P. (1988). An atypical neurocognitive profile in alcoholic fathers and their sons. *Journal of Studies on Alcohol, 49*(3), 240–244.

Wilkinson, D., & Carlen, P. (1980a). Chronic organic brain syndromes associated with alcoholism: Neuropsychological and other aspects. In Y. Israel, F. Glaser, H. Kalant, R. Popham, W. Schmidt, & R. Smart (Eds.), *Research advances in alcohol and drug problems* (Vol. 6). New York: Plenum Press.

Wilkinson, D., & Carlen, P. (1980b). Neuropsychological and neurological assessment of alcoholism: Discrimination between groups of alcoholics. *Journal of Studies on Alcohol, 41*, 129–139.

Wilson, G., & Abrams, D. (1977). Effects of alcohol on social anxiety and physiological arousal: Cognitive versus pharmacological processes. *Cognitive Therapy and Research, 1*, 195–210.

Wood, D., Reimherr, F., Wender, P., & Johnson, G. (1976). Diagnosis and treatment of minimal brain dysfunction in adults. *Archives of General Psychiatry, 33*, 1453–1460.

Wood, D., Wender, P., & Reimherr, F. (1983). The prevalence of attention deficit disorder, residual type, or minimal brain dysfunction, in a population of male alcoholic patients. *American Journal of Psychiatry, 140*, 95–98.

Workman-Daniels, K. L., & Hesselbrock, V. M. (1987). Childhood problem behavior and neuropsychological functioning in persons at risk for alcoholism. *Journal of Studies on Alcohol, 48*(3), 187–193.

Yeudall, L. (1980). A neuropsychological perspective of persistent juvenile delinquency and criminal behavior. *Annals of the New York Academy of Sciences, 347*, 349–255.

Zuckerman, M., Bone, R., Neary, R., Mangelsdorff, D., & Brustman, B. (1972). What is the sensation seeker? Personality and trait experience correlates of the Sensation Seeking Scales. *Journal of Consulting and Clinical Psychology, 39*, 308–321.

CHAPTER FIVE

Behavior Genetic Research and Risk for Alcoholism among Children of Alcoholics[1]

JOHN S. SEARLES

The children of alcoholics (COA) domain is often closely identified with research on the genetics of alcoholism. This is primarily because of quasi-genetic designs that compare behavioral, psychological, physiological, and neurocognitive characteristics of offspring of alcoholics and nonalcoholics, usually before the onset of overt alcoholic symptoms in the children. In addition, the results of other behavior genetic research, such as twin and adoption studies, have been used to assign a numerical risk of becoming an alcoholic asociated with being the child of an alcoholic. For example, based on the results of the Danish Adoption Study, the State of New York recently produced and distributed several public service messages that suggested that COAs have a fourfold increased risk of becoming alcoholics, compared with other children.

It is important to distinguish between the risk for alcoholism as a result of genetic transmission and the physical and psychological consequences of being exposed to alcoholic parents. While they are clearly not mutually exclusive, they can be independent. In the Danish Adoption Study, Goodwin and colleagues (Goodwin, Schulsinger, Hermansen, Guze, & Winokur, 1973; Goodwin et al., 1974) reported that male offspring of alcoholics were no more likely to become alcoholic if they were raised by their alcoholic parents than by nonalcoholic foster parents. However, Tarter, Hegedus, Goldstein, Shelly, and Alterman (1984) reported that children reared by alcoholic parents are at substantially greater risk of physical abuse and traumatic head injury than children raised by nonalcoholic parents. Individuals who are physically insulted and/or psychologically exploited as a result of parental substance abuse may develop psychiatric problems, including alcoholism, independent of any genetic liability (Searles, 1988).

[1]This chapter is adapted by permission of the publisher from Searles, J. S. (1988). The role of genetics in the pathogenesis of alcoholism. *Journal of Abnormal Psychology, 97,* 153–167. Copyright 1988 by the American Psychological Association.

This chapter outlines various methods that have been employed for separating the influences of genetics and environment and evaluates the results of the application of those methods in behavior genetic research as they relate to children of alcoholics. An evaluation of purported "high-risk" studies is also presented. These studies have generated considerable interest recently and the results of this body of research have theoretical implications for the etiology of alcoholism and practical implications for treatment of COAs. Finally, new approaches that incorporate the joint effects of environmental and genetic factors are discussed, as well as recently developed quantitative techniques that enhance data comprehension.

FAMILY STUDIES

Family or consanguinity studies represent the most basic behavior genetic research design. This design assumes that if a behavior or trait is under genetic control, this should be reflected in the correlation between the amount of genetic overlap and the phenotypic expression of the behavior or trait under study. Therefore, if alcoholism is genetically regulated, identical twins should be more concordant than fraternal twins, who should be as concordant as siblings, who in turn should be more concordant than half siblings, and so on. Indeed, this linear relationship has been found to hold for male but not for female alcoholics (Winokur, Reich, Rimmer, & Pitts, 1970). This gender difference is problematic for genetic models of alcoholism and is discussed at length in a later section of this chapter.

HALF-SIBLING STUDIES

The study of half-siblings, that is, siblings who have one parent in common, was initially undertaken as a subaltern substitute for adoption studies at a time when adoption records were sealed and unavailable to researchers. Only one published study concerning alcoholism has used the half-sibling method. Schuckit, Goodwin, and Winokur (1972) found that those half-siblings who shared an alcoholic parent were more likely to be alcholics themselves than half-siblings who did not share an alcholic parent. This was true regardless of the alcohol involvement of the foster parent. That is, there was no increased risk associated with living with an alcoholic foster parent. Although this design poses significant methodological problems, such as different degrees of genetic overlap and variations in exposure to a similar environment, it may be most useful in delineating nonshared environmental effects that are etiologically related to alcoholism. Merikangas (1988) has also called for an increased effort in half-sibling research in order to more accutately specify the genetic epidemiological nature of alcoholism and other psychopathologies.

TWIN STUDIES

The twin method relies on the fact that monozygotic (MZ), or identical, twins are 100% genetically similar, while dizygotic (DZ), or fraternal, twins are no more genetically alike than any two siblings (on the average, siblings share a 50% genetic overlap). The critical assumption for this approach is that both types of twins share equally variable environments. If this is so, then environmental effects should not differentially influence either type of twin, and observed differences in a trait or behavior could theoretically be ascribed to the closer genetic similarity of the MZ twins. Statistically, that portion of the phenotypic variance that is due to genetic influences (h^2) is usually taken as twice the difference between the intraclass correlation coefficients of MZ and DZ twins, $h^2 = 2(r_{MZ} - r_{DZ})$ (Falconer, 1960). It should be noted that the equal environment premise is controversial (Lewontin, Kamin, & Rose, 1983), although a number of empirical investigations support either the assumption itself or the notion that differential environments are uncorrelated with theoretically important constructs such as measured personality traits (Loehlin & Nichols, 1976; Rowe, 1983; Scarr & Carter-Saltzman, 1979). Kamin (1974) and Lewontin et al. (1983), however, maintain that differences in socially relevant traits and behaviors such as IQ are mediated almost entirely by environmental factors.

Although several twin studies that pertain to alcohol use and abuse have been reported, they do not converge on a consistent result; nor are they directly pertinent to the COA area. One possible use of this methodology that would be relevant to COAs is the study of the offspring of MZ twins who are concordant and discordant for alcoholism. Children of twins are genetic half-siblings and therefore offer a unique opportunity to investigate genetic and environmental effects in intact families of half-siblings (Corey & Nance, 1978). This approach has yet to be applied, probably because of intimidating logistical problems such as finding twins (or at least one of a pair) who are actually diagnosable as alcoholics. A first step in this direction has been taken by Pickens, Svikis, and McGue (1988), who are screening all admissions to alcohol treatment centers in Minnesota for twinships. Thus far, after evaluation of some 48,000 persons, 54 MZ and 70 DZ pairs have been recruited, with a mean age of 37 years. It should be noted that the focus of the study is on the twins themselves and not their children; however, this group does offer the possibility of instituting the twin half-sibling methodology in a sample of alcholics diagnosed according to DSM-III criteria (American Psychiatric Association, 1980).

ADOPTION STUDIES

The most powerful technique for separating the effects of environment and genetics is the adoption method. Assuming minimal maternal (biological) contact and no gene–environment (g–e) correlation, this technique permits the

independent assessment of genetic and environmental effects in the etiology of
alcoholism. The results of such studies bear a direct relation to COAs. Individuals may be at risk despite being reared in a home with nonalcoholic,
perhaps even abstaining, foster parents. The increasing attention these studies are
receiving from the scientific community, policy makers, and health-care providers and payers justifies an intensive examination of the methodology and results
of the key adoption studies in the etiology of alcoholism. These studies also have
important implications for treatment, such as the therapeutic effectiveness of
non-abstinence-oriented approaches, and for theory as in the viability of a
typology of alcoholisms. However, the four critical reviews of this literature
(Lester, 1988; Murray, Clifford, & Gurling, 1983; Peele, 1986; Searles, 1988)
all suggest that scientific and policy decisions based on these studies may be
premature.

The first adoption study concentrating on children of alcholic parents was
reported by Roe (1944) and Roe and Burks (1945). They compared the adult
adjustment patterns of 36 adoptees who had alcholic biological parents (usually
the father) with those of 25 adoptees who had what they term "normal parentage." The mean age of the former group at the time of the study was 32 years;
that of the latter group was 28 years. The investigators found no differences in
psychopathology or drinking patterns between the two groups, and neither group
manifested adjustment patterns dissimilar to the general population. These results obtained despite the fact that the adoptees with alcoholic parents were
placed in foster homes at an average age of 5.5 years, compared with 2.6 years
for the adoptees with nonalcoholic parents, *and* that the adoptive environments
of the children of alcoholics were in many respects less enriched than the
adoptive homes of the children of nonalcoholic parents (for example, fewer
affectionate foster fathers and fewer foster homes rated as providing a satis-
factory emotional background). Roe (1944) summarizes the findings in the
following manner:

> It must be concluded that the reported high incidence of inebriety and psy-
> chosis in the offspring of alcoholics is not explicable on the basis of any
> hereditary factor. It is clear that these children of alcoholic parentage, even
> though they had on the whole more disturbed early years and less desirable
> foster-homes than the children of normal parentage, nevertheless have suc-
> ceeded as adults in making life adjustments which are not significantly inferior
> in general to the adjustments made by the children of normal parentage under
> comparable conditions. Alcoholic parentage, then, does not preclude good
> adjustment; nor does it, under reasonably adequate life circumstances, make
> good adjustment more difficult (p. 391)

While this study is notable for not finding *either* a genetic or an environmental effect, several methodological problems should temper practical interpretation of the results. First, a null finding in a small sample size suggests
that it may be a function of insufficient statistical power. This is particularly

evident when clinically meaningful but statistically nonsignificant trends appear in the data, as when Roe (1944) reports that 28% of COAs compared with 8% of nonCOAs "got into serious difficulties with others than foster parents" (p. 381). Second, females constituted 42% of the children of alcoholics and 56% of the controls; since the genetic mechanism for transmission of alcoholism may be different for males and females, this gender distribution may mask any real effect present. Third, more than two thirds of the COAs were placed in rural homes, while only 28% of the nonCOAs were so placed. Since availability of alcohol has an obvious and direct relation to the development of alcohol problems, this could be an important factor in reducing group differences. It may also be that exposure to specific featues of an urban or suburban environment, such as higher daily stress levels and more drinking-related cues, may provoke a latent predisposition to alcoholism. Finally, the precision of the diagnosis of alcoholism in the biological parents is in question. Although Roe (1944) describes the biological fathers of the COA sample as "heavy drinkers with syndrome," no criteria are provided by which this assessment was made. The issue is complicated by the fact that "heavy drinking" or even "problem drinking" (depending on how it is defined) may not be on the same continuous dimension as alcoholism and, therefore, may be independent of genetic transmission. Ambiguity in the diagnosis of alcoholism has been a continuing problem, particulary in comparing results across studies with widely varying definitions and assessment techniques of alcoholism (such as self-reports, collateral reports, and serological results).

Despite these design weaknesses and methodological flaws, the Roe (1944) study demonstrates that early and sustained exposure (up to ten years) to an alcohologenic environment *even with a possible genetic predisposition* does not necessarily have inevitable and irreversible consequences for adult adjustment. This suggests that factors embedded in both the environment and the person may determine psychological adaptation and, perhaps, even physical well-being. The notion of g–e correlation will be expanded on later in this chapter.

The availability of extensive and objective information on both the biological and adoptive parents is crucial to the successful implementation of the adoption method. In the United States, this type of information is either extremely limited or nonexistent, especially for the biological parents and particularly for the biological father. For example, data gleaned from adoption records by the Iowa group (e.g., Cadoret, Cain, & Grove, 1980; Cadoret, O'Gorman, Troughton, & Heywood, 1985; Cadoret, Troughton, & O'Gorman, 1987) rely on behavioral and personological descriptions of the biological father provided by the mother. The veridicality of such second-hand data is suspect because it is susceptible to many sources of distortion, both systematic (as in confabulation or intentional underreporting or overreporting) and unsystematic (nonspecific memory errors, for instance).

Goodwin and colleagues (Goodwin et al., 1973, 1974; Goodwin, Schulsinger, Moller, Mednick, & Guze, 1977) have reported on a Danish cohort remarkable for the extensive criminal, medical, and personal records maintained on each individual in the population. Cloninger and colleagues (Cloninger, Bohman, & Sigvardsson, 1981; Bohman, Sigvardsson, & Cloninger, 1981) reported on similar information gathered from a Swedish sample. These two groups of researchers have had a profound impact on the scientific and lay understanding of the genetics of alcoholism. Of more immediate relevance to this book, much of the presumed scientific support for the concept of the risk of COAs for developing alcoholism is abstracted from the reports of these two groups of researchers. For example, as mentioned earlier, the popularly promulgated notion that COAs have a fourfold increased risk of becoming alcoholic has been extracted from the Danish Adoption Study reported by Goodwin et al. (1973, 1974). Because of the very large sample sizes (862 men and 913 women) and sophisticated analytic techniques, the results of the Swedish Adoption Study (Bohman et al., 1981; Cloninger et al., 1981) have received even more attention from the popular press, clinicians, paraprofessionals, and COA self-help groups. These studies have also been used to help support the disease concept of alcoholism, both medically and legally (Fingarette, 1988; Johnson, 1987).

Because of the weight placed on these studies it is important that the methodologies employed and the results obtained be thoroughly examined to exclude the possibility of artifactual explanation of the data. Such comprehensive examinations have found major flaws in the study designs and interpretation of the outcomes that may seriously limit the applicability of the results to children of alcoholics in particular and the genetics of alcoholism in general (Lester, 1988; Murray et al., 1983; Peele, 1986; Searles, 1988). A summary of these critiques is presented below.

Danish Adoption Study

The major difficulty of this study occurs in the definition of alcoholism. That is, Goodwin et al. (1973) categorized individuals as "moderate drinker," "heavy drinker," "problem drinker," or "alcoholic."[2] The fourfold increase in risk occurs only in the putative alcoholic category. In fact, more controls than probands are classified as heavy drinkers, and problem drinkers. If the problem-drinker and alcoholic categories are combined, there is no significant difference between the probands with alcoholic parents and the control adoptees without an alcoholic family history. This is especially important because the mean age of

---

[2]The last three categories are described as follows: Heavy drinker—for at least one year drank daily and had six or more drinks at least two or three times a month; or drank six or more drinks at least one time a week for over one year, but reported no problems. Problem drinker—meets criteria for heavy drinker; had problems from drinking, but too few to meet alcholism criteria. Alcoholic—heavy drinker who had problems in at least three of four areas: (1) Social disapproval of drinking by friends, parents; marital problems from drinking. (2) Job trouble; traffic arrests; other police trouble from drinking. (3) Frequent blackouts; tremor; withdrawal hallucinations or convulsions; delirium tremens. (4) Loss of control; morning drinking.

persons in the samples was 30 years, substantially younger than most alcoholics in treatment. This suggests the possibility that a proportion of those classified as problem drinkers and, perhaps, a lesser fraction of those classified as heavy drinkers will eventually meet the criteria for alcoholism; and since more individuals in these categories are from the control group, differences in rates of alcoholism are likely to dissipate. One simple way to address this issue would be to conduct a follow-up study, since all individuals in the two groups are now well beyond the peak period of lifetime risk for alcoholism. No such study has yet been published.

Other problems with the Danish study include higher than expected rates of foster parent psychopathology, high proband divorce rate, and possible prenatal effects (see Searles, 1988, for more details). Finally, while the increased risk among male COAs for becoming alcoholic themselves (although no differences were found among female probands and controls) is often emphasized, little mention is made of the fact that this risk did not increase for the brothers (full or half) of the adoptees who were raised by their biologial alcoholic parents. That is, being reared in an alcohologenic environment did not elevate the risk status over and above preexisting genetic factors (Goodwin et al., 1974). Even long-time exposure to the alcoholic parent (i.e., more than 14 years) was not associated with an increased risk for developing alcoholism. It is interesting to note that significantly more adopted sons exhibited personality disturbances and psychopathology than their brothers raised by the alcoholic parent. This finding, as well as the similarity of risk for alcholism among siblings who were and were not reared by their biological alcoholic parents may be problematic for sociological theories of the etiology of alcoholism and for the Adult Children of Alcoholics (ACOA) movement, which stresses the psychopathology-inducing nature of growing up in an alcoholic milieu.

There is one final, ironic note concerning the Danish study that bears mentioning. While the major result of the study (a fourfold increased risk of becoming an alcoholic) has been widely cited and used as a basis for organizing ACOA therapy groups, the principal author of the investigation, Donald Goodwin, has reservations about the implications for children of alcoholics (Sifford, 1989):

> Goodwin said that "all the stuff" that has been written in recent years about adult children of alcoholics has been, in his judgment, something akin to a hoax. Adult children of alcoholics are about like adult children of everybody else with a problem, he said, and it's hard to build a reasonable case for giving them extraordinary attention.
>
> Then why are they getting so much attention?
>
> Goodwin's answer: Therapists "invented" the concept that adult children of alcholics have special problems that can be treated through therapy. They were able to sell this concept to the public and now they are eligible for reimbursement from insurance companies. In short, said Goodwin, it was a way for therapists to tap into a new market and make money.

How do adult children of alcoholics react to Goodwin's position?

Not very well, he said, because it forces them to take responsibility for their lives—rather than presenting themselves as helpless victims of fate. But he has no desire to anger them, he said, and for that reason he has toned down what he says in public. (p. 5-C)

Swedish Adoption Study

The most influential set of results purporting to link both genetic and environmental factors to the etiology of alcohol abuse have been published by Cloninger and colleagues (Bohman et al., 1981; Cloninger, 1988; Cloninger et al., 1981. They have proposed two distinct types of alcoholism. Type 1, or milieu-limited alcoholism, is related to both mild and severe forms of alcohol abuse, requires both a genetic predisposition and an environmental releasor, and is the more common form, prevalent in 76% of the abusers in the Swedish sample. Type 2, or male-limited alcoholism, is associated with moderate alcohol abuse (but severe abuse and severe criminality in the fathers), is found exclusively in men, and is highly heritable (.90) but not influenced by environmental factors. Cloninger (1986, 1987b) has recently expanded the theoretical base of this work by proposing a new general theory of personality integrating both neurobiological structures and neurochemical brain systems (specifically, independently functioning monoamine neuromodulators) with behavioral manifestations and social personological constructs (novelty seeking harm avoidance, and reward dependence). Cloninger (1987b) has described the two types of alcohol abusers within this personality scheme as not just distinct but orthogonal. Thus, Type 1 alcohol abusers would be low in novelty seeking, high in harm avoidance, and high in reward dependence; while Type 2 alcoholics are described as high in novelty seeking, low in harm avoidance, and low in reward dependence. These are theoretically derived characterizations with limited empirical support (Cloninger, 1988). It is difficult to overestimate the influence that this research has had on the alcholism field. At the 1988 meeting of the Research Society on Alcoholism, virtually all paper presenters either were asked how their results would be affected by the Cloninger typology or extemporaneously related ways their results were compatible with it.

The adoption research conducted by this group was based on records that were even more extensive and objective than those screened in the Danish study and with a much larger sample size. Given the considerable theoretical and practical impact that the results have had, it is surprising that they have been accepted with very little critical examination. Although this is partly a function of the quality of the work (the higher the quality, the less there is to criticize), it also reflects on the proficiency of others to adequately evaluate the complex statistical procedures in relation to the obtained outcomes. Careful examination reveals several serious methodoligical difficulties and problematic interpretational ambiguities that need to be resolved before the results should be fully accepted (Bower, 1988).

The principal complication of the Swedish study is a consequence of the mechanism used to categorize the 151 (17.5% of the total) individuals who abused alcohol and the statistical consequences that follow from this classification. The adoptees were categorized as mild, moderate, or severe alcohol abusers based on the number of times they had been registered with the Temperance Board for insobriety or drinking-related problems (social, medical, or legal), and the their treatment history. The Temperance Board (one for each county) has no American analogue, but it presumably monitors and records all instances of alcohol-related problems such as family violence, traffic offenses, and medical diagnoses reported by legal and medical authorities as well as by family and friends. Mild abusers had a single lifetime registration with the Temperance Board without a treatment history; moderate abusers had two or three registrations and no treatment; severe abusers had four or more registrations, compulsory treatment for alcoholism (board mandated), or psychiatric hospitalization with a diagnosis of alcoholism. Several problems should be evident with this approach.

First, it is unclear what the criteria are for being reported to the Temperance Board. It is likely that the legal and medical authorities have one set of criteria (or two), while friends and family may each have their own idea of what should or should not be reported. There is no question that this data source is a significant improvement over those available in the United States; however, because the diagnosis of alcholism has varied so widely, it is important to precisely specify criteria to minimize ambiguity. For example, one or two reports to the Temperance Board may be identical to Goodwin et al.'s (1973) problem-drinker category, which *did not* show a genetic effect. In the Cloninger et al. (1981) classification system this group would be classified as either mild (one registration) or moderate (two registrations) abusers. In contrast to Goodwin et al. (1973), these categories exhibit varying degrees of genetic loading. These data may be reconciled by imposing some standard definitional criteria for alcohol abuse.

Second, the taxonomic scheme used by the Swedish group results in some serious interpretive anomalies. For example, Type 1 alcoholism encompasses both mild and severe abusers, while Type 2 includes exclusively male moderate abusers. The Type 1 alcoholic requires both a genetic predisposition *and* one of a limited set of environmental conditions; the Type 2 alcoholic requires only a genetic predisposition. The peculiar nature of the genetic mechanism implied by this classification should be evident: the most and least severe form of abuse are equally heritable and less heritable than a moderate form of abuse. The picture is further clouded by the abuse status of the biological parents (Searles, 1988).

Additional methodological difficulties in the Swedish data make unambiguous interpretation problematic. These include the relatively high rate of alcoholism in the biological parents compared with the general population, no age effects for the prevalence or onset of alcoholism, an underestimation of maternal and prenatal effects, and difficulties in generalizing from the study sample to other, more heterogeneous populations. Bohman has commented on this last point: "Sweden today is a stable country with a stable population, a high living standard, and a well developed social security system. We do not have the large differences between social classes that we find in other countries, including some states or cities in the United States, and this gives us an opportunity to study the importance of genetic factors. We cannot generalize our findings concerning criminality or alcohol abuse to the United States. The United States as a whole is a country with very different circumstances" (cited in Bohman, Cloninger, Sigvardsson, & von Knorring, 1983, pp. 275–276).

Finally, Littrell (1988) has pointed out critical statistical anomalies that may have a significant impact on the interpretation of the Swedish data. Until these and other serious problems (see Searles, 1988) are addressed, the heritability of alcholism and consequently the genetic impact of being a child of an alcoholic should be considered speculative.[3]

HIGH-RISK STUDIES

The research that is most directly relevant to COAs concerns the study of individuals at high risk to develop alcoholism because of their family background. That is, persons whose family pedigrees include relatives (usually, but not always, first or second degree) who can be identified as alcohol abusers are compared with persons whose family histories contain no relatives with alcohol disorders. The former group is designated high risk or family history positive (FHP, or FH+) while the latter group serves as controls and is designated family history negative (FHN, or FH–). In order not to confound the comparison with the deleterious effects that may result from the ingestion of large amounts of alcohol over time, the groups are typically equated for current drinking patterns and are initially studied prior to the possible onset of alcohol abuse; that is, members of both groups are normal social drinkers at the inception of the study.

It should be clear that high-risk study designs are not strictly within the behavior genetic domain because genetic and environmental factors are completely confounded. Any differences found between the two groups could be due either to genetic influences or to being reared in an environment that includes whatever consequences accrue from having an alcoholic relative. The only possible exceptions may be differences in biological parameters such as blood

---

[3]Even if there is a genetic subtype of alcohol abuse, the majority of alcoholics studied in past research (50%–80%) have no known family history of alcoholism. This suggests that unspecified environmental factors are at least as important in the etiology of alcoholism.

chemistry and variations in quantity of neutotransmitters. However, even these could conceivably be mediated environmentally through, for example, different early nutritional practices. Although these studies are outside the purview of the behavior genetic area, they are reviewed here because they are considered part of the general body of research encompassed under the heading of the genetics of alcoholism.

There are at least four major areas that comprise the high-risk domain: biological, psychological, neuropsychological, and electrophysiological. While the eventual goal of this research is to delineate those variables that may serve as presymptomatic markers for alcohol abuse, the results have been ambiguous. Some laboratories find consistent differences between persons in groups FHP and FHN, while others obtain mixed or null results. Each of these areas is discussed at length in other chapters of this volume. What follows is a distillation of pertinent research that relates directly to a genetic basis of alcoholism.

The search for biological markers, including differences in the metabolism of ethanol, has been disappointing. FHP individuals are indistinguishable from those designated FHN on absorption rate, clearance rate, time to peak blood alcohol concentration, and maximum blood alcohol concentration (Nagoshi & Wilson, 1987; Schuckit, 1981). No reliable differences in any single biological marker have been found to discriminate high-risk individuals from controls; however, Schuckit (1988) reported that FHN young men had higher levels of cortisol and ACTH following a challenge dose of ethanol, compared with FHP men. Although this finding needs to be replicated, it emphasizes the importance of employing multivariate techniques to more accurately detect interactive effects as well as real but subtle differences between FHP and FHN individuals.

One other research finding related to biological markers bears mentioning. Both von Knorring, Bohman, von Knorring, and Oreland (1985) and Pandey, Fawcett, Gibbons, Clark, and Davis (1988) have reported lower platelet monoamine oxidase (MAO) activity among alcoholics than in normal controls. Further, they reported that within the alcoholic sample they were able to distinguish two types of alcoholics that roughly conform diagnostically to the Cloninger group's Type 1 and Type 2 alcoholics. Those with lower platelet MAO activity were younger, had an earlier age of onset of alcoholic symptomatology, and had a greater degree of alcoholism among their family members than did those with relatively higher platelet MAO activity. Both groups of researchers suggested that since platelet MAO activity is under substantial genetic control, it may be a stable biological marker for alcoholism. However, neither of these studies has addressed the effects of long-term consumption on platelet MAO activity, nor have the results been successfully applied to COAs. Knop, Goodwin, Teasdale, Mikkelsen, and Schulsinger (1984) found no differences in platelet MAO activity between relatively large FHP and FHN samples (134 and 70 men, respectively). See Chan (Chapter 3, this volume) for an extensive discussion of these and other biological markers.

Another area of current intense research focus is on possible electrophysiological differences between FHPs (COAs) and FHNs (nonCOAs). Gabrielle et al. (1982) reported that sons of alcoholic fathers had significantly more relative beta wave activity than a control group. Compared with controls, FHP individuals have shown a reduction in the P300 wave following an alcohol challenge (Elmasian, Neville, Woods, Schuckit, & Bloom, 1982; Volavka, Pollock, Gabrielli, & Mednick, 1985). Begleiter, Porjesz, Bihari, and Kissin (1984) reported differences between preadolescent sons of alcoholics and age-matched sons of nonalcoholics in the amplitude of the P300 wave following presentation of a visual stimulus. The importance of this finding and its potential significance were enhanced by the young age of the subjects and the fact that these differences were evident prior to the onset of regular or even occasional drinking.

Although these results are provocative, not all the reports support this finding. Hill (1988) found differences in latency, but not amplitude, of the P300 wave in children of alcoholics who themselves were diagnosed as alcoholics, compared with a nonalcoholic sibling from the same alcoholic parent. Polich and Bloom (1988) in an attempt to replicate the Elmasian et al. (1982) study found no differences in P300 amplitude or latency in response to alcohol and placebo challenges between FHPs and FHNs who were matched for age, height, weight, college grade-point average, and current quantity and frequency of alcohol consumption. Negative results have also been reported by Neville and Schmidt (1985), Polich (1984), Polich and Bloom (1986, 1987), Polich, Haier, Buchsbaum, and Bloom (1988), and Whipple and Noble (1986). These contradictory findings suggest either that the P300 differences are not very robust, especially across different samples of FHP individuals, or that, since only a subset of the FHP individuals will actually progress to alcoholism, those who do will have evidenced marked presymptomatic electrophysiological differences. The former renders the P300 wave impotent as a marker for alcoholism; the latter awaits the results of the several longitudinal studies of high-risk individuals that are currently in progress.

The neuropsychological and cognitive literature pertaining to persons at presumed risk for alcoholism (such as COAs) is also marked by inconsistent results. There have been both positive and negative findings reported in virtually all subfields, including cognitive functioning, motor performance, intellectual ability, and memory. To illustrate the lability of obtained results, it is interesting to note that Hill, Armstrong, Steinhauer, Baughman, and Zubin (1987) reported greater static ataxia (body sway) in FHP individuals, while Nagoshi and Wilson (1987) reported no differences between FHP and FHN groups on the same measure at baseline or following ethanol ingestion. Both accounts were published in the same issue of the same journal. Furthermore, Schuckit (1985) has reported a *decrease* in static ataxia among FHP young men, compared with FHNs following an alcohol challenge.

Further examples of the variable results obtained in this area are contained in the following two titles and abstracts:

"Neuropsychological differences between male familial and nonfamilial alcoholics and nonalcoholics."

The hypothesis was tested that neuropsychological differences exist between males who have an alcoholic parent, sister, or brother (FH+) versus those who do not (FH–). Neuropsychological tests measuring verbal, learning/memory, abstracting/problem solving, and perceptual-motor performance were given to four groups of middle-aged subjects: alcoholic FH+ (n = 41); alcoholic FH– (n = 27); nonalcoholic FH+ (n = 19); nonalcoholic FH– (n = 43). FH+ subjects performed significantly poorer than FH– subjects on the abstracting/problem solving and perceptual-motor tasks, and approached significance on the verbal and learning/memory measures. Alcoholics performed more poorly than nonalcoholics on abstracting/problem solving and learning/memory tasks. There were no groups by family history significant interactions. From these results we suggest: (1) a performance deficit in abstracting/problem solving and possibly learning/memory may antedate the alcoholic stage in FH+ individuals; (2) alcoholism and positive family history of alcoholism have independent, additive deleterious effects on cognitive-perceptual functioning; and (3) future neuropsychological studies of alcoholism should consider the frequency of FH+ and FH– individuals in both alcoholic and control groups. (Schaeffer, Parsons, & Yohman, 1984, p. 347)

"Family history of alcoholism does not predict neuropsychological performance in alcoholics."

We examined the relationship of history of alcoholism in first-degree relatives to neuropsychological [NP] performance of alcoholics abstinent from several weeks to several years. Eighty-four men were assigned to four groups based on "strength" of family history of alcoholism. The groups were: (1) "strong history," a parent plus another first-degree relative positive; (2) "moderate," parent only positive; (3) "weak," nonparent first-degree relative only positive; and (4) "negative," no first-degree relative positive. There were no significant between group differences in NP performance. In other analyses, there were no NP differences between alcoholics classified positive or negative purely on [the] basis of paternal alcoholism, and no differences between subjects who had multigenerational versus unigenerational versus negative familial histories of alcoholism. It is concluded that genetic loading for alcoholism does not significantly affect the NP status of abstinent alcoholic groups equated for education, drinking history, and medical risk. (Reed, Grant, & Adams, 1987, p. 340)

Although the report by Schaeffer et al. (1984) is framed in such a way as to emphasize neuropsychological disparities, Reed et al. (1987) point out that the differences obtained by Schaeffer et al. (1984) occurred in the FHP/FHN nonalcoholic controls, not in the FHP/FHN alcoholic subjects.

Perhaps the most important consideration pertaining to neuropsychological effects in high-risk individuals in the hostile environment they may encounter as children while growing up in an alcoholic milieu. Sons of alcoholic fathers are six times more likely to suffer physical abuse from their fathers and are seven times more likely to have suffered loss of consciousness at least once as a result of a traumatic head injury (Tarter et al., 1984). Therefore, any neurocognitive differences found between FHPs and FHNs may be environmentally induced, at least in part, as a consequence of severe and/or repeated blows to the head.

The final area of research into markers for alcoholism concerns psychological aspects. Again, there have been conflicting reports as to the viability and robustness of FHP/FHN differences on traditional measures of personality and early psychological and behavioral pathognomonic signs (e.g., Morrison & Schuckit, 1983; Schuckit, 1982, 1983; Schulsinger, Knop, Goodwin, Teasdale, & Mikkelsen, 1986; Tarter et al., 1984). An area of recent theoretical and research interest concerns concurrent diagnoses of alcoholism and antisocial personality as well as the relationship among risk for alcoholism, early antisocial behavior, and childhood manifestations of hyperkinetic behavior/minimal brain dysfunction (Tarter, Alterman, & Edwards, 1985). Windle (Chapter 6, this volume) provides a comprehensive assessment of the relationship of these and other pertinent personological and temperamental factors to COA status (see also Searles, 1988).

The psychobiological theory recently advanced by Schuckit attempts to simultaneously account for and conceptually link data in several of the areas mentioned above; particularly the physiological and psychological differences between FHPs (COAs) and FHNs in response to challenge doses of ethanol (Schuckit, 1984, 1987, 1988b; Schuckit & Gold, 1988; Schuckit, Risch, & Gold, 1988). Schuckit and colleagues suggest that FHPs react subjectively less to moderate doses of ethanol (i.e., report feeling less intoxicated at the same objective blood alcohol concentration) and have concomitantly lower hormonal responses following alcohol consumption than do FHNs. This is despite the fact that both groups have identical blood alcohol concentrations. As mentioned above, Schuckit (1985) has also reported that FHNs show a greater increase in body sway following alcohol ingestion than do FHPs. The implication of this behavioral–physiological nexus is presumably that FHPs require more ethanol to experience an equivalent level of intoxication than FHNs, thus leading to an overall increase in the level of alcohol consumption by FHPs, which in turn could be related to an elevated risk for associated alcohol complications such as driving under the influence, marital discord, or job difficulties. Based on the electrophysiological differences between FHPs and FHNs that he and others (e.g. Begleiter et al., 1984) have found. Schuckit also suggests that ethanol may be differentially reinforcing to high- and low-risk individuals, such that FHPs are more sensitive to the rewarding effects of the drug.

This intriguing theory, vigorously advanced by Schuckit, appears to be internally consistent, logically merging findings across several disparate research domains. Also, if correct, the theory would afford a relatively simple technique for identifying potential alcoholics (FHPs/COAs), who could then be provided with information concerning their risk status. However, a close inspection of the premises, structure, and implications of the theory reveals several serious methodological flaws and theoretical peccadillos that need to be addressed, some of which have already been acknowledged by Schuckit (1987, 1988a, 1988b).

First, since only a subset of the individuals at presumed risk (COAs) will actually develop alcoholic symptoms, it is not clear how this theory will operationally identify those particular individuals. For whatever reason—luck of the genetic draw, coexisting protective biological or psychological factors, or idiosyncratic environmental influences—at least 75% of COAs will *not* encounter major difficulties with alcohol, a figure likely to be even greater, depending on the social class of this group, so this is a real concern.[4] Furthermore, the results of this research may be inapplicable to most alcoholics, since the majority of treated alcoholics have no family history of alcoholism. For example, 94 of the 151 (62%) male adoptees identified as alcohol abusers in the Swedish Adoption Study were not at genetic risk to develop alcoholism, while 19 of the 31 (61%) female adoptees developed alcoholism without associated genetic or congenital risk factors (Bohman et al., 1981; Cloninger et al., 1981).

Second, as documented above, there is a considerable body of research that does not replicate Schuckit's. While differences in experimental technique and specific subject populations may account for some of the disparity, it is difficult to reconcile many of the contradictory results. For example, Schuckit (1987) has emphasized the significance of FHP/FHN electrophysiological differences as an important component of the modulated reactance to alcohol hypothesis. This finding in particular has been notably labile across laboratories. This is most clearly illustrated in the report by Polich and Bloom (1988), who found no differences between FHPs and FHNs in an attempt to replicate Elmasian et al. (1982), who reported a lower P300 amplitude in FHPs than in FHNs.

Finally, Schuckit has maintained that any genetic liability is alcohol specific, without associated psychiatric disorders or other substance abuse. This seems incongruent with the notion of a biological basis of addiction, for which researchers have yet to locate specific alcohol receptor sites in the brain but have mapped a network of opiate receptors and endogenous opiates that indicate the existence of those sites.[5] Schuckit's position may be a function of the strict subject-screening process required by the protocol: no psychopathology, no history of chronic medical disorders, and no current or past alcohol or substance abuse. This procedure will yield relatively uncontaminated groups, which will serve to amplify significant findings, but it also may sacrifice much ecological validity by eliminating subjects who may be most at risk to develop alcohol

---

[4]There are many levels of concern implied here, including the relatively trivial unintentional denial of the pleasurable effects of alcohol consumption (e.g., wine with meals) as well as the possible positive medical side effects of moderate alcohol consumption. Perhaps the most important aspect of this issue is the unnecessary anxiety that could be produced in some individuals who may be needlessly fearful of the consequences of drinking in moderation.

[5]There have been reports that some of the metabolites of ethanol can compete for opiate receptor sites (Blum & Trachtenberg, 1988; Volpicelli, 1987). At this time, research results are sparse and theories of the brain action of ethanol are highly speculative. The ultimate goal of this line of research is to provide a biobehavioral theory of alcoholism that would take into account both biological and environmental factors.

and/or substance abuse problems. Schuckit's approach cannot be faulted on scientific grounds; however, it may be difficult to generalize the results beyond the narrow focus of the subject specifications. Since the groups are carefully matched along a number of sociodemographic, cognitive, and drinking-history dimensions, it will be difficult to ascribe any eventual group differences to early environmental influences or preadolescent personality factors. Both these areas are the subject of considerable current research interest (Cloninger, Sigvardsson, & Bohman, 1988; Tarter et al., 1985).

An associated problem concerns the impact of the study objectives on the subjects themselves. Many of the subjects in the study are likely to be aware of their risk status because of the amount of national exposure that Schuckit and the project have received (including a network television appearance on CBS's *Forty-Eight Hours,* July 6, 1989). The question arises: Are the subjects in this study likely to modulate their drinking *because* they are participants in an investigation of possible familial vulnerability to alcoholism? That is, does knowing that one is possibly at increased risk to develop alcoholism and is being monitored as part of a scientific research project alter the behavioral correlates and manifestations in such a way as to ameliorate that risk status?[6] This research paradigm may be more useful in identifying characteristics of those high-risk individuals who do not develop alcoholism.

A methodological dilemma posed by most high-risk research ventures in relation to its clinical application to COAs concerns the gender of the research subjects versus the gender of the COA clinical patient.

The overwhelming majority of clients/patients in COA groups, whether professionally directed or in self-help associations, are women, while men constitute most of the subject samples in research investigations. Since many reports suggest that male and female alcoholism may be independent and have different etiological pathways (e.g., Cloninger et al., 1981; Bohman et al., 1981), the research results may not be congruent with the clinical applications. This is not to imply that there is no experimental research on female COAs. For example, Lex, Lukas, Greenwald, and Mendelson (1988) reported significantly increased body sway in six FHN women compared with six FHP women following an alcohol challenge. While this parallels the result for men (Schuckit, 1985), Lex et al. (1988) also reported nonsignificant but consistently higher subjective ratings of intoxication for the FHP women—a finding directly opposite that for the men and therefore not in accord with the decreased intensity of reaction theory (Schuckit, 1984, 1987).

The fact that more men than women are research subjects reflects two

[6]Knowledge of risk status might also increase the likelihood of engaging in presymptomatic behaviors if the subject thinks a familial predisposition inevitably leads to alcoholism. This presupposes a fatalism and cognitive simplicity that, it is hoped, most individuals do not possess. It is particularly unlikely that many of the participants in Schuckit's study have this attitude, given that many of them are university students.

phenomena. First, there are some ethical questions concerning possible adverse physiological side effects of ethanol consumption (challenge doses of alcohol) by women of childbearing age, as well as potential psychological consequences of giving alcohol to individuals who are at putative high risk to develop alcoholism. This latter point also applies to studies of FHP males. Second, the prevalence of reported alcohol abuse is considerably higher among men than women. For example, in the Swedish Adoption Study 151 of the 862 men studied (17.5%) qualified as alcohol abusers, while only 31 of the 913 women investigated (3.4%) met alcohol-abuse criteria. This low prevalence imposes critical constraints on experimental design and methodological facility be requiring extremely large sample sizes for even moderate effects to be detected.[7]

The question remains, however: Why is there such a marked disparity between the gender composition of COAs in therapy and in research and epidemiological protocols? Several hypotheses are possible. Women may be more susceptible to the adverse psychological consequences of prolonged exposure to an alcoholic parent. This susceptibility could manifest itself constitutionally, socioculturally, or through some interactive process encompassing the two. Also as a result of having an alcoholic parent, women may be subject to more psychologically distressing physical insults, such as sexual abuse, that induce protracted and profound psychological disturbances. The adult pathognomonic indications of such enduring traumatic offenses may reflect some reported COA characteristics (e.g. low self-esteem, difficulty forming close interpersonal relationships), although it has been difficult to empirically demonstrate a coherent and distinct COA profile (see Searles and Windle, Chapter 1, this volume). Finally, male alcoholism and specific female psychopathology could be nonindependent subsets of divergent consequences of parental alcohol abuse. Again, the etiological basis for either could be rooted in genetic or environmental factors, or in a g–e correlation. It should be emphasized that this list of hypotheses is not exhaustive; other causal agents and motivational structures could be postulated. However, those discussed have the advantage of being empirically testable, with varying degrees of methodological complications.

GENE × ENVIRONMENT INTERACTION AND GENE–ENVIRONMENT CORRELATION

As mentioned above, it is quite possible that *both* genetic and environmental factors render a joint influence in the etiology of alcoholism. The behavior genetic model is based on phenotypic variability and assumes that this variability

---

[7]The ability to detect differences between groups, termed the power of the experiment, is a function of both the size of the effect and the size of the sample. Small but potentially important differences require large samples to be detected statistically; conversely, large effects can be ascertained with relatively small sample sizes.

can be decomposed into basic components attributable to genes and environment. The approach has been heavily criticized for what appears to be ignoring the obvious; that is, behavior is also a function of some complex gene × environment (G × E) interaction (Lewontin et al., 1983).[8] However, despite an active analytical search in the data from the Colorado Adoption Project, Plomin and DeFries (1985) have been unable to uncover any G × E interactions of significance that account for even a modest amount of variance. Plomin (1986) suggests this may be because of the age of the subjects (infants) and/or the quality of the measures, but he also points out that the search for meaningful G × E interactions in other areas (specifically, aptitude × treatment) has also proved fruitless despite long-term research efforts.

With respect to alcoholism, Cloninger et al. (1981) have reported what appears to be a genuine interaction between genetic predisposition to alcoholism and an alcohologenic environment. However, this finding may be an artifact of the nonstandard criteria they used to diagnose alcohol abuse (Searles, 1988). Although Cadoret, Cain, and Crowe (1983) have reported a significant G × E interaction in the development of antisocial behavior sometimes associated with alcohol abuse (Tarter, Alterman, & Edwards, 1985), this same group was unable to find any evidence for G × E interactions for alcoholism (Cadoret et al., 1985). It should be stressed that current measures of the environment are relatively unsophisticated and undifferentiated, compared with measures of phenotypic expression of personality. For example, the "environment" as measured by Cadoret et al. (1985) consisted of dichotomous indicators (present/absent) of alcohol, antisocial, or other psychiatric problems of the adoptive parents and siblings as well as gross measures (also dichotomous) of parental health, marital stability, socioeconomic status, and neighborhood. It may be that with more refined instruments, G × E interactions that are intuitively appealing but empirically elusive will be found. Zucker and colleagues (Zucker, 1987; Zucker & Lisansky-Gomberg, 1986; Zucker & Noll, 1987) have been active in suggesting and implementing innovative research approaches to assess the impact of G × E interactions in the development of alcohol and drug abuse. Recently, Bergeman, Plomin, McClearn, Pedersen, and Friberg (1988) reported several significant G × E interactions in 99 pairs of MZ twins reared apart, a subset drawn from the 750 pairs of twins that comprise the Swedish Twin Registry. This study is important for several reasons. First, it represents the first scientific account of significant G × E interactions, although no single interaction accounted for more than 7% of the total variance. Second, the mean age of the sample was approximately 59 years, providing some important, albeit retrospective, information on the influence of early environments on later personality development. Finally, through the use of hierarchical multiple regression the authors provide an innovative technique to test for G × E interactions unconfounded by main effects.

---

[8]In a trivial sense, behavior never occurs outside some context, but the term interaction here is meant in a statistical sense whereby phenotypic expression would be a function of genotypic structure at different measurable levels of the type of environment.

Much more theoretical and research effort has gone into the notion of g–e correlation (Jensen, 1976; Plomin, 1986; Plomin, DeFries, & Loehlin, 1977; Plomin, DeFries, & McClearn, 1980; Scarr & McCartney, 1983). Three distinct types of g–e correlations have been proposed (Plomin et al., 1977).

1. *Passive*. This refers to the fact that children are exposed to environments that are not independent of their inherited genes. For instance, highly educated, intelligent parents provide not only genetic material but also may provide environments for their children that may reflect and promote cognitive development and intellectual activity. Since adoptive families provide only environmental factors and nonadoptive families provide both genetic and environmental factors, it is possible to directly estimate the g–e correlation within a behavior genetic framework given adequate data. Because of data limitations in other traits, only IQ has been subjected to thorough systematic analysis (Loehlin & DeFries, 1987). Estimates of g–e correlations from existing data bases average about .20, a substantial effect. However, a limited analysis from the Colorado Adoption Project (Plomin & DeFries, 1985) yielded a .07 passive g–e correlation between infant temperament and environmental factors related to personal growth (Loehlin & DeFries, 1987). Since one focus of current theorizing on the etiology of alcoholism is on early temperament and activity level, this low figure assumes some significance. It appears that this type of g–e correlation may have much less of an impact on personality development than expected.

2. *Reactive/evocative*. Individuals react differently to different genotypes. For example, sociable children and shy children are responded to differently, thus creating a g–e correlation (assuming, of course, that sociability has a genetic component). It is possible to measure reactive g–e correlation by assessing the relationship between characteristics of the biological parents with measures of the adoptive home (selective placement effects are assumed to be negligible). Current estimates of reactive g–e correlations in the personality domain are in the .15 to .20 range for 7 of 28 correlations found to be significant in the Colorado Adoption Project data (Plomin & DeFries, 1985).

3. *Active/niche-seeking*. This refers to the notion that individuals will actively seek out environments that complement their genotypes. For example, extroverts are likely to engage in sociable activities while introverts are not. To date, no methods of assessing active g–e correlation have been developed. Theoretically, however, this type of g–e correlation can adequately account for the substantial similarity observed in monozygotic twins reared apart, including the fact that the most dissimilar pairs were those in which a range of potential environmental influences was not available to one twin.

The importance of g–e correlations is twofold. First, they provide measurement techniques for assessing the combined impact of genetics and environment on phenotypic variance. As long as one does not subscribe to an extreme interactionist position in which genetic and environmental influences are inextricably interwoven, genetic, environmental, and g–e correlated influences can be independently measured and their relative impact assessed.

Second, they fit a general model of development described by Scarr and

McCartney (1983). Passive g–e correlation is of major significance during infancy, because parents are the providers of both the infant's genes and a major proportion of its environment. As the child matures, this form of g–e correlation becomes less influential, and reactive and active forms predominate, with active g–e correlations assuming lifelong importance. This model parsimoniously accounts for some intriguing observations from extant data such as:

1. Higher than expected dizygotic twin correlations in early childhood.
2. The moderate adoptive sibling correlations in childhood that reduce to zero in late adolescence.
3. The above-mentioned similarity of monozygotic twins reared apart.

No one to date has directly examined the implications of g–e correlations for the etiology of alcoholism. There are several ways in which the impact of g–e correlations could be significant. First, passive g–e correlation could have a direct effect through the infant's ingestion of ethanol in the mother's milk. Certain genotypes may be more susceptible than others to the effects of alcohol. Also, an alcoholic mother may provide a hostile intrauterine environment before birth that can result in serious medical complications for the infant, such as fetal alcohol syndrome (FAS). While this could be construed as primarily a congenital effect, particular genotypes may be more vulnerable than others to the effects of alcohol.

Second, if alcohol abuse/dependence is associated with personality traits, and there is some evidence that at least primary alcoholism may be (Cadoret et al., 1984; Tarter, et al., 1985), then reactive g–e correlations could have an indirect effect through personality. Reactions to impulsive, extraverted children will certainly be different from those to children who are controlled and shy. For example, extraverted and shy children are likely to differ on the degree and extent of peer relationships, which may have a substantial influence on early drinking decisions (Kandel, 1984). This notion also applies to the active form of g–e correlation, where individuals choose their environments partly as a function of their genetic predispositions.

Third, some of the g–e correlations associated with alcoholism are likely to be negative, particularly the active form (Cattell, 1982). That is, being exposed to an alcoholic environment may result in an active selection of environments that avoid or preclude alcohol-related properties. In the passive sense, one parent may make special efforts to structure children's environments that emphasize sobriety if the other parent is an alcoholic. The idea of negative, compensatory g–e correlation has received little research attention in general, and none specific to the development of alcoholism.

These explications of G × E interaction and g–e correlation imply that they are quantifiable variance components that can be specified, estimated, and tested in behavior genetics analyses. Naturally, this assumes that these components are, in fact, extricable from the proper data; an assumption that remains controversial despite the increasing sophistication of behavior genetic techniques (Lewontin et al., 1983; Wilson, 1978).

SUGGESTIONS FOR FUTURE RESEARCH

In the current enthusiasm for genetic/biological models for the pathogenesis of disease, environmental influences may have been underemphasized as significant factors in the etiology of alcoholism. Unfortunately, methodologically rigorous studies of environmental influences in the etiology of alcohol abuse have been rare, with longitudinal studies even rarer. Kumpfer and DeMarsh (1986) have suggested several familial factors that may increase a child's risk for alcohol and/or drug abuse, such as degree of family conflict, degree of overt modeling of abuse, social isolation, and severity of parental neglect. While these factors could have a significant impact on the psychological and emotional development of the child, there are no studies that have systematically linked nongenetic familial influences to adult alcohol abuse despite the intuitive appeal of these social constructs. In fact, those factors that are associated with adolescent problem drinking are uncorrelated with adult drinking status (Temple & Fillmore, 1986), and degree of adolescent alcohol use is not predictive of adult abuse (Donovan, Jessor, & Jessor, 1983).

This suggests several independent but complementary hypotheses that implicitly call for a greater emphasis on individual differences:

1. Genetic influences may have differential developmental (i.e., age related) significance (Plomin, 1986). There are two important ideas embedded in this statement. First, genetic influences can change over the life course. Second, different genes may control different aspects of the same behavior. For example, social drinking may be under much less or qualitatively different genetic control than alcohol abuse.
2. Unique environmental factors play a major etiological role (Plomin & Daniels, 1987).
3. The g–e correlations (particularly the active sort) are instrumental in the development of alcohol disorders.
4. If the work reported by Bergeman et al. (1988) continues to yield theoretically meaningful results, G × E interaction may have a significant effect.
5. Alcohol abuse is the result of some complex function incorporating all of these factors.

This individual-difference perspective could provide a more profound understanding of the pathogenesis of alcohol abuse. Future research, then, should recognize not just the relative importance of individuals and environments but also the dynamic aspects of both. Explicit recognition of the importance of the nonstatic nature of the person–environment relationship will necessitate specific methodological improvements and conceptual reformulations, such as:

1. *More refined environmental measurement.* What is termed "environment" in most extant studies is usually not the complex, multifaceted construct that the word implies. It often is simply what is left after genetic factors are removed, or it reflects overly broad influences of crudely measured variables. For example, in the Swedish Adoption Study, four environmental variables were associated with alcohol abuse in the adoptees: reared by biological mother for more than 6 months, greater age at time of placement, extent of hospital care prior to placement, and ocupational status of the adoptive father. Only the occupational status of the foster father is related to the adoptive home environment. The environmental influences described by Cadoret et al (1985) have already been discussed. Environments need to be assessed with much greater specificity and precision than is currently being accomplished. The goal of more fine-grained analysis of the environment is to be able to accurately differentiate subtle G × E interactions and g–e correlations (Zucker & Noll, 1987; Zucker, in press).

2. *Systematic study of nonshared environmental influences.* Recently, behavior geneticists have begun to stress environmental variables as important factors in cognitive and personality development (see Plomin & Daniels, 1987, for a review of relevant studies). However, this environmental emphasis has not, for the most part, been in the customary sense of home and family as significant socialization agents. In a seminal paper, Rowe and Plomin (1981) discussed two sources of environmental influences. The first, called shared or between-family environment (E_2), acts to make individuals in the same family alike and is most similar to traditional conceptualizations of environment such as common child rearing practices. The second, called nonshared or within-family environment (E_1), acts in such a way as to make family members different from one another and reflects those forces that are unique to individual family members. With behavior genetic methods it is possible to estimate the relative influence of these two sources of environmental variance. For example, the correlation of adoptive and nonadoptive children in the same family milieu is a direct estimate of E_2, while one minus the intraclass correlation coefficient between monozygotic twins raised together ($1 - r_{MZT}$) is an estimate (although an underestimate for nontwins) of sources of variance that make them different from each other (E_1).

Data from both twin and adoption studies suggest that for dimensions of personality the between family environmental influence is essentially zero (Goldsmith, 1983; Rowe and Plomin, 1981). That is, personality as currently conceptualized and measured appears to be a function of genetic predispositions and nonshared environmental factors. Empirical support for this position is surprisingly compelling. Goldsmith (1983) presents estimates of heritability (h^2), E_1, and E_2 for ten different twin studies of personality. The means across all the studies for all scales are $h^2 = .40$, E_2 (shared) $= .07$, E_1 (nonshared) $= .54$. He also reviewed two well-known adoption studies. The mean adoptive sibling correlation for several personality variables was .09, which indicates that shared environment has a minimal impact. Studies of infant and childhood temperament, thought to be developmentally related to adult personality (Buss & Plomin, 1984), show a similar pattern. From these data Goldsmith (1983) concludes "common familial environment is not a potent source of similarity in a wide range of personality traits" (p. 341). Rowe and Plomin (1981) after their review of this area state: "In other words, whatever environmental variables influence personality—and they are substantial, accounting for half the variance of personality—they are not shared by siblings" (p. 522). Since both temperament and personality factors have been implicated in the etiology of some types of alcoholism, the significance of nonshared environmental influences could be substantial.

It should be noted that inappropriate conceptualization of environmental processes as well as inadequate measurement techniques may account for at least part of the failure to find significant familial environmental influences in the personality domain (Wachs, 1983). Also, direct measurement of nonshared environment has been rare. In most behavior genetic studies to date, E_1 is a residual term that also includes error variance.

3. *Sibling studies.* Because of the potential importance of E_1, multiple members of the same family should be included in future studies. Daniels and Plomin (1985) have developed the Sibling Inventory of Differential Exprience (SIDE) to assess nonshared environmental effects. Preliminary reports suggest that the SIDE is environmentally mediated and is sensitive to sibling differences in personality that are a function of E_1 (Daniels, 1986). The inclusion of siblings in high-risk studies may be particularly important. Also, with the decreasing availability of adoptees for study as a result of legal abortion and accessible birth control, half- and step-siblings could be utilized. Although this would require a significant increase over current methodological precision, the improvement in the generalizability of the results may offset the difficulties in solving problems such as variable exposure to environments and degree of genetic overlap.

4. *Studies of "resilient" children.* As mentioned previously, most individuals who are described as being at high risk for alcohol problems by virtue of their having an alcoholic parent do not actually develop alcoholism. Since the focus of much of the research in this area has been on the psychopathological aspects of the genetic and environmental sequelae, individuals who adapt successfully despite their vulnerability have rarely been studied systematically. Garmezy and colleagues (e.g., Garmezy, Masten, & Tellegen, 1984; Garmezy & Tellegen, 1984) have provided general models for the study of stress-resistant children. Werner and colleagues (Werner, 1986; Werner & Smith, 1982) have contributed substantially by reporting on a cohort of children from the island of Kauai who were followed over the course of 18 years. They were able to identify specific factors associated with being "vulnerable but invincible" with respect to learning and behavior problems, as well as reporting on a group of COAs who flourished despite their risk status. Both psychological variables

(such as scores on several scales of the California Psychological Inventory) and early environmental influences (such as birth of another sibling within two years), as well as potential g–e correlations (e.g., an infant perceived as cuddly and affectionate during its first year), significantly discriminated individuals who did and did not develop coping problems by age 18. This important study will continue to follow these individuals as they progress through the age of risk for alcoholism and psychopathology (Werner, 1986). Additional longitudinal investigations of personological attributes and environmental circumstances that contribute to effective adult adjustment despite an adverse risk status appear warranted. This would provide a much more complex, multifarious approach for characterizing the etiology of alcoholism than is currently being considered.

   5. *Expanded use of newly developed multivariate techniques.* Recent substantive advances in the multivariate analysis of data have yet to be applied directly to questions concerning the etiology of alcoholism in general and COAs in particular. Latent variable and causal analytic procedures have been used in the depiction and interpretation of adolescent substance use and its relation to early adult psychological development (Newcomb & Bentler, 1988). These procedures provide a significant enhancement in analytical precision compared with less sophisticated approaches. Perhaps the most important refinement is the ability to specify and test diverse models of various levels of complexity and statistically determine which fit the obtained data better. Also, these methods are particularly appropriate for tracking change over time (longitudinal data) and representing complex interrelationships among variables of interest. These techniques require relatively large sample sizes and multiple measures of the same construct in order to ensure model stability and precision, as well as error-free latent variable measurement.

   The use of these methods is made possible by increasingly complex computer technology, including high-speed processors and coprocessors that enhance algorhythmic accuracy and allow relatively rapid processing. While several programs are available on mainframe computers, a few have been developed that will perform confirmatory factor analysis as well as structural equation modelling on suitably equipped personal computers. For example, EQS (Bentler, 1985), LISCOMP (Muthen, 1988), and LISREL VII (Jöreskog & Sörbom, 1989) have been designed to perform these high-level statistical procedures on AT class (i.e., "286" processors) personal computers equipped with a math coprocessor. Thus, these powerful techniques are available to virtually any researcher who is willing to learn about their proper application and interpretation as well as their potential limitations (for a cogent critique of statistical model building in general see Freedman, 1987a, 1987b).

   Although this chapter presents a critical view of behavior genetic research on alcoholism, it should be remembered that all researchers in the alcohol field share similar goals: the alleviation of existing alcohol disorders and the eventual prevention of the development of alcoholism without socially engineered responses such as prohibition. Legitimate differences arise with respect to the methodological adequacy of extant research and the utility and efficacy of specific research programs. Critical reviews highlight methodological weaknesses and conceptual deficiencies in current strategies. Peel (1984, 1986) has been the most eloquent and outspoken critic of the genetic model of alcoholism as well as its medical corollary, the disease concept. Peele (1984, 1986) has suggested that both are fundamentally flawed and do not reflect empirical findings; neither concept has led to a greater understanding of the etiology of alcohol disorders, a genuine prevention effort, or an increase in the effectiveness of alcohol treatments. A secondary purpose of critical reviews is to suggest news, potentially fertile areas of research. My colleagues and I are in the process of implementing research programs that incorporate many of the suggestions in this chapter (Alterman, A., Searles, J. S., McLellan, A. T., & O'Brien, C. P., *Risk Factors and the Development of Problematic Drinking,* a project funded by the National Institute on Alcoholism and Alcohol Abuse; and Searles, J. S., *Environmental and Personality Correlates of Alcoholism: A Pilot Study,* funded by the Research Advisory Group of the U.S. Veterans Administration).

Regardless of their origin, alcohol-related difficulties have a substantial economic impact (Vaillant, 1983), as well as an inestimable social and emotional cost. The early identification of potential alcohol abusers and the eventual amelioration of the deleterious effects of alcoholism may be facilitated by the results of research in this area.

REFERENCES

American Psychiatric Association. (1980). *Diagnostic and statistical manual of mental disorders* (3rd ed.). Washington, DC: Author.

Begleiter, H., Porjesz, B., Bihari, B., & Kissin, B. (1984). Event-related brain potentials in boys at risk for alcoholism. *Science, 225,* 1493–1496.

Bentler, P. M. (1985). *Theory and implementation of EQS: A structural equations program.* Los Angeles: BMDP Statistical Software.

Bergeman, C. S., Plomin, R., McClearn, G. E., Pedersen, N. L., & Friberg, L. T. (1988). Genotype-environment interaction in personality development: Identical twins reared apart. *Psychology and Aging, 3,* 399–406.

Blum, K., & Trachtenberg, M. C. (1988). Alcoholism: Scientific basis of a neuropsychogenetic disease. *International Journal of the Addictions, 23,* 781–796.

Bohman, M., Cloninger, C. R., Sigvardsson, S., & von Knorring, A.-L. (1983). Gene-environment interaction in the psychopathology of Swedish adoptees: Studies of the origins of alcoholism and criminality. In S. B. Guze, F. J. Earls, & J. E. Barrett (Eds.), *Childhood psychopathology and development* (pp. 265–278). New York: Raven Press.

Bohman, M., Sigvardsson, S., & Cloninger, C. R. (1981). Maternal inheritance of alcohol abuse: Cross fostering analysis of adopted women. *Archives of General Psychiatry, 38,* 965–969.

Bower, B. (1988, July 30). Alcoholism's elusive genes. *Science News, 134,* 74.

Buss, A. H., & Plomin, R. (1984). *Temperament: Early developing personality traits.* Hillsdale, NJ: Erlbaum.

Cadoret, R. J., Cain, C. A., & Crowe, R. R. (1983). Evidence for gene–environment interaction in the development of adolescent antisocial behavior. *Behavior Genetics, 13,* 301–310.

124   J. S. Searles

Cadoret, R. J., Cain, C. A., & Grove, W. M. (1980). Development of alcoholism in adoptees raised apart from alcoholic biologic relatives. *Archives of General Psychiatry, 37,* 561–563.

Cadoret, T. J., O'Gorman, T. W., Troughton, E., & Heywood, R. (1985). Alcoholism and antisocial personality: Interrelationships, genetic and environmental factors. *Archives of General Psychiatry, 42,* 161–167.

Cadoret, R. J., Troughton, E., & O'Gorman, T. W. (1987). Genetic and environmental factors in alcohol abuse and antisocial personality. *Journal of Studies on Alcohol, 48,* 1–8.

Cattell, R. B. (1982). *The inheritance of personality and ability.* New York: Academic Press.

Cloninger, C. R. (1986). A unified biosocial theory of personality and its role in the development of anxiety states. *Psychiatric Developments, 3,* 167–226.

Cloninger, C. R. (1987a). A systematic method for clinical description and classification of personality variants. *Archives of General Psychiatry, 44,* 573–588.

Cloninger, C. R. (1987b). Neurogenetic adaptive mechanisms in alcoholism. *Science, 236,* 410–416.

Cloninger, C. R. (1988, June). *Types of alcoholism.* Paper presented at the annual meeting of the Research Society on Alcoholism, Wild Dunes, SC.

Cloninger, C. R., Bohman, M., & Sigvardsson, S. (1981). Inheritance of alcohol abuse: Cross fostering analysis of adopted men. *Archives of General Psychiatry, 38,* 861–868.

Cloninger, C. R., Sigvardsson, S., & Bohman, M. (1988). Childhood personality predicts alcohol abuse in young adults. *Alcoholism: Clinical and Experimental Research, 12,* 494–505.

Corey, L. A., & Nance, W. E. (1978). The monozygotic half-sib model: A tool for epidemiological research. In L. Gedda, P. Parisi, & W. E. Nance (Eds.), *Twin research: Psychology and methodology* (pp. 201–209). New York: Alan R. Liss.

Daniels, D. (1986). Differential experiences of siblings in the same family as predictors of adolescent sibling personality differences. *Journal of Personality and Social Psychology, 51,* 339–346.

Daniels, D., & Plomin, R. (1985). Differential experience of siblings in the same family. *Developmental Psychology, 21,* 747–760.

Donovan, J. E., Jessor, R., & Jessor, L. (1983). Problem drinking in adolescence and young adulthood: A follow-up study. *Journal of Studies on Alcohol, 44,* 109–137.

Elmasian, R., Neville, H., Woods, D., Schuckit, M. A., & Bloom, F. (1982). Event-related brain potentials of young men at risk for developing alcoholism. *Proceedings of the National Academy of Sciences, 79,* 7900–7903.

Falconer, D. S. (1960). *Introduction to quantitative genetics.* New York: Ronald Press.

Fingarette, H. (1988). *Heavy drinking: The myth of alcoholism as a disease.* Berkeley: University of California Press.

Freedman, D. A. (1987a). As others see us: A case study in path analysis. *Journal of Educational Statistics, 12,* 101–128.

Freedman, D. A. (1987b). A rejoinder on models, metaphors, and fables. *Journal of Educational Statistics, 12,* 206–223.

Gabrielli, W. F., Jr., Mednick, S. A., Volavka, J., Pollock, V. E., Schulsinger, F., & Ital, T. M. (1982). Electroencephalograms in children of alcoholic fathers. *Psychophysiology, 19,* 404–407.

Garmezy, N., Masten, A. S., Tellegen, A. (1984). The study of stress and competence in children: A building block for developmental psychopathology. *Child Development, 55,* 97–111.

Garmezy, N. & Tellegen, A. (1984). Studies of stress-resistant children: Methods, variables, and preliminary findings. In F. Morrison, C. Lord, & D. Keating (Eds.), *Advances in applied developmental psychology* (Vol. 1, pp. 231–287). New York: Academic Press.

Goldsmith, H. H. (1983). Genetic influences on personality from infancy to adulthood. *Child Development, 54,* 331–355.

Goodwin, D. W., Schulsinger, F., Hermansen, L., Guze, S. B., & Winokur, G. (1973). Alcohol problems in adoptees raised apart from biological parents. *Archives of General Psychiatry, 28,* 238–243.

Goodwin, D. W., Schulsinger, F., Moller, N., Hermansen, L., Winokur, G., & Guze, S. B. (1974). Drinking problems in adopted and nonadopted sons of alcoholics. *Archives of General Psychiatry, 31,* 164–169.

Goodwin, D. W., Schulsinger, F., Moller, N., Mednick, S., & Guze, S. (1977). Psychopathology in adopted and nonadopted daughters of alcoholics. *Archives of General Psychiatry, 34,* 1005–1009.

Hill, S. Y. (1988, June). *ERP and other biological markers in high risk three generation pedigrees.* Paper presented at the annual meeting of the Research Society on Alcoholism, Wild Dunes, SC.

Hill, S. Y., Armstrong, J., Steinhauer, S. R., Baughman, T., & Zubin, J. (1987). Static ataxia as a psychobiological marker for alcoholism. *Alcoholism: Clinical and Experimental Research, 11,* 345–348.

Jensen, A. R. (1976). The problem of genotype-environment correlation in the estimation of heritability from monozygotic and dizygotic twins. *Acta Geneticae Medicae et Gemellologiae, 25,* 86–89.

Johnson, D. (1987, October 25). High court faces alcoholism issue. *The New York Times,* p. 1.

Jöreskog, K. G., & Sörbom, D. (1989). LISREL VII users reference guide. Mooresville, IN: Scientific Software.

Kamin, L. J. (1974). *The science and politics of IQ.* Potomac, MD: Erlbaum.

Kandel, D. B. (1984). Family and peer processes in adolescent drug use. In S. A. Mednick, M. Harway, & K. M. Finello (Eds.), *Handbook of longitudinal research* (pp. 18–33). New York: Praeger.

Knop, J., Goodwin, D., Teasdale, T. W., Mikkelsen, U., & Schulsinger, F. (1984). A Danish prospective study of young males at high risk for alcoholism. In D. W. Goodwin, K. T. Van Dusen, & S. A. Mednick (Eds.), *Longitudinal research in alcoholism* (pp. 107–124). Boston: Kluwer-Nijhoff.

Kumpfer, K. L., & DeMarsh, J. (1986). Family environmental and genetic influences on children's future chemical dependency. In S. Griswold-Ezekoye, K. L. Kumpfer, & W. J. Bukoski (Eds.), *Childhood and chemical abuse: Prevention and intervention* (pp. 46–91). New York: Haworth Press.

Lester, D. (1988). Genetic theory: An assessment of the heritability of alcoholism. In C. D. Chaudron & D. A. Wilkinson (Eds.), *Theories of alcoholism* (pp. 1–28). Toronto: Addiction Research Foundation.

Lewontin, R. C., Kamin, L. J., & Rose, S. (1983) *Not in our genes.* New York: Pantheon.

Lex, B. W., Lukas, S. E., Greenwald, N. E., & Mendelson, J. H. (1988). Alcohol-induced changes in body sway in women at risk for alcoholism: A pilot study. *Journal of Studies on Alcohol, 49,* 346–356.

Littrell, J. (1988). The Swedish studies of the adopted children of alcoholics. *Journal of Studies on Alcohol, 49,* 491–499.

Loehlin, J. C., & DeFries, J. C. (1987). Genotype–environment correlation and IQ. *Behavior Genetics, 17,* 263–277.

Loehlin, J. C., & Nichols, R. C. (1976). *Heredity, environment, and personality.* Austin: University of Texas Press.

Merikangas, K. (1988, June). *Genetic epidemiologic study of DSM III alcohol abuse/dependence.* Paper presented at the annual meeting of the Research Society on Alcoholism, Wild Dunes, SC.

Morrison, C., & Schuckit, M. A. (1983). Locus of control in young men with alcoholic relatives and controls. *Journal of Clinical Psychiatry, 44,* 306–307.

Murray, R. M., Clifford, C. A., & Gurling, H. M. D. (1983). Twin and adoption studies: How good is the evidence for a genetic role? In M. Galanter (Ed.), *Recent developments in alcoholism* (Vol. 1, pp. 25–48). New York: Plenum Press.

Muthen, B. O. (1988). *LISCOMP: Analysis of linear structural equations with a comprehensive measurement model* (2nd ed.). Mooresville, IN: Scienfic Software

Nagoshi, C. T., & Wilson, J. R. (1987). Influence of family alcoholism history on alcohol metabolism, sensitivity, and tolerance. *Alcoholism: Clinical and Experimental Research, 11,* 392–398.

Neville, H. J., & Schmidt, A. L. (1985). Event-related brain potentials in subjects at risk for alcoholism. In N. Chang & H. Chao (Eds.), *Early identification of alcohol abuse* (Research Monograph No. 17, pp. 228–239). Rockville, MD: National Institute on Alcoholism and Alcohol Abuse.

Newcomb, M. D., & Bentler, P. M. (1988). *Consequences of adolescent drug use: Impact on the lives of young adults.* Newbury Park, CA: Sage Publications.

Pandey, G. N., Fawcett, J., Gibbons, R., Clark, D. C., & Davis, J. M. (1988). Platelet monoamine oxidase in alcoholism. *Biological Psychiatry, 24,* 15–24.

Peele, S. (1984). The cultural context of psychological approaches to alcoholism: Can we control the effects of alcohol. *American Psychologist, 39,* 1337–1351.

Peele, S. (1986). The implications and limitations of genetic models of alcoholism and other addictions. *Journal of Studies on Alcohol, 47,* 63–71.

Pickens, R., Svikis, S., & McGue, M. (1988, June). Twin study of factors in alcohol abuse. In J. Stabenau (Chair), *Genetic factors and lifetime risk for alcoholism.* Symposium conducted at the annual meeting of the Research Society on Alcoholism, Wild Dunes, SC.

Plomin, R. (1986). *Development, genetics, and psychology.* Hillsdale, NJ: Erlbaum.

Plomin, R., & Daniels, D. (1987). Why are children in the same family so different from one another? *Behavioral and Brain Sciences, 10,* 1–60.

Plomin, R., & DeFries, J. C. (1985). *Origins of individual differences in infancy: The Colorado Adoption Project.* Orlando, FL: Academic Press.

Plomin, R., DeFries, J. C., & Loehlin, J. C. (1977). Genotype-environment interaction and correlation in the analysis of human behavior. *Psychological Bulletin, 84,* 309–322.

Plomin, R., DeFries, J. C., & McClearn, G. E. (1980). *Behavioral genetics: A primer.* San Francisco: W. H. Freeman.

Polich, J. (1984). P300 latency reflects personal drinking history. *Psychophysiology, 21,* 592–593.

Polich, J., & Bloom, F. E. (1986). P300 and alcohol consumption in normals and individuals at risk for alcoholism. *Progress in Neuropsychopharmacology and Biological Psychiatry, 10,* 201–210.

Polich, J., & Bloom, F. E. (1987). P300 from normals and children of alcoholics. *Alcohol, 4,* 301–305.

Polich, J., & Bloom, F. E. (1988). Event-related brain potentials in individuals at high and low risk for developing alcoholism: Failure to replicate. *Alcoholism: Clinical and Experimental Research, 12,* 368–373.

Polich, J., Haier, R. J., Buchsbaum, M., & Bloom, F. E. (1988). Assessment of young men at risk for alcoholism with P300 from a visual discrimination task. *Journal of Studies on Alcohol, 49,* 186–190.

Reed, R., Grant, I., Adams, K. M. (1987). Family history of alcoholism does not predict neuropsychological performance in alcoholics. *Alcoholism: Clinical and Experimental Research, 11,* 340–344.

Roe, A. (1944). The adult adjustment of children of alcoholic parents raised in foster homes. *Quarterly Journal of Studies on Alcohol, 5,* 378–393.

Roe, A., & Burks, B. (1945). *Adult adjustment of foster children of alcoholic and psychotic parentage and the influence of the foster home* (Memoirs of the Section on Alcohol Studies, No. 3). New Haven, CT: Yale University Press.

Rowe, D. C. (1983). A biometrical analysis of family environment: A study of twin and singleton kinships. *Child Development, 54,* 416–423.

Rowe, D. C., & Plomin, R. (1981). The importance of non-shared (E_1) environmental influences in behavioral development. *Developmental Psychology, 17,* 517–531.

Scarr, S., & Carter-Saltzman, L. (1979). Twin method: Defense of a critical assumption. *Behavior Genetics, 9,* 527–542.

Scarr, S., & McCartney, K. (1983). How people make their own environments: A theory of genotype-environment effects. *Child Development, 54*, 424–435.

Schaeffer, K. W., Parsons, O. A., & Yohman, J. R. (1984). Neuropsychological differences between male familial and nonfamilial alcoholics and nonalcoholics. *Alcoholism: Clinical and Experimental Research, 8*, 347–351.

Schuckit, M. A. (1981). Peak blood alcohol levels in men at high risk for the future development of alcoholism. *Alcoholism: Clinical and Experimental Research, 5*, 64–66.

Schuckit, M. A. (1982). Anxiety and assertiveness in sons of alcoholics and controls. *Journal of Clinical Psychiatry, 43*, 238–239.

Schuckit, M. A. (1983). Extroversion and neuroticism in young men at higher and lower risk for alcoholism. *American Journal of Psychiatry, 140*, 1223–1224.

Schuckit, M. A. (1984). Subjective responses to alcohol in sons of alcoholics and controls. *Archives of General Psychiatry, 41*, 879–884.

Schuckit, M. A. (1985). Ethanol-induced changes in body sway in men at high alcoholism risk. *Archives of General Psychiatry, 42*, 375–379.

Schuckit, M. A. (1987). Biological vulnerability to alcoholism. *Journal of Consulting and Clinical Psychology, 55*, 301–309.

Schuckit, M. A. (1988a, June). *Changes in hormones after alcohol challenge in sons of alcoholics.* Paper presented at the annual meeting of the Research Society on Alcoholism, Wild Dunes, SC.

Schuckit, M. A. (1988b). Reactions to alcohol in sons of alcoholics and controls. *Alcoholism: Clinical and Experimental Research, 12*, 465–470.

Schuckit, M. A., & Gold, E. O. (1987). A simultaneous evaluation of multiple markers of ethanol/placebo challenges in sons of alcoholics and controls. *Archives of General Psychiatry, 45*, 211–216.

Schuckit, M. A. Goodwin, D. W., & Winokur, G. (1972). A study of alcoholism in half siblings. *American Journal of Psychiatry, 128*, 1132–1135.

Schuckit, M. A., Risch, S. C., & Gold, E. O. (1988). Alcohol consumption, ACTH level, and family history of alcoholism. *American Journal of Psychiatry, 145*, 1391–1395.

Schulsinger, F., Knop, J., Goodwn, D. W., Teasdale, T. W., & Mikkelsen, U. (1986). A prospective study of young men at risk for alcoholism: Social and psychological characteristics. *Archives of General Psychiatry, 43*, 755–760.

Searles, J. S. (1988). The role of genetics in the pathogenesis of alcoholism. *Journal of Abnormal Psychology, 97*, 153–167.

Sifford, D. (1989, January 2). A psychiatrist discusses creative writers and alcohol. *The Philadelphia Inquirer*, p. 5-C.

Tarter, R. E., Alterman, A. I., & Edwards, K. L. (1985). Vulnerability to alcoholism in men: A behavior genetic perspective. *Journal of Studies on Alcohol, 46*, 329–356.

Tarter, R. E., Hegedus, A. M., Goldstein, G., Shelly, C., & Alterman, A. I. (1984). Adolescent sons of alcoholics: Neuropsychological and personality characteristics. *Alcoholism: Clinical and Experimental Research, 8*, 216–222.

Temple, M. T., & Fillmore, K. M. (1986). The variability of drinking patterns and problems among young men, age 16–31: A longitudinal study. *International Journal of the Addictions, 20*, 1585–1620.

Vaillant, G. E. (1983). *The natural history of alcoholism.* Cambridge, MA: Harvard University Press.

Volavka, J., Pollock, V., Gabrielli, W. F., & Mednick, S. A. (1985). The EEG in persons at risk for alcoholism. In M. Galanter (Ed.), *Recent developments in alcoholism* (Vol. 3, pp. 21–36). New York: Plenum Press.

Volpicelli, J. R. (1987). Uncontrollable events and alcohol drinking. *British Journal of Addiction, 82*, 381–392.

von Knorring, A. L., Bohman, M., von Knorring, L., & Oreland, L. (1985). Platelet MAO activity as a biological marker in subgroups of alcoholism. *Acta Psychiatrica Scandinavica, 72*, 51–58.

Wachs, T. D. (1983). The use and abuse of environment in behavior genetic research. *Child Development, 54,* 416–423.

Werner, E. (1986). Resillient offspring of alcoholics: A longitudinal study from birth to age 18. *Journal of Studies on Alcohol, 47,* 34–40.

Werner, E. E., & Smith, R. S. (1982). *Vulnerable but invincible.* New York: McGraw Hill.

Whipple, S., & Noble, E. P. (1986). The effects of familial alcoholism on visual event-related potentials. *Psychophysiology, 23,* 470.

Wilson, E. O. (1978). The attempt to suppress human behavioral genetics. *Journal of General Education, 29,* 277–287.

Winokur, G., Reich, T., Rimmer, J., & Pitts, F. N. (1970). Alcoholism III: Diagnosis and family psychiatric illness. *Archives of General Psychiatry, 23,* 104–111.

Zucker, R. A. (1987). The four alcoholisms: A developmental account of the etiologic process. In P. C. Rivers (Ed.), *Alcohol and addictive behaviors: Nebraska symposium on motivation, 1986* (pp. 27–84). Lincoln: University of Nebraska Press.

Zucker, R. A. (in press). Is risk for alcoholism predictable? A probabilistic approach to a developmental problem. *Drugs and Society.*

Zucker, R. A., & Lisansky-Gomberg, E. S. (1986). Etiology of alcoholism reconsidered: The case for a biopsychosocial process. *American Psychologist, 41,* 783–793.

Zucker, R. A., & Noll, R. B. (1987). The interaction of child and environment in the early development of drug involvement: A far ranging review and a planned very early intervention. *Drugs and Society, 2,* 57–97.

CHAPTER SIX

Temperament and Personality Attributes of Children of Alcoholics

MICHAEL WINDLE

Across diverse theoretical orientations, temperament and personality frequently have been considered salient influences in the etiology of alcoholism (e.g., Blane, 1968; McClelland, Davis, Kalin, & Warner, 1972; Tarter, Alterman, & Edwards, 1985). While there is no paucity of research studies conducted on associations between temperament and personality attributes and alcoholism, there remains much controversy over the specificity and presumed psychological significance of temperament and personality attributes on alcoholic behaviors (e.g., Nathan, 1988; Vaillant & Milofsky, 1982; Zucker & Gomberg, 1986). Nevertheless, there is a consensus in the alcoholism literature regarding the futility of identifying a singular "alcoholic personality," and most researchers have adopted more heterogeneous, multifactorial models to represent the etiology of alcholism (e.g., Barnes, 1979; Cloninger, 1987; Graham & Strenger, 1988; Tarter et al., 1985; Zucker, 1987).

In this chapter, research pertinent to individual differences in temperament and personality among children of alcoholics (COAs) is selectively reviewed in three sections, sequenced, to a large extent, chronologically by the age groups referenced. First, research on the interrelationships between temperament attributes (such as hyperactivity) in childhood and problem drinking and alcoholism in adolescence and adulthood is presented. Second, research based on the family history method—that is, categorizing subjects as family history positive (FHP) versus family history negative (FHN) for parental alcoholism—is reviewed regarding possible differences in personality attributes between COAs and nonCOAs. Third, research pertaining to alcoholism typologies and coexisting psychiatric disorders among adults is discussed with regard to the role of temperament and personality factors influencing and being influenced by alcoholic behaviors. A methodological evaluation of the research reviewed is then provided, with suggestions for future research directions.

TEMPERAMENT STUDIES

Historical and contemporary approaches to temperament have provided a broad array of theoretical perspectives, with a range of alternative methods of defining and measuring temperament and with foci on different levels of analysis (e.g., Lerner & Lerner, 1986; Plomin & Dunn, 1986; Windle, 1988). For example, Rothbart and colleagues (e.g., Derryberry & Rothbart, 1984; Rothbart & Derryberry, 1981) have defined temperament as constitutional differences in reactivity and self-regulation. In this approach, reactivity refers to response parameters (such as threshold, latency, intensity) of the somatic, endocrine, autonomic, and central nervous systems, and self-regulation refers to higher-level affective–motivational processes. Buss and Plomin (1984) have focused on heritable temperament traits identified in infancy. Thomas and Chess (1977) and Lerner and Lerner (1983) and colleagues (e.g., Windle et al., 1986) have proposed a "goodness of fit" conceptualization of temperament in which developmental outcomes such as psychosocial adjustment are evaluated by measuring the congruity or incongruity between features of temperament and environmental demands. On the basis of this heterogeneity of approaches to temperament, several prominent investigators have proposed that temperament may be better viewed as a higher-order organizational concept, or rubric, analogous to cognition (Goldsmith et al., 1987). Viewing temperament as a higher-order concept may facilitate the organization and integration of concepts, variables, and research findings conducted by investigators from diverse theoretical positions who may be analyzing data at different levels of analysis.

Research on the association between temperament functioning in childhood among COAs and subsequent alcohol abuse and alcoholism has been limited in relation to the available range of contemporary perspectives and conceptual models (e.g., Lerner & Lerner, 1986; Plomin & Dunn, 1986). There are, nevertheless, two strands of research regarding temperament in childhood that are of relevance to alcohol abuse and alcoholism among COAs. The first strand of research has been reported in the psychiatric–clinical literature and centers on hyperactivity among COAs. The second strand of research has drawn on temperament dimensions identified by Thomas and Chess (1977) and Buss and Plomin (1984), and efforts have been made to conceptualize these childhood temperament dimensions as vulnerability or high-risk factors for subsequent alcoholic behaviors (e.g., Tarter et al., 1985). Research pertinent to each of these two strands of literature are discussed below with regard to their relevance for COAs.

Hyperactivity

Several studies using cross-sectional designs were completed in the early 1970s and suggested a higher prevalence of paternal alcoholism among hyperactive children seen at mental health clinics (e.g., Cantwell, 1972; Morrison & Stewart, 1971). For instance, Cantwell (1972) reported that 20% of fathers and 5% of mothers of 51 hyperactive children were alcoholic, compared with 10% of fathers of a control group. Morrison and Stewart (1971) studied differences in parental psychopathology among 59 hyperactive children and a matched control group of children with medical (nonpsychiatric) problems. For the hyperactive children, there was a higher prevalence of alcoholism and sociopathy among fathers and hysteria among mothers than in the control group. Further, there was a higher prevalence of hyperactivity among the parents and other family members (grandfathers, for example) of the hyperactive children relative to the prevalence among family members of the control group. Lund and Landesman-Dwyer (1979) and Fine, Yudin, Holmes, and Heinemann (1976) reported that COAs tended to manifest hyperactive symptoms such as high distractibility, poor emotional control, and difficulties delaying gratification (impulsivity). Morrison (1980) used a psychiatric control group of 91 children and a group of 140 hyperactive children to compare parental psychopathology. There were no differences between the parents of the two groups with respect to parental alcoholism, but more of the fathers of the hyperactive children manifested antisocial personality disorder and the mothers of the hyperactive children manifested a higher prevalence of Briquet syndrome (that is, a long history of multiple, medically unexplained somatic complaints).

Additional support for a relationship between childhood hyperactivity and parental alcoholism has been reported in a number of studies using the retrospective method. Goodwin, Schulsinger, Hermansen, Guze, and Winokur (1975) compared the retrospective reports of alcoholic and nonalcoholic Danish adoptees. The alcoholic adoptees ($N = 14$) reported higher levels of hyperactivity, truancy, antisocial behavior, shyness, aggression, disobedience, and friendlessness in childhood than nonalcoholic adoptees ($N = 119$). Although there were no differences in socioeconomic status, psychopathology, or drinking histories between the adopted families of the alcoholics and nonalcoholics, 10 of the 14 alcoholics had a biological parent who was alcoholic compared with no biological parents with alcoholism among the nonalcoholic adoptees. Therefore, alcoholism in a biological parent was associated with higher levels of childhood hyperactivity and adult alcoholism for adopted children, that is, for COAs who were not raised by their alcoholic parent(s). Cantwell (1975) and Morrison and Stewart (1971) also have reported data that suggest that paternal alcoholism is associated with higher prevalence of hyperactivity among children reared by nonalcoholic adoptive parents. Retrospective reports by alcoholics have also suggested that COAs tend to manifest more hyperactivity symptoms during childhood than alcoholics who report no family history of alcoholism (e.g., Alterman, Petrarulo, Tarter, & McGowan, 1982; Tarter, McBride, Buonpane, & Schneider, 1977). Wood, Reinherr, Wender, and Johnson (1976) interviewed the mothers of a sample of alcoholics about their alcoholic offspring and reported that a retrospective diagnosis indicated that one third of these alcoholics manifested attentional deficit disorder (or, for our purposes, hyperactivity symptomatology).

However, an interesting set of studies by Huessy and Howell (1985) encourages caution in interpreting these studies based on the retrospective method. Huessy and Howell conducted two studies, one using the retrospective method with alcoholics and a second using a longitudinal follow-up design of 369 subjects who had or had not manifested symptoms of hyperactivity (attentional deficit disorder) during elementary school. The findings from the retrospective reports of alcoholics paralleled the research findings of the studies cited previously, indicating a high prevalence of hyperactivity among the alcoholics. However, the longitudinal follow-up study indicated no differences in self-reported levels of alcohol use among the two adult groups that had been classified according to hyperactivity or nonhyperactivity in childhood. This finding raises questions about the validity and generalizability of the research based on cross-sectional and retrospective studies of clinical samples of hyperactive children and alcoholics. A limitation of the Huessy and Howell follow-up study is that the average age of adult respondents was 22 years, possibly too young for group differences to emerge with respect to the expression of alcoholism. The findings do, nevertheless, strongly suggest that future research would benefit from the use of longitudinal research designs to see if they corroborate findings using cross-sectional research designs and the retrospective method.

The cross-sectional research findings and those using the retrospective method are fairly consistent in suggesting some link between parental alcoholism, offspring hyperactivity, and the subsequent development of alcoholism among offspring. A simplified model reflecting this link is shown in Figure 6.1. However, research conducted from the late 1970s to the present has "muddied" the model, and a more complicated one has emerged. For purposes of direct comparison, this alternative model is shown in Figure 6.2. Research supportive of the latter is presented below.

As American psychiatric nomenclature has evolved over the years, the symptoms (criteria) and diagnosis of hyperactivity have repeatedly undergone change, often in the direction of differentiation and the identification of more highly integrated and reliably measured subtypes. In DSM-III-R (American Psychiatric Association, 1987), disordered childhood behaviors historically referred to under the rubric of hyperactivity or minimal brain dysfunction are categorized as three conduct disorders (undersocialized aggression, socialized

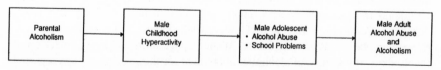

FIGURE 6.1. Early model of influence of parental alcoholism on offspring hyperactivity and alcohol abuse/alcoholism.

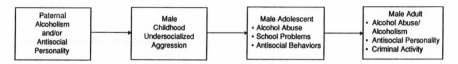

FIGURE 6.2. Influence of paternal alcoholism and/or antisocial personality on offspring problem behavior and alcohol abuse/alcoholism.

aggression, and a residual undifferentiated type) and attention-deficit hyperactivity disorder (ADHD). Reviews of research studies on the reliability, validity, and usefulness of these separate diagnostic entities have been provided by Hinshaw (1987) and Quay (1986).

Initial research studies examining relationships between parental psychopathology (e.g., alcoholism) and childhood aggression and hyperactivity have been generally supportive of the distinctive childhood psychopathology categories of DSM-III-R. Stewart, DeBlois, and Cummings (1980) examined paternal psychopathology among 126 males aged 5 to 15 years who were diagnosed as (1) unsocialized aggressive, (2) unsocialized aggressive and hyperactive, (3) hyperactive, or as having (4) other psychiatric disorders. Paternal alcoholism *and* antisocial behavior (e.g., aggression, arrest, imprisonment) were significantly associated with unsocialized aggressive diagnoses, and no association was found between these paternal characteristics and a diagnosis of hyperactivity among offspring. Similar findings were reported by Stewart, DeBlois, and Singer (1979) in that paternal alcoholism and antisocial behaviors were more highly associated with an offspring diagnosis of unsocialized aggression than with an offspring diagnosis of hyperactivity. August, Stewart, and Holmes (1983) studied differences in the behavior of hyperactive children categorized as either FHP (having a family history of *either* alcoholism *or* antisocial personality disorder) or FHN (no evidence of parental psychopathology for alcoholism or antisocial personality disorder). The research findings indicated that both groups of hyperactive children were inattentive and highly reactive, but that the FHP children manifested higher rates of conduct disturbance and aggression. Further, the FHP hyperactive children had siblings with a higher prevalence of conduct disorders than did the FHN hyperactive children.

Evidence supporting the differential adolescent outcome of childhood hyperactivity versus conduct disorder has been provided in two longitudinal studies. August et al. (1983) conducted a 4-year follow-up study of boys who had previously been categorized either as "purely" hyperactive (manifesting symptoms of inattention and impulsivity) or as undersocialized and aggressive. At the time of the follow-up, the hyperactive boys continued to have difficulties related to task orientation and impulsivity, but they did not have difficulties related to aggressive, antisocial behavior. The undersocialized and aggressive group also manifested a pattern of continuity in that they continued to have problems related to task orientation and impulsivity, but they were characterized further as more aggressive, noncompliant, egocentric, antisocial, and as consuming more alcohol. Blouin, Bornstein, and Trites (1978) identified a sample of hyperactive children and a control group of children the same age who had school difficulties unrelated to hyperactivity. A 5-year follow-up of these two groups when they were teenagers indicated that the hyperactive children, some of whom were manifesting aggressive, undersocialized behavior patterns, were consuming larger quantities of alcohol, especially hard liquor, than the control group. Moreover, the parents of the hyperactive children reported a larger number of conduct problems among their children than did the parents of the control group. Although neither of these two follow-up studies contains data relevant to family history of alcoholism, both suggest across-time linkages between undersocialized, aggressive behavior in childhood and subsequent problem behavior, including heavy alcohol consumption, in adolescence. These findings are also consistent with several major longitudinal studies of alcoholism that have found that undersocialized, aggressive behavior in childhood is often predictive of adult alcohol abuse and alcoholism (e.g., Jones, 1968; McCord & McCord, 1960; Robins, 1966; Vaillant, 1983).

As is quite common in most research endeavors, initial broad-based models require modifications and qualifications to more adequately account for the ensuing empirical findings. In this instance, regarding the relations between parental alcoholism, offspring hyperactivity, and the subsequent development of alcoholism in offspring, several modifications and qualifications have been suggested. For example, the emphasis has shifted from parental alcoholism and psychopathology to paternal alcoholism and antisocial behavior. In addition, hyperactivity behaviors have been divided into those characteristic of attentional deficits (e.g., distractibility, poor impulse control) and those characteristic of conduct disordered behavior (e.g., undersocialized aggression). The conceptual model in Figure 6.2 is a revision of the Figure 6.1 model, based on extant empirical findings. The revised model suggests that paternal alcoholism and/or antisocial personality disorder contributes to conduct-disordered behavior among male offspring, which in turn contributes to adolescent alcohol abuse, school problems, and delinquent activity, which in turn contributes to adult alcoholism, antisocial personality disorder, and criminality. Research questions abound with respect to the testing of features of the conceptual model presented in Figure 6.2. For instance, el-Guebaly and Orford (1979) have suggested that parental alcoholism often coexists with other indicators of dysfunction, such as poverty and family disorganization, and that few studies have examined the single versus conjoint influences of such factors on alcoholism among COAs. A second research question pertains to why only some COAs develop conduct disorders in childhood and others do not. A third research question pertains to the moderating influences (e.g., income, family conflict, community resources) that may increase or attenuate risk for conduct disordered behavior and subsequent alcoholism among COAs. These three research domains as well as others will be facilitated by the use of prospective research designs that attempt to chart the alternative developmental pathways toward and away from disordered childhood behaviors, aberrant activities, in adolescence, and alcoholism and antisocial behavior in adulthood.

Vulnerability and Protective Factors

The research on hyperactivity, conduct-disordered behavior, and parental alcoholism was pursued principally within the psychiatric–clinical literature and focused, in a general sense, on possible family links between parental alcoholism and offsprings' disordered behaviors. An alternative approach to the conceptualization and measurement of temperament has been to identify normally distributed temperament attributes (rather than categorically defined diagnostic entities) and to assess the heritability and functional significance of these attributes in relation to given outcomes such as alcohol use, or depression (e.g., Buss & Plomin, 1984; Thomas & Chess, 1977). The potential relevance of this alternative temperament approach to COAs is represented in two conceptual models.

Tarter et al. (1985) have developed a vulnerability model of alcoholism by conceptually integrating behavior genetic research findings on temperament and high-risk research findings within the alcoholism literature. More specifically, they identified six dimensions of temperament that were presumed or had been demonstrated to be highly heritable or constitutional in origin: activity level, attention-span persistence, soothability (facility to be calmed following distress), emotionality, reaction to food (propensity to seek out new and different-tasting foods), and sociability. A literature review suggested that deviations on these six temperament dimensions were associated with a prealcoholic profile, which in turn suggested that deviations on these dimensions may predispose persons or make them vulnerable to the development of alcoholism. Tarter et al. then proceded to provide an integrated neurobiological theory that detailed the proposed mechanisms underlying such temperamental vulnerability to alcoholism.

Thus, in contrast to the psychiatric–clinical approach, which focused on diagnostic entities (e.g., hyperactivity), the approach of Tarter et al. (1985) suggests that the measurement of multiple heritable temperament dimensions and their neurobehavioral substrate may facilitate the identification of premorbid or prealcoholic temperament profiles. Given that the proposed temperament attributes are heritable, they are conceptualized as vulnerability or high-risk factors that may influence the origin, development, and alcoholic outcomes of COAs. This model requires additional conceptual elaboration and empirical testing.

A second conceptual model based more on multiple, normally distributed temperament attributes than on psychiatric classification has been developed by Thomas and Chess (1977) and elaborated by Lerner and colleagues (Lerner & Lerner, 1983; Windle et al., 1986). The particular model proposed is referred to as the goodness of fit model of person–context relations. Unlike the psychiatric–

clinical model or the model of Tarter et al. (1985), the goodness of fit model proposes that it is necessary to examine features of the person (such as temperament) *in relation to* features of context (such as the demands or expectations of a given school or home environment). The emphasis of the goodness of fit model is, therefore, on the bidirectional effects of persons on their environments and of environments on the developing person (Lerner & Busch-Rossnagel, 1981).

Although it is not universal, Thomas and Chess (1977) identified a "difficult temperament profile" among white, middle-class children who manifested a pattern of slow adaptability, withdrawal responses, negative mood, high intensity of reactions, and biological irregularity. Children with this profile had more behavior problems with parents, peers, and teachers and were more likely to be referred to mental health clinics. Secondary analyses of data from the New York Longitudinal Study also have indicated that children manifesting the difficult temperament profile are more likely to use tobacco, alcohol, and marijuana in young adulthood (Lerner & Vicary, 1984). Quinton and Rutter (1985) have reported that children manifesting a particular constellation of difficult temperament attributes were more likely to have family criticism and hostility directed toward them. With respect to COAs, Werner (1986) reported that an affectionate temperament style in COA infants predicted resiliency and an absence of learning or behavior problems at age 18. COAs who were not identified as manifesting this affectionate temperament style during infancy had more than twice as many learning and behavior problems at age 18. Werner proposed that the affectionate temperament in infancy may have fostered positive social exchanges with family members and others and thus to have influenced the quality of the caregiving environment. The affectionate temperamental style was conceptualized by Werner as a protective factor.

Although few studies to date have been completed using the goodness of fit model of temperament–context relations among COAs or alcoholics in general, it has the potential of stimulating thought and research questions about the manner in which vulnerability and protective factors influence and are influenced by physical and social contexts. This model or some version of it may be necessary to understand and to predict why some COAs become alcoholics and some do not, as well as to identify processes (e.g., hostile exchanges) that may serve as targets for prevention/intervention efforts. Such an orientation moves from the simple identification of prodromal characteristics toward a contextual mapping of heterogeneous developmental processes.

PERSONALITY STUDIES

Relative to the few studies currently completed in some research domains concerning COAs (e.g., biochemical markers), there are a growing number of studies that have examined differences in personality attributes between COAs and nonCOAs. The research design typically used in these studies is cross-sectional and involves statistical comparisons (e.g., *t* tests, analyses of variance) between FHP and FHN subjects identified as having an alcoholic biological parent, typically the father, or as not having an alcoholic parent. The sampling of the specific personality attributes measured in the COA literature appears to have been selected primarily from the larger research literature on personality and alcoholism (e.g., Barnes, 1979; Cox, 1983; Miller, 1976). That is, the selection of personality attributes to study for possible differences between FHP and FHN samples was based principally on prior findings regarding significant associations between personality attributes and drinking behavior in both general population and alcohol treatment samples. The major research question investigated in these COA studies was whether those personality characteristics that have been associated with problem drinking and alcoholism in the personality–alcoholism research literature differentiate COAs from nonCOAs. If such differences could be found, and in the direction suggested by prior research, then (1) personality attributes (some of which may be highly heritable) that differentiate COAs from nonCOAs may indicate premorbid personality functioning, and (2) the identification of these premorbid personality characteristics would facilitate early detection and pave the way for prevention and interventions to subvert the development of problem drinking and/or alcoholism.

Table 6.1 provides a summary of 27 studies that assess differences between FHP and FHN subjects with regard to a range of personality attributes. For purposes of discussion, personality attributes are categorized as follows: (1) negative affective attributes, such as neuroticism, anxiety, or distress; (2) positive affective attributes, such as extraversion, sociability, or assertiveness; (3) cognitive–perceptual attributes, such as field dependence–field independence, dispositional self-awareness, or locus of control; (4) behavioral undercontrol attributes, such as aggression, rebelliousness, or impulsivity; and (5) a residual category for attributes such as sensation seeking or Type A personality.

Negative Affective Attributes

Barnes (1979, 1983) reviewed a number of research studies that used various standardized measures to suggest that neuroticism and domain-associated variables such as anxiety, distress, generalized fear, and heightened emotionality are associated with alcoholism. Whie the direction of the causal relations between alcoholism and neuroticism was questioned by Barnes (that is, whether neuroticism was a cause or a consequence of alcoholism), several studies using the FHP–FHN high-risk research design examined whether neuroticism and associated attributes (e.g., anxiety, heightened emotionality) differed for the two family history groups. No statistically significant differences between FHP and FHN subjects were found in three of four studies (Finn & Pihl, 1987; Knop, Teasdale, Schulsinger, & Goodwin, 1985; Schuckit, 1982), whereas mixed results were found in the fourth study (Finn & Pihl, 1989). In the fourth study,

TABLE 6.1. Personality Differences between Children with and without Alcoholic Parents

Study	Sample(s)	Personality trait measure	General finding
Alterman, Bridges, & Tarter (1986)	17 FHP and 17 FHN college males between 18–23 years of age	MAC Sensation seeking	No statistically significant differences. Higher level of sensation seeking in FHN group.
Alterman, Searles, & Hall (1989)	27 FHP (father or mother alcoholic), 26 FHP (second-degree relative alcoholic), and 30 FHN college males between 17–22 years of age	Adolescent antisocial behavior MAC Sensation seeking CPBCL	No statistically significant differences. No statistically significant differences. No statistically significant differences. No statistically significant differences on three subscales; statistically significant difference ($p < .05$) on attentional and social problems subscale.
Berkowitz & Perkins (1988)	155 FHP and 700 FHN college freshmen and sophomores; most between 18–20 years of age; males and females	Self-deprecation; impulsiveness; lack of tension, other-directedness; independence/autonomy; need for social support; sociability; directiveness	Significant differences only for self-deprecation for females and independence/autonomy for males.
Callan & Jackson (1986)	14 FHP, 21 FHP (recovered alcoholic fathers), and 35 FHN subjects; mean age, 13.5–13.6 years for each group	Perceived happiness Self-esteem Locus of control	Children of recovered alcoholics happier than FHP group. No statistically significant differences No statistically significant differences.
Chassin, Mann, & Sher (1988)	200 FHP and 747 FHN high-school students; 53.1% male; 97% white	Dispositional self-awareness	Self-awareness not significantly associated with family history of alcoholism.

138

Study	Sample	Measure	Results
Drejer, Theilgaard, Teasdale, Schulsinger, & Goodwin (1985)	134 FHP and 70 FHN males 18–19 years of age	Field dependence (EFT)	No statistically significant differences.
Finn, Martin, & Pihl (1987)	G-1: 12 FHP (multigenerational family history of alcoholism), G-2: 12 FHP (previous generation only), and G-3: 12 FHN nonalcoholic males; mean age, 24.3 years	Alexithymia	G-1 more alexithymic than G-2 and G-3.
Finn & Pihl (1987)	G-1: 12 FHP (multigenerational family history of alcoholism), G-2: 12 FHP (previous generation only), and G-3: 12 FHN nonalcoholic males; mean age, 23.9 years	Neuroticism Extraversion (EPI) Fear Distress Emotionality Activity Sociability (EAS; Buss & Plomin, 1984)	G-1 more neurotic than G-3. No statistically significant differences. No statistically significant differences. No statistically significant differences. G-2 more emotional than G-3. No statistically significant differences. No statistically significant differences.
Finn & Pihl (1989)	G-1: 10 FHP (multigenerational family history of alcoholism) and G-2: 10 FHP (previous generation only) nonalcoholic males; mean age, 24.1 years	Neuroticism Extraversion (EPI) Alexithymia	No statistically significant differences. No statistically significant differences. G-1 more alexithymic than G-2.
Franks & Thacker (1979)	15 FHP and 15 FHN chronic alcoholics	MMPI	All 30 had elevated scores for schizophrenia, extraversion, and depression; average intercorrelation among these three subscales significantly higher among FHPs ($r = .72$).

(continued)

139

TABLE 6.1. (Continued)

Study	Sample(s)	Personality trait measure	General finding
Hennecke (1984)	30 FHP and 30 FHN subjects 10–12 years of age	Stimulus augmenting	Incidence of stimulus augmenting higher in FHP group.
		Field dependence	No statistically significant differences.
Kern, Hassett, Collipp, Bridges, Solomon, & Condren (1981)	20 FHP and 20 FHN subjects 8–13 years of age	Locus of control	FHP group more externally oriented.
Knop, Teasdale, Schulsinger, & Goodwin (1985)	134 FHP and 70 FHN males 19–20 years of age	Impulsivity	FHP group more impulsive.
		Nervous anxiety	No statistically significant differences.
		Violent	No statistically significant differences.
		Independent	No statistically significant differences.
		Withdrawn (based on teacher ratings)	No statistically significant differences.
Mann, Chassin, & Sher (1987)	200 FHP and 750 FHN high-school students; 53.1% male; 97% white	Presumed personality risk (items from CPI socialization subscale and items from MMPI MAC)	FHP group higher on presumed personality risk.
Manning, Balson, & Xenakis (1986)	Study 1: 46 nonalcoholic mothers, FHP husband alcoholic, and 65 FHN matched controls	Type A	Greater impatience–aggression in FHP group.
	Study 2: 104 military fathers and 104 FHN controls	Type A (JAS)	No statistically significant differences.
	Study 3: 70 FHP and 70 FHN subjects	Type A	No statistically significant differences.

Study	Sample	Variables	Results
McKenna & Pickens (1983)	1,929 alcoholics in treatment; 1,411 males; 518 females	MMPI subscales	*Number* of alcoholic parents associated with elevated profiles; sociopathic tendencies higher and situational depression lower in relation to number of alcoholic parents; MAC scores *not* associated with number of alcoholic parents.
Morrison & Schuckit (1983)	25 FHP and 25 FHN male college students and nonacademic staff 21–25 years of age	Locus of control	No statistically significant differences.
Prewett, Spence, & Chaknis (1981)	15 FHP and 15 FHN subjects 7–12 years of age; 8 males, 7 females in each group	Locus of control	FHP group more externally oriented.
Saunders & Schuckit (1981)	30 FHP and 30 FHN males 20–25 years of age	MMPI subscales MAC (A Mac) Rosenberg (A Ros) Revised (A Rev)	Differences on only one A Mac subscale—FHP group lower in interpersonal competence.
Schuckit (1982)	30 FHP and 30 FHN male college students and nonacademic staff 21–25 years of age	Anxiety Assertiveness	No statistically significant differences for either trait.
Schuckit (1983)	32 FHP and 32 FHN male college students and nonacademic staff 21–25 years of age	Extraversion Neuroticism (EPI)	No statistically significant differences for either trait.
Schuckit & Penn (1985)	8 FHP and 8 FHN male college students and nonacademic staff 21–25 years of age	Field dependence (RFT)	No statistically significant differences.
Schulsinger, Knop, Goodwin, Teasdale, & Mikkelsen (1986)	134 FHP and 70 FHN males 19–20 years of age	Impulsivity (psychological interview)	FH group *somewhat* more impulsive ($p = .08$). *(continued)*

TABLE 6.1. (Continued)

Study	Sample(s)	Personality trait measure	General finding
Sher & McCrady (1984)	105 alcoholics in day treatment; 69 males, mean age, 38 years; 42 females, mean age, 40 years	MMPI MAC	MAC correlated with severity of alcohol abuse; subscale scores of school maladjustment for males and females, and extraversion exhibitionism for males associated with parental alcoholism.
Tarter, Hegedus, Winsten, & Alterman (1984)	16 FHP and 25 FHN white, male delinquents	Impulsivity (MFFT) MMPI (short form)	FHP group *less* impulsive. FHP group higher on subscales of hysteria, hypochondriasis, and depression, though not in pathological ranges.
Tarter, Jacob, Hill, Hegedus, & Carra (1986)	35 FHP, 31 FHN, and 27 sons of depressed fathers; average age, 13 years	Field dependence (RFT)	No statistically significant differences.
Werner (1986)	20 FHP *with* problems at age 18 (70% males) and 29 FHP *without* problems at age 18 (27.6% males)	CPI	FHP group *without* problems report a greater sense of well-being; more responsible, socialized, and caring; more self-controlled and a higher tolerance of individual differences; more achievement oriented and more intellectually efficient.
		Locus of control (both assessed in Grade 12)	No statistically significant differences.

Note. FHP, family history positive; FHN, family history negative; MAC, MacAndrew Alcoholism Scale; CPBCL, Childhood Problem Behavior Checklist; EFT, Embedded Figures Test; EPI, Eysenck Personality Inventory; EAS, Emotionality, Activity, Sociability Measure; MMPI, Minnesota Multiphasic Personality Inventory; CPI, California Personality Inventory; JAS, Jenkins Activity Scale; RFT, Rod-and-Frame Test; MFFT, Matching Familiar Figures Test.

Finn and Pihl used a three- rather than two-group design by forming two FHP groups, one with a family history of alcoholism in the previous generation only (unigenerational) and one with a family history of alcoholism in the previous and *preceding* generations (e.g., grandparents of COAs). This latter group was referred to as a multigenerational family history positive group. Comparisons between these two FHP groups and a FHN group for a measure of neuroticism indicated that the multigenerational FHP group, but not the unigenerational FHP group, was more neurotic than the FHN group. For the same sample, no statistically significant differences were found with regard to the variables of fear or distress; however, the unigenerational FHP subjects, but not the multi-generational ones, rated themselves higher than FHNs in emotionality. In sum, the evidence currently available is not very potent in supporting neuroticism as a personality attribute differentiating COAs from nonCOAs.

Positive Affective Attributes

Five studies have focused on personality differences between COAs and non-COAs with respect to components of positive affect. Callan and Jackson (1986) compared children's responses on self-esteem and perceived happiness for two FHP groups (one consisting of children of recovered alcoholic fathers and one consisting of children of nonrecovered alcoholic fathers) and one FHN group. Prior research has indicated that lower self-esteem is associated with alcoholism in both men and women, although the direction of the effect is not clear (e.g., Beckman, 1978; Cox, 1979). The three-group comparisons by Callan and Jackson indicated no statistically significant differences for self-esteem, though, not surprisingly, children of the recovered alcoholic fathers reported higher levels of happiness than children of the nonrecovered alcoholic fathers.

Three studies have assessed possible differences between COAs and non-COAs regarding the socially outgoing, gregarious personality attributes of extraversion, sociability, and activity level (Finn & Pihl, 1987, 1989; Schuckit, 1983). In none of the three studies, which included the multigenerational FHP group in the Finn and Pihl studies, did COAs differ significantly from nonCOAs. Additionally, Schuckit (1982) examined differences between COAs and non-COAs regarding the personality attribute of assertiveness. Some prior research has suggested that low assertiveness may be reflective of impaired social skills and/or low social competence, which may contribute to feelings of personal inadequacy and to a lack of social support to facilitate coping with stressful life events (e.g., Pentz, 1985). Schuckit (1982) reported no significant differences between COAs and nonCOAs on the assertiveness measure.

While meager support for the existence of premorbid personality differences among COAs and nonCOAs is provided in these five studies of positive affective attributes, it should be noted that such differences may be manifested after, rather than before chronic alcohol consumption. The research question then becomes whether COAs are more vulnerable than nonCOAs to lower self-esteem and depressed affect after chronic alcohol consumption, and whether the personality attributes of COAs are more state-susceptible to the influences of heavy alcohol consumption than those of nonCOAs. Keehn (1970) reported that alcoholics tend to rate themselves as more highly extraverted when drinking than when not drinking, suggesting a possible state-dependent relationship between alcohol consumption and extraverted behavior.

Cognitive–Perceptual Attributes

Five separate cognitive–perceptual personality attributes have been studied using the FHP–FHN research design. These personality attributes are referred to as cognitive–perceptual because they refer to characteristic ways of perceiving, remembering, and organizing information, and to subjective-reflection processes regarding the self. Consistent with the research literature pertaining to cognitive styles (e.g., Messick, 1969; Witkin, Karp, & Goodenough, 1959), individual differences in these cognitive–perceptual attributes are presumed to be relatively stable dispositions that influence the manner or form of cognition.

Four COA studies have been reported regarding *field independence* (FI) and *field dependence* (FD), the most widely researched cognitive style dimension in the psychological literature (Witkin & Goodenough, 1977). FI individuals tend to manifest better analytical abilities, are better able to restructure the perceptual field, and utilize a wider range of cognitive strategies in problem solving (Green, 1985). FD individuals tend to rely on global features of the perceptual field, have difficulties identifying hidden figures in an embedded context, and underutilize optimal cognitive strategies in problem solving. Research studies with alcoholic samples reviewed by Tarter (1975) indicated that field dependence was more characteristic of alcoholics, and it was suggested that the FD disposition may be an etiologic agent in the development of alcoholism (though the causal relations were ambiguous, because FD may have preceded or been the consequence of chronic alcohol consumption). In none of the four studies using the high-risk research design did the children of alcoholics score higher in the direction of field dependence; no statistically significant differences were found to reliably discriminate FHP and FHN subjects (Drejer, Theilgaard, Teasdale, Schulsinger, & Goodwin, 1985; Hennecke, 1984; Schuckit & Penn, 1985; Tarter, Jacob, Hill, Hegedus, & Carra, 1986). On the basis of these four studies, it appears unlikely that FD is a predisposing factor for the development of alcoholism, at least for COA samples within the early- to late-adolescent age range investigated in these studies.

Nevertheless, there are alternative explanations that need to be investigated further with regard to FD as a predisposing factor for alcoholism. For example, it is possible that the usefulness of FD as a marker for alcoholism may not be salient until the peak years of alcoholic risk (around age 35–43). It also has been proposed that the FI–FD attribute is highly associated with intelligence and is better viewed as a cognitive attribute than as a personality attribute (see Tarter, Laird, & Moss, Chapter 4, this volume, for a further discussion of cognitive variables). If viewed in this light, higher field dependence among alcoholics reported in the literature (e.g., Witkin et al., 1959) may be the consequence of prolonged alcohol consumption and may reflect neurotoxic central nervous system (CNS) effects caused by chronic ethanol ingestion (e.g., Ryan & Butters, 1983).

A second cognitive style investigated with COAs has referred to individual differences in the modulation of stimulus intensity, with the two poles of the cognitive style being *stimulus-intensity reduction* and *stimulus-intensity augmentation* (Petrie, 1967). According to Petrie, augmenters typically increase, amplify, or overestimate their perceptual experience, whereas reducers typically decrease, attenuate, or underestimate their perceptual experience. Some research has suggested that alcoholics often are stimulus-intensity augmenters, though the evidence is still limited (Barnes, 1983). In a study using the high-risk research design, Hennecke (1984) reported that stimulus-intensity augmenters were statistically more highly represented among a sample of FHP 10- to 12-year-olds than among a sample of FHN 10- to 12-year-olds. Thus, before alcohol consumption, COAs, more so than a matched group of nonCOAs, manifested a cognitive style that has shown some moderate associations with adult alcoholism. One might therefore theorize that stimulus-intensity augmenters are attracted to ethanol because of its disinhibiting effects on the CNS, which intensifies perceptual experience. The stimulus-intensity augmentation disposition may, therefore, influence parameters of drinking behavior (e.g., frequency, quantity) and the time-course and eventual outcome of drinking careers. Hennecke has suggested that further study be directed toward the interrelations between stimulus-intensity modulation and the influence of ethanol on the CNS.

A third cognitive attribute studied with the FHP–FHN research design is *dispositional self-awareness* (e.g., Chassin, Mann, & Sher, 1988). Dispositional self-awareness refers to individual differences in the cognitive monitoring of one's own behavior and ranges from low to high levels of self-awareness (Hull, 1981, 1987). Hull proposed that persons high in self-awareness who are receiving failure feedback tend to drink alcohol to reduce the negative self-referenced failure feedback. Alcohol consumption is, therefore, motivated by self-regulatory behavior on the part of the individual to avoid undesirable, painful states of self-awareness.

Chassin et al. (1988) investigated the interrelations among family history of alcohol abuse, dispositional self-awareness, alcohol consumption, and alcohol problems in a relatively large sample of high-school students. Family history of alcohol abuse was not significantly associated with dispositional self-awareness for the high-school students ($r = .02$), though both variables (i.e., family history of alcohol abuse and self-awareness) manifested significant "main effects" and a statistically significant interaction effect in the prediction of alcohol consumption and adverse consequences of alcohol consumption. While not supportive of high dispositional self-awareness as a premorbid alcoholic attribute among COAs, Chassin et al. interpreted the significant interaction effect as suggestive of a moderating role for dispositional self-awareness with regard to the relationship between family history of alcoholism and alcoholic outcome. More specifically, Chassin et al. proposed that high dispositional self-awareness may function as a protective factor (rather than as a vulnerability factor), moderating the relationship between family history of alcohol abuse and subsequent adult alcoholic outcome.

The research findings of Chassin et al. (1988) are important for two major reasons. First, they suggest that dispositional self-awareness may best be conceptualized as a moderator, rather than as a mediator, for the interrelation between family history of alcoholism and future alcoholic outcome. That is, dispositional self-awareness may moderate alcoholic outcome by interacting with family history of alcoholism rather than directly accounting for the interrelation between the two. Baron and Kenny (1986) have provided some useful conceptual and methodological distinctions for moderators amd mediators, ones that may be applied in future research for the role not only of dispositional self-awareness, but also of other personality and temperament attributes with regard to their effect on alcohol consumption and adverse consequences. It is possible through alternative conceptual approaches and statistical modeling techniques to analyze the influence of personality (and temperament) attributes on alcohol-related behaviors as direct effects, indirect effects, interaction effects, bidirectional effects, etc. Such alternative conceptualizations and statistical models may facilitate the specification and testing of more complex models regarding personality and alcohol-abuse relationships.

Second, the research findings of Chassin et al. (1988) identify dispositional self-awareness as a possible protective factor moderating the relationship between family history of alcoholism and alcohol abuse. Most of the emphasis in the alcoholism literature (of which the COA literature is a subset) has been on the identification of vulnerability factors. The identification of protective factors may be equally useful in understanding the heterogeneous developmental pathways toward and away from alcoholism and may provide a more balanced picture of individual outcomes. In addition, knowledge of protective factors may facilitate the design of prevention and intervention programs that seek to enhance or optimize specific protective factors (e.g., social competence).

The fourth cognitive–perceptual attribute that some researchers (e.g., Segal, Huba, & Singer, 1980) have referred to as a cognitive style dimension is *locus of control*. Locus of control refers to an individual's belief in the relative control one's personal actions have on environmental outcomes. Individuals who believe that environmental outcomes are attributable to fate, chance, or forces primarily beyond their control are characterized as exhibiting an external locus of control orientation. Individuals who believe that environmental outcomes are attributable, in large part, to their own actions and who view themselves as influential agents, are characterized as exibiting an internal locus of control orientation (Lefcourt, 1976; Rotter, 1966). Within the alcoholism literature, some studies have suggested that an external locus of control orientation is more highly associated with alcoholism. The psychodynamic processes involved suggest that individuals may consume large quantities of alcohol to compensate (or to regulate mood) for anxiety or depression associated with feelings of lack of control over environmental contingencies. Further, loss of control over drinking may be a specific instance of the generalized external locus of control orientation. While theoretically cogent, the empirical research on locus of control and alcoholism is inconsistent and questions have arisen regarding the generality versus specificity of the locus of control construct with regard to alcohol consumption and alcoholism (Barnes, 1983).

Four studies using the FHP–FHN research design have been conducted with the locus of control construct and, similar to the conclusions of Barnes (1983) regarding the general alcoholism literature, have produced contradictory findings. Callan and Jackson (1986) and Morrison and Schuckit (1983) reported no statistically significant differences between FHP and FHN samples on locus of control for early adolescents and young adults, respectively. However, with samples somewhat younger in age than those in the Callan and Jackson study, two studies have indicated that FHP children are more externally oriented than FHN children (Kern et al., 1981; Prewett, Spence, & Chaknis, 1981). A fifth study, by Werner (1986), investigated differences in locus of control for FHP adolescents *with* and *without* psychological problems at age 18. No statistically significant differences in locus of control were found between these two FHP groups. In sum, there is some evidence suggesting that COAs may have a predisposition toward an external locus of control orientation; however, the evidence at the current time is mixed and the strongest findings are for those comparisons among COAs who are the youngest in age. While limited to speculation because of the cross-sectional nature of the extant data, it is possible that the alcoholic family environments of COAs may undermine beliefs about locus of control in childhood, but that as the cognitive, social, and physical resources of children develop in adolescence and adulthood, and as the children engage more frequently in nonfamilial social contexts (e.g., school, work settings), generalized expectancies about locus of control may shift more toward that of the general population. Prospective research design studies are required to address more adequately the issues associated with locus of control, family history of alcoholism, and alcoholic outcomes.

A fifth cognitive–perceptual personality attribute that may be categorized as a cognitive style dimension in the broad sense intended in this section is *alexithymia,* which means "without words for moods or feelings" (Apfel & Sifneos, 1979). More specifically, persons described as manifesting alexithymia have difficulty expressing emotions, are deficient in fantasizing, think in concrete terms, typically use action rather than thinking as a coping style, and intrapsychically are characterized by repression and denial (Finn & Pihl, 1989).

Thus, in alexithymia there appears to be a high degree of incongruity (or lack of synchrony) between autonomic nervous system (ANS) functioning, corresponding cognitive states, and appropriate psychomotor responses (e.g., verbal articulation of emotional state). Most of the research on alexithymia has been conducted in psychosomatic medicine, with alexithymic persons typically manifesting more stress-related disorders (Martin & Pihl, 1985). With regard to alcoholics, Rybakowski, Ziolkowski, Zasadzka, and Brzezinski (1988) reported that 78 of 100 alcoholic male inpatients manifested an alexithymic personality pattern, a prevalence pattern that is higher than that reported for psychosomatic patients. Finn and Pihl (1987, 1989) also found that men with a multi-generational history of alcoholism tend to manifest higher levels of alexithymia than men with a unigenerational history of alcoholism or men who were FHN for alcoholism. Finn and Pihl (1987) also reported heightened cardiovascular reactivity for men with a multigenerational history of alcoholism. Given these two findings, Finn, Martin, and Pihl (1987) have proposed that high levels of alexithymia may predispose *some* individuals toward alcoholism because the ingestion of alcohol may reduce the heightened reactivity of the ANS. Thus, alexithymia may be associated with high ANS reactivity levels among men with multigenerational family histories of alcoholism, and heavy alcohol consumption may reduce and regulate the heightened levels of ANS activation.

The underlying conceptual model of Finn and Pihl (1987) regarding alexithymia and individual differences in ANS reactivity shares some features with research being conducted in other laboratories around the country. For example, research on the stress-dampening response of alcohol consumption by Levenson (1987) and Sher and Levenson (1982) has suggested individual differences in the reinforcing properties of ethanol on ANS reactivity levels. Thus, some subjects (e.g., COAs; aggressive, antisocial types) may be at increased risk for alcoholism because of the greater reinforcement that ethanol affords them in reducing stress-related ANS (hyper)activity. In a somewhat related vein, Kagan, Reznick, and Snidman (1986) have identified relatively stable patterns of cardiovascular reactivity among young children that are associated consistently with the temperament dimension of behavioral inhibition. Kagan et al. propose that the behavioral inhibition temperament dimension is related to aspects of cognitive and social development, with persistent manifestations of anxiety and fearfulness among those most behaviorally inhibited. Recent behavior genetic research (e.g., Carmelli, Chesney, Ward, & Rosenman, 1985; Ditto, 1987) also has indicated familial similarity of cardiovascular reactivity to stress for both twin and nontwin sibling pairs. The focus on individual differences in ANS reactivity levels, their origin, and their psychological and social significance for drinking behaviors, differential pathways to alcoholism, and to other emotional problems (e.g., neurotic disorders) is in the early phases of study but appears to be promising in integrating functioning at the biological and psychosocial levels.

With respect specifically to alexithymia, Sher (1987) has noted that the heightened ANS reactivity tendency of alexithymics to somatize is more characteristic of female than male offspring of alcoholics (e.g., Cloninger, Bohman, Sigvardsson, & von Knorring, 1985). However, Cloninger (1987) has noted that medical complications (e.g., cirrhosis and other liver problems) are common among a subset of male alcoholics (Type 1 milieu-limited). Given that no data were collected on females and that all subjects were nonalcoholic males in the studies of Finn and Pihl, it is not possible at this time to know the relative prevalence of this disposition among men and women in general, or among male and female alcoholics in particular. The sample sizes of the studies conducted by Finn and Pihl were small, the age ranges were restricted, and only nonalcoholic males were assessed. Future research on alexithymia will benefit by including larger, more representative samples covering a wider age range. In addition, more attention needs to be directed toward differences between uni- and multi-generational FHP samples in terms of prevalence, different developmental pathways, and probable adult outcomes.

Behavioral Undercontrol Attributes

A number of longitudinal studies have indicated an association between pre-alcoholic characteristics of aggression, risk taking, impulsivity, rebelliousness, nonconventionality, and subsequent adult alcohol abuse and alcoholism (e.g., Jones, 1968; Loper, Kammeier, & Hoffman, 1973; McCord & McCord, 1960; Robins, 1986; Vaillant, 1983). On the basis of these longitudinal findings, several studies have investigated possible differences between COAs and non-COAs with respect to these attributes, which I refer to collectively as behavioral undercontrolling attributes. Most of these COA studies have used the Minnesota Multiphasic Personality Inventory (MMPI) and have analyzed differences with respect to elevations of specific subscales, or they have used the MacAndrew Alcoholism Scale (MAC; MacAndrew, 1965), a derived subscale of the MMPI that measures features of aggression, risk taking, and extraversion. The MAC has been found to correlate with alcohol abuse and in most of these COA studies mean level comparisons were made for FHP and FHN subjects (e.g., Graham & Strenger, 1988; Preng & Clopton, 1986).

In general, the results of COA studies using the MMPI and the MAC have suggested that FHP subjects differ from FHN subjects on several subscale scores, though there are some findings to the contrary. With an alcoholic treatment sample, Sher and McCrady (1984) reported that (1) the MAC correlated significantly with severity of alcohol abuse, (2) the MMPI subscale scores of school maladjustment differed for men and women, and (3) extraversion/exhibitionism for men was associated with parental alcoholism. With a large high-school sample, Mann, Chassin, and Sher (1987) reported that FHP adolescents scored higher on a dimension they referred to as "presumed personality risk." Presumed personality risk scores were derived from items of the MAC and items from the California Personality Inventory socialization subscale, with both sets of items keyed to aggressive, impulsive, antisocial activity. Saunders and Schuckit (1981) also analyzed possible COA and nonCOA differences on the MMPI and MAC for nonalcoholic young adult males. They found that FHP subjects differed only on the MAC subscale of interpersonal competence, with FHP subjects scoring lower than FHN subjects.

Evidence not supporting these general findings for relationships between family history of alcoholism and MMPI and MAC subscale scores also have been reported. Alterman et al. (1986) and Alterman, Searles, and Hall (1989) reported no statistically significant differences for FHP and FHN college males on the MAC; however, in the 1986 study FHP subjects did report engaging in more antisocial activities (e.g., lying, stealing, running away from home, fighting) than FHN subjects. McKenna and Pickens (1983) studied more than 1,900 alcoholics in treatment and found that the MAC was not associated with the number of alcoholic parents. The number of alcoholic parents was, however, associated with MMPI subscale scores reflecting sociopathic tendencies and situational depression. Similarly, with a sample of male delinquents, Tarter, Hegedus, Winsten, and Alterman (1984) reported that FHP subjects have elevated subscale scores on hysteria, hypochondriasis, and depression, although none of these scores were in the pathological range. Franks and Thacker (1979) found that *both* FHP and FHN chronic alcoholics had elevated MMPI subscale scores on schizophrenia, extraversion, and depression, though the average intercorrelation among these three subscale scores was significantly higher ($r = .72$) among FHP subjects.

Although suggesting some possible differences between COAs and non-COAs on MMPI subscale scores and on the MAC, the last five studies cited raise questions regarding the generality of relationships between MMPI subscale scores and family history of alcoholism. Furthermore, given the longitudinal research findings cited earlier (e.g., Jones, 1968; Loper et al., 1973; Vaillant 1983), one might expect at least somewhat elevated scores on the psychopathic deviate subscale of the MMPI for COAs. Future COA research with the MMPI (and the MAC) will need to be conducted to resolve contradictory findings and to substantiate further the utility of the measure as a useful identifier of prealcoholic characteristics for the population in general, and for COAs in particular. Graham and Strenger (1988) have offered several suggestions for future alcoholic studies with the MMPI, including identification of subtypes of alcoholics based on MMPI subscale scores; such alternative approaches may be used as well with COAs to identify discriminable patterns that may be associated with adult outcomes such as alcoholism or antisocial personality disorder.

A limited number of additional, non-MMPI-based personality research studies concerned with behavioral undercontrol among COAs have been conducted with reference to impulsivity. On the basis of data collected from a Danish longitudinal study, teachers in a blinded study rated FHP subjects as more impulsive than FHN subjects (Knop et al., 1985). With the same data set, but on the basis of a psychological interview rather than the teacher ratings, FHP subjects tended to be rated somewhat more impulsive than FHN subjects, though the difference was not statistically significant (Schulsinger, Knop, Goodwin, Teasdale, & Mikkelsen, 1986). With a sample of white, male delinquents, Tarter, Hegedus, Winsten, and Alterman (1984) reported that FHN subjects were *more* impulsive than FHP subjects, though as suggested by Sher (1987), delinquency and impulsivity are highly intercorrelated among delinquents and this intercorrelation may negate or attenuate group differences in family history of alcoholism.

On the basis of the COA literature, it is difficult to draw any solid conclusions on behavioral undercontrol attributes as predisposing personality factors associated with family history of alcoholism. Clearly the findings of some family history of alcoholism studies (e.g., Knop et al., 1985; Mann et al., 1987; Sher & McCrady, 1984) are supportive, and considered in conjunction with previous longitudinal studies in the alcoholism literature (e.g., Jones, 1968; McCord & McCord, 1960; Robins, 1966) are likely to stimulate additional research pertinent to behavioral undercontrol attributes. However, in addition to several more methodologically oriented issues to be discussed later in the evaluation section (e.g., nonrepresentative samples, few longitudinal research designs), there are a number of conceptual issues that need to be addressed in clarifying what is intended by behavioral undercontrol attributes. Behavioral undercontrol has become an umbrella term for psychological constructs such as impulsivity, aggression, inattention, hyperactivity, antisocial behavior, delinquent activity, deviance proneness, and problem behavior. Many of these terms reference quite different psychological and behavioral constructs, have different antecedents, correlates, and consequences, have different implications both legally and with respect to psychiatric diagnoses, and take on different psychological meanings at different times in the lifespan. For example, Buss and Plomin (1984) and others (e.g., Schalling & Asberg, 1985) have indicated that impulsivity, in and of itself, is a multidimensional construct that includes components such as inhibitory behavioral control (e.g., delay of gratification), rapid decision making, high distractibility, and monotony avoidance.

Similarly, Block and Gjerde (1986) provided some clarity and distinctions between undercontrolling behavioral styles and antisocial behavior. Block and Gjerde have proposed that

> By viewing an antisocial disposition largely in terms of insufficient impulse control, important psychological insights regarding different kinds of antisocial behavior may be lost. Conceiving of antisocial behavior in broader terms, involving rejection or unawareness of the social contract, inability to empathize with unfortunate others, and an absence of inhibitions regarding the manipulation and exploitation of others, one can readily see how an individual—antisocial in this latter way—could well have sufficient ability to modulate impulse. (pp. 179–180)

Block and Gjerde proceed to cite research literature (e.g., Megargee, 1966) that suggests that extremely violent criminals manifest a more controlled personal style than either nonassaultive criminals or normal individuals. The authors also reported on a longitudinal study with data they had collected that indicated that antisocial behavior, and not an undercontrolling personality style, predicts illegal substance use. The two key features of antisocial behavior involved in the prediction of illegal substance use were a lack of empathy and poor interpersonal relations.

It would be beneficial to state explicitly the nature of the relationship between items (or manifest indicators) and psychological constructs. Listings of problem behavior (e.g., substance use, poor grades, precocious sexual activity) are used frequently to refer to personality characteristics of behavioral undercontrol (e.g., deviance proneness). Two problems can arise with this approach. The first concerns tautological reasoning that suggests persons are deviance prone because they are abusing alcohol and that they are abusing alcohol because they are deviance prone. This presents formidable problems for the personality researcher who seeks to describe stable personality dispositions of those adolescents (the majority) who "mature out" of the problem behaviors of adolescence. Second is the pressing question of whether a range of aberrant behaviors or antisocial activities should be referred to as reflecting a personality construct. Nathan (1988) presented six characteristics (internal, unique, enduring, active, causal, and integrating) frequently used to describe personality attributes and argued that *antisocial behavior,* and not *antisocial personality,* is often identified as an antecedent to alcoholism. Clearly this sort of critical analysis is consonant with the arguments of Block and Gjerde (1986) regarding the need for clarity of measured constructs. In pursuing research on the interrelations between behavioral undercontrol attributes and alcoholism, and with respect to possible differences in family history of alcoholism, it is necessary to do some fine tuning regarding the conceptualization of psychological constructs. Such conceptual fine tuning needs to go hand-in-hand with measures developed to reflect the proposed constructs. Through such efforts, the probability of attaining stable, replicable research findings is likely to be greatly enhanced.

Residual Category of Personality Attributes

In addition to the personality attributes categorized above into four domains, several other personality attributes have been studied using the FHP–FHN research design. Manning, Balson, and Xenakis (1986) investigated the prevalence of the Type A personality pattern among COAs. The Type A personality pattern, which has been associated with increased risk for coronary heart disease (e.g., Friedman & Rosenman, 1974), is characterized by extreme competitiveness, a sense of time urgency, impatience, aggression, and a low threshold for hostility. On the basis of clinical reports (rather than empirical studies), Manning et al. noted a consistent theme that suggested the Type A behavior pattern was a characteristic response of some COAs to parental alcoholism. More specifically, Woititz (1977) suggested that some COAs tend to develop an overreactive response style to uncontrollable changes in the environment (e.g., some behaviors of alcoholic parents). Thus, the development of the Type A personality pattern among COAs was presumed to reflect a reactive, maladaptive response to uncontrollable and unpleasurable stressful life events associated with parental alcoholism.

Manning et al. (1986) reported the results of three studies examining possible differences between COAs (FHP) and nonCOAs (FHN). Self-reports and parental ratings were used as methods of measurement and the scales were representative of those used in the Type A research literature (e.g., the Jenkins Activity Survey). Overall, the three studies did not lend support to the notion of a higher prevalence of Type A personalities among COAs. Rather, the FHP and FHN subjects tended to manifest highly similar prevalence rates.

Sensation seeking is a second personality attribute studied with the FHP–FHN research design. Sensation-seeking personalities are characterized by a disposition toward thrill seeking, searching for novelty, high external stimulation, and exhilarating and varied nonconventional activities (Zuckerman, 1979). Sensation seeking has been shown to be correlated with alcohol and drug use and abuse, though not with alcoholism (e.g., Zuckerman, 1979). Researchers have often characterized this personality attribute under the rubric of behavioral undercontrol. However, most of the undercontrolled behaviors do, by definition, involve deviant or problematic behavior. There is nothing intrinsic in sensation-seeking behavior that *necessarily* leads to deviance; in fact, most of the non-drug-related items on the sensation-seeking scale (Zuckerman, 1978) reflect a preference for exhilarating activities (e.g., parachute jumping) rather than deviant acts. In one study with a sample of college males, Alterman et al. (1986) found that FHP subjects manifested higher levels of sensation seeking than FHN subjects; however, a replication study indicated no group differences on sensation seeking for FHP and FHN samples (Alterman et al., 1989). Additional research needs to be conducted to resolve these contradictory findings and to see if higher sensation-seeking scores of FHPs (should they exist) facilitate the prediction of adult alcoholism. Prospective research designs will facilitate such efforts and properly designed studies may reveal the direct and indirect roles sensation seeking may play in the development of alcoholism.

ADULT COEXISTING DISORDERS

In addition to research conducted on temperament and personality attributes among COAs, a third research area of relevance pertains to adult alcoholic typological approaches, some of which refer to the cooccurrence or coexistence of psychiatric disorders (e.g., Alterman & Tarter, 1986; Cloninger et al., 1985;

Hesselbrock, 1986; Penick et al., 1984, Zucker, 1987). Although there are differences in the conceptualization and measurement of continuous tempera- ment and personality attributes (the principal focus of this chapter) and of discrete psychiatric diagnostic entities (e.g., clinical depression), for purposes of completeness a sampling of the psychiatric diagnostic research is provided below. Furthermore, this research is of relevance to the study of alcoholism among high-risk groups such as COAs. The sampling of typological research is limited to that of Cloninger and colleagues (Cloninger, 1987; Cloninger et al., 1985) and to Zucker (1987), with no intent to minimize the contributions of others (e.g., Alterman & Tarter, 1986; Hesselbrock, 1986; Penick et al., 1984).

Cloninger and colleagues (Cloninger, 1987; Cloninger et al., 1985) have used data from a Swedish adoptee study to develop, among other contributions, distinguishing characteristics of two types of alcoholism. The first type, referred to as Type 1, or milieu-limited, is characterized by the onset of alcohol problems *after* age 25, infrequent fighting and arrests when drinking, frequent psycholog- ical dependence (loss of control over drinking), heightened guilt and fear about alcohol dependence, and a family history of adult-onset paternal alcoholism *not* characterized by antisocial behavior or criminal activity. The second type, referred to as Type 2, or male-limited, is characterized by the onset of alcohol problems *before* age 25, frequent fighting and arrests when drinking, infrequent psychological dependence, infrequent guilt and fear about alcohol dependence, and a family history of paternal alcoholism *and* antisocial activity, in some instances criminal activity.

Thus, the research of Cloninger et al. (1985) suggests two rather distinct etiologic pathways to alcoholism that are contingent on age of problem onset, amount of antisocial behavior, degree of psychological dependency and guilt feelings, and parental history of alcoholism and antisocial activity. Further, the adoptee research design has permitted Cloninger et al. (1985) to investigate additive and interactive genetic and environmental influences with respect to alcoholism (see Searles, Chapter 5, this volume, for a more detailed discussion of behavior genetic studies). However, of particular interest to this chapter is Cloninger's (1987) neurobiological personality theory and the relationship of the proposed personality traits to milieu-limited and male-limited alcoholic types.

Cloninger (1987) proposes a tridimensional model of personality function- ing, with a brain system and primary monoamine neuromodulator (e.g., dopa- mine, serotonin, norepinephrine) associated with each personality dimension. The three personality dimensions and associated brain systems are (1) novelty seeking—behavioral activation, (2) harm avoidance—behavioral inhibition, and (3) reward dependence—behavioral maintenance. Although other personality researchers (e.g., Eysenck, 1967; Gray, 1981; Zuckerman, 1979) have proposed neurobiological approaches, Cloninger's approach is unique in that it suggests that variations in these three personality traits underlie milieu-limited and male- limited alcoholic types. More specifically, Cloninger posits that the prototypic personality pattern of milieu-limited alcoholics is one of low novelty seeking, high harm avoidance, and high reward dependence. This translates into a personality pattern characterized by (1) emotional dependency, heightened sentimentality, amd a high sensitivity to social cues (attributes of high reward dependence); (2) apprehensiveness, pessimism, inhibition, and shyness (attributes of high harm avoidance); and (3) rigidity, orderliness, and high attention to detail (attributes of low novelty seeking). Collectively, this personality profile may be characterized as passive-dependent or neurotic.

The prototypic personality pattern of male-limited alcoholics is one of high novelty seeking, low harm avoidance, and low reward dependence. Male-limited alcoholics display a personality pattern of (1) high impulsivity, high excitability, disorderliness, and distractibility (attributes of high novelty seeking); (2) confidence, relaxation, optimism, uninhibition, and carefreeness (attributes of low harm avoidance); (3) social detachment, emotional coolness, tough-mindedness, and independence (attributes of low-reward dependence). Collectively, this personality profile corresponds to an antisocial alcoholism type.

Cloninger's (1987) tridimensional theory offers a coherent and integrated approach to the study of relationships between neurobiologically based, heritable personality traits and the differential expression of alcoholism. Future COA and high-risk research will need to investigate further the internal features of the theory (e.g., the adequacy of the hypothesized brain–behavior relations), familial transmission mechanisms, and the strength of the two personality profiles to predict specific types of alcoholism.

Whereas Cloninger (1987) has posed two alcoholic types, Zucker (1987) has compiled, analyzed, and integrated a range of typological studies, including Cloninger's, and has suggested that current evidence merits the consideration of four alcoholic types. One type is referred to as *antisocial alcoholism;* its etiologic process parallels salient features of the male-limited type described by Cloninger et al. (1985) and others (e.g., Lewis, Rice, & Helzer, 1983; Penick et al., 1984), except that here women can also be classified as antisocial alcoholics. A second type is referred to as *developmentally cumulative alcoholism,* characterized by relatively continuous heavy drinking from adolescence onward. This form of alcoholism is observed in both males and females and, while there are some deleterious social consequences (e.g., career and marital difficulties), serious antisocial behavior and criminal activity are much less frequent than for antisocial alcoholics. A third type is referred to as *developmentally limited alcoholism,* characterized by a pattern of frequent, heavy drinking during early adulthood. However, a reduction in alcohol consumption levels characterizes this pattern as these persons marry, establish a more stable life structure, and adopt adult social roles (e.g., husband, wife, mother, father, family financial provider). A fourth type is referred to as *negative affect alcoholism* and is more common among females than males. A family history of unipolar affective disorder is implicated as one of the etiologic agents in this type of alcoholism, and heavy alcohol consumption is presumably related to coping with or enhancing close interpersonal relationships.

Zucker (1987) cites a number of research studies in support of the four alcoholic types and the reader is referred to this contribution for further information. There are, however, a few general points to be made about the typological approach used by Zucker (and others) and its implications for COA and high-risk research. First, the typological approach of Zucker suggests that there are multiple etiologic pathways to alcoholism. Further, specific personality attributes such as depressed affect and antisocial personality behaviors may influence the time course and specific form of the alcoholism expressed. Genetic, environmental, and gene×environment interactions and correlations of COAs and other high-risk groups regarding these personality attributes and alcoholic manifestations may thus be an area worthy of future study. Second, a family history of unipolar affective disorder was implicated for the negative affect alcoholism type, suggesting that other forms of parental psychopathology may be influential in specific types of alcoholism. Finn, Kleinman, and Pihl (1988) have also provided data that suggest that family history of alcoholism is predictive of other nonalcoholic psychiatric disorders. Third, the typology of Zucker emphasizes the possible differential pathways to alcoholisms for men and women. Robins (1986) has further supported this position with regard to conduct disordered behaviors and has discussed socialization differences between men and women that may influence both antecedent and consequent conditions. Using data from the Epidemiologic Catchment Area Survey, Helzer and Pryzbeck (1988) reported some tantalizing findings regarding sex differences in the sequence of lifetime alcoholism and clinical depression. For men, alcoholism preceded the onset of depression in 78% of the cases where both disorders were reported to have occurred. For women, depression preceded the onset of alcoholism in 66% of the cases where both disorders were reported. Further, for both men and women, alcoholism was less severe if depression preceded alcoholism, rather than alcoholism preceding depression.

The typological approach offers one vehicle for exploring the heterogeneity of alcoholisms. By examining commonalities and differences in alternative developmental pathways to alcoholism, it may be possible to more specifically identify the ways in which risk factors, for example being the child of an alcoholic, are expressed and modified by personality attributes and a range of life conditions.

CRITIQUE AND FUTURE DIRECTIONS

In evaluating the range of COA research pertaining to temperament and personality, three major areas are considered: (1) specific criticisms of COA personality studies using the FHP–FHN research design, (2) conceptually restricted models of temperament and personality, and (3) limited use of prospective research designs and the underutilization of multivariate statistical models. These three areas are interconnected and, considered collectively, converge on a common theme that suggests a need for a multivariate conceptualization of the possible effects of temperament and personality on alcoholic behavior and, conversely, of alcoholic behavior on temperament and personality.

FHP–FHN Personality Studies

Although 27 personality studies using the FHP–FHN research design were summarized in Table 6.1, there are a number of limitations that restrict the generalizability of the findings. Three specific problems pertain to sampling issues. First, the sample size in a large number of the studies was small, thus limiting the power to detect statistically significant differences between FHP and FHN groups. In more than half of the personality studies, fewer than 30 subjects were in each of the two family history groups. Relatively potent group differences would need to exist in order to detect statistically significant differences between groups with samples of fewer than 30 subjects per group. Second, the samples usually were unrepresentative, consisting of college students, children of nonacademic staff members at universities, delinquents, and chronic alcoholics. With respect to college student samples, representativeness issues may be especially acute with regard to COAs, because poorer school performance and academic difficulties (e.g., Knop et al., 1985; Miller & Jang, 1977) may reduce their representation in college settings. Third, the age range selected for group comparisons may not be optimal for assessing alcoholic drinking patterns, which for many alcoholics appear at an age later than that typically associated with college attendance.

Additional difficulties arise in generalizing these personality findings using the FHP–FHN research design because different measurement techniques were used to define family history categorization. A positive family history of alcoholism could have resulted from a single question, "Did either of your parents have a drinking problem?," from the use of diagnostic criteria for parental alcoholism (with or without collateral support), or from medical records of those with a history of alcoholic treatment. Further, estimates based on medical records are biased because only 10%–15% of alcoholics are "selected" into treatment. Variations in the criteria to define family history groups, biased samples, and small sample size may contribute to the unreliability of the findings.

The sample of personality measures and the method of measurement also have been restricted in these FHP–FHN studies. With regard to personality measures, there has been a tendency to use only a few of the many available multidimensional standardized personality measures or to create composite scores without proper psychometric scale development. While there are clear advantages in using identical measures in different studies for purposes of replication and comparability, it is equally important to determine whether group differences or similarities are generalizable beyond a given test to the *construct* being assessed. That is, are the results attributable to differences or similarities in the construct, or to differences or similarities that are test-specific? In addition, the research on temperament and personality attributes in recently formulated etiologic theories of alcoholism (e.g., Cloninger, 1987; Tarter et al., 1985) has yet to be sufficiently evaluated. With regard to method of measurement, all studies were conducted using self-report measures without collaterals. Whereas collateral informants are increasingly being used in studies to support validity claims regarding drinking behavior, this approach is little used in the alcoholism research to support personality claims of subjects. Further, with some notable exceptions (e.g., Finn & Pihl, 1987; Levenson, 1987; Sher & Levenson, 1982), other methods of measuring personality, such as physiological measures and behavioral observation techniques, have been used infrequently.

Conceptually Restricted Models of Temperament and Personality

The dominant conceptual model of the relationship between temperament and personality attributes and alcoholism in the COA literature (and in the alcoholism literature in general) has been essentially a premorbid trait model. The research focus has been on the identification of temperament and personality factors that are most highly associated with the subsequent expression of alcoholism. In general, this conceptual approach has assumed that temperament and personality attributes are biologically based (often heritable), relatively stable across situations and time, and capable of respectable levels of prediction of alcoholism *without* the inclusion of other variables.

An alternative model may be more useful in the description, explanation, and prediction of alcoholic behavior among COAs and others, specifically a reciprocally interactive (transactional) model of temperament and personality development. Space constraints limit a comprehensive articulation of such a transactional model (see Windle & Searles, Chapter 9, this volume), but several key features are noted here. For purposes of comparison with the assumptions of the premorbid trait model, the transactional model assumes that temperament and personality attributes are coherent, dispositional features of human behavior *typically* associated with emotional (versus intellectual) functioning. As in the premorbid trait model, there is a presumed biological basis of the attributes. However, in the premorbid trait model, the biological basis is often assumed to underlie and to be the *cause of* the stability of temperament and personality attributes; for the proposed transactional model, there are presumed biological processes associated with temperament and personality attributes, but these processes are not necessarily assumed to be the cause of stability (or change, for that matter). Rather, the stability and change (or continuity and discontinuity) of temperament and personality behavior is attributable to the biopsychosocial conditions and reciprocal exchange processes that foster alternative developmental trajectories. Further, if the temperament and personality attributes are heritable, then this is a population characteristic of the attribute, but this characteristic of the attribute ensures neither the stability of the genotype or phenotype (because these may systematically change over time) nor the stability of the behavior (for which heritability is not a requirement). Angoff (1988) has noted that there are many instances in which heritable traits manifest nonstable phenotypic patterns and many instances in which nonheritable, environmentally influenced behaviors are resistant to change. As such, the research question associated with the stability and change of temperament and personality attributes is not one of either–or (that is, of whether temperament is stable or not), but rather of the specification of conditions that contribute to such behavior patterns.

In contrast to the causal linear-sequence approach posed by the premorbid trait model, a transactional model assumes that behaviors are bidirectionally influenced and may change over time. Thus, temperament and personality attributes may be influential in initial tendencies to drink alcohol, but many other factors, including the influence of ethanol on biological systems (e.g., alcohol sensitivity) and persistent environmental stressors, may influence consumption patterns, which may in turn influence the overt expression of temperament and personality attributes. Again, the research question becomes one of identifying not the single causal sequence relating temperament and personality to alcohol consumption, but rather the conditions under which various patterns occur and for what attributes.

In addition, given that a transactional model assumes reciprocally interactive exchange processes, a multivariate, rather than a univariate research approach is adopted. That is, other salient variables in addition to temperament and personality attributes are assumed to influence complex behaviors associated with alcohol abuse and alcoholism. Temperament and personality attributes may be conceptualized more flexibly (and tested statistically) as direct effects, indirect effects, moderators, mediators, etc. To provide but a few examples, temperament and personality attributes may influence coping styles, stressful life events, psychiatric status, positive and negative affect, parent and peer relationships, and job skills—all of which may be related directly or indirectly to patterns of alcohol use and abuse.

Research Designs and Statistical Models

Few of the studies conducted with COAs have used prospective research designs. This, of course, limits the power and specificity of conclusions regarding the influences of being a child of an alcoholic. While the usefulness of prospective research designs has been cited in numerous sources (e.g., Goodwin, van Dusen, & Mednick, 1984; Zucker & Gomberg, 1986), two sampling issues should be highlighted that have an important bearing on the planning and conduct of future research with COAs. Neither of these sampling issues pertains to sampling strategies associated with person representativeness, because issues associated with this problem were discussed briefly earlier (e.g., the representativeness of college samples).

The first sampling issue pertains to an adequate sampling of factors that, if not measured, can confound resulting research findings. In particular, much of the existing research on COAs has not adequately accounted for alternative, so-called third-variable influences that can create spurious correlations between childhood status variables (e.g., being a COA) and subsequent outcomes (e.g., alcoholism). This issue is of particular importance in COA research to discriminate among those common and unique factors (genetic and/or environmental) associated with being children of alcoholics versus children with parents who divorce, versus children with affectively disordered parents, versus children who are physically abused, etc. Given that most of the existing research suggests complex, differential, and multidetermined outcomes among COAs, it is of importance to identify the factors that are most prominent in predicting alcoholism and to target prevention and intervention accordingly.

The second sampling issue pertains to the age range selected for COA studies. Many of the COA studies reviewed in the personality section used college students. In addition to the (person) sample representativeness problems, more systematic thought needs to be given to *when* (i.e., at what age) we would expect to observe differences on *what* variables. Empirical studies on COAs are increasing and the analysis, evaluation, and integration of research findings may provide conditions for more theory-driven formulations for assessing the influences of being a COA. The central point here is that it is as important in terms of etiologic theories or prevention/intervention strategies to sample appropriate follow-up periods for presumed effects as it is to sample persons or other variables.

With a few exceptions, statistical models used to analyze COA data have been limited to univariate analyses of variance (ANOVAs) or to bivariate measures of association (e.g., Pearson correlations). These statistical procedures are warranted for the establishment of bivariate relations between variables and to test hypotheses within the limitations of an ANOVA framework. However, even though COA research is in its nascent stage of development, complex hypotheses and statistical relations are emerging that support a multifactorial representation. Furthermore, recommendations are increasingly being forwarded to conduct longitudinal research, of which many applications require more sophisticated statistical models. Covariance structure models, which include path analytic models, confirmatory factor analytic models, and latent variable models are likely to be used more frequently by COA researchers (e.g., Bentler, 1980; Jöreskog & Sörbom, 1984). A survey of other approaches to statistical modeling, hypothesis testing, and model fit evaluation are provided by Nesselroade and Cattell (1987). In order to test statistically the complex hypotheses that are being proposed in COA research, it will be necessary to use correspondingly more complex statistical models.

SUMMARY

Empirical research was reviewed for children of alcoholics with regard to possible differences in temperament and personality functioning between COAs and nonCOAs. Some of the initial research in the childhood temperament literature indicated that parental alcoholism was associated with offspring hyperactivity, which in turn was associated with eventual alcohol abuse or alcoholism in the offspring. Subsequent research suggested much more specificity in terms of the relationship between parental psychiatric status and offspring childhood and adult psychiatric status. More specifically, paternal alcoholism, antisocial behavior, and criminal activity were associated with male offspring childhood undersocialized aggression, which in turn was associated with adult offspring alcoholism, antisocial behavior, and criminal activity.

Twenty-seven studies using the family history research design (i.e., family history positive or negative for alcoholism) were reviewed regarding possible personality differences. In many studies, no statistically significant differences were found. However, a large number of these studies were plagued by shortcomings such as small sample size, limited representativeness of sample, and restricted age ranges that may not correspond to the expression of some types of alcoholism. Three personality domains where some significant group differences were found were locus of control, alexithymia, and behavioral undercontrol. There was some tendency for early adolescent COAs to report a more external locus of control orientation than nonCOAs. There was also some suggestive evidence that COAs may be more alexithymic, that is, they may manifest a behavioral style characterized by heightened cardiovascular arousal and asynchrony of cognitive, emotional, and psychomotor systems. Finally, there was mixed support for COAs displaying a personality style of behavioral undercontrol (e.g., impulsivity, antisocial behavior, distractibility). In the case of behavioral undercontrol, it was suggested that future research focus on conceptual clarity in defining and measuring constructs under the rubric of behavioral undercontrol.

Some research from the adult alcoholism literature was reviewed and related to COA research. More specifically, research by Cloninger and associates (Cloninger et al., 1985) regarding Type 1 (milieu-limited) and Type 2 (male-limited) alcoholics was cited briefly, and Cloninger's (1987) tridimensional personality theory and its implications for COA research were presented. Zucker's (1987) typological approach was outlined to provide a sense of the range of alcoholic patterns currently being considered, with the possibility that COAs may have some representation in each of these alcoholic types.

A critical evaluation of COA research on temperament and personality identified several limitations. In brief, there have been problems regarding the sampling of persons, variables, and measurement occasions. Further, the conceptual model typically has been one principally concerned with the identification of premorbid temperament and personality attributes. An alternative, reciprocally interactive transactional model was proposed as more useful in delineating multivariate patterns of continuity and discontinuity with respect to temperament, personality, and alcohol variables. A final recommendation was made to use multivariate statistical models to correspond with the multifactorial etiologic models evolving in the alcoholism literature.

REFERENCES

Alterman, A. I., Bridges, K. R., & Tarter, R. E. (1986). Drinking behavior of high risk college men: Contradictory preliminary findings. *Alcoholism: Clinical and Experimental Research, 10,* 305–310.

Alterman, A. I., Petrarulo, E., Tarter, R. E., & McCowan, J. (1982). Hyperactivity and alcoholism: Familial and behavioral correlates. *Addictive Behavior, 7,* 413–421.

Alterman, A. I., Searles, J. S., & Hall, J. G. (1989). Failure to find differences in drinking behavior as a function of familial risk for alcoholism: A replication. *Journal of Abnormal Psychology, 98,* 1–4.

Alterman, A. I., & Tarter, R. E. (1986). An examination of selected typologies. In M. Galanter (Ed.), *Recent developments in alcoholism* (Vol. 4, pp. 169–189). New York: Plenum Press.

American Psychiatric Association. (1987). *Diagnostic and statistical manual of mental disorders* (3rd ed., rev.). Washington, DC: Author.

Angoff, W. H. (1988). The nature–nurture debate, aptitudes, and group differences. *American Psychologist, 43,* 713–720.

Apfel, R. J., & Sifneos, P. E. (1978). Alexithymia: Concept and measurement. *Psychotherapy and Psychosomatics, 32,* 180–190.

August, G. J., Stewart, M. A., & Holmes, C. S. (1983). A four-year follow-up of hyperactive boys with and without conduct disorder. *British Journal of Psychiatry, 143,* 192–198.

Barnes, G. E. (1979). The alcoholic personality: A reanalysis of the literature. *Journal of Studies on Alcohol, 40,* 571–634.

Barnes, G. E. (1983). Clinical and personality characteristics. In B. Kissin & H. Begleiter (Eds.), *The pathogenesis of alcoholism: Psychosocial factors* (Vol. 6, pp. 113–196). New York: Plenum Press.

Baron, R. M., & Kenny, D. A. (1986). The moderator–mediator variable distinction in social psychological research: Conceptual, strategic, and statistical considerations, *Journal of Personality and Social Psychology, 51,* 1173–1182.

Beckman, L. J. (1978). Self-esteem of women alcoholics. *Journal of Studies on Alcohol, 39,* 491–498.

Bentler, P. M. (1980). Multivariate analysis with latent variables: Causal modeling. *Annual Review of Psychology, 31,* 419–456.

Berkowitz, A., & Perkins, H. W. (1988). Personality characteristics of children of alcoholics. *Journal of Consulting and Clinical Psychology, 56,* 206–209.

Blane, H. T. (1968). *The personality of the alcoholic: Guises of dependency.* New York: Harper.

Block, J., & Gjerde, P. F. (1986). Distinguishing between antisocial behavior and undercontrol. In D. Olweus, J. Block, & M. Radke-Yarrow (Eds.), *Development of antisocial and prosocial behavior* (pp. 177–206). New York: Academic Press.

Blouin, A., Bornstein, R., & Trites, R. (1978). Teenage alcohol use among hyperactive children: A five-year follow-up study. *Journal of Pediatric Psychology, 3,* 188–194.

Buss, A. H., & Plomin, R. (1984). *Temperament: Early developing personality traits.* Hillsdale, NJ: Erlbaum.

Callan, V. J., & Jackson, D. (1986). Children of alcoholic fathers and recovered alcoholic fathers: Personal and family functioning. *Journal of Studies on Alcohol, 47,* 180–182.

Cantwell, D. P. (1972). Psychiatric illness in the families of hyperactive children. *Archives of General Psychiatry, 27,* 414–417.

Cantwell, D. P. (1975). Genetic studies of hyperactive children: Psychiatric illness in biological and adopting parents. In R. R. Fieve, D. Rosenthal, & H. Brill (Eds.), *Genetic studies of hyperactive children: Psychiatric illness in biologic and adopting parents* (pp. 273–280). Baltimore: Johns Hopkins University Press.

Carmelli, D., Chesney, M. A., Ward, M. M., & Rosenman, R. H. (1985). Twin similarity in cardiovascular stress response. *Health Psychology, 4,* 413–423.

Chassin, L., Mann, L. M., & Sher, K. J. (1988). Self-awareness theory, family history of alcoholism, and adolescent alcohol involvement. *Journal of Abnormal Psychology, 97,* 206–217.

Cloninger, C. R. (1987). Neurogenetic adaptive mechanisms in alcoholism. *Science, 236,* 410–416.

Cloninger, C. R., Bohman, M., Sigvardsson, S., & von Knorring, A. L. (1985). Psychopathology in adopted-out children of alcoholics: The Stockholm Adoption Study. In M. Galanter (Ed.), *Recent developments in alcoholism* (Vol. 3, pp. 37–51). New York: Plenum Press.

Cox, W. M. (1979). The alcoholic personality: A review of the evidence. In B. A. Maher (Ed.), *Progress in experimental personality research* (Vol. 9, pp. 89–148). New York: Academic Press.

Cox, W. M. (Ed.). (1983). *Identifying and measuring alcoholic personality characteristics.* San Francisco: Jossey–Bass.

Derryberry, D., & Rothbart, M. K. (1984). Emotion, attention, and temperament. In C. E. Izard, J. Kagan, & R. B. Zajonc (Eds.), *Emotions, cognition, and behavior* (pp. 132–166). New York: Cambridge University Press.

Ditto, B. (1987). Sibling similarities in cardiovascular reactivity to stress. *Psychophysiology, 24,* 353–360.

Drejer, K., Theilgaard, A., Teasdale, T. W., Schulsinger, F., & Goodwin, D. W. (1985). A prospective study of young men at high risk for alcoholism: Neuropsychological assessment. *Alcoholism: Clinical and Experimental Research, 9,* 498–502.

el-Guebaly, N., & Offord, D. R. (1979). On being the offspring of an alcoholic: An update. *Alcoholism: Clinical and Experimental Research, 3,* 148–157.

Eysenck, H. J. (1967). *The biological basis of personality.* Springfield, IL: Charles C. Thomas.

Fine, E. W., Yudin, L. W., Holmes, J., & Heinemann, S. (1976). Behavioral disorders in children with parental alcoholism. *Annals of the New York Academy of Sciences, 273,* 507–517.

Finn, P. R., Kleinman, I., & Pihl, R. O. (1988). *The life-time prevalence of psychopathology in men with multigenerational family histories of alcoholism.* Manuscript submitted for publication.

Finn, P. R., Martin, J., & Pihl, R. O. (1987). Alexithymia in males at high genetic risk for alcoholism. *Psychotherapy and Psychosomatics, 47,* 18–21.

Finn, P. R., & Pihl, R. O. (1987). Men at high risk for alcoholism: The effect of alcohol on cardiovascular response to unavoidable shock. *Journal of Abnormal Psychology, 96,* 230–236.

Finn, P. R., & Pihl, R. O. (1989). Risk for alcoholism: A comparison between two different groups of sons of alcoholics on cardiovascular reactivity and sensitivity to alcohol. *Alcoholism: Clinical and Experimental Research, 12,* 742–747.

Franks, D. D., & Thacker, B. T. (1979). Assessing familial factors in alcoholism from MMPI profiles. *American Journal of Psychiatry, 136,* 1084–1085.

Freidman, M., & Rosenman, R. (1974). *Type A behavior and your heart.* New York: Knopf.

Goldsmith, H. H., Buss, A. H., Plomin, R., Rothbart, M. K., Thomas, A., Chess, S., Hinde, R. A., & McCall, R. B. (1987). Roundtable: What is temperament? Four approaches. *Child Development, 58,* 505–529.

Goodwin, D. W., Schulsinger, F., Hermansen, L., Guze, S. B., & Winokur, G. (1975). Alcoholism and the hyperactive child syndrome. *Journal of Nervous and Mental Disease, 160,* 349–353.

Goodwin, D. W., Van Dusen, K. T., & Mednick, S. A. (Eds.). (1984). *Longitudinal research in alcoholism*. Hingham, MA: Kluwer-Nijhoff.

Graham, J. R., & Strenger, V. E. (1988). MMPI characteristics of alcoholics: A review. *Journal of Consulting and Clinical Psychology, 56*, 197–205.

Gray, J. A. (1981). *The neuropsychology of anxiety: An enquiry into the functions of the septo-hippocampal system*. Oxford: Oxford University Press.

Green, K. W. (1985). *Cognitive style: A review of the literature*. Technical Report 1. Chicago: Johnson O'Connor Research Foundation.

Helzer, J. E., & Pryzbeck, T. R. (1988). The co-occurrence of alcoholism with other psychiatric disorders in the general population and its impact on treatment. *Journal of Studies on Alcohol, 49*, 219–224.

Hennecke, L. (1984). Stimulus augmenting and field dependence in children of alcoholic fathers. *Journal of Studies on Alcohol, 45*, 486–492.

Hesselbrock, M. N. (1986). Childhood behavior problems and adult antisocial personality disorder in alcoholism. In R. E. Meyer (Ed.), *Psychopathology and addictive disorders* (pp. 78–94). New York: Guilford Press.

Hinshaw, S. P. (1987). On the distinction between attentional deficits/hyperactivity and conduct problems/aggression in child psychopathology. *Psychological Bulletin, 101*, 443–463.

Huessy, H. R., & Howell, D. C. (1985). Relationship between adult alcoholism and childhood behavior disorders. *Psychiatric Journal of the University of Ottawa, 10*, 114–119.

Hull, J. G. (1981). A self-awareness model of the causes and effects of alcohol consumption. *Journal of Abnormal Psychology, 90*, 586–600.

Hull, J. G. (1987). Self-awareness model. In H. T. Blane & K. E. Leonard (Eds.), *Psychological theories of drinking and alcoholism* (pp. 272–304). New York: Guilford Press.

Jones, M. (1968). Personality correlates and antecedents of drinking patterns in adult males. *Journal of Consulting and Clinical Psychology, 32*, 2–12.

Jöreskog, K. G., & Sörbom, D. (1984). *LISREL VI: Analysis of linear structural relationships by maximum likelihood, instrumental variables, and least squares methods*. Mooresville, IN: Scientific Software.

Kagan, J., Reznick, J. S., & Snidman, N. (1986). Temperamental inhibition in early childhood. In R. Plomin & J. Dunn (Eds.), *The study of temperament: Changes, continuities and challenges* (pp. 53–66). Hillsdale, NJ: Erlbaum.

Keehn, J. D. (1970). Neuroticism and extraversion; chronic alcoholics' reports on effects of drinking. *Psychological Reports, 27*, 767–770.

Kern, J. C., Hassett, C. A., Collipp, P. J., Bridges, C., Solomon, M., & Condren, R. J. (1981). Children of alcoholics: Locus of control, mental age, and zinc level. *Journal of Psychiatric Treatment and Evaluation, 3*, 169–173.

Knop, J., Teasdale, T. W., Schulsinger, F., & Goodwin, D. W. (1985). A prospective study of young men at high risk for alcoholism: School behavior and achievement. *Journal of Studies on Alcohol, 46*, 273–278.

Lefcourt, H. M. (1976). *Locus of control: Current trends in theory and research*. Hillsdale, NJ: Erlbaum.

Lerner, J. V., & Lerner, R. M. (1983). Temperament and adaptation across life: Theoretical and empirical issues. In P. B. Baltes & O. G. Brim, Jr. (Eds.), *Life-span development and behavior* (Vol. 5, pp. 197–231). New York: Academic Press.

Lerner, J. V., & Lerner, R. M. (Eds.) (1986). *Temperament and social interaction in infants and children*. San Francisco: Jossey-Bass.

Lerner, J. V., & Vicary, J. R. (1984). Difficult temperament and drug use: Analyses from the New York Longitudinal Study. *Journal of Drug Education, 14*, 1–8.

Lerner, R. M., & Busch-Rossnagel, N. (Eds.). (1981). *Individuals as producers of their development: A life-span perspective*. New York: Academic Press.

Levenson, R. W. (1987). Alcohol, affect, and physiology: Positive effects in the early stages of drinking. In E. Gottheil, K. A. Druley, S. Pashko, & S. P. Weinstein (Eds.), *Stress and addiction* (pp. 173–196). New York: Brunner/Mazel.

Lewis, C. E., Rice, J., & Helzer, J. E. (1983). Diagnostic interactions: Alcoholism and antisocial personality. *Journal of Nervous and Mental Disorders, 171,* 105–113.

Loper, R. G., Kammeier, M. L., & Hoffman, H. (1973). MMPI characteristics of college freshmen males who later became alcoholics. *Journal of Abnormal Psychology, 82,* 159–162.

Lund, C., & Landesman-Dwyer, S. (1979). Pre-delinquent and disturbed adolescents: The role of parental alcoholism. In M. Galanter (Ed.), *Currents in alcoholism* (Vol. 5, pp. 339–348). New York: Grune & Stratton.

MacAndrew, C. (1965). The differentiation of male alcoholic outpatients from nonalcoholic psychiatric outpatients by means of the MMPI. *Quarterly Journal of Studies on Alcohol, 26,* 238–246.

Mann, L. M., Chassin, L., & Sher, K. J. (1987). Alcohol expectancies and the risk for alcoholism. *Journal of Consulting and Clinical Psychology, 55,* 411–417.

Manning, D. T., Balson, P. M., & Xenakis, S. (1986). The prevalence of Type A personality in the children of alcoholics. *Alcoholism: Clinical and Experimental Research, 10,* 184–189.

Martin, J. B., & Pihl, R. O. (1985). The stress-alexithymia hypothesis: Theoretical and empirical considerations. *Psychotherapy and Psychosomatics, 43,* 169–176.

McClelland D. C., Davis, W. N., Kalin, R., & Warner, E. (1972). *The drinking man: Alcohol and human motivation.* New York: Free Press.

McCord, W., & McCord, J. (1960). *Origins of alcoholism.* Stanford, CA: Stanford University Press.

McKenna, T., & Pickens, R. (1983). Personality characteristics of alcoholic children of alcoholics. *Journal of Studies on Alcohol, 44,* 688–700.

Megargee, E. I. (1966). Undercontrolled and overcontrolled personality types in extreme antisocial aggression. *Psychological Monographs, 80* (3, Whole No. 66).

Messick, S. (1969). Measures of cognitive styles and personality and their potential for educational practice. In K. Ingendamp (Ed.), *Developments in educational testing* (pp. 329–341). London: University of London Press.

Miller, D., & Jang, M. (1977). Children of alcoholics: A 20-year longitudinal study. *Social Work Research Abstracts, 13,* 23–29.

Miller, W. R. (1976). Alcoholism scales and objective assessment methods: A review. *Psychological Bulletin, 83,* 649–674.

Morrison, J. R. (1980). Adult psychiatric disorders in parents of hyperactive children. *American Journal of Psychiatry, 137,* 825–827.

Morrison, J. R., & Schuckit, M. A. (1983). Locus of control in young men with alcoholic relatives and controls. *Journal of Clinical Psychiatry, 44,* 306–307.

Morrison, J. R., & Stewart, M. A. (1971). A family study of the hyperactive child syndrome. *Biological Psychiatry, 3,* 189–195.

Nathan, P. E. (1988). The addictive personality is the behavior of the addict. *Journal of Consulting and Clinical Psychology, 56,* 183–188.

Nesselroade, J. R., & Cattell, R. B. (1987). *Handbook of multivariate experimental psychology* (2nd ed.). New York: Plenum Press.

Penick, E. C., Powell, B. J., Othmer, E., Bingham. S. F., Rice, A. S., & Liese, B. S. (1984). Subtyping alcoholics by coexisting psychiatric syndromes: Course, family history, outcome. In D. W. Goodwin, R. T. Van Dusen, & S. A. Mednick (Eds.), *Longitudinal research in alcoholism* (pp. 167–196). Hingham, MA: Kluwer-Nijhoff.

Pentz, M. A. (1985). Social competence and self-efficacy as determinants of substance use in adolescence. In S. Shiffman & T. A. Wills (Eds.), *Coping and substance use* (pp. 117–142). New York: Academic Press.

Petrie, A. (1967). *Individuality in pain and suffering.* Chicago: University of Chicago Press.

Plomin, R., & Dunn, J. (Eds.). (1986). *The study of temperament: Changes, continuities, and challenges.* Hillsdale, NJ: Erlbaum.

Preng, K. W., & Clopton, J. R. (19860. The MacAndrew Scale: Clinical application and theoretical issues. *Journal of Studies on Alcohol, 47,* 228–236.

Prewett, M. J., Spence, R., & Chaknis, M. (1981). Attribution of causality by children with alcoholic parents. *International Journal of the Addictions, 16,* 367–370.

Quay, H. C. (1986). Conduct disorders. In H. C. Quay & J. S. Werry (Eds.), *Psychopathological disorders of childhood* (3rd ed., pp. 35–72). New York: Wiley.

Quinton, D., & Rutter, M. (1985). Family pathology and child psychiatric disorder: A four-year prospective study. In A. R. Nicol (Ed.), *Longitudinal studies in child psychology and psychiatry* (pp. 91–134). New York: Wiley.

Robins, L. N. (1966). *Deviant children grown up.* Baltimore: Williams & Wilkins.

Robins, L. N. (1986). The consequences of conduct disorder in girls. In D. Olweus, J. Block, & M. Radke-Yarrow (Eds.), *Development of antisocial and prosocial behavior* (pp. 385–414). New York: Academic Press.

Rothbart, M., & Derryberry, D. (1981). Development of individual differences in temperament. In M. Lamb & A. Brown (Eds.), *Advances in developmental psychiatry* (pp. 37–86). Boston: Erlbaum.

Rotter, J. B. (1966). Generalized expectancies for internal versus external control of reinforcement. *Psychological Monographs, 80* (1, Whole No. 609).

Ryan, C., & Butters, N. (1983). Cognitive deficits in alcoholics. In B. Kissin & H. Begleiter (Eds.), *The pathogenesis of alcoholism* (Vol. 7, pp. 485–538). New York: Plenum Press.

Rybakowski, J., Ziolkowski, M., Zasadzka, T., & Brzezinski, R. (1988). High prevalence of alexithymia in male patients with alcohol dependence. *Drug and Alcohol Dependence, 21,* 133–136.

Saunders, G. R., & Schuckit, M. A. (1981). MMPI scores in young men with alcoholic relatives and controls. *Journal of Nervous and Mental Disease, 169,* 456–458.

Schalling, D., & Asberg, M. (1985). Biological and psychological correlates of impulsiveness and monotony avoidance. In J. Strelau, F. H. Farley, & A. Gale (Eds.), *The biological basis of personality and behavior* (Vol. 1, 181–194). New York: Hemisphere.

Schuckit, M. A. (1982). Anxiety and assertiveness in sons of alcoholics and controls. *Journal of Clinical Psychiatry, 43,* 238–239.

Schuckit, M. A. (1983). Extroversion and neuroticism in young men at higher and lower risk for alcoholism. *American Journal of Psychiatry, 140,* 1223–1224.

Schuckit, M. A., & Penn, N. E. (1985). Performance on the rod and frame test for men at elevated risk for alcoholism, and controls: A pilot study. *American Journal of Drug and Alcohol Abuse, 11,* 113–118.

Schulsinger, F., Knop, J., Goodwin, D. W., Teasdale, T. W., & Mikkelsen, U. (1986). A prospective study of young men at high risk for alcoholism: Social and psychological characteristics. *Archives of General Psychiatry, 43,* 755–760.

Segal, B., Huba, G. J., & Singer, J. L. (1980). *Drugs, daydreaming, and personality.* Hillsdale, NJ: Erlbaum.

Sher, K. J. (1987). *What we know and do not know about COAs: A research update.* Paper presented at the MacArthur Foundation Meeting on Children of Alcoholics, Princeton, NJ.

Sher, K. J., & Levenson, R. W. (1982). Risk for alcoholism and individual differences in the stress-response-dampening effect of alcohol. *Journal of Abnormal Psychology, 91,* 350–368.

Sher, K. J., & McCrady, B. S. (1984). The McAndrew alcoholism scale: Severity of alcohol abuse and parental alcoholism. *Addictive Behaviors, 9,* 99–102.

Stewart, M. A., DeBlois, C. S., & Cummings, C. (1980). Psychiatric disorder in the parents of hyperactive boys and those with conduct disorders. *Journal of Child Psychology Psychiatry, 21,* 283–292.

Stewart, M. A., DeBlois, C. S., & Singer, S. (1979). Alcoholism and hyperactivity revisited: A preliminary report. In M. Galanter (Ed.), *Currents in alcoholism* (Vol. 5, pp. 349–357). New York: Grune & Stratton.

Tarter, R. E. (1975). Psychological deficit in chronic alcoholics: A review. *International Journal of the Addictions, 10,* 327–368.

Tarter, R. E., Alterman, A. I., & Edwards, K. L. (1985). Vulnerability to alcoholism in men: A behavior-genetic perspective. *Journal of Studies on Alcohol, 46,* 329–356.

Tarter, R. E., Hegedus, A. M., Goldstein, G., Shelly, C., & Alterman, A. I. (1984). Adolescent sons of alcoholics: Neuropsychological and personality characteristics. *Alcoholism: Clinical and Experimental Research, 8,* 216–222.

Tarter, R. E., Hegedus, A., Winsten, N., & Alterman, A. I. (1984). Neuropsychological, personality, and familial characteristics of physically abused juvenile delinquents. *Journal of the American Academy of Child Psychiatry, 23,* 668–674.

Tarter, R. E., Jacob, T., Hill, S., Hegedus, A. M., & Carra, J. (1986). Perceptual field dependency: Predisposing trait or consequence of alcoholism. *Journal of Studies on Alcohol, 47,* 498–499.

Tarter, R. E., McBride, H., Buonpane, N., & Schneider, D. U. (1977). Differentiation of alcoholics. *Archives of General Psychiatry, 34,* 761–768.

Thomas, A., & Chess, S. (1977). *Temperament and development.* New York: Brunner/Mazel.

Vaillant, G. (1983). *The natural history of alcoholism.* Cambridge, MA: Harvard University Press.

Vaillant, G. E., & Milofsky, E. S. (1982). The etiology of alcoholism: A prospective viewpoint. *American Psychologist, 37,* 494–503.

Werner, E. E. (1986). Resilient offspring of alcoholics: A longitudinal study from birth to age 18. *Journal of Studies on Alcohol, 47,* 34–40.

Windle, M. (1988). Psychometric strategies of measures of temperament: A methodological critique. *International Journal of Behavioral Development, 11,* 171–201.

Windle, M., Hooker, K., Lernerz, K., East, P. L., Lerner, J. V., & Lerner, R. M. (1986). Temperament, perceived competence, and depression in early- and late-adolescents. *Developmental Psychology, 22,* 384–392.

Witkin, H. A., & Goodenough, D. R. (1977). Field dependence and interpersonal behavior. *Psychological Bulletin, 84,* 661–689.

Witkin, H. A., Karp, S. A., & Goodenough, D. R. (1959). Dependence in alcoholics. *Quarterly Journal of Studies on Alcohol, 20,* 493–504.

Woititz, J. G. (1977). *Adult children of alcoholics.* Hollywood, FL: Health Communication.

Wood, D. R., Reimherr, F. W., Wender, P. H., & Johnson, G. E. (1976). Diagnosis and treatment of minimal brain dysfunction in adults: A preliminary report. *Archives of General Psychiatry, 33,* 1453–1460.

Zucker, R. A. (1987). The four alcoholisms: A developmental account of the etiologic process. In P. C. Rivers (Ed.), *Nebraska symposium on motivation, 1986: Vol. 34. Alcohol and addictive behaviors* (pp. 27–84). Lincoln: University of Nebraska Press.

Zucker, R. A., & Gomberg, E. S. L. (1986). Etiology of alcoholism reconsidered: The case for a biopsychosocial process. *American Psychologist, 41,* 783–793.

Zuckerman, M. (1978). Sensation seeking. In H. London & J. Exner (Eds.), *Dimensions of personality.* New York: Wiley.

Zuckerman, M. (1979). *Sensation seeking: Beyond the optimal level of arousal* (pp. 487–559). Hillsdale, NJ: Erlbaum.

CHAPTER SEVEN

Family Factors and Adjustment of Children of Alcoholics

RUTH ANN SEILHAMER
THEODORE JACOB

In the early 1970s several child and family clinicians published reports aimed at alerting mental health professionals to an underacknowledged and little-understood phenomenon: the impact of parental alcoholism on children. These writers labeled children of alcoholics a "hidden tragedy" (Bosma, 1972), a "neglected problem" (Sloboda 1974), and the "unseen casualties" (Cork, 1969). While these writers targeted the seeming apathy of their time, interest in such children can be documented as long ago as in the days of Aristotle (Warner & Rosett, 1975). Concern was also expressed in England during the 1700s, when high infant morbidity and mortality coincided with the gin epidemic, and was rekindled in the early 1800s, when familial effects related to the alcohol "disease" received attention. For most of the 20th century, influences such as the suppressing effect of Prohibition on alcohol research, the more predominant individual approaches in the mental health field, and the social stigma attached to familial alcoholism served to dampen interest in children of alcoholics (Russell, Henderson, & Blume, 1984).

During the past 15 years there has been a vigorous movement to remedy this oversight, as evidenced in a growing literature; the formation of special-interest groups of national scope, such as the National Association for Children of Alcoholics and the Children of Alcoholics Foundation, Inc.; numerous conferences on national, state, and regional levels; and the development of model programs aimed at treatment and prevention, such as Al-Ateen, and the Cambridge–Somerville Program for Alcoholism Rehabilitation (DiCicco, Davis, Travis, & Orenstein, 1983–1984).

Although the increased clinical focus on the needs of children of alcoholics has produced a wealth of descriptive and sympathetic reports, the current literature lacks comprehensive theories and sound empirical research. Clinicians continue to call for data-based investigations to guide treatment efforts, resource allocations, and prevention policies. In a 1984 interview, Robert G. Niven, director of the National Institute on Alcohol Abuse and Alcoholism, spoke of this need:

> We need to know more about the nature of the effects of parental alcoholism . . . before we can begin to prescribe specific interventions or treatments. . . . It is imperative that we encourage research that looks at the impact of parental alcoholism on children, using objective measures. (Hindman & Small, 1984, p. 4)

Although the emphasis has been on the victimization of these children, many reports, including several critical literature reviews, point to considerable heterogeneity among children of alcoholics (Burk & Sher, 1988; el-Guebaly & Offord, 1979, 1980; Heller, Sher, & Benson, 1982; Jacob, Favorini, Meisel, & Anderson, 1978; Russell et al., 1984; West & Prinz, 1987; Woodside, 1988). Obviously, estimates that approach 29 million children of alcoholics in the United States (Woodside, 1988) suggest substantial variability. Moreover, descriptions of nonsymptomatic children of alcoholics, many of whom exhibit extraordinary coping skills, have earned them the label of "invulnerables" or "superkids." However, other writers claim that the exaggerated coping styles of many of these children lead to dysfunction in adulthood (Black, 1979; Brown, 1986; Gravitz & Bowden, 1984).

Despite the uncertainties that prevail, there is a general consensus that children of alcoholics are a population at risk. They are overrepresented in the caseloads of medical, psychiatric, and child guidance clinics; in the juvenile justice system; and in cases of child abuse (Russell et al., 1984). There is little doubt that the deluge of descriptive literature over the past two decades has established an awareness of the needs of these children. However, equivocal research findings and a wide spectrum of outcomes across medical, psychiatric, neuropsychological, and psychosocial domains have generated much uncertainty about the actual nature of impairment of children of alcoholics. The critical issue at this time is the clarification of the parameters of risk, those biological and psychosocial factors that mediate vulnerability. Although specific childhood outcomes are undoubtedly determined by a highly variable and complex interplay of many factors, this chapter focuses on the literature that has explored the association of family processes and child adjustment in families of alcoholics. The study of interaction patterns in families of alcoholics is a relatively new area that has generated fresh insights and hypotheses. Based primarily on a behavioral-systems perspective, this approach contends that a complete understanding of dysfunctional behavior must include a consideration of the interpersonal relationships in which family members develop and function. To the extent that family interaction patterns, which are protectively or detrimentally related to child risk status, can be identified, treatment efforts will be grounded in more substantiated information.

OUTCOME STUDIES

Most of the literature by far, on children of alcoholics consists of outcome studies, and these reports are generally categorized into health issues, alcohol-related issues, and psychosocial difficulties (e.g., Deutsch, DiCicco, & Mills, 1982; O'Gorman, 1981). Health-related issues have focused on the *in utero* sequelae of maternal drinking, such as the fetal alcohol syndrome (Graham-Clay, 1983; Holzman, 1982; Smith, 1979; Warner & Rosett, 1975); on child abuse and neglect (el-Guebaly & Offord, 1977, 1979; Hindman, 1979; Orme & Rimmer, 1981; Wilson, 1982); on neurological and neuropsychological deficits associated with minimal brain disorder and hyperactivity (Alterman, Petrarulo, Tarter, & McCowan, 1982; Bell & Cohen, 1981; Hesselbrock, Stabenau, & Hesselbrock, 1984; Morrison & Stewart, 1973; Tarter, McBride, Buonpane, & Schneider, 1977); and on scattered reports of increased physical and psychosomatic complaints among children of alcoholics (Biek, 1981; Chafetz, Blane, & Hill, 1971; el-Guebaly & Offord, 1979; Nylander, 1960; Rydelius, 1981).

The second area of attention, alcohol-related issues, consists primarily of reports describing the increased risk for alcoholism among children of alcoholics. Two relatively distinct bodies of research have developed: studies that focus on genetic influences in the intergenerational transmission of alcoholism and studies that are concerned with environmental influences in the etiology of alcoholism. Efforts to produce evidence for a genetic factor have been based on studies that examine rates of alcoholism in ethnic groups, identical versus fraternal twins, adopted children of alcoholic parents, and half-siblings (Cadoret, Gain, & Grove, 1980; Cadoret & Gath, 1978; Cloninger, Reich, & Yokoyama, 1983; Goodwin, Schulsinger, Hermansen, Guze, & Winokur, 1973; Kaij, 1960; Partanen, Bruun, & Markkanen, 1966; Schuckit, Goodwin & Winokur, 1972). In turn, compelling findings from these studies have spurred a search for mechanisms or markers by which a genetic risk is expressed, including endocrine, neurochemical, motor, neurological, and cognitive–perceptual functions (see Russell et al., 1984, for a review of 119 studies of genetically influenced characteristics related to alcohol).

While these studies present data that support a genetically based propensity for alcoholism, they are not completely explanatory. For example, they fail to account for the 40%–50% discordant rate in identical twins, and they do not explain the large proportion of alcoholics with no ancestry of alcoholism (Cadoret et al., 1980). In a critical review of the literature, Searles (1988; also see Chapter 5, this volume) discusses the methodological and conceptual shortcomings that limit conclusions, noting that "environmental influences may have been underemphasized as significant factors in the etiology of alcoholism" (p. 163).

In comparison with genetic studies, the literature on family environmental influences in the etiology of alcoholism is much less rigorous. Although clinical observations describe the deleterious effects of living in a home with alcoholism, there is a lack of guiding conceptualizations and systematic investigations of the actual processes and events that occur within these families.

A notable effort in this area has been the work of Wolin and Bennett and their colleagues (Wolin, Bennett, & Noonan, 1979; Wolin, Bennett, Noonan, & Teitelbaum, 1980), who have examined how the preservation versus disruption of family rituals is associated with the subsequent drinking status of offspring. In an attempt to elucidate environmental influences that potentiate the transmission of alcoholism across generations, these researchers focused on how families preserve ritualized patterns of behavior. Rituals refer to the specific ways a family carries out everyday activities (such as meals), the ways it marks transitional events (births, marriages, deaths), and how it celebrates special events such as holidays. Specifically, these researchers hypothesized that families that are able to maintain family rituals despite a parent's alcohol problem are less likely to produce children with an alcohol problem. These families are labeled "distinctive" in contrast to "subsumptive" families in which alcoholism has disrupted or altered family rituals. The ritual theory was supported in an initial study of 25 families wherein transmitter families fell primarily into the subsumptive category and nontransmitter families fell primarily into the distinctive category (Wolin et al., 1980). In a later report on 68 children in 30 alcoholic families, Bennett and Wolin (1986) found that transmission was less likely for both sons and daughters who had low to moderate contact with the alcoholic family of origin and who had a high degree of "deliberateness" in selecting and establishing rituals in their own marriages. Although these preliminary results are in need of replication with demographically broader and larger samples, they underscore the viability of identifying distinct family behavioral patterns that may lead to specific child outcomes.

The efforts of Wolin et al. represent an important contribution to much-needed theory-building in this area. However, as mentioned, the family ritual model currently lacks sufficient empirical validation and exemplifies the immaturity that characterizes this area of study. Moreover, although several theorists have proposed integrative models that include both nature and nurture (Cloninger, 1983; Cloninger, Bohman, & Sigvardsson, 1981; Goodwin, 1979), the alcohol-risk literature continues its split developmental path with a critical lack of efforts to explore the interactive effects of genetics and environment.

The final area of interest has focused on the possible psychiatric and psychosocial disturbances of children of alcoholics. This domain, described and summarized by several reviewers (Adler & Raphael, 1983; Deutsch et al., 1982; el-Guebaly & Offord, 1977; Jacob et al., 1978; O'Gorman, 1981; Russell et al., 1984; West & Prinz, 1987; Wilson, 1982; Wilson & Orford, 1978; Woodside, 1988), encompasses interpersonal relationships, academic performance, self-concept, role acquisition, coping behaviors, personality profiles, and psychopathology. Again, the emphasis here is on children of alcoholics as casualties, although methodological limitations in this literature undermine confidence in such an interpretation. Among the problems are (1) a critical lack of adequate control groups, especially psychiatric groups that would allow for the determination of specific effects; (2) a lack of assessment of stress factors found to correlate with alcoholism, such as marital conflict, unemployment, family violence, separations, and relocations; (3) a need for an evaluation of the mental health status of the nondrinking parent since his or her capability to be a protective agent could significantly influence child outcome; (4) vague and inconsistent criteria for diagnosing alcoholism; and (5) little attention to drinking-related variables such as duration, severity, consumption pattern, location of drinking, and interaction of sex of drinking parent with sex of child. Moreover, samples are often small and unrepresentative of children of alcoholics in the general population, drawn from clinical or judicial systems, and assessed by indirect sources with retrospective reports of dubious reliability and validity.

Notwithstanding these methodological inadequacies, many reviewers over the past decade have affirmed the assumption of increased risk for children of alcoholics. In a 1978 review of empirical studies, Jacob and colleagues found modest to moderate support for significantly greater psychosocial problems in offspring of alcoholics (Jacob et al., 1978). More recently, West and Prinz (1987) concluded that "the findings taken as a whole support the contention that alcoholism is associated with heightened incidence of child symptomatology" (p. 214). Likewise, Russell et al. (1984) state that collectively "studies convincingly demonstrate that children of alcoholics are at a particularly high risk for emotional and behavioral problems" (p. 52). All of these authors, however, also stress that the interpretation of results should be tempered by the methodological difficulties mentioned above.

MODERATORS OF OUTCOME

Although surveys of the literature on outcome have fostered an impression of poor psychosocial adjustment of children of alcoholics, several recent reports have been more skeptical. Heller et al. (1982) caution against "risk overprediction" that can occur by (1) the use of biased samples, (2) a focus on childhood or adolescent symptoms that have unknown predictability for adult functioning, and (3) inattention to the segment of alcoholics' offspring who are "copers." These authors suggest several sampling methods that would produce more generalizable information, and they encourage research aimed at identifying the distinguishing characteristics of nonsymptomatic offspring.

Several empirical studies have found that a substantial proportion of children of alcoholics are faring well in comparison with children of nonalcoholics. For example, Jacob and Leonard (1986) found that only a minority of children of alcoholics scored in the impaired range on the Achenbach Child Behavior Checklist (CBCL; Achenbach, 1978). These researchers compared parent CBCL reports of 296 demographically similar children in 134 families, including 100 children of alcoholics, 105 children of normal controls, and 91 children of depressives. Although they found that sons and daughters of alcoholic and of depressed fathers were rated by both parents as more problematic, the mean CBCL values of disturbed groups were within the normal range, supporting refutations of predestined adverse outcome for "vulnerable" children. A within-group analysis of children of alcoholics indicated that impaired versus nonimpaired children of alcoholics had parents with elevated measures of psychopathology and/or fathers with more alcohol-related difficulties.

Currently, we are analyzing the CBCL reports of parents who participated in a separate study in which selection criteria were less stringent; that is, fathers had more secondary Research Diagnostic Criteria (RDC) diagnoses (Spitzer & Endicott, 1977) and mothers were more variable in terms of current psychopathology and drinking status. Our preliminary analyses replicate our original findings: Children whose alcoholic parents have more psychiatric disturbance, including more problematic drinking, exhibit more dysfunction on CBCL scores than children of depressed or normal controls.

In a study of 70 young adults with and without alcoholic parents, Clair and Genest (1987) found that many children of alcoholics functioned on a level comparable to or better than that of children of nonalcoholics, despite reporting more disruptive, less cohesive family environments and a lack of supportive parental guidance. Generalizability of results, however, is limited by use of subjects who were predominantly females drawn from a university setting.

The resiliency of children of alcoholics has also been supported in a longitudinal study of Hawaiian children who were followed from infancy to age 18 (Werner, 1986). From a cohort of 698 children, 49 were identified as having an alcoholic father ($n = 38$), an alcoholic mother ($n = 6$), or alcoholism in both parents ($n = 5$). It was found that 59% of these children had no serious adjustment problems by age 18, despite the fact that most were raised in chronic poverty. Moreover, it was found that 72% of the resilient group were females and 70% of the problem group were males. Besides sex of the child, other predictors of outcome included competency of the mother (particularly with regard to drinking status), quality of early caregiving, degree of family conflict in early childhood, intelligence level, and academic performance.

Werner's results are similar to the findings of Miller and Jang (1977), who reported on a 20-year study of 259 children who also came from disadvantaged environments, 147 of whom had an alcoholic parent. These researchers reported that a "true predictive course of intergenerational transmission" (p. 29) could not be traced, with outcome moderated by sex of the child, sex of the alcoholic parent, early childhood crises, and socialization failure in adolescence. Although more children of alcoholics were heavy drinkers than children of nonalcoholics (36% versus 16%), the authors note that predictability of definitive adult alcoholism was limited by the short drinking histories of their young-adult sample.

These longitudinal studies highlight the age factor in the "risk overprediction" warning by Heller et al. (1982). Given that alcohol consumption typically peaks during young adulthood, follow-up assessments of subjects in their early

20s may lead to an overestimation of intergenerational transmission of alcoholism. Several investigators have analyzed various aspects of this issue in considerable detail (Blane, 1979; Donovan, Jessor, & Jessor, 1983; Kandel & Logan, 1984).

We have recently conducted a 5-year follow-up of 150 families who participated in a broad-based family interaction study (Jacob, Seilhamer, & Rushe, 1989). A preliminary analysis of 140 adult children, who represent 22 families of male alcoholics, 18 families of male depressives, and 18 normal control families, found significantly elevated rates of lifetime alcoholism among adult offspring in all three groups. (This diagnosis pertained to 26% of adult sons of alcoholics, 20% of adult sons of depressives, and 11% of adult sons of normal controls.) However, most of these offspring would fail to meet DSM-III-R (American Psychiatric Association, 1987) criteria for alcohol dependence because of the requirements for tolerance and withdrawal, phenomena that require a relatively protracted drinking history. Nevertheless, these offspring would meet DSM-III-R criteria for alcohol abuse, which requires one month's duration of problem drinking. Scores on Feighner criteria (Feighner et al., 1972) and the Alcohol Use Questionnaire (Horn, Skinner, Wanberg, & Foster, 1982) also support high rates of alcohol abuse, but not alcohol dependence, in young adult males and reveal that abusive consumption is primarily exhibited in disruptive social behavior (e.g., legal difficulties, traffic violations, job losses, or aggressive behavior, all of which are associated with drinking). This is particularly evident among sons of alcoholics, who report a higher degree of social impairment than sons of depressives or of controls.

We have recently completed data collection and plan within-group analyses and further stratification of the larger sample by sex and age. A critical issue, however, is that much of the sample has not passed through the period of risk for alcoholism. The median age of the adult offspring in the subset described above is 23 years, and 26% of the offspring are minors with a median age of 15. Because many of these alcohol-abusing offspring "mature out" as they pass through the period of risk, we can not yet determine which of the offspring will exhibit continued or exacerbated pathological patterns of alcohol abuse. Given this uncertainty, an accurate and effective tracking of the course of alcohol abuse requires continued longitudinal assessment of a substantial number of offspring through the risk period.

Studies of families of recovered alcoholics also argue for the resiliency of offspring. In a comparison of parental reports of alcoholics regarding their children's emotional and health functioning, Moos and Billings (1982) found no significant differences between the children of 28 recovered alcoholics and the children of 59 community control families. However, the children of 23 relapsed alcoholics (as measured by rehospitalization or resumption of severe drinking at 6-month and 2-year follow-up) had twice as much emotional disturbance as controls. Furthermore, child emotional disturbance was significantly related to a family life characterized by conflict, use of avoidance in coping styles, low cohesiveness, lack of organization, and occurrence of negative life events.

Ratings of family life also distinguished children of drinking alcoholics from children of recovered alcoholics and controls in a study by Callan and Jackson (1986). The direct reports of 21 children of recovered alcoholics, 14 children of current alcoholics, and 35 controls did not differ on measures of self-esteem and locus of control, but children of current alcoholics described their family life as significantly less happy and less cohesive.

In summary, although empirical reports are limited, several outcome studies have demonstrated that children of alcoholics vary widely with regard to psychosocial adjustment and that many exhibit adequate to superior functioning. Moreover, studies of children of recovered alcoholics suggest that maladjustment is situation-related rather than an irreparable injury, as many descriptive reports have contended. Several factors that influence outcome have been suggested, including individual characteristics of the child (sex, temperament, intellectual level) and parent (extent of alcohol problems, emotional stability, coping style), as well as features of the family environment (cohesiveness, conflict). Again, interpretation of results is hampered by biased sampling, indirect child assessment, unsubstantiated global ratings, and insufficient life-span assessment. The most critical gaps are conceptual; that is, there is a lack of theoretical perspectives that offer explanations and of rationales that link specific family processes to child outcome.

A process model proposed by Moore (1982) is an exception to the mainstream focus on static outcome variables. In developing a conceptual framework from which to study the effects of parental alcoholism on children, Moore (1982) proposed that the child's adjustment is dependent on the chronicity and severity of disruption of three primary factors: the quality and style of the relationship between parent and child, the style and consistency of parental supervision, and the level and style of direct parental socialization. According to this model, there are secondary factors that mediate child adjustment by disrupting these primary factors. Secondary factors include marital conflict, family crises, social isolation, unemployment, and alcoholism. Thus, child adjustment would vary as a function of the impact of such secondary factors on the parental role. As numerous clinical observations and descriptive accounts have detailed, alcoholic parenting is often characterized by an inadequate affectional bond, inconsistent discipline, and poor social modeling. Moreover, alcoholism is a particularly detrimental factor because of its tertiary role in the genesis and perpetuation of other family stressors such as marital conflict and dissolution, social isolation, unemployment, and financial hardship. In a survey of the child adjustment literature, Moore (1982) notes a common association of these family stressors and alcoholism. In a recent review of alcoholics' offspring, West and Prinz (1987) note that parental alcoholism "may increase the child's risk of experiencing other family stressors, which in turn lead to negative outcomes" (p. 209). They note that a combination of stressors "may potentiate each other, resulting in much more risk . . . than . . . a simple summation of the effects of separate stressors considered singly" (p. 209).

Ackerman (1983) offers a similar conceptual framework for understanding how alcoholism affects children by disrupting vital parental functions. Regardless of whether the mother or the father is alcoholic, the emotional strain on both parents interferes with their ability to offer a nurturing and consistent environment. In the Eriksonian tradition, Ackerman describes how deficient parenting thwarts resolution of normal stage-related crises. Depending on the child's developmental stage when abusive drinking emerges and on the extent of parental role impairment, the child will fail to achieve a secure self-concept characterized by self-esteem, self-control, and autonomy. There are few concrete data on how child adjustment is influenced by the interaction of child variables (age, sex, temperament, intellectual level), parental variables (sex of alcoholic parent, drinking pattern and duration) and "buffers" in the child's environment.

Figure 7.1 is a schematic representation of the pathways by which parental alcoholism has been proposed to influence child outcome. The act of consuming alcoholic beverages results in three main effects involving ethanol, the family, and role modeling.

Ethanol effects. In the short run, excessive ethanol alters the cognition, affective state, and behavioral responses of the alcoholic parent. Such impairments as mood disturbances, memory lapses, aggressive outbursts, and motor dysfunctions incapacitate the individual as an effective parent. In the long run, chronic ingestion of alcohol could engender or aggravate a host of medical problems, which in turn may compound financial problems, create absences due to hospitalization, and lead to chronic illnesses that further hamper parenting functions.

Family effects. As thoroughly described and usually sympathetically portrayed in the literature, drinking leads directly to multiple family stressors

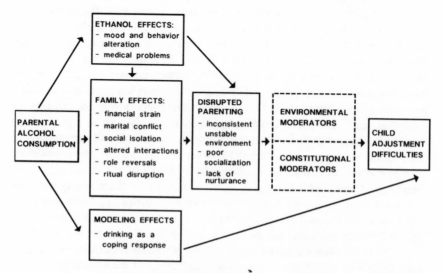

FIGURE 7.1 Influence of parental alcoholism on offspring adjustment.

including financial strain, marital dissension, isolation from extended family and community support, overburdening of the nonalcoholic parent, "parentification" of children, and disruption of day-to-day as well as major religious or cultural rituals. Moreover, as described below, altered family interactions include changes of affective expression and problem resolution. In turn, these changes affect the ability of both parents to provide a consistent, cohesive, and supportive environment in which children can mature in an adaptive developmental progression.

Modeling effects. Independent of its interference with parenting functions, alcohol consumption can directly influence a child's adjustment by becoming the model for coping responses or by dint of its sociocultural significance as a marker of adult passage or sex role expression. With reference to the acquisition of drinking behavior, Zucker (1976) suggests that modeling effects of parental drinking are tempered by the child's age and personality, peer influences, and parental interactions in drinking contexts.

In a highly idiosyncratic way, these primary effects of alcohol consumption interact to produce a family environment characterized by varying degrees of deficiencies in organization, cohesiveness, predictability, discipline, emotional sustenance, and training in basic life skills. Eventual child adjustment, however, is also determined by a filter of mediators that can temper or magnify the effects of disruptive parenting. Several buffers or "escape routes" have been suggested; these generally fall into the environmental or constitutional categories. Constitutional moderators encompass such variables as sex, age, intellectual level, temperament, and genetic propensities. Environmental moderators include sex of the nonalcoholic parent, psychiatric status of the nonalcoholic parent, duration and intensity of exposure to drinking, treatment experience, peer influences, supportive social institutions, and informal social resources (Miller & Jang, 1977).

Although the emphasis in Figure 7.1 is unidirectional (with parental alcohol consumption leading to child adjustment difficulties), reciprocal effects are quite plausible. To the extent that the abusive drinking of the alcoholic parent is exacerbated by social stressors, child adjustment problems (as well as other family stressors) may lead to increased consumption.

Considering the complexity and diversity of factors as well as their additive and synergistic effects, it is little wonder that child adjustment is highly variable. Empirical research is needed that will provide reliable and valid data regarding these processes, so that more relevant and effective prevention and treatment programs can be developed.

FAMILY PROCESS STUDIES

In the last 10 years, a systems–interactional perspective has generated increasing interest among alcohol researchers and clinicians in efforts to disentangle the complex association of abusive drinking, family processes, and outcome on individual, dyadic, and systemic levels (Jacob & Seilhamer, 1987). Earlier efforts in this area consisted mainly of studies of marital dyads. Based primarily on retrospective self-reports, characteristics of the relationship were inferred from comparisons of spouses' perception of their relationship (Drewery & Rae, 1969; Mitchell, 1959; Tamerin, Toler, DeWolfe, Packer, & Neuman, 1973). As direct observation procedures became the preferred method for gathering "valid" data, researchers examined family interactive behavior in contrived laboratory settings. In these contexts, the outcomes of "games" or standard problem-solving tasks were interpreted as measurable consequences of family interactive processes (Gorad, McCourt, & Cobb, 1971; Kennedy, 1976). Again only marital dyads were involved, and the number of studies was extremely small. More recently, investigators have begun to study families in less synthetic contexts by observing family interactions during personally relevant, affect-laden discussions and naturalistic home settings that include parents and children (Jacob et al., 1989).

Although the study of family interactions involving alcoholic members is still in an early stage of development, this theoretical–methodological perspective has already generated a number of hypotheses. The most influential effort in the field has been the extended work of Steinglass and colleagues over the past 15 years. The life history model proposed by Steinglass (1980) is a synthesis of developmental and behavior–systems concepts, a model that evolved from observations of ongoing family processes in both natural home settings and creative laboratory experiments.

The life history model embodies two earlier concepts proposed by Steinglass, namely, the adaptive consequences model and the alcohol maintenance model (Steinglass, Weiner, & Mendelson, 1971; Steinglass, Davis, & Berenson, 1977). The adaptive consequences model was derived from observations of family dyads under drinking and nondrinking conditions. Steinglass found that couples interacted quite differently under these two conditions; intoxication served to suppress or sanction the expression of feelings or the enactment of certain behaviors. Consequently, interpersonal conflicts were reduced, alleviating relationship tensions and providing a short-term solution or "adaptation." On a broader scale, the alcohol maintenance model proposes that the stability, or homeostasis, of the family system relies on cycles of intoxication and sobriety. Thus, alcohol use is reinforced and, in turn, intoxication perpetuates certain interactive patterns that may be adaptive in the broadest sense.

In an effort to validate a family interaction model based on stages of alcohol consumption (e.g., wet, dry), Steinglass (1981) observed 31 alcoholic families within the home setting. Two trained observers remained in the home throughout nine 4-hour periods, and each recorded the behaviors of a targeted family member. In all cases these targets were the parents, and thus results are based on parental behavior as indices or markers of intrafamilial processes. Additionally, Steinglass (1979) assessed the problem-solving behavior of 17 of these 31 families who had a child 12 years of age or older living at home. He found that differences in dimensions of family cohesiveness were related to drinking phase (wet or dry) of the alcoholic parent.

In a study that served to pilot an extensive research investigation of alcoholic families, Jacob, Ritchey, Cvitkovic, and Blane (1981) compared the interactions of eight alcoholic families during discussions generated by the Revealed Differences Questionnaire (Strodbeck, 1951). Family units consisted of both parents and two of their children who were between 10 and 18 years of age. Analyses of mother–children and father–children interchanges revealed between-group differences in parental instrumentality. Briefly, alcoholic fathers were less instrumental (i.e., displayed less problem-solving behavior) than control fathers, and mothers with alcoholic spouses were more instrumental than mothers in control families. Unfortunately, these authors did not examine whether this role-reversal phenomenon was also characteristic of interactions that engaged both parents and children.

In an extended study, Krahn, Jacob, and Leonard (1989) examined the parent–child interactions of a larger sample that included untreated, intact families of 39 male alcoholics, 35 male depressives, and 35 nondisturbed (no RDC diagnosis) parents. Videotaped discussion sessions involved dyadic (mother–father, mother–child, father–child) and triadic (mother–father–child) combinations under drinking and nondrinking conditions. Groups were demographically similar, and the children's ages ranged from 10 to 17 years. Role reversals were not found in this sample, but several other significant findings were reported, with group differences most evident in the father–child interactions. Although alcoholic and depressed father–child dyads were not significantly different, nondistressed dyads exhibited higher rates of congeniality and problem solving. The authors suggested that distressed fathers less frequently model problem solving, and their children therefore have less opportunity for learning effective problem resolution. Moreover, the consumption of alcohol was found to have unique effects on alcoholic families. First, maternal positivity in the alcoholic group increased in the drinking condition, particularly in mother–son interactions. The authors suggested that mothers may exhibit more compensatory behavior in drinking situations, or that the familiarity of a drinking context makes them more comfortable. Second, alcohol exerted more of an influence on levels of positivity in mother–child dyads in families where the father had steady drinking patterns, compared with families with fathers who had a pattern of episodic drinking.

These reports of Jacob et al. (1978) and Steinglass (1979, 1980, 1981) reveal that there are demonstrated differences between alcoholic and control families in the quality of parent–child interactions. It was also shown that, in a laboratory setting, the problem-solving and affective behaviors of alcoholic families vary with the drinking phase of the alcoholic parent.

A major difficulty with the Jacob and Steinglass research designs is that they are cross-sectional and offer no information about how family processes vary over time. Also, in the Steinglass analysis, the predictor variable (i.e., the wet or dry phase distinction) is based on macroscopic, or relatively long-term, stages of alcohol consumption. This broad categorization is not conducive to an understanding of more microscopic, ongoing family processes that may change with day-to-day cycles of intoxicated and sober states.

In an effort to discern how alcohol consumption affected family relationships on a day-to-day basis, Dunn (1984) collected daily reports of drinking, marital satisfaction, and psychiatric symptoms from eight couples for 3 months. This effort evolved from an earlier cross-sectional study indicating that husbands' recent alcohol consumption was significantly related to wives' reports of marital satisfaction and psychiatric symptoms (Jacob, Dunn, & Leonard, 1983); consumption levels correlated positively with marital satisfaction and negatively with symptomatology. The longitudinal effort included only steady drinkers because the cross-sectional correlations were substantiated only for alcoholics whose drinking history indicated a steady consumption pattern. Eight dyads with steady-drinking alcoholic husbands were involved, four of whom were in-home drinkers and four of whom were out-of-home drinkers. (This distinction was made in order to evaluate the influence of drinking location, since it was felt that the episodic–steady dichotomy may have been confounded by drinking location.) Data were then subjected to univariate and bivariate time series analyses, allowing for an interpretation of the temporal covariation of alcohol consumption and marital stability, and the direction of effects of these variables.

Results indicated that for two of three clearly defined in-home drinkers, alcohol consumption was positively associated with wives' marital satisfaction, whereas with all out-of-home drinkers, marital satisfaction declined for all wives following their spouses' alcohol consumption. Notwithstanding the need for larger sample replication, this study suggests further refinement of the adaptive consequences model by proposing that drinking pattern and location can be potent mediators of relationship functioning in alcoholic families. To the extent that the consumption pattern is predictable and incorporated into family life, drinking is likely to be associated with positive consequences (Dunn, Jacob, Hummon, & Seilhamer, 1987). Alternatively, the chaotic and unpredictable course of episodic drinking (i.e., the heavy weekend drinking by fathers who characterized the out-of-home group) appears to have more of a destabilizing influence on relationships.

In a similar effort that focused on parent–child interactions, Seilhamer (1987) collected daily reports of relationship satisfaction, child symptoms, and parent drinking for 85 days from eight father–son dyads. Time series analyses showed that in six of eight families, the child's daily satisfaction rating with the father–child relationship was causally related to father's level of daily alcohol consumption. That is, the child's daily satisfaction with his father was better predicted by knowledge of the father's drinking level than it was by just knowing how the child usually feels about his father from day to day. Moreover, it was found that the bivariate relationships obtained in six of the eight parent–child dyads were congruent with bivariate processes in the marital dyad. That is, when the parent–child relationship was negatively affected by the father's drinking, the marital relationship was also negatively affected. The long-term drinking histories of these fathers suggest that the response congruence between family subsystems reflects the extent to which the father's drinking is incorporated into family life on a day-to-day basis.

In addition to a possible historical effect, synchrony between subsystems was most evident in families with negative associations between the father's alcohol consumption level and dyadic relationship satisfaction. This raises questions about the ability of negatively affected mothers to act as buffering influences for their children, and also about the transfer of effects between the marital dyad and the parent-child dyad. Although these points raise provocative issues, their exploration suggests the need for higher-order multivariate analyses. Nevertheless, an empirical demonstration of the correspondence between family subsystems in their reactions to the father's drinking is of interest in its own right.

The Seilhamer findings did not support the steady in-home versus episodic out-of-home distinction in parent–child relationships that was found in the marital relationships described by Jacob and Leonard (1988) and Dunn (1984). There are several possible explanations for this failure to replicate. First, the number of family dyads was small in both the Dunn study and the Seilhamer effort, and therefore inconsistencies may be due to limited sampling. Another explanation relates to the degree of psychosocial disturbance found in these groups. While episodic drinkers in the studies of Dunn and Jacob had more disturbances than steady drinkers, the opposite was true of the groups in the Seilhamer study. That is, the steady in-home drinkers in this latter effort had more disturbances than the episodic out-of-home drinkers.

The steady–episodic dichotomy described by Jacob and colleagues is a distinction that needs validation with larger and more heterogenous samples. Nevertheless, these studies demonstrate that the drinking patterns of the alcoholic husband/father may be an important moderator of family relationship functioning. Clearly, identification of family processes linked to various consumption patterns would have important clinical implications.

SUMMARY

Thus far, neither the multifaceted literature on children of alcoholics nor the burgeoning field of family interaction research has provided an empirically substantiated understanding of the conditions under which family interactive processes mediate the relationship between parental drinking and adverse child outcome. However, some provocative hypotheses relating alcoholism and family interactions have been generated by various theoretical frameworks and the limited empirical literature.

First, Wolin et al. (1979, 1980) have suggested that children of alcoholics will fare better to the extent that the family can insulate its rituals from the disruptive effects of alcoholism. Second, Steinglass's (1980) developmental model of dry, wet, and transitional phases proposes that families engage in discernible, qualitatively distinct patterns of interaction that are adaptive to these phases. Third, the work of Dunn et al. (1987) and Seilhamer (1987) suggests that drinking pattern and location can be potent predictors of family interactions and relationship satisfaction. Finally, Moore's (1982) model suggests that alcohol consumption, via its disruption of primary parenting functions, alters the parent–child relationship in ways that lead to adverse child adjustment.

In accord with Moore's (1982) framework, the accumulated literature on children of alcoholics suggests that relationship changes effected by parental alcohol consumption are of a pernicious nature. Moreover, the chronicity of alcoholism would predict extended disruption of nurturance and socialization of children and ultimately, negative child adjustment. However, Steinglass's adaptive consequence model, based on clinical observations of family interactions during sober and intoxicated states, suggests that drinking in some family systems may actually serve to ease tensions or enhance the expression of emotion. Although this process may be maladaptive in the long run (by preventing resolution of stage-related tasks and progression along a normal family developmental path), the short-term consequences can be construed as positive. In sum, these theories suggest that: (1) there is an *ongoing* association between parental drinking and the parent–child relationship, (2) this association involves a *causal* relationship, in that drinking/intoxication effects disturbances in the parent–child relationship, and (3) while parental alcoholism is assumed to cause negative outcomes for children in the long run, the quality of the parent–child relationship during day-to-day cycles of sobriety and intoxication may vary with drinking pattern and consumption level. Further empirical tests of these theories are needed if current understanding of parent–child relationships in alcoholic homes is to move beyond the stage of casual speculation.

REFERENCES

Achenbach, T. M. (1978). The Child Behavior Profile: I. Boys aged 6–11. *Journal of Consulting and Clinical Psychology, 46*, 478–488.
Ackerman, R. J. (1983). *Children of alcoholics; A guidebook for educators, therapists, and parents* (2nd ed.). Holmes Beach, FL: Learning Publications.
Adler, R., & Raphael B., (1983). Children of alcoholics, *Australian and New Zealand Journal of Psychiatry, 17,* 3–8.
Alterman, A., Petrarulo, E., Tarter, R., & McCowan, J. (1982). Hyperactivity and alcoholism: Familial and behavioral correlates. *Addictive Behaviors, 7,* 413–421.
American Psychiatric Association. (1987). *Diagnostic and statistical manual of mental disorders* (3rd ed., rev.). Washington, DC: Author.
Bell, G., & Cohen, R. (1981). The Bristol Social Adjustment Guide: Comparison between the offspring of alcoholic and non-alcoholic mothers. *British Journal of Clinical Psychology, 20,* 93–95.

Bennett, L. A., & Wolin, S. J. (1986). Daughters and sons of alcoholics: Developmental paths in transmission. *Alcoholism, 22*(1), 3–15.

Biek, J. E. (1981). Screening test for identifying adolescents adversely affected by a parental drinking problem. *Journal of Adolescent Health Care, 2,* 107–113.

Black, C. (1979). Children of alcoholics. *Alcohol Health and Research World, 4*(1), 23–27.

Blane, H. T. (1979). Middle-age alcoholics and young drinkers. In H. T. Blane & M. E. Chafetz (Eds.), *Youth, alcohol, and social policy* (pp. 5–38). New York: Plenum Press.

Bosma, W. (1972). Children of alcoholics—a hidden tragedy. *Maryland State Medical Journal, 21*(1), 34–36.

Brown, S. (1986). Children with an alcoholic parent. In N. J. Estes & M. E. Heinemann (Eds.), *Alcoholism, developmental consequences, and interventions* (3rd ed., pp. 207–220). St. Louis: C. V. Mosby.

Burk, J. P., & Sher, K. J. (1988) The "forgotten children" revisited: Neglected areas of COA research. *Clinical Psychology Review, 8,*(3), 285–302.

Cadoret, R. J., Cain, C. A., & Grove, W. M. (1980). Development of alcoholism in adoptees raised apart from alcoholic biologic relatives. *Archives of General Psychiatry, 37,* 561–563.

Cadoret, R. J., & Gath, A. (1978). An inheritance of alcoholism in adoptees. *British Journal of Psychiatry, 132,* 252–258.

Callan, V. J. & Jackson, D. (1986). Children of alcoholic fathers and recovered alcoholic fathers: Personal and family functioning. *Journal of Studies on Alcohol, 47,* 180–182.

Chafetz, M. E., Blane, H. T. & Hill (1971). Children of alcoholics: Observations in a child guidance clinic. *Quarterly Journal of Studies on Alcohol, 32,* 687–698.

Clair, D., & Genest, M. (1987). Variables associated with the adjustment of offspring of alcoholic fathers. *Journal of Studies on Alcohol, 48,* 345–355.

Cloninger, C. R. (1983). Genetic and environmental factors in the development of alcoholism. *Journal of Psychiatric Treatment and Evaluation, 5,* 487–496.

Cloninger, C. R., Bohman, M., & Sigvardsson, S. (1981). Inheritance of alcohol abuse: Cross fostering analyses of adopted men. *Archives of General Psychiatry, 38,* 861–868.

Cloninger, C. R., Reich, T., & Yokoyama, S. (1983). Genetic diversity, genome organization, and investigation of the etiology of psychiatric diseases. *Psychiatric Developments, 3,* 225–246.

Cork, R. M. (1969). *The forgotten children: A study of children with alcoholic parents.* Toronto: Alcoholism and Drug Addiction Research Foundation of Ontario.

Deutsch, C., DiCicco, L., & Mills, D. J. (1982). Services for children of alcoholic parents. *Prevention, intervention and treatment: Concerns and models* (Alcohol and Health Research Monograph No. 3; DHHS Publication No. (ADM) 82-1192, pp. 147–173). Rockville, MD: U.S. Department of Health and Human Services.

DiCicco, M. S., Davis, R., Travis, J., & Orenstein, A. (1983–1984). Recruiting children from alcoholic families into a peer education program. *Alcohol Health and Research World, 8*(2), 28–34.

Donovan, J. E., Jessor, L. & Jessor, L. (1983). Problem drinking in adolescence and young adulthood: A follow-up study. *Journal of Studies on Alcohol, 44,* 109–137.

Drewery, J., & Rae, J. B. (1969). A group comparison of alcoholic and nonalcoholic marriages using the interpersonal perception technique. *British Journal of Psychiatry, 115,* 287–300.

Dunn, N. J. (1984). *Patterns of alcohol abuse and family stability.* Unpublished doctoral dissertation, University of Pittsburgh.

Dunn, N. J., Jacob, T., Hummon, N., & Seilhamer, R. A. (1987). Marital stability in alcoholic-spouse relationships as a function of drinking pattern and location. *Journal of Abnormal Psychology, 96,* 99–107.

el-Guebaly, N., & Offord, D. R. (1977). The offspring of alcoholics: A critical review. *American Journal of Psychiatry, 134,* 357–365.

el-Guebaly, N., & Offord, D. R. (1979). On being the offspring of an alcoholic: An update. *Alcoholism: Clinical and Experimental Research, 3,* 148–157.

el-Guebaly, N., & Offord, D. R. (1980). The competent offspring of psychiatrically ill parents. *Canadian Journal of Psychiatry, 25,* 457–463.

Feighner, J., Robins, E., Guze, S., Woodruff, R., Winokur, G., & Munoz, R. (1972). Diagnostic criteria for use in psychiatric research. *Archives of General Psychiatry, 26,* 57–63.

Goodwin, D. W. (1979). Alcoholism and heredity: A review and hypothesis. *Archives of General Psychiatry, 36,* 57–61.

Goodwin, D. W., Schulsinger, F., Hermansen, L., Guze, S. B., & Winokur, G. (1973). Alcohol problems in adoptees raised apart from alcoholic biological parents. *Archives of General Psychiatry, 28,* 238–243.

Gorad, S., McCourt, W. & Cobb, J. (1971). A communications approach to alcoholism. *Quarterly Journal of Studies on Alcohol, 32,* 651–668.

Graham-Clay, S. (1983). Fetal Alcohol Syndrome: A review of the current human research. *Canada's Mental Health, 31*(2), 2–5.

Gravitz, H., & Bowden, J. (1984). Therapeutic issues of adult children of alcoholics. *Alcohol Health and Research World, 8*(4), 25–29.

Heller, K., Sher, K. J., & Benson, C. S. (1982). Problems associated with risk overprediction in studies of offspring of alcoholics: Implications for prevention. *Clinical Psychology Review, 2,* 183–200.

Hesselbrock, V. M., Stabenau, J. R., & Hesselbrock, M. N. (1984). Minimal brain dysfunction and neuropsychological test performance in offspring of alcoholics. In M. Galanter & D. W. Goodwin (Eds.), *Recent developments in alcoholism* (Vol. 3, pp. 65–80). New York: Grune & Stratton.

Hindman, M. (1979). Family violence. *Alcohol Health and Research World, 4*(1), 2–11.

Hindman, M., & Small, J. (1984). Children of alcoholics: An interview with the NIAAA director. *Alcohol Health and Research World, 4*(1), 3–5.

Holzman, I. R. (1982). Fetal alcohol syndrome (FAS)—A review. *Journal of Children in Contemporary Society, 15,* 13–19.

Horn, J. L., Skinner, H. A., Wanberg, K., & Foster, F. M. (1982). *Alcohol Use Questionnaire (ADS).* Toronto: Addiction Research Foundation.

Jacob, T., Dunn, N. J., & Leonard, K. (1983). Patterns of alcohol abuse and family stability. *Alcoholism and Experimental Research, 7,* 382–385.

Jacob, T., Favorini, A., Meisel S., & Anderson, C. (1978). The spouse, children, and family interactions of the alcoholic: Substantive findings and methodological issues. *Journal of Studies on Alcohol, 39,* 1231–1251.

Jacob, T., & Leonard, K. (1986). Psychosocial functioning in children of alcoholic fathers, depressed fathers and control fathers. *Journal of Studies on Alcohol, 47,* 373–380.

Jacob, T., & Leonard, K. (1988). Alcoholic-spouse interaction as a function of alcoholism subtype and alcohol consumption interaction. *Journal of Abnormal Psychology, 97*(2), 231–237.

Jacob, T., Ritchey, D., Cvitkovic, J., & Blane, H. (1981). Communication styles of alcoholic and nonalcoholic families when drinking and not drinking. *Journal of Studies on Alcohol, 42,* 466–482.

Jacob, T., & Seilhamer, R. A. (1987). Alcoholism and family interaction. In T. Jacob (Ed.), *Family interaction and psychopathology: Theories, methods, and findings* (pp. 535–580). New York: Plenum Press.

Jacob, T., Seilhamer, R. A., & Rushe, R. (1989). Alcoholism and family interaction: an experimental paradigm. *American Journal of Drug and Alcohol Abuse, 15*(1), 73–91.

Kaij, L. (1960). *Alcoholism in twins: Studies on the etiology and sequels of abuse of alcohol.* Stockholm: Almqvist & Wiksell.

Kandel, D., & Logan, J. (1984). Patterns of drug use from adolescence to young adulthood. I. Periods of risk for initiation, continued use, and discontinuation. *American Journal of Public Health, 74,* 660–666.

Kennedy, D. L. (1976). Behavior of alcoholics and spouses in a simulation game situation. *Journal of Nervous and Mental Disease, 162,* 23–34.

Krahn, G. & Jacob, T., & Leonard, K. (1989). *Parent–child interactions in families with alcoholic fathers.* Unpublished manuscript.

Miller, D., & Jang, M. (1977). Children of alcoholics: A 20-year longitudinal study. *Social Work Research Abstracts, 13,* 23–29.

Mitchell, H. E. (1959). The interrelatedness of alcoholism and marital conflict. *American Journal of Orthopsychiatry, 28,* 888–891.

Moore, D. R. (1982). *Alcohol and family interaction: Child adjustment issues.* Unpublished manuscript.

Moos, R. H., & Billings, A. G. (1982). Children of alcoholics during the recovery process: alcoholic and matched control families. *Addictive Behaviors, 7,* 155–163.

Morrison, J., & Stewart, M. (1973). The psychiatric status of the legal families of adopted hyperactive children. *Archives of General Psychiatry, 28,* 888–891.

Nylander, I. (1960). Children of alcoholic fathers. *Acta Paediatrica Scandinavica, 49* (Suppl. 121), 1–134.

O'Gorman, P. (1981). Prevention issues involving children of alcoholics. In Department of Health and Human Services, *Services for children of alcoholics* (NIAAA Research Monograph No. 4; DHHS Publication No. (ADM) 81-1007, pp. 81–100). Rockville, MD: National Institute on Alcohol Abuse and Alcoholism.

Orme, T. C. & Rimmer, J. (1981). Alcoholism and child abuse: A review. *Journal of Studies on Alcohol, 42,* 273–287.

Partanen, J., Bruun, K., & Markkanen, T. (1966). *Inheritance of drinking behavior: A study of intelligence, personality, and use of alcohol in adult twins* (Finnish Foundation for Alcohol Studies Publication No. 14). Helsinki: Finnish Foundation for Alcohol Studies.

Russell, M., Henderson, C., & Blume, S. B. (1984). *Children of alcoholics; A review of the literature.* New York: Children of Alcoholics Foundation.

Rydelius, P. (1981). Children of alcoholic fathers: Their social adjustment and their health status over 20 years. *Acta Paediatrica Scandinavica* (Suppl. 286), 1–89.

Schuckit, M., Goodwin, D., & Winokur, G. (1972). A study of alcoholism in half-siblings. *American Journal of Psychiatry, 127,* 1653–1658.

Searles, J. S. (1988). The role of genetics in the pathogenesis of alcoholism. *Journal of Abnormal Psychology, 97,* 153–167.

Seilhamer, R. A. (1987). *Patterns of consumption and parent–child relationships in families of alcoholics.* Unpublished doctoral dissertation, University of Pittsburgh.

Sloboda, S. B. (1974). The children of alcoholics: A neglected problem. *Hospital and Community Psychiatry, 25,* 605–606.

Spitzer, R., & Endicott, J. (1977). *Research diagnostic criteria (RDC) for selected groups of functional disorders* (3rd ed.). New York: Biometrics Research, New York State Psychiatric Institute.

Smith, I. E. (1979). Fetal alcohol syndrome: A review. *Journal of the Medical Association of Georgia,* pp. 799–804.

Steinglass, P. (1979). The alcoholic family in the interaction laboratory. *Journal of Nervous and Mental Disease, 167,* 428–436.

Steinglass, P. (1980). A life history model of the alcoholic family. *Family Process, 19,* 211–226.

Steinglass, P. (1981). The alcoholic family at home: Patterns of interaction in dry, wet, and transitional stages of alcoholism. *Archives of General Psychiatry, 38,* 578–584.

Steinglass, P., Davis, D., & Berenson, D. (1977). Observations of conjointly hospitalized "alcoholic couples" during sobriety and intoxication: Implications for theory and therapy. *Family Process, 16,* 1–16.

Steinglass, P., Weiner, S., & Mendelson, J. H. (1971). A systems approach to alcoholism: A model and its clinical application. *Archives of General Psychiatry, 24,* 401–408.

Strodbeck, F. (1951). Husband–wife interaction over revealed differences. *American Sociological Review, 16,* 468–478.

Tamerin, J. S., Toler, A., DeWolfe, J., Packer, L., & Neuman, C. P. (1973). Spouses' perception of their alcoholic partners; A retrospective view of alcoholics by themselves and their spouses. *Proceedings of the Third Annual Alcoholism Conference of the National Institute on Alcohol Abuse and Alcoholism* pp. 33–49.

Tarter, R., McBride, H., Buonpane, N., & Schneider, D. (1977). Differentiation of alcoholics: Childhood history of minimal brain dysfunction, family history, and drinking patterns. *Archives of General Psychiatry, 34,* 761–768.

Warner, R., & Rosett, H. L. (1975). The effects of drinking on offspring: An historical survey of the American and British literature. *Journal of Studies on Alcohol, 36,* 1395–1420.

Werner, E. E. (1986). Resilient offspring of alcoholics; A longitudinal study from birth to age 18. *Journal of Studies on Alcohol, 47,* 34–40.

West, M. O., & Prinz, R. J. (1987). Parental alcoholism and childhood psychopathology. *Psychological Bulletin, 102,* 204–218.

Wilson, C. (1982). The impact on children. In J. Orford & J. Harwin (Eds.), *Alcohol and the family* (pp. 151–166). London: Croom Helm.

Wilson, C., & Orford, J. (1978). Children of alcoholics: Report of a preliminary study and comments on the literature. *Journal of Studies of Alcohol, 39,* 121–142.

Wolin, S. J., Bennett, L. A., & Noonan, D. L. (1979). Family rituals and the recurrence of alcoholism over generations. *American Journal of Psychiatry, 136,* 589–593.

Wolin, S. J., Bennett, L. A., Noonan, D. L., & Teitelbaum, M. A. (1980). Disrupted family rituals. *Journal of Studies on Alcohol, 41,* 199–214.

Woodside, M. (1988). Research on children of alcoholics: past and future. *British Journal of Addiction, 83,* 785–792.

Zucker, R. A. (1976). Parental influences on the drinking patterns of their children. In M. Greenblatt & M. Schuckit (Eds.), *Alcoholism problems in women and children* (pp. 211–238). New York: Grune & Stratton.

CHAPTER EIGHT

Prevention and Treatment Approaches for Children of Alcoholics

CAROL N. WILLIAMS

The purpose of this chapter is to critique the research literature on prevention and treatment programs for children of alcoholics (COAs). Unfortunately, empirical studies on prevention and treatment for COAs are almost nonexistent. Far more questions than answers exist, and the field is best characterized as being in the descriptive stage. Little research has been completed on the conceptualization of problems and issues facing children of alcoholics or on the efficacy of COA prevention and treatment programs that have been proposed in either the popular or the professional literature. Research in this area is faced with two major obstacles: One is the nascent nature of theory development and the other is the considerable confusion over what exactly constitutes prevention efforts as opposed to intervention and treatment efforts with this high-risk group.

That the field is at this stage is normal. Research needs to go through a developmental process before rigorous scientific studies can be conducted. Currently, a variety of clinical observations, descriptive studies, and suggestions for interventions exist. Research in the addictions field in general is weak on theory, but even more so in the case of the relatively new domain of COAs. As a result, the field is in the process of inductive (or grounded) theory development constructed from many discrete observations.

Out of these facts, beliefs, and observations, several systematic sets of ideas or models and constructs will be formulated that can be tested, shaped, and reshaped until they fit the observations fairly well. Kuhn (1970) postulated that every scientific field emerges in a disparate, uncoordinated manner, with lines of investigation and theoretical ideas developing autonomous and competitive positions, until a particular set of ideas assumes the status of a paradigm. This paradigm then acquires dominance in the field until a shift to another, more explanatory, paradigm occurs.

Studies on children of alcoholics can be considered "preparadigmatic" in that no one set of ideas has dominance over another and many lines of inquiry appear to be equally legitimate. The field is on the verge of developing and

188 C. N. Williams

empirically testing models of prevention, intervention, and treatment based on the wealth of clinical descriptive data available. This chapter will organize the findings from the literature in these three areas and suggest research issues that need to be addressed.

A lack of clarity exists, however, regarding what exactly constitutes prevention and treatment programs for COAs. Examples of some unclear definitions of these terms are evident from a 1979 symposium on services for children of alcoholics (Department of Health and Human Services, 1981). Treatment was defined as "the process of providing services needed by the child. It is not necessarily a formal therapy program, but it may include activities usually thought of as 'prevention.' . . . The problem assessment and definition stage of the treatment process have some unique aspects for the children of the alcoholic parent. . . . There may be no presenting problem, no visible symptoms, no accurate developmental history, or no history at all" (p. 23).

The definition of prevention is just as obscure. "Due to its targeting on specific areas for intervention, prevention has an orientation similar to treatment [but] somewhat more expanded than treatment. As a *treatment strategy, prevention* should . . ." (p. 30, emphasis added). This last statement, in which prevention is defined as a treatment strategy, illustrates the confusion as to exactly what is being done: Are we treating COAs for their exposure to parental alcoholism, preventing their development of future alcoholism, or accomplishing some combination of both? The symposium's definition of prevention was thought to improve on the one developed by the National Council on Alcoholism (1976), which stated that "primary prevention of alcohol misuse, abuse, and alcoholism means to permanently forestall the development of these conditions."

Given the lack of clarity regarding the goals of prevention, intervention, and treatment and the lack of specific operationalizations of goals and terms necessary to conduct evaluation outcome research in these three areas, it is not surprising that confusion exists as to what is trying to be accomplished with whom and how it should be optimally researched. Part of the problem may be due to the belief by some that all COAs are impaired and in need of intervention simply because they lived with an alcoholic parent, regardless of whether they are symptomatic or not. Examples of this belief are the proposal by Cermak (1984) for a new DSM diagnostic category of codependency for family members of alcoholics and the challenge by Balis (1986) that the appearance of competence among COAs is illusory. Others warn against the risk of overprediction; because some members of a group show symptoms does not mean that the group as a whole should be defined as high risk (Heller, Sher, & Benson, 1982).

A public health model provides a useful organizational scheme to clarify the goals and objectives of programs for COAs and facilitates the conceptualization and design of appropriate evaluation and outcome studies for these programs. The model can be conceived in two ways: as primary, secondary, and tertiary prevention or as prevention, intervention, and treatment programs, both of which relate to providing a comprehensive continuum of care dependent on where in the continuum of substance use the individuals fall.

Primary prevention targets the general population proactively, before people ever begin to drink or before they display any evidence of problems from drinking (see Figure 8.1). The goal is to keep people problem-free and at low risk. Secondary prevention, or intervention, efforts occur when symptoms of a problem related to substance use first appear. The goal is early detection of problems and interruption and reversal of these problems or risk behaviors (see Figure 8.2). Tertiary prevention, also called treatment, occurs when serious dysfunction from substance use is present. The goal is to prevent further deterioration and dysfunction in the person and to minimize the impact of the dysfunction on those surrounding that person (see Figure 8.3).

PHASE I. PRIMARY PREVENTION

A. Broad-Based Primary Prevention Settings

Media	Community-Based	Educational	Work	Social/Recreational	Health Care

Goal: Alcoholism reduction in the general population includes messages for COAs at all age levels and at single (e.g., family history of alcoholism) and multiple (family history positive, low socioeconomic status, etc.) levels of risk. For some COAs (particularly resilient ones) risk information may be all that is needed to deter development of alcoholism and other dysfunctions.

Research Questions: What are the most effective programs and settings for channeling this information, and at what level of risk is this approach sufficient to prevent alcoholism for COAs?

B. High-Risk Population

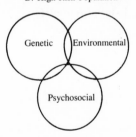

Domains of Risk Factors

Goal: Identification as high-risk by self or others from awareness-raising and training provided in general education. Receive more specific education about increased risks. Prevention efforts targeted specifically to characteristics of this group.

Research Questions: For which symptomless COAs are targeted prevention programs sufficient to prevent development of alcoholism and other dysfunctions? What is the most effective combination of educational techniques and settings? What are the most effective means of identifying and referring those in need of secondary and tertiary prevention programs?

FIGURE 8.1. Issues pertaining to primary prevention of alcoholism with COAs.

PHASE II. SECONDARY PREVENTION (INTERVENTION)

Symptom Areas

Cognitive	Psychological/ Affective	Physical	Behavioral	Substance Use
Lower IQ Low achievement Neurological deficits	Coping problems Depression Low self-esteem	Illnesses Accidents Psychosomatic complaints	Impulsivity Aggression Acting-out behaviors Delinquency	Heavy alcohol or drug use

Goals: Screening for COAs manifesting symptoms of alcohol abuse or other disorders in a variety of settings, such as special education classrooms, child guidance clinics, health care settings, criminal justice system, youth agencies.

Research Questions: What are the best screening tools for which settings? Does intervention into symptoms associated with increased risk for alcoholism decrease the number of developmental problems and incidence of drug and alcohol abuse? How do COAs who develop symptoms differ from COAs who do not develop symptoms? What constitutes the best intervention programs in which settings for what specific constellation of risk factors?

FIGURE 8.2 Issues pertaining to secondary prevention of alcoholism with COAs.

All three efforts can use similar techniques such as education, individual, group, and family sessions, skills building, and values clarification, but the content and the purpose of each endeavor is different. Because of the strong intergenerational transmission patterns of alcoholism, the concepts of primary, secondary, and tertiary prevention are especially useful, since interventions at any of these levels can have long-term preventive effects on several generations of the family.

PHASE III. TERTIARY PREVENTION (TREATMENT)

Treatment of Alcoholic Family	Treatment of Alcoholic COA

Goal: Treatment of the person who has developed alcoholism as part of a family unit or treatment of alcoholic COA to arrest the disorder and prevent transmission.

Research Questions: Which family-systems treatment techniques, in combination with which constellation of family characteristics, are most effective for preventing alcoholism and other dysfunctions in the child? Do alcoholic COAs need different treatment components to arrest their alcoholism and its intergenerational transmission than do alcoholics who do not have an alcoholic heritage?

FIGURE 8.3. Issues pertaining to tertiary prevention of alcoholism with COAs.

PRIMARY PREVENTION PROGRAMS

The National Council on Alcoholism's definition of primary prevention as preventing a problem before it begins is compatible with a public health model definition. Prevention programs for COAs have two major objectives: to deter the development of drinking problems and to deter the development of antecedent risk factors associated with the subsequent development of drinking problems or other dysfunctional patterns of behavior. Broad-brush prevention programs are aimed at the population in general, which is considered to be on a continuum of risk from very slight to extreme.

Two models of prevention have been proposed. The distribution of consumption model states that decreases in the amount of drinking are effected through societal control of availability of alcohol. This includes such measures as price increases, banning "happy hours," shortening the hours of sale, and raising the legal drinking age (Parker & Harman, 1980). According to Ledermann (1956), reductions in overall societal drinking levels lead to decreases in the number of heavy and problem drinkers. Presumably, the number of children adversely affected by alcohol-related problems in their families as well as the number who develop problems in the future would also be reduced. The efficacy of this prevention strategy for COAs has not yet been tested, although the distribution of consumption model has been shown to be effective in reducing alcohol-related problems (Romelsjö & Ågren, 1985).

The sociocultural model focuses on education and "strengthening" individuals through information, clarification of values, and various skill-building techniques so that these individuals choose abstinence or moderation of drinking, thereby lowering their risk for development of alcohol-related problems (Heath, 1980). Such primary prevention campaigns can be mounted through the media, community-based prevention programs, and in specific settings such as schools, work, physicians' offices, and recreational activities or social clubs. Some of the major alcohol education messages of such campaigns are the awareness of the risks facing COAs, knowledge of symptoms of dysfunction, what prevention measures can be taken, and where to seek more information or obtain professional help. An example of the impact of a media event was the 1987 television documentary on inherited risks for addiction to alcohol and other drugs, which generated 800 phone calls, 80 letters, and 1,950 requests for copies of the videocassettes (Casement, 1987).

Such measures help educate all COAs, both identified and unidentified, whether they are displaying symptoms or not. Caregivers and others in the lives of COAs are also educated to recognize that these children are at increased risk. A primary prevention approach avoids issues of stigmatization and harmful labeling of children and provides an opportunity for identification of children in need of further education or intervention. Unfortunately, the effectiveness of such programs on the functioning of COAs is largely unknown.

A study by the New York State Division of Alcoholism (Lillis, 1987) is suggestive of the potential usefulness of a primary prevention effort. A survey of 2,000 persons was conducted using a random digit dialing sampling method. Although 17% of the respondents stated that one or both parents were alcoholic, only 5% of those sampled were aware that COAs were at increased risk for developing alcoholism. The most interesting aspect of this study, though, was that knowledge did, in fact, seem to influence behavior. Those COAs ignorant of their increased risk drank three times as much and seven times as often as did COAs aware of their increased risk for the development of alcoholism. They also were more likely to drink to the point of intoxication than were members of the informed group.

For some COAs, a general informational message regarding their increased risk may be all that is required to reduce their risk for alcoholism. It must be remembered that a majority of COAs do *not* develop alcoholism and are symptomless. Primary prevention messages may be adequate to meet their low-risk needs. The overwhelming majority of the literature on COAs is based on self-identified or clinical samples of help-seeking COAs whose needs have been described primarily by clinicians. Some evidence suggests that this clinical focus has skewed the perception of COAs in the general population (Barnard & Spoentgen, 1986; Heller et al., 1984).

Community-Based Prevention

One of the most promising models for prevention has evolved from the heart-health prevention programs, where whole communities are targeted for massive risk-reduction prevention campaigns in which the incidence of and risks for cardiovascular disease have actually decreased (Johnson & Solis, 1983; Perry, Klepp, & Shultz, 1988). Similar efforts are being explored for reduction of alcohol problems, but the final results are not yet available (Waters, 1984). The components of these programs include "mass media compaigns, community-based organization, adult education, youth education, health professional education, and mass screening of health medical services" (Johnson & Solis, p. 105). Benard (1986) summarizes the characteristics of effective prevention programs as: (1) integrated into multiple systems within the total community, (2) targeted to all youth as opposed to just high-risk individuals, (3) part of a broader health promotion campaign, (4) of sufficient duration and intensity, and (5) encouraging participation and personal responsibility. Strategies for accomplishing these goals are also provided.

The arguments for mounting community-wide prevention programs that include components targeted to COAs are similar to those for mounting such programs against cardiovascular disease. One justification is that by targeting high-risk groups only, a larger group of potential cases would be neglected (Perry et al., 1988). The majority of people are distributed in the midrange of risk factors rather than at either extreme, and it is easier to effect moderate changes in behavior and attitudes than large ones.

Comprehensive community programs can lead to indirect effects that also influence risk factors. For example, healthy lifestyles education that teaches stress reduction techniques can secondarily result in decreased excessive drinking as a means of handling stress, which in turn decreases the risk of developing alcohol problems. Finally, because of easy access, most prevention programs have been implemented in school systems. However, children are out of school more than they are in school, and family and social factors and community values may exert greater influence on their behavior (Johnson & Solis, 1983).

Community prevention efforts can occur in a multitude of settings with all ages of COAs. Some strategies that have been suggested are as follows: literature in physicians' waiting rooms or school nurses' offices (Scavnicky-Mylant, 1987; Triplett & Arbeson, 1983); self-help and other COA-specific books promoted in libraries and book stores (Manning, 1987); and incorporation of information into health-promotion campaigns at the worksite (Woodside, 1986) and in parenting classes (O'Gorman & Oliver-Diaz, 1987). All can be effective vehicles for promoting prevention and education.

Even when children are not directly targeted in these prevention programs, they can indirectly benefit from them by the increased awareness of those around them and possible reduction of excessive drinking in the community at large. Little systematic attention has been paid to prevention efforts for COAs at this level, and virtually no research has been conducted to evaluate the effectiveness of these approaches for COAs. Given the potential benefits derived from these prevention efforts, community prevention research is an important endeavor to evaluate the efficacy of various approaches and of specific components.

School Settings

Many of the major alcohol education curricula for schools address familial alcoholism in their lesson plans. The Cambridge and Somerville Program for Alcoholism Rehabilitation (CASPAR) Alcohol Education Program curriculum is one of the most aggressive in terms of offering out-of-school, time-limited groups for children from alcoholic families. DiCicco (1981) believed that "CASPAR's work with children of alcoholics is a natural and even inevitable outgrowth of its school-based primary prevention program. We are convinced that there is no shortcut that will prove comparably effective: a school-based primary prevention network is the key to systematic work with children of alcoholics before their troubles become obvious and more difficult to reverse. And trained teachers, rather than guidance counselors or school nurses, are the heart of that prevention network" (p. 47).

All students receive alcohol education in the classroom that includes general information on alcoholic families. They could then self-refer or be referred by teachers, other students, or agency personnel to after-school groups to gain more information on alcohol in general or about alcoholic families specifically. A strong component of this after-school program depends on the use of trained peer leaders who are themselves COAs to help run the groups. DiCicco and colleagues (DiCicco, Davis, Hogan, MacLean, & Orenstein, 1984; DiCicco, Davis, Travis, & Orenstein, 1984) found that students were reluctant to join the children of alcoholic families group, but they constituted one fourth of the basic alcohol education group.

When asked what they had learned and how self-disclosive they could be, children in the alcoholic families group reported the highest percentage of positive learning experiences. COAs in the basic alcohol education group, however, consistently reported more positive responses to the group than did children from families without alcoholism. A higher precentage of COAs in the basic group also reported that they had learned useful information and indicated that they should drink differently, and were actually drinking less, as a result of the group experience than did nonCOAs or children in the COA group. The implications were that, although COAs seemed to gain more from groups dealing directly with familial alcoholism, more children were willing to attend an educational group that did not identify them and still were able to gain useful information.

More outcome research has been conducted on alcohol education approaches in general, the findings of which should be useful in developing programs for COAs. In a meta-analysis of 143 education programs, Tobler (1986) reported that peer-based prevention programs produced the most favorable outcomes, followed by alternative programs that provided either non-drug-oriented leisure activities or remedial help for high-risk youth. Unfortunately, one of the discouraging aspects of classroom education has been the lack of long-term behavioral change recorded as an outcome of alcohol and drug education (Hopkins, Mauss, Kearney, & Weisheit, 1988; Mauss, Hopkins, Weisheit, & Kearney, 1988). The implications with regard to education programs for COAs are unknown and in need of systematic investigation.

SECONDARY PREVENTION (INTERVENTION) PROGRAMS

Secondary prevention is intervention in the earliest stages of problem development, with high-risk groups often being specifically targeted for identification and intervention. There are two main goals for interventions with COAs. One is to identify and address early symptoms of problem drinking in order to prevent development of more serious drinking problems. The second is to detect and alter dysfunctional behaviors and coping skills that may be predisposing risk factors for problem drinking or other life problems. The bulk of both the popular literature (Black, 1982; Wegscheider, 1981; Woititz, 1983) and the scientific literature (el-Guebaly & Offord, 1977; Russell, Henderson, & Blume, 1985) on COAs has described how COAs differ from other children in terms of psychosocial and physical functioning, with COAs almost always displaying lower levels of adaptive functioning and more disadvantaged environmental circumstances.

Myriad problems exist with these descriptions. They are usually based on clinical impressions or on small research sample sizes selected on the basis of convenience rather than as a representative or general population-based sample. Standardized instruments are rarely used and the criteria for parental alcoholism are often unspecified. Comparison groups of children with psychiatric or other problems (e.g., divorced parents, chronic illness) as well as those with no apparent problems are underutilized. The specificity of characteristics of children from alcoholic families compared with children from other types of disrupted families needs further exploration. Study results are often reported simply as differences in percentages between groups of children. The statistical significance or confidence limits for the differences are often not reported.

Despite these shortcomings, a surprising consistency in the description of characteristics of children from alcoholic homes has emerged, suggesting convergent validity from these diverse studies. These characteristics have been reviewed extensively elsewhere (Kumpfer, 1987; Russell et al., 1985; Tarter, Alterman, & Edwards, 1985). The differences can be briefly summarized as follows. Far more is known about male COAs than female children, possibly because males are more likely to manifest attention-attracting symptoms than females. In addition to being at increased genetic risk for alcoholism (but see Searles, Chapter 5, this volume), COAs also experienced more psychosocial deficits than children from nonalcoholic homes. They displayed lower levels of self-esteem, greater impulsivity and hyperactivity, greater external locus of control, more illness, accidents and psychosomatic complaints, and more conduct disorders and academic problems than did children from nonalcoholic homes.

Environmental risk factors for these children were also elevated. Alcoholic families were more likely to be disrupted by divorce, separation, absence of parent or removal of child from the home, and greater financial instability. Higher prevalence of sexual and physical abuse, as well as neglect and inadequate parenting were also reported, and children appeared to develop fewer support systems to mitigate some of these effects.

In response to these problems, a variety of interventions have been developed for all ages of COAs. Although techniques may differ, many programs have similar basic components. Group settings appear to be preferred for addressing issues of familial alcoholism (Hawley & Brown, 1981; Miller, 1983; Morehouse, 1986). Because of family denial of alcoholism and "rules" not to talk about any problems outside the family, as well as the outright lies and excuse-making that occur as part of the process of protecting family secrets, children found it quite liberating to be with other children who had the same problems as they. The isolation of some children was often so great that they did not talk to even their siblings about what was happening (Owen, Rosenberg, & Barkley, 1985). Groups provided a great sense of relief and affirmation that they were not "crazy," and that peers had experienced and felt the same things.

The tasks of group interventions can best be summarized as overcoming the three cardinal family rules of COAs outlined by Black (1982): "Don't talk, don't trust, don't feel." Most group programs consist of four basic components: education about alcoholism and its effects on the family; identification and expression of feelings; development of healthy social interactions with children and adults; and development of healthy problem-solving and coping skills (Bingham & Bargar, 1985). To date, empirical assessments of groups are practically nonexistent. Mostly subjective impressions of the value of groups have been reported. The results of a few programs that conducted a more stringent assessment are reviewed in this section.

Groups for Young Children

Dinklage and Plummer (1985) evaluated a 20-week, 1-hour-a-week group for 13 children of alcoholics (mean age, 9.7 years) referred to a child guidance clinic for other problems. They employed the Nowicki–Strickland Locus of Control Scale (Nowicki & Strickland, 1972) and developed an alcohol awareness test, an adaptive behavior checklist, and a test of coping strategies to be administered before and after the group intervention (a pre- and posttest research design). The children's parents completed the Personality Inventory for Children (PIC; Wirt, Seat, & Broen, 1977) at pretest, but many refused to fill it out at posttest, stating that it was too long and complicated. The children filled out the Piers–Harris Self-Concept Scale (Piers, 1984) at posttest.

Significant increases in knowledge about alcoholism and positive coping strategies were reported between the pre- and posttest sessions. Trends toward greater adaptive behavior and internal locus of control occurred, although these two results were not statistically significant. The parents' ratings of the children on the PIC were in the maladaptive range at pretest, yet the children's self-concept scores on the Piers–Harris scale at posttest were in the normal range.

Anderson and Quast (1983) also used the PIC for 50 boys and girls from 6 to 12 years of age who had a parent in an inpatient alcoholism program. The children were significantly more maladaptive than normative samples on the Family, Adjustment, and Anxiety Scales. Based on these findings, an 18-hour, 12-week cognitive-behavior modification skills-training program for children and a rational-emotive therapy group for parents was developed. The program was implemented with 18 children whose parents were in an alcoholism outpatient aftercare program. Anderson and Quast (1983) concluded that "all children improved in their ability to understand and practice the self-counseling principles taught" (p. 184), but specifically what these skills were and the magnitude of the pre- to posttest change were not specified.

Woodward (1985) assessed pre- and posttest results and 8-month outcome of a 6-week group for COAs that consisted of weekly meetings of a child group, a parent group, and a family group in a mental health clinic setting. This treatment group ($n = 20$) of COAs received alcohol education, psychosocial education, and psychotherapeutic interventions. The group was compared with three other groups: COAs not in treatment ($n = 13$), nonCOAs whose parents were receiving mental health services ($n = 6$), and nonCOAs whose parents had *not* received mental health services in the last 5 years ($n = 13$). The Conners Parent Checklist, the PIC, the Nowicki–Strickland Locus of Control Scale, the Piers–Harris Self-Concept Scale, and the Walker Problem Behavior Checklist (Walker, 1970) were used.

No significant treatment effects were recorded for increased alcohol knowledge, changes in attitudes, peer relations, or school behavior. Positive changes were reported in social skills and achievement; for some of the behaviors on the Conners Parent Checklist that reflected emotional development, less acting out, and lower dysphoric behavior; and for mothers' but not fathers' impression that the home environment had improved. The modest effects may have been a function of the small, unequal group sizes, the brevity of the intervention, the insensitivity of the instruments to measure change over time, and the fact that the nonCOAs may still have come from families disrupted by mental health problems.

Adolescent Groups

Deckman and Downs (1982) described a group intervention for three boys and five girls between 13 and 17 years of age who had been referred to a COA group by youth service agencies. The most difficult problems with the COA adolescents involved establishing and maintaining boundaries and rules for acceptable behavior. The youths acted angry and disruptive, yet rated their group experience as being "very good or excellent," with overcoming isolation as the best aspect of it.

Kern, Tippman, Fortgang, and Paul (1977) described an unsuccessful attempt to use psychodrama, role-play, and puppetry with three mothers and eight COA teenagers in a 16-hour, 8-week group. The teenagers were unwilling to participate with their mothers, and separate groups for mothers and teenagers were recommended. Morehouse (1979) advocated the use of in-school student assistance programs for students displaying problems or adjustment difficulties. Those identified by student assistance counselors as children of alcoholics could then be referred to groups specifically addressing the issues and consequences of familial alcoholism.

Several dissertations have investigated the effectiveness of Al-Ateen for COAs. Hughes (1977) compared three groups of 25 adolescents each. Group 1 consisted of adolescents (mean age, 15 years) who were not members of Al-Ateen or receiving any services. Fourteen of them were recruited as they entered their first Al-Ateen meeting. Groups 2 and 3 were matched to Group 1 by age, sex, grade level, and father's occupational level, but Group 2 had no parental alcoholism and Group 3 was composed of members of Al-Ateen and matched to Group 1 on number and sex of alcoholic parents as well. How long the individuals in Group 3 had been members of the organization and the method used to determine parental alcoholism and its severity were not reported.

The COA group receiving no services displayed significantly lower self-esteem and more impairment on the Profile of Mood States (McNair, Lorr, & Droppelman, 1981) than did either of the other two groups. Both the Al-Ateen and the non-Al-Ateen COAs were more likely to have been in trouble with the law and more reported that they were not working up to their academic ability than did subjects in the group with no alcoholic parents. Apparently, Al-Ateen helped adolescents achieve more positive self-esteem and mood states, but behavior was less affected.

Peitler (1980) randomly assigned 14- to 16-year-old sons of alcoholics to one of three treatment conditions. Thirty-six boys, half of whom were under the age 8 when their fathers developed alcoholism, were assigned to group treatment, Al-Ateen, or no treatment. The California Test of Personality (Thorpe, Clark, & Tiegs, 1939) was administered at pre- and posttest in each treatment condition with special emphasis on the measurement of self-worth, withdrawal tendencies, and antisocial tendencies.

The group that was younger at the time of the father's development of alcoholism showed greater impairment in all three areas of functioning than did the older group. Group counseling proved to be more effective than Al-Ateen in improving feelings of self-worth and decreasing antisocial tendencies. When compared with the no-treatment group, boys in Al-Ateen and group treatment who were younger at the time of their father's alcoholism showed increased self-worth. None of the treatments reduced the withdrawal tendencies of the boys who were older when their fathers developed alcoholism.

Barnard and Spoentgen (1986) sought to understand the differences between COAs who sought treatment and those who did not. They used the Children of Alcoholics Screening Test (Jones, 1982) to screen college students in a required general psychology course into non-treatment-seeking COAs and nonCOAs. These two groups were compared with 21 students in three COA campus groups that met for a total of 12 hours over an 8-week period. The Personal Orientation Inventory (Shostrom, 1974) was administered at the beginning and at the end of the semester to all the groups.

The treatment-seeking group tended to be older than the other two groups and scored significantly lower than the other two on inner-directedness, self-regard and acceptance, feeling reactivity, and capacity for intimate contact. They also reported more parental loss due to death or separation as well as fewer financial resources. Surprisingly, the non-treatment-seeking COAs showed a greater capacity for intimate contact but otherwise were very similar to the nonCOA group. Treatment-seeking COAs displayed significant improvement on pretest–posttest assessments of inner-directedness, self-regard, and capacity for intimate contact. The authors concluded that some COAs were more resilient than others and that the more impaired COAs were the treatment seekers. Unfortunately, the components of treatment were not well described, nor was the durability of these changes measured.

Adult Groups

Cermak and Brown (1982) described a more intensive group (20 weeks, 90 minutes per session) for adult COAs recruited from clinic caseloads and newspaper advertisements. The reasons clients gave for joining the group were to sever identity with parents, face fears of developing alcoholism, overcome feelings of guilt and overresponsibility, and break the patterns of family denial. The therapists defined issues of control as the most important ones facing the clients, in addition to difficulties with trust of self and others and the need for personal validation. Brown and Beletsis (1986) proposed that clients transferred unresolved family dynamics onto the therapy group and then worked out their issues within that context. Although adult COA groups are probably the most numerous of all extant COA groups, the least amount of outcome research has been forthcoming about the efficacy and specificity of their intentions.

Resilient Children

Implications for interventions can be gleaned from unimpaired as well as impaired children. Garmezy (1984) proposed that it is just as important to understand why children do *not* get sick as it is to know why and how they do get sick. Intervention programs should focus on more than just the alleviation of symptoms that lead to dysfunction or alcoholism. It would be helpful to identify and foster proactive protective factors that could increase resistance to dysfunctional behavior such as low self-esteem, poor peer relations, and alcoholism. One of the most important findings from research on children resilient in the face of adversity was that a child's temperament and ability to interact positively with adults greatly increased that child's chances for becoming competent and successful as an adult (Kauffman, Grunebaum, Cohler, & Gamer, 1979; Pellegrini et al., 1986; Rutter, 1979; Thomas & Chess, 1977, 1984; Werner, 1985, 1986).

Even in families with parents impaired by alcoholism, mental illness, or poverty, the appealing (e.g., easy temperament) baby and child were able to elicit what little nurturance the caretaker could give and were able to build positive interactional patterns with adults to develop a supportive, protective social system. Such children experienced fewer negative life events, had higher self-esteem, and had greater goal orientation and achievement than children unable to elicit such support. Children unable to elicit support were more likely to develop substance abuse or mental disorders (Johnson, 1985). Overcoming such adversities can have a positive "steeling" effect (Bleuler, 1978; Eisenstadt, 1978; Sheehy, 1986). No research has been conducted on how to incorporate these qualities found in resilient children into prevention and intervention programs for COAs, but it is an important area of future inquiry.

TERTIARY (TREATMENT) PROGRAMS

The principal purpose of tertiary prevention is to halt further deterioration or dysfunction in impaired persons and to help them regain their health. Second, the impact of the impairment on those surrounding the person should also be mitigated as a result of the primary patient's treatment. This section will focus on two types of treatment programs for COAs: family therapy, in which the whole family is identified as the patient, and treatment of alcoholic COAs.

Family Therapy

Family systems theory, developed in the early 1960s, posits that family members behave in patterned ways, such that change in the functioning of one member is automatically compensated for by change in one or more other family members. Bowen (1974) described three states of system functioning: healthy adaptive functioning, overfunctioning of one or more members when decompensated states occur in other members, and unproductive dysfunctional states in which "an organ that functions for another for long periods of time does not return to normal so easily" (p. 116). Alcoholism is viewed as a dysfunction that causes imbalance in the family system and "when it is possible to modify the family relationship system, the alcoholic dysfunction is alleviated, even though the dysfunctional one may not have been part of the therapy" (p. 117). This rationale is often used for intervening with children of alcoholics even when the parent or parents are not in treatment. Changes in the rigidly patterned behavior can cause enough discomfort to make the alcoholic or other family members seek treatment. Jackson (1954) was one of the first to describe the developmental process whereby families attempted to cope with an alcoholic's progression into and recovery from alcoholism.

The effectiveness of specific family treatment approaches with alcoholics has not been systematically researched. A few studies have been conducted on the effect of the alcoholic's recovery on the family's functioning, with mixed results. Moos and Billings (1982) studied the intact families of 51 alcoholics admitted to an inpatient treatment program who had nonadult children living in the home. These families were followed for 18 months after treatment and divided into recovered ($n = 28$) and relapsed ($n = 23$) groups. The alcoholic families were matched to community control families from the same census tracts. Only the parents filled out the Health and Daily Living Form (Moos, Cronkite, Billings, & Finney, 1987) and the Family Environment Scale (Moos & Moos, 1981), so that reports of the children's functioning were second-hand.

Children of recovered alcoholics were reported to be functioning as well as the children in the community control group. Children of relapsed alcoholics experienced more emotional and physical problems than did the other two groups, and their families were judged to be lower on family cohesion, expressiveness, parental congruence, and family activities. Children's emotional health was related to parental emotional, vocational, and physical functioning and handling of stress. Filstead, McElfresh, and Anderson (1981) included the self-reporting of children aged 9 years and older and reported comparable findings in terms of differences between the families of unrecovered alcoholics and Moos's normative control group on the Family Environment Scale.

Using the self-reports of 54 teenagers with an alcoholic parent in treatment (26 recovered parents) matched to 54 community control group teenagers, McLachlan, Walderman, and Thomas (1973) concluded that the relationships between alcoholic parents and children were more impaired than those of the control groups, but that the children of alcoholics did not evidence greater personality, intellectual, or academic disturbance. The impairment was reversible with the parent's recovery from alcoholism, except for a low self-concept among teenagers with an alcoholic father, whether he was recovered or not.

Callan and Jackson (1985) studied 35 adolescent children of alcoholic fathers (21 of whom were recovered) in Al-Ateen and compared them with 35 matched control children. Children of recovered parents and control group parents scored higher on levels of family happiness, cohesiveness, trust, and affection than did children of unrecovered fathers, but all adolescents scored similarly on measures of self-esteem and locus of control. COAs were less happy with their lives, however, than was the community control group of nonCOA children. Booz-Allen & Hamilton, Inc. (1974), in interviews with 50 adolescent and adult COAs, also found that they were generally unhappy and that those with recovered parents were not functioning better than those whose parents had not recovered.

A significant issue that relates to recovery from alcoholism is whether or not children should be included in the therapy sessions. All too often, the term "family therapy" is used when in fact counseling of couples is occurring and the children are not part of the process (although they may be the subject of sessions). Reasons for the lack of child involvement are varied: therapist resistance, parental or child resistance, lack of insurance coverage or clinical resources, and belief that treatment of the parent will have a trickle-down effect and be sufficient for adequate functioning of the child (Cable, Noel, & Swanson, 1986).

Meeks and Kelly (1970) reported that inclusion of the children in the therapy sessions was beneficial and Dulfano (1982) suggested that it was imperative. In order to determine the efficacy and impact on the child's health and functioning, several issues require further research efforts, such as exclusion or inclusion of the child in family therapy, at what age, at what stage of the parent's recovery process, for how long, and at what intensity.

In an effort to understand how communication patterns may differ between alcoholic and nonalcoholic families, Jacob, Ritchey, Cvitkovic, and Blane (1981) compared the verbal and nonverbal communication patterns of eight families with an alcoholic father and eight families with a nonalcoholic, nondisturbed father in both drinking and nondrinking laboratory situations. Families were recruited from newspaper advertisements. Few differences between the families were found. Mothers in alcoholic families were more instrumental in problem-solving; the fathers' influences were equal to those of his children.

Alcoholic families also expressed greater negativity during drinking sessions than did the comparison families, who became more convivial under the drinking condition. The alcoholic fathers did not drink significantly more than the nonalcoholic fathers in the laboratory situations where alcohol was available. The lack of strong findings may be indicative of the fact that alcoholic families in the general population may not be as impaired as those in treatment situations. Treatment samples have typically been used to characterize family functioning of COAs in the existing clinical descriptions.

Steinglass, Bennett, Wolin, and Reiss (1987) reached conclusions similar to those of Jacob et al. (1981) in their naturalistic studies of alcoholic families recruited from the general population. Their research lays the groundwork for developing clinical interventions with alcoholic families that can then be evaluated for effectiveness. An understanding of the dynamics of alcoholic families under a variety of situations is essential in order to detect levels of impairment and risk factors and match treatment components to them so that changes and outcomes resulting from treatment can be optimized.

Steinglass et al. (1987) reported that protective factors were operating in some families where some members were not particularly affected by the drinking. These families were called "families with alcoholism." Other families had reorganized around the central theme of drinking and were vulnerable to its disruption, showing greater psychiatric symptomatology, rigidity, highly patterned behavior, and susceptibility to intergenerational transmission of alcoholism. These families were labeled "alcoholic families."

The important variables to be addressed in these families were: (1) stage of alcoholism and family life development—early, middle, or late; (2) family temperament with regard to energy level, sense of boundaries, and flexibility of behavior; (3) rituals, routines, rules, and affective expressiveness; and (4) type of family—stable wet, stable dry, or alternator between the two states. The conclusions that these four variables differentiated best among alcoholic families were based on observations of general population families recruited through advertisements, not on families already in alcoholism treatment. The alcoholic member had to meet stringent criteria for alcoholism.

Many families were observed in their own homes over a period of time in both drinking and sober conditions. The focus was on the marital dyad, although it was evident that children were present in at least some of the sessions. An understanding of the stages of alcoholic family development is important to the development and evaluation of intervention and treatment programs and is presented in more detail below.

   The identity-formation stage: Early phase. Adult COAs, like other persons in the general population, have choices when they first marry and begin the development of a family identity. Those most deliberate in their choice not to incorporate their alcoholic family heritage into their nuclear family identity are the most likely to be protected from developing alcoholism. The family heritage study, conducted by Bennett and colleagues (Bennett & McAvity, 1985; Bennett, Wolin, Reiss, & Teitelbaum, 1987), interviewed a minimum of two adult siblings and their spouses from 30 families in which at least one parent was an alcoholic. The variables most predictive of familial transmission of alcoholism were whether the child was the son of an alcoholic father (risk); whether there was a high level of deliberateness in choosing family heritage (protective); whether the spouse's family dinner ritual level was high (protective); and whether the child's dinner ritual was kept distinctive, that is, not disrupted by the drinking (protective).

   An earlier study by Wolin, Bennett, Noonan, and Teitelbaum (1980) found that alcoholic families able to maintain family rituals such as dinners, holidays, and traditions without disruption by drinking were less likely to transmit alcoholism to their offspring (who at the time of the study were in their early 20s and not yet fully through the age of risk). Finkelstein (1986) reported that in interviews with alcoholic and nonalcoholic daughters of alcoholics, talking about disrupted family rituals was more painful and difficult for them than talking about incidences of physical and sexual abuse.

   A potentially useful strategy would be to develop and evaluate an intervention program for young adult COAs who are just beginning to develop marital difficulties. The intervention would teach them how to develop and maintain family rituals, and to detach or "unmesh" themselves from their alcoholic family of origin so as to protect their marriage from developing an alcoholic family identity.

   Consolidation of alcoholic family identity: Middle phase. The "maintenance activities of the middle phase are built around alcohol related behaviors as a central core" (Steinglass et al., 1987, p. 143) with the purpose of developing homeostasis. Middle-phase families exhibited predictable behavior patterns during intoxicated and sober states, and the behaviors were often mutually exclusive. They had "a remarkable intolerance for uncertainty" so that "a [middle-stage] family can be characterized as unusually rigid, unusually quick to respond to any challenge to the status quo, unusually inflexible in its response patterns" (p. 174). Many families of COAs described in the literature appear to be in this stage of development.

   Alcohol was often used for short-term problem solving by middle-stage families. Steinglass illustrated this point with the story of a mother whose requests for emergency medical treatment for her son were ignored when she was sober and timid but met when she became intoxicated and aggressive. However, as Steinglass pointed out, "active drinking alone is not the critical element determining home behavior, since both stable wet and alternator families contained actively drinking alcoholic members." Family temperament (energy level, boundaries, flexibility of behavior) and regulatory behavior (rules, rituals, affective expressiveness) are equally important variables for the discrimination of types of alcoholic families.

Using discriminant function analysis with the variables of family regulatory behavior and drinking patterns, Steinglass (1981) was able to correctly classify 74% of the families as stable wet, stable dry, or alternator. Those in alternator families were most at risk for emotional and familial problems. These findings are consistent with self-reports by COAs (Cork, 1969; Finkelstein, 1986) in that the COAs were not so much upset by the parental drinking *per se* as by the other behaviors in the home that engendered feelings of being rejected, unloved, ignored, and upset by the parental quarrels and inconsistency.

Family heritage transmission: Late phase. Families go through a time of crisis as the children prepare to leave home and relationships need to be renegotiated. Crises also occur around the loss of alcohol if the family develops into a stable dry family. Whether they are aware of it or not, families face major developmental tasks and decisions about what the family identity is and what heritage will be passed to the next generation: stable wet, where growth has been stunted; stable dry, which is still organized around alcohol—fear of it, fear of return to drinking, etc.; or family growth beyond preoccupation with drinking.

In addition to addressing the emotional impact of growing up in an alcoholic family, adult COAs need to understand the nature of their family heritage in order to prevent transmission of unhealthy behavior and attitudes to their own families. The effectiveness of the incorporation of Steinglass and colleagues' findings into family treatment methods needs to be tested empirically. Another important issue that should be addressed is the inadequate parenting many COAs receive and the need to learn new parenting skills to disrupt the intergenerational transmission of alcoholic family dynamics (O'Gorman & Oliver-Diaz, 1987; Williams, 1987).

The Steinglass family observations were complex and economically costly, but it is unfortunate that no comparison group families with other disorders (e.g., psychiatric controls) or no apparent problems were systematically observed to assess the specificity of the family regulatory behavior to alcoholic families. Few studies of the efficacy of family treatment with alcoholics exist, and none takes into account many of the variables Steinglass et al. (1987) found to be important.

Other variables, not studied by Steinglass, are also important in the study of families. For instance, in his studies of families of drug abusers, Kauffman (1985) found that ethnicity had a powerful effect on family function and roles. Jewish and Italian families were totally enmeshed (overinvolved, lacking in

personal boundary definition), whereas white Anglo-Saxon Protestants and ma-
triarchical black families were quite disengaged (lacking involvement, emotionally distant and rigid). Based on a review of the clinical literature on family
therapy with alcoholics, Janzen (1978) concluded that the overall results were
positive, and O'Shea and Phelps (1985) concluded that in the few studies where
multiple family therapy groups have been evaluated, the results were promising.

Kumpfer and DeMarsh (1986; DeMarsh & Kumpfer, 1986) stated that
intervention with families of substance-abusing parents was the most important
strategy for preventing substance abuse among the children. They conducted one
of the few studies assessing the effectiveness of a parenting program that targeted
opiate, narcotic, and poly-drug-abusing parents. Sixty drug-dependent parents
and their children who were in a family-based prevention program were compared with 60 families randomly selected from a stratified cluster sample from an
urban county. A battery of standardized tests were administered, including the
Family Environment Scale, the Family Adaptability and Cohesion Evaluation
Scales (Olson, Portner, & Bell, 1982), the Spanier Marital Adjustment Scale
(Spanier, 1976), the Cowen Parent Attitude Test (Cowen, Huser, Beach, &
Rappaport, 1970), the Beck Depression Inventory (Beck, 1978), the Family
Inventory of Life Events (McCubbin, Patterson, & Wilson, 1980), the Achen-
bach Child Behavior Checklist (Achenbach & Edelbrock, 1979), and child and
parent questionnaires.

Preliminary analyses of differences between the families with drug abuse
and the community families indicated that the children of drug-abusing parents
were significantly more disobedient, isolated, lonely, and unable to make friends
or talk about their families to outsiders than were the community children.
Drug-abusing families were significantly more conflictual, depressed, inconsistent in discipline, and lax in transmitting moral, religious, and social
responsibility values to their children. The drug abusers' marital dyad was more
enmeshed but the parents spent half as much time in activities with their children
as did the community parents.

The Family Skills Training Program developed by Kumpfer and DeMarsh
(1986) targeted three areas of risk for the child: family function, children's
behavioral problems, and children's expressiveness. Significant improvement
between pretest and posttest in all three areas of functioning were reported.
Improved family functioning consisted of increased communication among
members, improved sibling relations, clarity of family rules, and increased
parental social contacts.

Parents stated that their children were better behaved and showed fewer
problem behaviors and less impulsivity after the training than before. The
children also significantly increased their ability to show and verbalize emotion
and appropriately ask for attention and help when needed. Follow-up to ascertain
the degree children and parents were able to maintain these changes is needed,
but the study is a promising beginning in the field of outcome research with
children of substance abusers.

Much of the family treatment literature is still at the case study level, and the impact of therapy on the children in the family is rarely addressed. As Olson et al. (1982) summarized, the problem with family research is "the emphasis on clinical intuitive data, lack of comparable control groups, unrepresentative client samples, nonstandardized data collection techniques, lack of triangulation of data sources" (p. 53), and lack of theoretical foundations for choosing dependent variables. The majority of families studied are intact, white, and middle class. It is not clear which techniques work best with single-parent, blended, or minority families, and how long changes in family and child functioning can be maintained.

Nor is the specificity of these characteristics to alcoholic families well known as compared with other disturbed or nonproblem families. Riddell (1988) characterized the differences between multiproblem families and alcoholic families as being in the areas of communication, acting-out behavior in the child, ability to express feelings and develop trust, and willingness to accept professional help. Persons in alcoholic families exhibited greater impairments in all these areas except for child behavior. More COAs than multiproblem children were high academic achievers and "super responsible."

In attempting to understand why so little research on families and children of alcoholics has occurred, Cermak and Brown (1982) hypothesized that "to document serious or potentially serious effects on children growing up in an alcoholic environment is to challenge the too easy acceptance of [alcohol's] use, to intrude into the privacy of the family, and to open our eyes to unpleasantness" (p. 385).

Alcoholic COAs

Adolescents

Little overlap exists between the extensive research conducted on adolescents with alcohol problems and COAs with drinking problems, although the descriptions of adolescent problem drinkers and adolescent COAs are quite similar. Bry (1983) believed that the number of high-risk factors a child faced was more predictive of substance abuse than what the exact constellation or nature of those risk factors were. She found a high correlation between the number of risk factors and the probability of adolescent substance abuse. For instance, only 4% of adolescents with no risk factors reported substance abuse problems, versus 100% of adolescents with five or six risk factors.

Brook, Whiteman, and Gordon (1983) reported that risk factors in the three domains of family, personality, and peer group operated independently, and evidence of a precursor in any one of the domains was predictive of the development of adolescent substance abuse. These findings would corroborate the increased risk of COAs for developing alcoholism, although adolescent COAs also deliberately choose not to drink because of the known risks. Morehouse (1984) discussed some of the clinical issues faced by substance-abusing COAs, such as parental resistance to acknowledgment of the adolescent's drinking problem and need for treatment, and the excess guilt, fear, and stigma that may accompany a COA's drinking.

In general, adolescent substance abuse has not proved to be predictive of adult substance abuse (Donovan, Jessor, & Jessor, 1983; Temple & Fillmore, 1986), but how true this is for COAs has not been studied. Also, most of the studies on adolescent substance abusers have not examined the differential characteristics of adolescents with positive family histories of alcoholism.

Adults

The findings of a number of studies conducted in treatment settings that compared family history positive adult alcoholics and family history negative ones suggested that alcoholic COAs were more impaired in a number of areas (Frances, Timm, & Bucky, 1980; Hesselbrock, Stabeneau, Hesselbrock, Meyer, & Babor, 1982; McKenna & Pickens, 1981, 1983; Penick, Read, Crowley, & Powell, 1978). COAs began drinking at an earlier age with more severe consequences and evidenced greater psychopathology, more life problems, and fewer coping skills than family negative alcoholics.

Haver (1987) found that a significantly poorer outcome and borderline personality disorder in 44 women alcoholics was associated with mothers being alcoholic, but not with fathers, in a 3- to 10-year follow-up after treatment. The implications of these more severe deficiencies for treatment planning are rarely addressed in programs. Long-term studies have not assessed possible differential treatment outcomes for family positive and negative alcoholics, nor the possible need for special treatment components to address the effects of familial alcoholism in addition to the individual's alcoholism.

Alcoholic COAs must overcome a double set of deficits for their own health and that of their children. Silvestri, Pratt, Klabanoff, and Gully (1988) reported that recovering alcoholic COAs were unable to address the effects of living in alcoholic families as children until long after they had gained sobriety and been in individual therapy. Unresolved childhood issues did not surface until after sobriety was achieved. The length of time before an alcoholic should begin dealing with childhood issues and what, if any, special treatment components are needed to aid recovery of both the individual and the family are open for exploration.

RECOMMENDATIONS FOR FUTURE RESEARCH

Many exciting possibilities exist for the study of effective prevention, intervention, and treatment programs for COAs. Few empirical studies have been conducted, so research opportunities are abundant. Issues that need to be ad-

dressed have been identified in each section, but following are overall suggestions for future research considerations.

1. *Clarification of program purpose and audience.* It is essential that the
program purpose and target audience be clearly specified. One program cannot
be all things to all persons; outcomes may be obscured if the goals, objectives,
and audience are not clearly defined as being targeted for prevention, intervention, or treatment. Although the same techniques may be used in each type of
program, the content will vary. Better definition and operationalization of specific components of prevention, intervention, and treatment programs, as well as
the beliefs, behaviors, and risk factors they are trying to affect, are important in
order to measure outcomes and assess what works with whom under what
conditions. It is not enough that a group is being run and everyone "feels good"
about it.

2. *Better identification of specific risk factors and degree of children's
impairment.* Without matching the components of the program to the needs of
the children, good programs can be judged to be ineffective and inefficient. The
interaction between the child's characteristics and the program intervention need
to be taken into account. One child may be more impaired and have a greater
number of risk factors than another. He or she may make a great deal of progress
because of the program, but still not be functioning at the level of a child who
shows only marginal gain from the program but who began it with a fairly high
level of functioning. If individual differences and baseline levels of risk factors
and functioning are not taken into account, they may be masked by group effects,
making it difficult to determine what worked best for whom (McCrady & Sher,
1985).

Factors that protect a child from the development of alcoholism need to be
identified as well as factors that render a child vulnerable to its development or
that of other disorders. Table 8.1 specifies some of the major risk factors that
need to be measured in three domains of interest: family characteristics, child's
attributes, and environmental aspects. Obviously, no one study can address all
the variables listed; however, these variables need to be carefully considered
when choices are being made as to what attitudes, attributes, or behaviors a
program is trying to change and how that change will be measured.

3. *Standardized instruments for assessment of baseline measures and
changes over time.* To assess the number and degree of risk factors facing the
child, as well as his or her strengths and weaknesses, more sophisticated
screening tools need to be developed and standardized instruments employed in
assessment. Use of standardized instruments would allow for comparison of
results across studies, comparisons to normed, non-alcohol-related groups, and
consistent measures of change over time.

4. *Incorporation of evaluation components.* Process as well as outcome
evaluation needs to be conducted. Little is known about the effect of setting
(school, clinic, other), staffing (social worker, peer, teacher), or intensity and
duration of groups on outcome. Program philosophies and theoretical orienta-

TABLE 8.1. Risk Factors for Development of Alcoholism

Family characteristics
  Socioeconomic status, ethnic group
  Type of alcoholic home (wet, dry, alternator)
  Stage of alcoholism, use of other drugs, presence of other disorders
  Length of time alcoholism a problem, length and stability of sobriety
  Number of generations and number of family members with alcohol problems
  Family constellation
    Nuclear, blended, single parent, extended
    Number of biological siblings, half- and stepsiblings, birth order

Child characteristics
  Age
  Sex
  Psychosocial, affective, and cognitive functioning
  Social competence
  Achievement levels
  Temperament
  Number of years exposed to alcoholism, intensity of exposure, age at first exposure
  Developmental stage
  Number of illnesses, accidents, somatic complaints

Environmental influences
  Peer support system, number of friends
  Mentors, mitigating conditions
  Major positive and negative life events
  Relationships with parents, relatives, siblings
  Caretaker characteristics and parenting skills

tions are rarely delineated. Problems of client recruitment and retention, program implementation, and how well measures are matched to the program content are rarely addressed. The most effective timing of education or intervention programs is unknown. At what age or stage of symptom development are groups most useful? The vast majority of literature has been written about white COAs. How critical issues may differ for COAs from other ethnic groups and how programs should be adapted for them needs immediate attention. All these issues are important in understanding differential outcomes.

5. *Population-based research.* More needs to be known about COAs in the general population who have not sought treatment. The accuracy of generalizations from a self-identified help-seeking group to those not seeking help is unknown. It appears that they may not have the same needs or impairments as COAs who identify themselves as needing intervention. Much of the literature describes COAs as if they are a homogeneous group by virtue of having alcoholic parents and assumes that a prescribed set of issues and techniques will meet all their needs. Most of the clinically based samples discussed have been chosen based on convenience. Their representativeness regarding COAs in the general population is unknown. More studies comparing children from alcoholic families with children from families with other disruptive psychiatric and physical disorders need to be conducted, as well as comparisons with families without diagnos-

able problems. Sample sizes have tended to be small. Power analyses (Cohen, 1977) should be conducted to ensure that sample sizes are large enough to detect the effect size being sought, especially if a large number of risk factors are being measured.

6. *Interdisciplinary collaboration.* Researchers studying the effects of familial alcoholism on the emotional, behavioral, and physical development of COAs, as well as the risk factors and protective factors that influence their development of substance abuse problems, have much to learn from colleagues in other disciplines and areas of child development. Studies on COAs would benefit from collaboration with researchers in the fields of child development and epidemiology and etiology of psychiatric disorders. By the same token, researchers in those disciplines need to address and document the issues of familial alcoholism in their studies.

7. *Elaboration of research designs.* The majority of the literature on programs for COAs has consisted of identification of the issues facing these children and recommendations for what issues programs should address. Many of the same authors and issues are cited repeatedly. It is now time for even the simplest programs to begin conducting pre-, post-, and follow-up testing to clarify what is being gained and maintained by their members beyond good feelings.

Ideally, the research that needs to be conducted would carefully measure the child's functioning at baseline and randomly assign him or her to one of five possible conditions: no (or delayed) treatment; alcoholic parent and spouse only in treatment; children's group only; family counseling with all members; and a combination of individual, family, and group counseling. Process evaluation of each condition would occur, as well as repeated measures of change at the completion of the program and every 6 months for a minimum of 2 years afterward to assess stability of change. An epidemiological population-based study using contingency table analysis of alcoholic and nonalcoholic siblings by low- and high-risk status has never been done but would add greatly to knowledge about COAs.

New Directions

Awareness of COAs as a special population has been slow to develop. One of the first and still one of the most poignant books written about the effect of parental alcoholism on children is *The Forgotten Children* (Cork, 1969). It was not until the late 1970s, when clinicians began describing clients who did not have alcoholism problems themselves but who came from alcoholic families and seemed to be manifesting a particular set of characteristics (e.g., low self-esteem, inability to achieve intimacy), that general interest in the area began to emerge.

The issues of COAs appear to strike a responsive chord in the general public, especially among caregivers. Interest in the issues grew from a grass-roots, not academic, origin, which may partially explain the lack of programmatic research. In 1982, the National Association for Children of Alcoholics (NACOA) was founded primarily by clinicians who had been writing and lecturing on the phenomenon of COAs. It now has more than 6,000 members. The *U.S. Journal of Alcohol and Drug Dependence* worked closely with the NACOA to sponsor hundreds of national and regional conferences on adult COAs, and publishes a large volume of popular literature on the subject.

The Children of Alcoholics Foundation was established in 1983 for the purpose of raising public awareness about COAs and promoting an increased research effort, as well as disseminating information on current research. Al-Anon, a nonprofessional self-help group traditionally focused on spouses of alcoholics, began sponsoring groups for adult COAs, although not before some lively discussion about whether such groups were within their purview. The number of groups worldwide grew from 6 in 1981 to 1,100 in 1987 (Al-Anon, 1986). Al-Ateen experienced similar growth.

The issues facing COAs have appeared in most major news and popular magazines. A number of celebrities and movie stars have disclosed what it was like to have an alcoholic parent. A COA movement is unfolding that has evangelical overtones similar to those of a religious conversion experience. This evangelical undercurrent could have adverse consequences on research findings if they are not in accord with popular belief, similar to the controversy over the publication of the Rand Report (Armor, Polich, & Stambul, 1978) and other studies discussing issues of "controlled drinking."

Major new research initiatives are needed on prevention, intervention, and treatment programs using both process and outcome measures. These initiatives have been slow in developing. As a step in the right direction, the Department of Health and Human Services Office of Substance Abuse Prevention has just begun to require that process evaluation strategies be incorporated into all applications submitted to it. Closer collaboration between program developers and evaluation researchers during the developmental process of program models should be encouraged so that goals and objectives can be operationalized more effectively and COAs can be followed over time to assess the stability of changes. This collaboration can be accomplished through the use of university graduate programs as well as through public and private sources of funding. Such collaboration provides the best opportunity for learning more about program processes and outcomes in the areas of prevention, intervention, and treatment for COAs. Perhaps in 5 years a greater body of knowledge about what programs and techniques are effective in the prevention of alcoholism in COAs will have accumulated so that the many gaps and unresolved issues in this chapter can be addressed.

REFERENCES

Achenbach, T. M., & Edelbrock, C. S. (1979). The child behavior profile: Boys aged 12 to 16 and girls aged 6 to 11 and 12 to 16. *Journal of Clinical Psychology, 41*, 223–232.
Al-Anon Family Group Headquarters, Inc. (1986). Inside Al-Anon. *Newsletter, 9*(6).

Anderson, E. E., & Quast, W. (1983). Young children in alcoholic familes: A mental health needs-assessment and an intervention/prevention strategy. *Journal of Primary Prevention, 3,* 174–187.

Armor, D. J., Polich, M., & Stambul, H. B. (1978). *Alcoholism and treatment.* New York: Wiley.

Balis, S. A. (1987). Illusion and reality: Issues in the treatment of adult children of alcoholics. *Alcoholism Treatment Quarterly, 3,* 67–91.

Barnard, C. P., & Spoentgen, P. (1986). Children of alcoholics: Characteristics and treatment. *Alcoholism Treatment Quarterly, 3,* 47–65.

Beck, A. T. (1978). *Beck Inventory.* Philadelphia: Center for Cognitive Therapy.

Benard, B. (1986). Characteristics of effective prevention programs. *Prevention Forum, 6*(4). Springfield, IL: AHTDS Prevention Resource Center.

Bennett, L. A. & McAvity, J. J. (1985). Family research: A case for interviewing couples. In G. Handel (Ed.), *The psychosocial interior of the family* (3rd ed.). New York: Aldine.

Bennett, L. A., Wolin, S. J., Reiss, D., & Teitelbaum, M. (1987). Couples at risk for alcoholism recurrence: Protective influences. *Family Process, 26,* 111–129.

Bingham, A., & Bargar, J. (1985). Children of alcoholic families: A group treatment approach for latency age children. *Journal of Psychosocial Nursing, 23,* 13–15.

Black, C. (1982). *It will never happen to me* (1st ed.). Denver: M.A.C. Printing and Publications Division.

Bleuler, M. (1978). *The schizophrenic disorders: Longterm patient and family studies.* New Haven, CT: Yale University Press.

Booz-Allen & Hamilton, Inc. (1974). *An assessment of the needs and resources for children of alcoholic parents.* National Institute of Alcohol Abuse and Alcoholism. Springfield, VA: National Technical Information Service.

Bowen, M. (1974). Alcoholism as viewed through family systems theory and family psychotherapy. *Annals of the New York Academy of Sciences, 233,* 115–122.

Brook, J. S., Whiteman, M., & Gordon, A. S. (1983). Stages of drug use in adolescence: Personality, peer, and family correlates. *Developmental Psychology, 19,* 269–277.

Brown, S., & Beletsis, S. (1986). The development of family transference in groups for the adult children of alcoholics. *International Journal of Group Psychotherapy, 36,* 97–114.

Bry, B. H. (1983). Empirical foundations of family-based approaches to adolescent substance abuse. In T. J. Glynn, C. G. Leukefeld, & J. P. Ludford (Eds.), *Preventing adolescent drug abuse: Intervention strategies* (NIDA Research Monograph No. 47, pp. 154–170; DHHS Publication No. (ADM) 83-600601). Rockville, MD: U.S. Department of Health and Human Services.

Cable, L. C., Noel, N. E., & Swanson, S. C. (1986). Clinical intervention with children of alcohol abusers. In D. C. Lewis & C. N. Williams (Eds.), *Providing care for children of alcoholics: Clinical and research perspectives* (pp. 65–79). Pompano Beach, FL: Health Communications.

Callan, V. J., & Jackson, D. (1986). Children of alcoholic fathers and recovered alcoholic fathers: Personal and family functioning. *Journal of Studies on Alcohol, 47,* 2, 180–182.

Casement, M. R. (1987). Out of the darkness: Informing the public about inherited vulnerability to alcoholism. *Alcohol Health and Research World, 12*(2), 114–119.

Cermak, T. L. (1984). Children of alcoholics and the case for a new diagnostic category of codependency. *Alcohol Health and Research World, 8,* 38–42.

Cermak, T. L., & Brown, S. (1982). Interactional group therapy with the adult children of alcoholics. *International Journal of Group Psychotherapy, 32,* 375–389.

Cohen, J. (1977). *Statistical power analysis for the behavioral sciences.* New York: Academic Press.

Cork, R. M. (1969). *The forgotten children: A study of children with alcoholic parents.* Toronto: Paperjacks.

Cowen, E. L., Huser, J., Beach, D. R., & Rappaport, J. (1970). Parental perceptions of young children and their relation to indexes of adjustment. *Journal of Consulting and Clinical Psychology, 34,* 97–103.

Deckman, J. & Downs, B. (1982). A group treatment approach for adolescent children of alcoholic parents, *Social Work with Groups, 5,* 73–77.

DeMarsh, J. & Kumpfer, K. L. (1986). Family-oriented interventions for the prevention of chemical dependency in children and adolescents. In S. Ezekoye, K. Kumpfer, & W. Bukoski (Eds.), *Childhood and chemical abuse: Prevention intervention*. New York: Haworth Press.

Department of Health and Human Services. (1981). *Services for children of alcoholics* (NIAAA Research Monograph No. 4; DHHS Publication No. (ADM) 81-1007). Rockville, MD: National Institute on Alcohol Abuse and Alcoholism.

DiCicco, L. (1981). Children of alcoholic parents: Issues in identification. In Department of Health and Human Services, *Services for children of alcoholics* (NIAAA Research Monograph No. 4, pp. 44–59; DHHS Publication No. (ADM) 81-1007). Rockville, MD: National Institute on Alcohol Abuse and Alcoholism.

DiCicco, L., Davis, R. B., Hogan, J., MacLean, A., & Orenstein, A. (1984). Group experiences for children of alcoholics. *Alcohol Health and Research World, 8*(4), 20–24.

DiCicco, L., Davis, R., Travis, J., & Orenstein, A. (1984). Recruiting children from alcoholic families into a peer education program. *Alcohol Health and Research World, 8*(2), 28–34.

Dinklage, S. & Plummer, K. (1985). *New skills for children from alcohol troubled families*. Pawtucket, RI: Rhode Island Youth Guidance Center.

Donovan, J., Jessor, R., & Jessor, L. (1983). Problem drinking in adolescence and young adulthood: A follow-up study. *Journal of Studies on Alcohol, 44*(1), 1983.

Dulfano, C. (1982). *Families, alcoholism and recovery: Ten stories*. Center City, MN: Hazelden Foundation.

Eisenstadt, J. M. (1978). Parental loss and genius. *American Psychologist, 33*, 211–223.

el-Guebaly, N. & Offord, D. R. (1977). The offspring of alcoholics: A critical review. *American Journal of Psychiatry, 134*, 357–365.

Filstead, W. J., McElfresh, O. & Anderson, C. (1981). Comparing the family environments of alcoholic and "normal" families. *Journal of Drug and Alcohol Education, 26*(2), 24–31.

Finkelstein, N. (1986). *Effects of parental alcoholism, family violence and social support on the intergenerational transmission of alcoholism in adult women*. Dissertation, Heller School, Brandeis University, Waltham, MA.

Frances, R. J., Timm, S. & Bucky, S. (1980). Studies of familial and nonfamilial alcoholism. *Archives of General Psychiatry, 37*, 564–566.

Garmezy, N. (1984). Children vulnerable to major mental disorders: Risk and protective factors. In L. Grinspoon (Ed.), *Psychiatry update, III* (pp. 91–107). Washington, DC: American Psychiatric Press.

Haver, B. (1987). Female alcoholics V: The relationship between family history of alcoholism and outcome 3–10 years after treatment. *Acta Psychiatrica Scandinavica, 76*, 21–27.

Hawley, N. P., & Brown, E. L. (1981). The use of group treatment with children of alcoholics. *Journal of Contemporary Social Work, 62*, 40–46.

Heath, D. B. (1980). A critical review of the sociocultural model of alcohol use. In T. C. Harford, D. A. Parker, & L. Light (Eds.), *Normative approaches to the prevention of alcohol abuse and alcoholism* (NIAAA Research Monograph No. 3, pp. 1–18; DHEW Publication No. (ADM) 79-600168). Rockville, MD: National Institute on Alcohol Abuse and Alcoholism.

Heller, K., Sher, K. J., and Benson, C. S. (1982). Problems associated with risk overprediction in studies of offspring of alcoholics: Implications for prevention. *Social Psychology Review, 2*, 183–200.

Hesselbrock, V. M., Stabenau, J. R., Hesselbrock, M. N., Meyer, R. E., & Babor, T. F. (1982). The nature of alcoholism in patients with different family histories for alcoholism. *Progress in Neuro-Psychopharmacology and Biological Psychiatry, 6*, 607–614.

Hopkins, R. H., Mauss, A. L., Kearney, K. A., & Weisheit, R. A. (1988). Comprehensive evaluation of a model alcohol education curriculum. *Journal of Studies on Alcohol, 49*(1), 38–50.

Hughes, J. M. (1977). Adolescent children of alcoholic parents and the relationship of Alateen to these children. *Journal of Consulting and Clinical Psychology, 45*, 946–947.

Jackson, J. K. (1954). The adjustment of the family to the crisis of alcoholism. *Quarterly Journal of Studies on Alcohol, 15*, 562–586.

Jacob, T., Ritchey, D., Cvitkovic, J., & Blane, H. (1981). Communication styles of alcoholic and nonalcoholic families when drinking and not drinking. *Journal of Studies on Alcohol, 42,* 466–482.

Janzen, C. (1978). Family treatment for alcoholism: A review. *Social Work, 23,* 135–141.

Johnson, C. A., & Solis, J. (1983). Comprehensive community programs for drug abuse prevention: Implications of the community heart disease prevention programs for future research. In T. J. Glynn, C. G. Leukefeld, & J. P. Ludford (Eds.), *Preventing adolescent drug abuse: Intervention strategies* (NIDA Research Monograph No. 47, pp. 76–114; DHHS Publication No. (ADM) 83-60061). Rockville, MD: U.S. Department of Health and Human Services.

Johnson, J. (1985). *Risk and protective factors in children vulnerable to alcohol abuse.* Paper presented at the panel on children of alcoholics at the National Council on Alcoholism Forum. Washington, DC.

Jones, J. W. (1982). *The children of alcoholics screening test,* 1–22. Park Ridge, IL: London House Consultants, Inc.

Kauffman, C., Grunebaum, H., Cohler, B., & Gamer, E. (1979). Superkids: Competent children of psychotic mothers. *American Journal of Psychiatry, 136,* 1398–1402.

Kaufman, E. (1985). Family systems and family therapy of substance abuse: An overview of two decades of research and clinical experience. *International Journal of the Addictions, 20*(6 & 7), 897–916.

Kern, J. C., Tippman, J., Fortgang, J., & Paul, S. R. (1977). A treatment approach for children of alcoholics. *Journal of Drug Education, 7*(3), 207–218.

Kuhn, T. S. (1970). *The structure of scientific revolutions* (2nd ed.). Chicago: University of Chicago Press.

Kumpfer, K. L. (1987). Special populations: Etiology and prevention of vulnerability to chemical dependency in children of substance abusers. In B. S. Brown & A. R. Mills (Eds.), *Youth at high risk for substance abuse* (pp. 1–72; DHHS Publication No. (ADM) 87-1537). Rockville, MD: U.S. Department of Health and Human Services.

Kumpfer, K. L., & DeMarsh, J. (1986). Family-oriented interventions for the prevention of chemical dependency in children and adolescents. In S. Ezekoye, K. Kumpfer, & W. Bukoski (Eds.), *Childhood and chemical abuse: Prevention and intervention,* New York: Haworth Press.

Ledermann, S. (1956). *Alcool, alcoolisme, alcoolisation: Donnés scientifiques de caractère physiologique, économique et social.* Paris: Presses Universitaires de France.

Lillis, R. P. (1987). Comparison of children of alcoholics' and non-children of alcoholics' perception of risk and alcohol consumption. Policy Brief No. 87–4, New York State Division of Alcoholism and Alcohol Abuse.

Manning, D. T. (1987). Books as therapy for children of alcoholics. *Child Welfare, 66,* 35–43.

Mauss, A. L., Hopkins, R. H., Weisheit, R. A., & Kearney, K. A. (1988). The problematic prospects for prevention in the classroom: Should alcohol education programs be expected to reduce drinking by youth? *Journal of Studies on Alcohol, 49*(1), 51–61.

McCrady, B. S., & Sher, K. (1985). Treatment variables. In B. S. McCrady, N. E. Noel, & T. D. Nirenberg (Eds.), *Future directions in alcohol abuse treatment research* (Research Monograph No. 15, pp. 48–62; DHHS Publication No. (ADM) 85-1322). Washington, DC: U.S. Government Printing Office.

McCubbin, H. I., Patterson, J. M., & Wilson, L. (1980). *Family Inventory of Life Events and Changes (FILE), Form A.* St. Paul, MN: Family Social Science.

McKenna, T., & Pickens, R. (1981). Alcoholic children of alcoholics. *Journal of Studies on Alcohol, 42*(11), 1021–1029.

McKenna, T., & Pickens, R. (1983). Personality characteristics of alcoholic children of alcoholics. *Journal of Studies on Alcohol, 44*(4), 689–700.

McLachlan, J. C. F., Walderman, R. L., & Thomas, S. (1973). *A study of teenagers with alcoholic parents* (Research Monograph No. 3). Toronto: Donwood Institute.

McNair, D. M., Lorr, M., & Droppelman, L. F. (1981). *EITS Manual for the Profile of Mood States.* San Diego, CA: Educational and Industrial Testing Service.

Meeks, D. E., & Kelly, C. (1970). Family therapy with the families of recovering alcoholics. *Quarterly Journal of Studies on Alcohol, 31*, 399–413.

Miller, N. (1983). Group psychotherapy in a school setting for adolescent children of alcoholics. *Group, 7*, 34–40.

Moos, R. H. & Billings, A. G. (1982). Children of alcoholics during the recovery process: Alcoholic and matched control families. *Addictive Behaviors, 7*, 155–163.

Moos, R. H., Cronkite, R. C., Billings, A. G., & Finney, J. W. (1987). *Health and Daily Living Form (revised)*. Palo Alto, CA: Social Ecology Laboratory, Veterans Administration and Stanford University.

Moos, R. H. & Moos, B. S. (1981). *Family Environment Scale Manual*. Palo Alto, CA: Consulting Psychologists Press.

Morehouse, E. R. (1979). Working in the schools with children of alcoholic parents. *Health and Social Work, 4*, 145–162.

Morehouse, E. R. (1984). Working with alcohol-abusing children of alcoholics. *Alcohol Health and Research World, 8*, 14–18.

Morehouse, E. R. (1986). Counseling adolescent children of alcoholics in groups. In R. Ackerman (Ed.), *Growing in the shadow* (pp. 125–142). Pompano Beach, FL: Health Communications.

National Council on Alcoholism. (1976). American Medical Society on Alcoholism: Committee on Definitions. *Annals of Internal Medicine, 85*, 6.

Nowicki, S. & Strickland, B. R. (1972). A Locus of Control Scale. *Journal of Consulting and Clinical Psychology, 39*, 1972.

O'Gorman, P., & Oliver-Diaz, P. (1987). *Breaking the cycle of addiction*. Pompano Beach, FL: Health Communications.

Olson, D. H., Portner, J., & Bell, R. (1982). *Family Adaptability and Cohesion Evaluation Scales (FACES II)*. St. Paul, MN: Family Social Service.

O'Shea, M. D., & Phelps, R. (1985). Multiple family therapy: Current status and critical appraisal. *Family Process, 24*, 555–582.

Owen, S. M., Rosenberg, J., & Barkley, D. (1985). Bottled up children: A group treatment approach for children of alcoholics. *Group, 9*(3), 31–42.

Parker, D. A., & Harman, M. S. (1980). A critique of the distribution of consumption model of prevention. In T. C. Harford, D. A. Parker, & L. Light (Eds.), *Normative approaches to the prevention of alcohol abuse and alcoholism* (NIAAA Research Monograph No. 3, pp. 67–88; DHEW Publication No. (ADM) 79-600168). Rockville, MD: National Institute on Alcohol Abuse and Alcoholism.

Peitler, E. J. (1980). A comparison of the effectiveness of group counseling and Alateen on the psychological adjustment of two groups of adolescent sons of alcoholic fathers. *Dissertation Abstracts International, 41*, 1520-B.

Pellegrini, D., Kosisky, S., Nackman, D., Cytryn, L., McKnew, D. H., Gershon, E., Homovit, J., & Cammuso, K. (1986). Personal and social resources in children of patients with bipolar affective disorder and children of normal control subjects. *American Journal of Psychiatry, 143*(7), 856–861.

Penick, E. C., Read, M. R., Crowley, P. A., & Powell, B. J. (1978). Differentiation of alcoholics by family history. *Journal of Studies on Alcohol, 39*(11), 1944–1948.

Perry, C. L., Klepp, K. I., & Shultz, J. M. (1988). Primary prevention of cardiovascular disease: Communitywide strategies for youth. *Journal of Consulting and Clinical Psychology, 56*(3), 358–364.

Piers, E. V. (1984). *Piers–Harris Children's Self-Concept Scale: Revised manual 1984*. Los Angeles: Western Psychological Services.

Riddell, A. M. (1988). "I never knew there were so many of us": A model early intervention alcohol program. *Alcohol Health and Research World, 12*(2), 110–113.

Romelsjö, A. & Ågren, G. (1985). Has mortality related to alcohol decreased in Sweden? *British Medical Journal, 291*, 167–170.

Russell, M., Henderson, C., & Blume, S. B. (1985). *Children of alcoholics: A review of the literature*. New York: Children of Alcoholics Foundation.

Rutter, M. (1979). Protective factors in children's responses to stress and disadvantage. In M. W. Kent & J. E. Rolf (Eds.), *Primary prevention of psychopathology: Social competence in children, 3*. Hanover, NH: University Press of New England.

Scavnicky-Mylant, M. (1987). School-based nursing intervention with children of alcoholics. *School Nurse*, Sept/Oct, 9–14.

Sheehy, G. (1987). *Spirit of survival*. Toronto, Canada: Bantam Books.

Shostrom, E. E. (1974). *Manual for the Personal Orientation Inventory*. San Diego, CA: Edits Publishers.

Silvestri, W., Pratt, V., Klabanoff, V., & Gully, A. (1988). *Sharing childhood experiences: A study of alcoholic counselors who are adult children of alcoholics*. Presented at the Society for Study of Social Problems Annual Conference, Atlanta, GA.

Spanier, G. B. (1976). Measuring dyadic adjustment: New scales for assessing the quality of marriage and similar dyads. *Journal of Marriage and the Family*, 15–28.

Steinglass, P. (1981). The alcoholic family at home: Patterns of interaction in wet, dry, and transitional phases of alcoholism. *Archives of General Psychiatry, 38*, 578–584.

Steinglass, P., Bennett, L. A., Wolin, S. J., & Reiss, D. (1987). *The alcoholic family*. New York: Basic Books.

Tartar, R. E., Alterman, A. I., & Edwards, K. L. (1985). Vulnerability to alcoholism in men: A behavior-genetic perspective. *Journal of Studies on Alcohol, 46*(4), 329–356.

Temple, M. T. & Fillmore, K. M. (1986). The variability of drinking patterns and problems among young men age 16–31: A longitudinal study. *International Journal of the Addictions, 20*, 1595–1620.

Thomas, A., & Chess, S. (1977). *Temperament and development*. New York: Brunner/Mazel.

Thomas, A., & Chess, S. (1984). Genesis and evolution of behavioral disorders: From infancy to early adult life. *American Journal of Psychiatry, 141*, 1–9.

Thorpe, L. P., Clark, W. W., & Tiegs, E. W. (1939). *California Test of Personality*. Monterey, CA: CTB/McGraw-Hill.

Tobler, N. S. (1986). Meta-analysis of 143 adolescent drug prevention programs: Quantitative outcome results of program participants compared to a control or comparison group. *Journal of Drug Issues, 16*(4), 537–567.

Triplett, J. L., & Arbeson, S. W. (1983). Working with children of alcoholics. *Pediatric Nursing, 9*, 317–320.

Walker, H. M. (1970). *Walker Problem Behavior Checklist*. Los Angeles: Western Psychological Services.

Waters, W. J. (1984). *The Alcohol-Related Injury Project: A five-year study*. CDC/NIAAA Cooperative Agreement U50/CC100832-003 awarded to the Rhode Island Department of Public Health.

Wegscheider, S. (1981). *Another chance: Hope and help for the alcoholic family*. Palo Alto, CA: Science & Behavior Books.

Werner, E. E. (1985). Stress and protective factors in children's lives. In A. R. Nicol (Ed.), *Longitudinal studies of child psychology and psychiatry* (pp. 335–355). New York: Wiley.

Werner, E. E. (1986). Resilient offspring of alcoholics: A longitudinal study from birth to age 18. *Journal of Studies of Alcohol, 47*, 34–40.

Williams, C. N. (1987). Child care practices in alcoholic families. *Alcohol Health and Research World, 2*(4), 74–77.

Wirt, R. D., Seat, P. D., & Broen, W. E. (1977). *Personality Inventory for Children*. Los Angeles: Western Psychological Services.

Woititz, J. G. (1983). *Adult children of alcoholics*. Hollywood, FL: Health Communications.

Wolin, S. J., Bennett, L. A., Noonan, D. L., & Teitelbaum, M. A. (1980). Disrupted family rituals. *Journal of Studies of Alcohol, 41*(3), 199–214.

Woodside, M. (1986). *Children of alcoholics on the job*. New York: Children of Alcoholics Foundation.

Woodward, B. S. (1985). An assessment of a prevention program for children of alcoholics. *Dissertation Abstracts International, 45*, 2324-B.

CHAPTER NINE

Summary, Integration, and Future Directions: Toward a Life-Span Perspective

MICHAEL WINDLE
JOHN S. SEARLES

The authors of previous chapters in this book have reviewed and evaluated conceptual models and empirical data on children of alcoholics (COAs) from multiple disciplinary perspectives (biochemical, behavior genetic, family, among others). The number and range of empirical studies have varied for different disciplinary areas, but in each instance promising research directions were suggested for future inquiry. The stimulative, or heuristic, value of a given body of research is a significant feature to consider when predicting the longevity of an area under investigation and in evaluating the potential usefulness of the contributions contained therein. As a general comment on the COA research literature, we conclude that there have been a number of very promising initial studies that have been of heuristic value and that appear to be useful for etiologic theories of alcoholism, with implications for targeted prevention and intervention strategies. It is also important, however, to recognize that the COA research literature is in its infancy as a body of knowledge, that many contradictory findings have been reported within each of the disciplinary domains, that relatively few theoretical approaches have been articulated formally with propositions tested to any degree of certainty, and that little evidence exists to suggest the kinds of preventions and interventions that are most likely to be helpful for COAs. Further, while there have been a few exciting and promising theoretical approaches cutting across disciplines (e.g., Cloninger, 1987; Tarter, Alterman, & Edwards, 1985), there currently does not exist a comprehensive formulation, orientation, or perspective to integrate research findings across the multiple disciplines.

The purpose of this summary, integration, and future directions chapter is twofold. First, a succinct description of some common themes across the substantive chapters in the book is provided. That is, despite differences in levels or units of analysis, historical traditions, and methodological approaches, several themes emerged as salient to address in future COA research. Second, a life-span developmental perspective (Baltes, 1987; Baltes, Reese, & Nesselroade, 1977; Lerner, 1984) is presented as a possible integrative orientation to organize the literature, to more closely tie theoretical or conceptual models and alternative methodological approaches, and to provide a coherent framework for considering research that seeks to examine relations within and *between* levels of analysis. In this last instance, information is presented on ways of conceptualizing the interlevel relations of the human organism, with multiple levels of discriminable behavior (e.g., biochemical, physiological, psychological), embedded within dynamic, historical, and socioenvironmental contexts.

COMMON THEMES ACROSS SUBSTANTIVE DOMAINS

Seven common themes surfaced repeatedly across the substantive chapters in this volume. These themes included theoretical and methodological problems and issues, as well as concerns with practical applications. Each of these themes, with exemplars from some of the chapters, is presented below.

The Need for Biopsychosocial Models

In contrast to much prior theorizing about the etiologic basis of alcoholism, it is evident from the COA research reviewed and evaluated in this book (as well as from the general alcoholism literature; e.g., Peele, 1985; Zucker, 1987) that "single cause" explanatory accounts of alcoholism (e.g., the alcoholic personality) are inadequate and that multifactorial models are required. The behavior genetic research reviewed in Chapter 5 by Searles provides support for both genetic and environmental factors as influential agents in the etiology of alcoholism. However, as Searles points out, little systematic research has been conducted on well-defined and well-measured environmental constructs, and consequently little is known about the influence of specific environments (or their features) on alcoholic outcomes. With better measures of the physical and social environmments that people inhabit, behavior genetic models are moving toward conceptual and methodological models that attempt to account for gene–environment relations over time (e.g., interactional and correlational models; see Scarr & McCartney, 1983). Such biopsychosocial models may be extremely useful in disentangling genetic and environmental effects, in studying their interrelations over time, and in providing information on developmental pathways toward and away from alcoholism.

In Chapter 3, Chan discussed biochemical markers and their potential usefulness for COAs and others at high risk for alcoholism. Chan did, however, suggest that a better understanding of the environment is required to explain why some persons who are at high risk (e.g., COAs) become alcoholics whereas others do not. Searles (Chapter 5) outlined a developmental model of genotype

(G) and environmental (E) relations proposed by Scarr and McCartney (1983). Early in human development, G × E relations are described as passive, because the infant or young child has limited personal resources to control his or her environment. During middle childhood, G × E relations are described as evocative, that is, individuals in one's social environment respond to one's features of individuality (e.g., physical appearance, temperament). During adolescence and beyond, G × E relations are described as active, or niche picking, because individuals have more personal resources to select and shape environments that are consonant with their inherited dispositions.

In Chapter 6, Windle presented a goodness of fit model of person–context relations (e.g., Lerner & Lerner, 1983; Thomas & Chess, 1981) in which physical and social contexts are viewed as essential to understanding human development. Individual characteristics, such as temperament or personality, are conceptualized as embedded within contexts (e.g., family) and individuals are seen as influential agents who both shape and are shaped by the multiple contexts they inhabit. The research reviewed by Seilhamer and Jacob (Chapter 7) suggests the importance of studying salient events and behavioral interactional processes within the family as determinants of alcoholic expression, while simultaneously recognizing that other psychological and environmental variables may moderate alcohol abuse and alcoholism among COAs.

Although several biopsychosocial models have recently been conceptualized (e.g., Peele, 1985; Zucker, 1976), very little research has examined the conjoint (multivariate) influences of risk variables for COAs, or included variables from more than one level of analysis. For example, what is the prevalence of alcoholism among COAs who manifest neurophysiological risk (i.e., attenuated P300 response), an undercontrolling temperamental style, and are reared in a "subsumptive" family (one in which the alcoholic's behavior dominates family functioning)? What kinds of social interactional patterns within and outside the family characterize COAs with this risk profile? More specific questions may be pursued in future research regarding which risk factors function to amplify or potentiate other risk factors, and delineating necessary and sufficient conditions that influence alcoholic expression (or nonexpression) among COAs.

Measurement of Alcoholism, Problem Drinking, and Family History of Alcoholism

Difficulties surrounding the conceptualization and measurement of alcohol abuse and alcoholism are pervasive in the field of alcohol studies and have an intimate link with COA research in that such definitions establish inclusionary and exclusionary criteria for COA status. Russell, in Chapter 2, reviewed some of the manifold ways that problem drinking, alcohol abuse, and alcohol dependence have been defined in various COA studies, thus introducing sources of systematic bias that preclude truly meaningful comparisons of prevalence across studies. Similarly, Searles, in Chapter 5, identified criteria used in the Swedish Adoption Study that may yield results that are culture-specific and not generalizable as standard criteria. In Chapter 3, Chan discussed some biological parameters that may be useful in the early detection of alcoholism and reviewed some research literature on the convergence between self-report measures of alcohol-related problems and biological indices. Russell also reviewed material related to alternative approaches to assessing alcoholic family history status, including the family interview method, the family history method, and single item (yes–no) questions regarding problem drinking among parents.

Although comparisons across studies are limited by the nonequivalent measurement of constructs, there does appear to be *some* convergence across recent studies with regard to the domains assessed. For instance, the domains of alcohol consumption (e.g., quantity–frequency measures, number of heavy drinking days), adverse social consequences (e.g., conflict with family members or employers), and dependency symptoms (e.g., morning shakes) are used in many clinical–psychiatric and treatment studies, as well as, increasingly, in community surveys. Further, methodological studies focused on the interrelationships between alternative methods of measurement (e.g., biological parameters, self-report) and the relative strengths and weakness of specific measures, for specific populations, for specified time intervals are on the increase and should prove fruitful in selecting particular measures for well-defined purposes. Another area of interest for COA research is the investigation of possible differential risk for children of alcoholics as a function of uni- versus multigenerational history of alcoholism (e.g., Alterman, Searles, & Hall, 1989; Finn & Pihl, 1987). This research obviously requires an alcoholic family history method that assesses alcohol abuse and alcoholism in extended family members of COAs, with methods (e.g., collateral informants) for determining the reliability and validity of such information.

Multivariate Statistical Models

Advances in computer technology have contributed to the development and mass distribution of statistical software programs that enable scientists to routinely use relatively sophisticated statistical procedures. In the not-too-distant past, the thought of doing, for instance, a factor analysis of 20 variables (with a hand calculator) may have appeared a nightmarish task, whereas results for such an application now are produced (typically) in a manner of moments. One specific statistical area that is being used more frequently in the biomedical and behavioral sciences involves multivariate models, often with particular reference to longitudinal research design applications.

Within alcoholism research in general, and COA research in particular, prospective longitudinal research designs often have been proposed as not only preferable, but essential to investigate alternative developmental pathways leading toward or away from alcoholism. In most instances, such longitudinal data are optimally analyzed via some multivariate model (e.g., Nesselroade & Baltes, 1979). Both Windle and Searles, in their respective chapters, identified covariance structure modeling (e.g., Bentler, 1985; Jöreskog & Sörbom, 1984) as a useful methodology for analyzing cross-temporal relationships among variables and establishing plausible and testable models regarding the causal direction of effects. Covariance structure models, which are also sometimes referred to as structural equation models, "causal" models, and (erroneously) as LISREL models, permit the specification, estimation, and statistical goodness of fit evaluation of a range of multivariate models (e.g., path analytic models, confirmatory factor analytic models, structural equation models with latent variables). Many of these multivariate models may be used to address issues of concern with longitudinal data (e.g., stability and change of behavior, lagged causal effects) as well as with cross-sectional data (e.g., simultaneous group analysis).

Applications of covariance structure models with COAs may be useful, for example, in testing formally alternative hypothesized models regarding the direct and indirect effects of proposed salient risk or protective variables. To illustrate with a relatively easy but substantively useful example, one could evaluate the statistical adequacy of a model that postulated that alcohol-associated family stress influenced problem drinking *indirectly* by lowering COAs' self-esteem with a model that postulated that alcohol-associated family stress influenced problem drinking among COAs directly (or with a third model, in which significant effects are hypothesized for *both* direct and indirect effects). Goodness of statistical fit indices could be evaluated to determine the relative adequacy of the alternatively specified models to reproduce the observed data. By expanding the number of risk factors and the number of possible outcome variables (e.g., alcohol abuse, illicit drug abuse, antisocial behaviors) with longitudinal data would enable investigators to hypothesize, test, and evaluate a range of models to inform them about the multivariate structure of their data. Family history of alcoholism could be specified in proposed models (i.e., as a dichotomous variable) and evaluated with respect to its direct and indirect influences on variables such as temperament and antisocial behaviors, as well as on the expression of alcoholic behaviors. In addition, recent advances in covariance structure modeling have included specifications for the assessment of $G \times E$ interactions (e.g., Boomsma & Molenaar, 1986; Molenaar & Boomsma, 1987), thus enabling investigators to model relations such as those discussed by Searles in Chapter 5.

Several other applications with multivariate models were also mentioned by contributors to this volume. Chan (Chapter 3) identified the quadratic discriminant function analysis model as one that has increased the sensitivity and discriminatory power of biochemical variables for classifying alcoholics. Seilhamer and Jacob (Chapter 7) mentioned the use of time series models to evaluate features of dyadic relations (e.g., relation between father's drinking and offspring's mood quality). And Williams (Chapter 8) alluded to the need for rigorous multivariate statistical models to conduct evaluation research studies on prevention and intervention programs. In sum, a consensus emerged from the contributors of this volume that efforts to address the significant events and heterogeneous processes associated with being a COA will be facilitated by the use of prospective longitudinal research designs and multivariate statistical models.

Typological Research

All of the chapters in this volume have, to varying degrees, referred to typological approaches to alcoholism. Most prominent among the typological approaches cited was that of Cloninger and colleagues (e.g., Cloninger, Bohman, & Sigvardsson, 1981), though other approaches (e.g., Goodwin, Schulsinger, Hermansen, Guze, & Winokur, 1973; Zucker, 1987) were also discussed. The typological approach is significant for the identification of differential etiologic pathways, for the accurate diagnosis and treatment of alcoholics, and for possible implications for offspring (i.e., for COAs). Russell (Chapter 2) points out that the prevalence of alcoholism among COAs may vary according to alcoholic subtype, with rates of transmission to sons of "male-limited" alcoholics as high as 9:1. Tarter, Laird, and Moss (Chapter 4) provided a neuropsychological theory to account for the neurobiological basis of vulnerability for male-limited alcoholics. Searles (Chapter 5) evaluated critically the research of Goodwin and colleagues and Cloninger et al. (1981) from a behavior genetic perspective. Alternative conceptual and statistical models (e.g., G × E interactions and correlations) were proposed to address some of the dynamic features of development that may account for diverse developmental trajectories and alcoholic outcomes.

It is clear that typological research will continue to influence research on alcoholism in general and COAs in particular because of its implications for the etiology, time course, and treatment of alcoholics and associated risk for COAs. Knowledge of differences in etiology, time course, and phenotypic expression may facilitate optimal matching of a range of treatments for alcoholics, whose prognosis may differ according to alcoholic subtype. The end result may be a significant improvement in recovery rates as well as a longer duration of recovery for alcoholics who relapse. Similarly, it is possible that alcoholic subtypes may be influential in determining particular preventions and interventions for COAs. For example, the offspring of antisocial alcoholics may be exposed to neglect and/or violence directed toward them or their mothers and may need different kinds of intervention than the offspring of a milder alcoholic subtype. Similarly, different interventions may be indicated for COAs with pathologically depressed mothers and/or fathers. We are in the nascent stages of developing and evaluating prevention and intervention research with COAs (see Williams, Chapter 8), but the specifics required in designing programs may be facilitated by knowledge of parental alcoholism subtypes.

Age, Sex, and Racial Group Differences

With a few exceptions, variation in alcohol expression among COAs has not been systematically evaluated for combinations of age, sex and race. Cloninger et al.'s (1981) research indicates a specific male parental alcoholism pattern, or type, characterized by early onset of drinking problems, rapid evolvement toward alcoholism, and criminal activities. This male-limited pattern was associated with a moderate alcoholism pattern in male offspring. Further, female offspring of the parental male-limited pattern were *not* at increased risk for alcoholism relative to normal population estimates. A second alcoholism pattern reported by Cloninger et al. was referred to as milieu-limited, and was characterized by later onset of drinking problems and a lack of criminal activity. Zucker (1987), similarly, has described different alcoholism patterns influenced by age of problem onset and has included an affectively depressed alcoholic type that is more frequent among female alcoholics.

However, the generalizability of findings for the alcoholic subtypes proposed by Cloninger et al. (1981) and by Zucker (1987) is still a matter for empirical inquiry. As noted by Russell in Chapter 2, the prevalence of such alcoholic subtypes currently is unknown, and part of the reason for this is that studies have often been conducted on nonrepresentative samples. We do know, nevertheless, that for many of the substantive domains covered in this volume, age, sex, and racial group differences do exist. For example, Chan (Chapter 3) indicates that men have lower mean corpuscular volume (MCV) levels than women, and that MCV is a better indicator of excessive alcohol consumption in women. Chalmers, Chanarin, MacDermott, and Levi (1980) have also suggested that women are more susceptible than men to the hematological toxicity of ethanol. There are also age changes in some prominent blood variables often used to assess alcoholism, such as MCV and mean corpuscular hemoglobin. Rates of childhood and adult behavior problems (e.g., hyperactivity, antisocial behaviors, depression), which may moderate the expression of alcoholism, differ for age, sex, and racial groups (e.g., Gelfand & Peterson, 1985; Kazdin, 1987). Family functioning and responsivity to prevention and intervention programs are influenced by age, sex, and race.

The lack of information regarding variation in age, sex, and race for alcoholic risk among COAs needs to be examined systematically in future research. Even if prevalence was found to be similar for particular combinations (e.g., white and black males), this would not necessarily indicate that similar etiologic pathways preceded alcoholic expression. An understanding of the heterogeneous pathways toward and away from alcoholism for COAs remains a major research objective that may facilitate assessment, diagnosis, and treatment.

Protective Factors

The notion of protective factors can be conceptualized in a health promotion (versus disease) model. That is, whereas the disease model orients one toward the identification of negative characteristics (e.g., vulnerability or risk factors) that may predict subsequent dysfunction, the health promotion model orients one toward the identification of positive characteristics (e.g., protective factors) that may predict successful adaptation to stressful life circumstances or potential environmental assaults. The general research question directing inquiries to protective factors can be posed as: Given that a set of persons inherit susceptibility to or are exposed to particular negative conditions (of genetic and/or environmental origin), what factors differentiate those who do *not* manifest subsequent dysfunction from those who do? Specific negative conditions that have been investigated include low socioeconomic status, psychiatric status of parents (e.g., schizophrenia), intellectual and socioemotional development of offspring following parental divorce, and psychosocial adjustment among World War II concentration camp survivors (e.g., Anthony & Cohler, 1987; Antonovsky, 1979; Garmezy & Rutter, 1983).

Much of the children of alcoholics literature has focused on vulnerability or risk factors and conceptualizations have emphasized both genetic and environmental factors as influential in adequately explaining COA risk (e.g., Cloninger et al., 1981; Tarter et al., 1985). Nevertheless, several protective factors have been identified and discussed in this volume. Chan (Chapter 3), for example, cites evidence regarding higher levels of acetaldehyde in *some* Oriental subjects that results in a flushing reaction following alcohol consumption and that may deter further ethanol ingestion (see Chi, Lubben, & Kitano, 1989, for a discussion of offsetting cultural factors). Although this flushing response appears specific to some Orientals, it is conceivable that there may be other biochemical markers that function to protect persons from increasing their alcohol consumption. Windle (Chapter 6) cited the longitudinal research of Werner (1986), who had found that an affectionate temperament style in infancy among COAs raised in poverty differentiated those COAs who at age 18 years manifested adjustment versus maladjustment. The affectionate temperament style was thought to moderate the quality of the early caregiving environment and thus to protect the infants from neglect or abuse that may have resulted otherwise. Seilhamer and Jacob (Chapter 7) cited research by Wolin, Bennett, and Noonan (1979) indicating that certain types of alcoholic families may protect offspring from the subsequent development of alcoholism. "Distinctive" families, which are able to maintain family rituals (e.g., daily routines, ways of celebrating holidays) despite a parent's alcoholic problem, are viewed as decreasing the alcoholic risk for offspring relative to "subsumptive" families. Subsumptive families are unable to maintain family rituals and the parent's alcoholic problem often dominates the structure and function of family activities.

Many conceptual and methodological issues remain regarding distinctions between vulnerability (risk) and protective factors (e.g., Anthony & Cohler, 1987; Rutter, 1987). For example, should vulnerability and protective factors be viewed along a unidimensional continuum, or as discrete, multidimensional factors? COAs are often exposed to a range of risk factors associated with parental alcoholism (e.g., poor role model for learning coping skills, marital conflict, poverty from parental job loss, physical and/or emotional abuse), many of which vary in terms of duration and intensity. A more adequate causal account of the variability in outcomes among COAs is likely to be enhanced by the study of risk and protective factors, their potentiating and attenuating capabilities, and their conjoint (interactive) influences. Thus, the vulnerability and protective factors paradigm may be used frequently in future investigations of alcoholic risk among COAs.

Practical Applications

A number of the contributions in this volume have identified ways that ongoing research with COAs can be applied to increase early awareness of vulnerability and to the early detection of possible alcoholic risk. Chan (Chapter 3) proposes that the development of a biochemical profile of alcoholic risk may facilitate physicians and health-care personnel in the early detection of persons at risk for alcoholism. On a practical level, physicians are not likely to administer a battery of tests to determine alcoholic risk. However, if biochemical risk profiles could be obtained easily through the standard analysis of routinely sampled blood, the health-care community may be able to intervene early in the alcoholic process and prevent the development of alcoholism in at least some of their patients. Windle (Chapter 6) identified some childhood temperament and personality attributes (e.g., aggression, antisocial behavior) that are associated, to some extent, with subsequent alcohol-related problems for COAs and nonCOAs. The early detection of such attributes could encourage early prevention efforts with regard to alcohol use, and information could be provided to parents to monitor more closely their offspring's behavior with regard to alcohol use and other problem behaviors (e.g., poor school performance, delinquency).

The results of research reviewed by Seilhamer and Jacob (Chapter 7), especially with regard to family interactional processes, are relevant for therapeutic interventions with alcoholics, in particular for interventions based on the family systems approach. A series of studies conducted by Jacob and collaborators (e.g., Jacob, 1987; Jacob & Leonard, 1988) have used naturalistic behavior observation methods to study interactional patterns among alcoholic, depressed, and normal (control group) families. Differentiating factors within alcoholic families include drinking style (steady versus binge drinking) and standard location (in-home versus out-of-home) of drinking. Differences in these factors were found to be associated systematically with different interactional processes among family members. Information regarding influential factors in familial interactional patterns may provide targets for intervention. Williams (Chapter 8) offers several ways of designing, implementing, and evaluating prevention and intervention programs so as to assess what is working with whom, why it is working, and how long the intervention is expected to last. As noted by Williams, this area of research with COAs has been largely neglected, and we know very little about the effectiveness of alternative prevention and intervention programs with COAs.

INTEGRATION: LIFE-SPAN DEVELOPMENTAL PERSPECTIVES

It is premature to form one specific theory regarding the etiology and time course of alcoholism among COAs. As evidenced in earlier sections of this chapter and in the previous chapters of this book, COA status can contribute to alcoholic risk in numerous ways, singly or in combination, and at different levels of analysis. Further, based on extant data, it appears that alcoholism is best conceptualized as multifactorial, or multidetermined, yielding single-cause explanations (e.g., single gene locus, alcoholic personality) inadequate. This does not suggest, however, that an integrative, unifying approach, or perspective, would not be useful to organize conceptually existing studies and to provide some directive influence on future studies. The authors propose that a life-span developmental perspective (e.g., Baltes, 1987; Lerner, 1984) would be well-suited to this task.

As noted by Baltes (1987), the life-span perspective is not a singular theory, but rather a flexibly oriented set of concepts and propositions about human development with implications for research design, statistical models, and the interpretation of findings. Further, multiple theoretical models can be subsumed under a life-span perspective, as well as a plurality of research methods. A description of some of the salient concepts and propositions of a life-span perspective are presented below, with relevant examples provided for the study of children of alcoholics. Specifically, six concepts are outlined along with some implications for COA research: (1) life-span development; (2) multidimensionality, multidirectionality, and multiple causality; (3) plasticity of development; (4) historical embeddedness; (5) contextualism; and (6) development as a multidisciplinary endeavor.

Life-Span Development

A fundamental objective of the life-span perspective is the investigation of lifelong processes associated with intraindividual change and with interindividual differences manifest in that change (e.g., Baltes et al., 1977). There are two key components of this objective. First, a focus on intraindividual change centers attention on within-person variability and on systematic behavior change processes across the life span. Stability reflects one kind of change, namely, no change. It is recognized that all individuals do not manifest identical (or necessarily similar) patterns of within-person change. A source of variability in the patterns of within-person change may be attributable to interindividual differences, for instance in genetic make-up and/or the family environment. Over the course of the life span such interindividual differences, expressed and fostered in persons' interactions with variable environments, contribute to (and potentiate) alternative patterns of intraindividual change. Thus, the life-span approach attempts to identify common and unique features of human development that are manifest in time-ordered behavior change processes.

By lifelong process, reference is made to the notion that development does not cease after childhood or early adolescence, but continues across the life span, producing diverse developmental pathways. The diverse developmental pathways are influenced by shared and unique characteristics of individuals, and their contexts as individuals shape and are shaped by the range of physical and social contexts they encounter across time (e.g., Lerner & Busch-Rossnagel, 1981). Although this notion of development as a lifelong process may appear self-evident, it is important to note that an implicit, and perhaps explicit, assumption of much biomedical and social science research before the 1970s (and in some circles today) was that development from late adolescence through middle-to-late adulthood was characterized by stability, and that aging was characterized by inevitable decline. An abundance of literature exists today contradicting both stability claims of adult development and the inevitable decline among older adults (e.g., Baltes & Schaie, 1976; Labouvie-Vief, 1982; Neugarten, 1973).

A perspective emphasizing lifelong development may be relevant for the study of COAs in several ways. For example, there is considerable evidence that alcoholics manifest different drinking styles (episodic versus steady), with different patterns of associated behaviors (e.g., violence, passivity), for different lengths of time, and with differences in cessation, maintenance, and relapse patterns (e.g., Jacob & Leonard, 1988; Marlatt & Gordon, 1985). The relative disruptiveness of these variations in parental alcoholism on offspring's age-associated developmental tasks have not been examined systematically. That is, some developmentalists, such as Havighurst (1972) and Erikson (1959), have suggested that there are salient life tasks to be confronted and resolved at different stages of the life span. Middle childhood, for instance, is characterized by tasks such as learning to get along with agemates, developing concepts necessary for everyday living and developing a sense of morality and set of values, whereas adolescence is characterized by tasks such as establishing independence of parents, selecting and preparing for an occupation, and preparing for marriage and family life. Failure to resolve, or master, tasks at one developmental stage may serve to undermine, or at least delay, the successful resolution of tasks at later stages, thus disrupting one's sense of self-efficacy or perceived competence, and therefore disturbing basic person–environmental adaptational processes.

Therefore, the study of relations between features of parental alcoholism and their influence on COA adaptation to age-associated life tasks may facilitate the identification of which characteristics are most (and least) detrimental to COAs at specific ages with respect to which kinds of developmental tasks. Further, given comparable environmental "presses" (e.g., specific attributes of parental alcoholism), this paradigm facilitates the assessment of personal (e.g., temperament) and social (e.g., emotional support) factors that protect some persons from undesirable outcomes. This approach has been useful in studying children of divorce, where sex, age, and postdivorce relations with both parents have been found to influence psychosocial development and adjustment of offspring (e.g., Hetherington, Cox, & Cox, 1982). Within the COA literature, age of the COA respondent generally has been examined only with respect to age of onset of drinking. While age of onset of drinking may be a salient event to investigate, it would be beneficial to examine other age-associated features of development, including salient environmental characteristics (e.g., parental alcoholism characteristics) and their differential impact on various age-associated life tasks.

A second application that may benefit from the use of a life-span perspective is the study of adult children of alcoholics (ACOAs). Current estimates suggest that there are more than 22 million ACOAs (Woodside, 1988). However, current knowledge of the psychosocial functioning of ACOAs is based on two biased sample sources. One source is based on alcoholic treatment samples, where ACOAs are overrepresented. Alcoholic treatment samples represent only 10%–15% of all alcoholics (e.g., Vaillant, 1983), and measurement procedures for assessing parental alcoholism are often suspect; therefore, generalizability is limited (see Russell, Chapter 2). A second source is based on ACOAs attending self-help groups or obtaining professional therapy. Again generalizability is a major issue because those seeking assistance are not likely to be representative of the population of ACOAs (in fact, the majority attending such sessions are women, whereas the behavior genetic literature indicates that the majority of alcoholic COAs are men; see Searles, Chapter 5). Nevertheless, it is generally not disputed that at least some ACOAs may be encountering difficulties that are directly or indirectly related to being reared in an alcoholic family.

A life-span perspective may be beneficial in orienting one toward the difficulties of ACOAs in two ways. First, ACOAs can be envisioned in the context of multiple, age-associated life tasks and an assessment can be made of their current functioning with regard to these tasks. Second, by understanding the variations in parental alcoholism and the possible disruption of specific age-associated tasks, light may be shed on some of the current difficulties. For example, problems in establishing intimate relations with a significant other may be associated with a failure to resolve critical issues or to attain appropriate social skills during a period in childhood or adolescence when parental alcoholism had its most detrimental impact. Although parental alcoholism (or divorce or death of a parent) may alter the conditions necessary to optimally master salient age-associated life tasks, many persons still manage to do so, either with or without some delay. The study of interindividual differences and patterns of intraindividual change may facilitate the investigation of unique life histories and the understanding of different developmental patterns that result in some ACOAs having difficulties in adulthood while others remain well adjusted.

Multidimensionality, Multidirectionality, and Multiple Causality

These three concepts suggest that human development is best viewed as a multivariate endeavor, consisting of the study of multiple constructs that may each manifest different rates of change and alternative developmental forms (multidirectionality), and that many variables of scientific interest are likely to be caused by multiple factors. If behavior is studied over time, this implies that the use of multivariate statistical models will facilitate the study of time-ordered structural relations between multiple causes and multiple effects. The chapters in this volume have identified a number of variables that can be considered vulnerability or risk factors. In evaluating these vulnerability factors it is important to consider their presumed causal status and the possibilities of their conjoint influences. The life-span developmental view facilitates this effort by emphasizing the multivariate nature of causes and effects across multiple levels of the organism (e.g., Lerner, 1984) and by recognizing that the presumed risk of assumed vulnerability factors may vary across the life span.

With regard to vulnerability factors identified for COAs, it is possible that some of these (e.g., low-amplitude P300 response, lower serum prolactin levels following an ethanol challenge, hyperactivity) may be conceptualized as putative causal variables, whereas others may be simply viewed as indicators or identifiers, without any attendant causal status. For instance, if the low-amplitude P300 response characterizes the cortical response pattern of male COAs (e.g., Begleiter, Porjesz, Bihari, & Kissin, 1984), does this reflect a causal agent that, if somehow reversed (i.e., P300 response amplitude increased), would decrease alcoholic risk for COAs? Or does the low-amplitude P300 response serve as a more generalized indicator of neurological dysfunction, possibly through some polygenic pattern that, in and of itself, has no direct explanatory value with regard to alcoholism among COAs or expresses itself only within the context of other putative causal factors?

It is useful to consider the causal status of vulnerability factors for two purposes. One is that it is desirable as a science to move beyond the study of descriptive differences between groups (e.g., COAs and nonCOAs), toward the investigation of causal explanatory processes and mechanisms. A second purpose is that in developing our conceptual models and research strategies, it is likely that the study of the interrelationships and conjoint influences of risk factors will become more prevalent, with the probable consequence of increasing the precision of prediction. That is, in disentangling alternative developmental pathways to alcoholism among COAs, it is important to understand the nature of the possible multiple causes (e.g., Hilborn & Stearns, 1982). For example, it would be useful to establish a taxonomy of necessary and sufficient conditions for the occurrence of alcoholism or its subtypes. Not all risk factors are likely to be involved in the expression of alcoholism among COAs, but knowing which ones are associated with which specific patterns could facilitate our understanding of heterogeneous etiological pathways and contribute to differential programs of prevention and intervention.

Plasticity of Development

Lerner (1984) has referred to plasticity as "the evolutionary and ontogenetic processes by which one develops one's capacity to modify one's behavior to adjust to, or fit, the demands of a particular context" (p. 10). Lerner (1984) and Gollin (1981) provided extensive reviews of literature indicating the plasticity of human behavior at multiple levels of analysis (e.g., neuronal, neurochemical) and across the life span. (This is not to suggest unbridled plasticity, because constraints are imposed by both nature and nurture.) Further, evidence is provided by Lerner and by Gollin that suggests that there may be (critical) periods in the life span during which some behaviors are more malleable or plastic than at others.

There are four important implications associated with this conceptualization of plasticity. First, developmental change occurs across the life span, though there are individual differences in rates of change and highest levels attained as a function of intraindividual functioning. Second, there is heterogeneity associated with behaviors for any age group because of initial differences, variability in developmental timing, and within-person variability. Third, there are distinct behavioral domains that have different rates and particular features of developmental change. As such, *domain specificity* is required in the design, timing, and implementation of preventions and interventions. Fourth, intervention has the potential to influence change positively in planned and unplanned ways as well as, inadvertently, negatively. This is commonly referred to as a double-edged sword because it is sometimes difficult to foresee how changes in one behavior may, in addition or instead, produce undesirable changes in other behaviors.

The implications of the plasticity concept for COA research are multiple. The consequences of events in childhood (e.g., events associated with parental alcoholism) are continually transformed by later experiences and thus persons are perceived as capable of overcoming adversities associated with an alcoholic rearing environment. There are, of course, individual differences in nature and nurture constraints, and manifestations in patterns of intraindividual change. The critical periods concept, which is still in need of further study with respect to human behaviors across the life span, may be useful in identifying specific periods during which COAs may be particularly vulnerable to developmental disruption. The notion of distinct behavioral domains, possibly each with its own developmental trajectory, suggests differential vulnerability for specific risk factors (e.g., neuropsychological vulnerability, temperament vulnerability) at different points in the life span (e.g., early childhood hyperactivity, early adolescent neuropsychological dysfunction); similarly, alternative prevention and intervention efforts may target specific age-associated behavioral domains. Finally, concern with the double-edged sword of prevention and intervention is especially pertinent to COAs because the development of early COA awareness programs of alcoholic risk could, if not sensitively and accurately presented, contribute to the establishment and expression of self-fulfilling prophecies. A similar concern has been expressed with regard to ACOAs, in that current adult nonalcoholic problems (e.g., poor interpersonal relations, low self-esteem) may be inaccurately attributed to being the child of an alcoholic. To the extent that such causal attributions are viewed as legitimizing one's current state of subjective distress and helplessness, they may undermine efforts to correctly identify and properly treat the sources of discomfort.

Historical Embeddedness

This concept refers to the bidirectional (though not necessarily symmetric) relationships between individual development (ontogenesis) and evolutionary development, with the latter reflected concurrently in biocultural change (e.g., Baltes, 1987; Riegel, 1975). More simply stated (at the expense of a more expanded account of long-term evolutionary development and its interrelatedness with ontogenesis), this concept refers to the fact that persons develop in specific sociohistorical periods. Further, they influence and are influenced by particulars of that period that may differentiate their developmental pattern from that of persons living in other historical periods. Similarly, major historical events (e.g., wars, natural disasters) may be differentially consequential for development, depending on characteristics (e.g., age, sex) of persons living in the same historical period. In the latter case, studies have been conducted to examine such differences, for example in Elder's (1974) study of the life-span development of children and adolescents after the Great Depression. In a related vein, sociologists and developmental psychologists often have studied cohort differences in personality, intelligence, and other social factors to assess the respective influences of historical cohort and age factors (e.g., Nesselroade & Baltes, 1974; Riley, 1976; Schaie, 1970).

The significance of the concept of historical embeddedness is pertinent to COA research for three reasons. First, in two studies cited by Russell (Chapter 3), secular trends were observed in the ages at which alcohol-related problems arose. Robins et al. (1984) reported that the life-time prevalence of alcohol abuse and dependence was higher among those under 44 years of age than those over 44 years. In a study of alcoholism among COAs, Reich, Cloninger, Van Eerdewegh, Rice, and Mullaney (1988) found that transmission was highest for the youngest cohorts and that the relatives of the younger cohort of alcoholics had a higher life-time prevalence of alcoholism and an earlier age of onset than the relatives of the older cohort of alcoholics. These cohort differences suggest that nongenetic sociohistorical influences contributed to the differential rates for the respective younger and older cohorts. A range of factors could be implicated in such cohort differences, including the availability and price of alcoholic substances, the glamorization of alcohol on television and radio, and the extensiveness of drug use in the culture. All of these factors are features of the sociohistorical context in which individual development occurs and which may influence alcoholic risk among COAs.

A second reason that historical embeddedness may be a useful concept for COA research is that not only are characteristics relating directly to alcohol consumption increasing, but other secular trends may exacerbate conditions that directly or indirectly influence alcoholic risk. For example, secular changes in the composition of families, including single-parent households and higher divorce rates, may contribute to familial stress and dysfunction through poverty, lack of parental role models, or insufficient social support. Smaller family sizes may reduce potential sources of (sibling) support among COAs as well as reduce the number of potential targets of physical or emotional abuse by an alcoholic parent. The lack of respectable wage employment opportunities for high-school dropouts and non-college-bound adolescents in contemporary society may contribute to the selection of higher paying pursuits, such as selling drugs, which indeed may increase alcoholic risk.

A third reason that historical embeddedness may be a useful concept for COA research is that it views persons as influential agents in shaping, to some extent, historical conditions. This view contrasts sharply with some perspectives in which persons are viewed as passive recipients of ongoing historical conditions, or as influential actors within their own spheres of life, but impotent to influence larger sociohistorical conditions either individually or collectively.

In sum, sociohistorical conditions provide an active, and to some extent malleable, background for individual development. The investigation of sources of variation associated with cohort differences and secular trends may facilitate the understanding of alcoholic expression or nonexpression among COAs by using a broader sociohistorical backdrop to evaluate stability and change of alcoholic behavior.

Contextualism

In addition to general sociohistorical conditions and their contextual influences on human development, three other classes of salient life events have been identified (e.g., Baltes, 1987; Lerner, 1984). The first is referred to as *normative age-graded events*, and they are characterized by their age-associated sequences and commonality of directionality across individuals. Features of biological maturation (e.g., onset of puberty, menopause) and age-associated socialization events (e.g., beginning school, marriage, retirement) exemplify such age-graded events. *History-graded events* are salient occurrences (eg., war, epidemics) that may have both short- and long-term effects on sociocultural conditions and on individual development. *Nonnormative events* are salient occurrences that are not typical for many persons and are not clearly associated with either ontogenesis or general sociohistorical events (e.g., accidents, illnesses, divorce).

The study of normative age-graded events is significant for COAs to the extent that COAs are "off-time" with regard to age-graded events and that the consequences of this are meaningful (e.g., Neugarten & Hagestad, 1987; Riley, 1976). History-graded events are significant to the extent that these have differential consequences for COAs. However, it is the study of nonnormative events that we propose may be of most interest to COA investigators. There are two reasons for this. First, the families of at least some COAs are likely to be exposed to an increased range of familial stressors (multiproblem families) because of parental alcoholism (e.g., parental job loss, low income, violence in some instances, marital conflict) and are, therefore, likely to experience an increased number of nonnormative events (e.g., divorce, family violence, police contact). The psychosocial developmental significance of some nonnormative events may be quite substantial, and may impede psychosocial development and adjustment. Thus, the etiologic focus for COAs and ACOAs shifts from a sole focus on parental alcoholism toward person–environmental processes associated with nonnormative life events (e.g., physical or sexual abuse) that may have significantly altered psychosocial development.

The second reason that nonnormative life events may be of interest to COA investigators is related to some recent research findings in behavior genetics (Plomin, 1986, 1989; Plomin & Daniels, 1987). The phenotypic variance of traits in behavior genetic models can be conceptualized as consisting of three substantive components—hereditary, shared (familial) environmental influences, and nonshared environmental influences. On the basis of data regarding sibling similarity, Plomin concluded that (1) children reared in the same family are not very similar; (2) siblings are more likely to be different than similar with regard to several domains of psychology (e.g., personality, cognitive abilities, psychopathology); (3) family environment does not contribute to similarities that do exist between siblings; and (4) environmental influences appear to operate on an individual-by-individual basis (or are attributable to nonshared environmental influences). Similar results were also recently obtained for a sample of older adults using an adoption/twin design to compare temperamental similarity for monozygotic and dizygotic twins reared together and reared apart (Plomin, Pedersen, McClearn, Nesselroade, & Bergeman, 1988). Twins reared together showed no greater similarity than twins reared apart, and environmental variation was attributable to nonshared sources. The implication of this sibling research is that familial and nonfamilial experiential factors are differentially influencing a range of behaviors for individual siblings, and that familial (and nonfamilial) influences are not uniformly influencing the behaviors of siblings in the same family.

This focus on nonshared environmental influences as significant factors in individual development dovetails, to some degree, with the concept of non-normative events in the life-span perspective (Plomin, 1986). That is, both highlight the role of unique environmental events or factors that may contribute to variable developmental pathways. For COAs, unique environmental factors, of which nonnormative events may be one class, may account for some of the variation in developmental pathways toward and away from alcoholism. Future research should be directed toward the identification of nonnormative events and the developmental processes they influence and are influenced by.

Development as a Multidisciplinary Endeavor

This proposition identifies the limitations of any singular discipline to account adequately for human development, or in this instance, for the development of alcoholism among COAs. A multidisciplinary approach has generally character-ized the field of alcohol studies, with contributions from disciplines such as epidemiology, molecular genetics, biochemistry, pharmacology, neuropsycholo-gy, psychophysiology, clinical psychology, sociology, and anthropology. There-fore, the conceptual orientation of a life-span developmental perspective is highly compatible with the field of alcohol studies. There are, nevertheless, two major directions suggested by the life-span perspective that currently have received relatively little attention among alcohol researchers in general, and COA researchers in particular.

First, most research has tended to focus on one level of analysis, rather than investigating interlevel relations (e.g., Lerner, 1984; Riegel, 1975; Schneirla, 1957). For example, epidemiological research has tended to collect extensive data on alcohol use and alcohol problems via self-report (or interview) methods and has excluded data pertaining to family functioning, personalty attributes, biochemical parameters, etc. (Admittedly, there are some practical con-siderations involved in collecting multiple-level data with general population samples, but it may be possible to select subgroups, based on defining character-istics such as family history of alcoholism, and do more intensive and extensive measurement.) Similarly, some family-oriented alcoholism research has ex-cluded the assessment of temperament attributes, even though such attributes may be influential in determining interactional patterns and other features of family functioning (e.g., Belsky, Lerner, & Spanier, 1984; Rutter, 1988; Tho-mas & Chess, 1977). Most COA research in temperament has also excluded measurements of family functioning, even though it is possible that given temperament attributes may be most highly associated with problem drinking in particular kinds of families (e.g., subsumptive families or families in which inconsistent discipline or coercive parental management styles are used). Studies such as those completed by Sher and Levenson (1982) and Finn and Pihl (1987), and those proposed by Cloninger (1987) and Tarter et al. (1985, and see Chapter 4) exemplify approaches that seek to investigate interlevel relationships between biological–biochemical variables (e.g., heart rate, levels of neurotransmitter substances) and personality functioning in terms of alcoholic behaviors.

It is important to note that by studying interlevel relationships we are not proposing a radical reductionistic philosophy (e.g., Bunge & Ardila, 1987). That is, we are not proposing that family functioning can be reduced to temperamental functioning, which in turn can be reduced to biochemistry, etc. Rather, we propose that there are emergent properties at various levels of analysis that do not yield to explanation by *sole reference* to constituent elements at a lower level in the hierarchy. What we are saying is that such interlevel relationships are related to varying degrees, depending on the specific behavior selected for study, and that a more comprehensive understanding of the expression of alcoholism in COAs and nonCOAs may be facilitated by investigating these interlevel relationships.

A second research direction implied by the adoption of a multidisciplinary life-span approach is the study of multiple variable influences over time. Although there have been a limited number of multivariate longitudinal research design studies with COAs, this limitation has been duly noted and studies are under way that will help clarify the heterogeneous developmental pathways of COAs. Furthermore, properly designed and implemented studies may facilitate the resolution of some perennial issues in alcoholism (e.g., whether personality is a cause or a consequence of alcoholism) and contribute to a better understanding of cross-temporal patterns of stability and change.

CONCLUSIONS

The study of COAs has engaged a range of researchers and practitioners from many different metatheoretical orientations and disciplines. The previous chapters in this volume have provided reviews and evaluations of specific domains of COA research, assessing both conceptual models and empirical data. This final chapter provides a list of some of the common themes that emerged across two or more of the chapters. We propose that these commonalities are significant in identifying central concerns of COA research and that they may assist in providing guidance for future research. A life-span developmental perspective was also presented as a vehicle to assist in the organization and integration of current COA research and in positing some future research questions. The multidisciplinary focus of the life-span developmental perspective was viewed as highly compatible with research being conducted in alcohol studies, as was the emphasis on multivariate longitudinal research designs. In closing, we propose that COA research is still in its infancy as a research domain, but that the early development can be characterized as healthy. With further fostering by a range of multidisciplinary researchers and practitioners, we look forward to the maturation of the COA field.

REFERENCES

Alterman, A. I., Searles, J. S., & Hall, J. G. (1989). Failure to find differences in drinking behavior as a function of familial risk for alcoholism: A replication. *Journal of Abnormal Psychology, 98*, 1–4.

Anthony, E. J., & Cohler, B. J. (Eds.). (1987). *The invulnerable child.* New York: Guilford.

Antonovsky, A. (1979). *Health, stress, and coping.* San Francisco: Jossey-Bass.

Baltes, P. B. (1987). Theoretical propositions of life-span developmental psychology: On the dynamics between growth and decline. *Developmental Psychology, 23*, 611–626.

Baltes, P. B., Reese, H. W., & Nesselroade, J. R. (1977). *Life-span developmental psychology: Introduction to research methods.* Monterey, CA: Brooks/Cole.

Baltes, P. B., & Schaie, K. W. (1976). On the plasticity of intelligence in adulthood and old age: Where Horn and Donaldson fail. *American Psychologist, 31*, 720–725.

Begleiter, H., Porjesz, B., Bihari, B., & Kissin, B. (1984). Event-related brain potentials in boys at risk for alcoholism. *Science, 225*, 1493–1496.

Belsky, J., Lerner, R. M., & Spanier, G. B. (1984). *The child in the family.* Reading, MA: Addison–Wesley.

Bentler, P. M. (1985). *Theory and implementation of EQS, a structural equations program.* Los Angeles: BMDP Statistical Software.

Boomsma, D. I., & Moleanaar, P. C. M. (1986). Using LISREL to analyze genetic and environmental covariate structure. *Behavior Genetics, 16*, 237–250.

Bunge, M., & Ardila, R. (1987). *Philosophy of psychology.* New York: Springer-Verlag.

Chalmers, D. M., Chanarin, I., MacDermott, S., & Levi, A. J. (1980). Sex-related differences in the haematological effects of excessive alcohol consumption. *Journal of Clinical Pathology, 33*, 3–7.

Chi, I., Lubben, J. E., & Kitano, H. H. L. (1989). Differences in drinking behavior among three Asian-American groups. *Journal of Studies on Alcohol, 50*, 15–23.

Cloninger, C. R. (1987). Neurogenetic adaptive mechanisms in alcoholism. *Science, 236*, 410–416.

Cloninger, C. R., Bohman, M., & Sigvardsson, S. (1981). Inheritance of alcohol abuse: Cross fostering analysis of adopted men. *Archives of General Psychiatry, 38*, 861–868.

Elder, G. H., Jr. (1974). *Children of the Great Depression.* Chicago: University of Chicago Press.

Erikson, E. H. (1959). *Identity and the life cycle* (Psychological Issues Monograph No. 1). New York: International Universities Press.

Finn, P. R., & Pihl, R. O. (1987). Men at high risk for alcoholism: The effect of alcohol on cardiovascular response to unavoidable shock. *Journal of Abnormal Psychology, 96*, 230–236.

Garmezy, N., & Rutter, M. (1983). *Stress, coping, and development in children.* New York: McGraw-Hill.

Gelfand, D. M., & Peterson, L. (1985). *Child development and psychopathology.* Beverly HIlls, CA: Sage.

Gollin, E. S. (1981). Development and plasticity. In E. S. Gollin (Ed.), *Behavioral and biological aspects of variations in development* (pp. 231–251). New York: Academic Press.

Goodwin, D. W., Schulsinger, F., Hermansen, L., Guze, S. B., & Winokur, G. (1973). Alcohol problems in adoptees raised apart from alcoholic biological parents. *Archives of General Psychiatry, 34*, 751–755.

Havighurst, R. J. (1972). *Developmental tasks and education* (3rd ed.). New York: McKay. (Original work published in 1948)

Hetherington, E. M., Cox, M., & Cox, R. (1982). Effects of divorce on parents and children. In M. E. Lamb (Ed.), *Nontraditional families: Parenting and child development* (pp. 233–288). Hillsdale, NJ: Erlbaum.

Hilborn, R., & Stearns, S. C. (1982). On inference in ecology and evolutionary biology: The problem of multiple causes. *Acta Biotheoretica, 31,* 145–164.

Jacob, T. (1987). Alcoholism: A family interaction perspective. In P. C. Rivers (Ed.), *Nebraska symposium on motivation, 1986: Vol. 34. Alcohol and addictive behaviors* (pp. 159–206). Lincoln: University of Nebraska Press.

Jacob, T., & Leonard, K. (1988). Alcoholic–spouse interaction as a function of alcoholism subtype and alcohol consumption interaction. *Journal of Abnormal Psychology, 97,* 231–237.

Jöreskog, K. G., & Sörbom, D. (1984). *LISREL VI: Analysis of linear structural relationships by maximum likelihood, instrumental variables, and least squares methods.* Mooresville, IN: Scientific Software.

Kazdin, A. E. (1987). *Conduct disorders in childhood and adolescence.* Beverly Hills, CA: Sage.

Labouvie-Vief, G. (1982). Dynamic development and mature autonomy: A theoretical prologue. *Human Development, 25,* 161–191.

Lerner, J. V., & Lerner, R. M. (1983). Temperament and adaptation across life: Theoretical and empirical issues. In P. B. Baltes & O. G. Brim, Jr. (Eds.), *Life-span development and behavior* (Vol. 5, pp. 197–231). New York: Academic Press.

Lerner, R. M. (1984). *On the nature of human plasticity.* New York: Cambridge University Press.

Lerner, R. M., & Busch-Rossnagel, N. A. (1981). Individuals as producers of their development: Conceptual and empirical bases. In R. Lerner & N. Busch-Rossnagel (Eds.), *Individuals as producers of their development: A life-span perspective* (pp. 1–36). New York: Academic Press.

Marlatt, G. A., & Gordon, J. R. (Eds.). (1985). *Relapse prevention: Maintenance strategies in the treatment of addictive behaviors.* New York: Guilford.

Moleanaar, P. C. M., & Boomsma, D. I. (1987). Application of nonlinear factor analysis to genotype-environment interaction. *Behavior Genetics, 17,* 71–80.

Nesselroade, J. R., & Baltes, P. B. (1974). Adolescent personality development and historical change: 1970–1972. *Monographs of the Society for Research in Child Development, 39* (1, Serial No. 154).

Nesselroade, J. R., & Baltes, P. B. (Eds.). (1979). *Longitudinal research in the study of behavior and development.* New York: Academic Press.

Neugarten, B. L. (1973). Personality change in late life: A developmental perspective. In C. Eisdorfer & M. P. Lawton (Eds.), *The psychology of adult development and aging* (pp. 311–335). Washington, DC: American Psychological Association.

Neugarten, B. L., & Hagestad, G. O. (1976). Age and the life course. In R. H. Binstock & E. Shanas (Eds.), *Handbook of aging and the social sciences* (pp. 35–55). New York: Van Nostrand Reinhold.

Peele, S. (Ed.) (1985). *The meaning of addiction: A compulsive experience and its interpretation.* Lexington, MA: Lexington Books.

Plomin, R. (1986). *Development, genetics, and psychology.* Hillsdale, NJ: Erlbaum.

Plomin, R. (1989). Environment and genes: Determinants of behavior. *American Psychologist, 44,* 105–111.

Plomin, R., & Daniels, D. (1987). Why are two children in the same family so different from each other? *Behavioral and Brain Sciences, 10,* 1–16.

Plomin, R., Pedersen, N. L., McClearn, G. E., Nesselroade, J. R., & Bergeman, C. S. (1988). EAS temperaments during the last half of the life span: Twins reared apart and twins reared together. *Psychology and Aging, 3,* 43–50.

Reich, T., Cloninger, C. R., Van Eerdewegh, P., Rice, J. P., & Mullaney, J. (1988). Secular trends in the familial transmission of alcoholism. *Alcoholism: Clinical and Experimental Research, 12,* 458–464.

Riegel, K. F. (1975). Toward a dialectical theory of development. *Human Development, 18,* 50–64.

Riley, M. W. (1976). Age strata in social systems. In R. H. Binstock & E. Shanas (Eds.), *Handbook of aging and the social sciences* (pp. 189–217). New York: Van Nostrand Reinhold.

Robins, L. N., Helzer, J. E., Weissman, M. M., Orvaschel, H., Gruenberg, H., Burke, J. D., Jr., & Regier, D. A. (1984). Lifetime prevalence of specific psychiatric disorders in three sites. *Archives of General Psychiatry, 41,* 948–959.

Rutter, M. (1987). Psychosocial resilience and protective mechanisms. *American Journal of Orthopsychiatry, 57,* 316–331.

Rutter, M. (1988). Epidemiological approaches to developmental psychopathology. *Archives of General Psychiatry, 45,* 486–495.

Scarr, S., & McCartney, K. (1983). How people make their own environments: A theory of genotype × environment effects. *Child Development, 54,* 424–435.

Schaie, K. W. (1970). A reinterpretation of age-related changes in cognitive structure and functioning. In R. L. Goulet & P. B. Baltes (Eds.), *Life-span developmental psychology: Research and theory* (pp. 485–507). New York: Academic Press.

Schneirla, T. (1957). The concept of development in comparative psychology. In D. Harris (Ed.), *The concept of development.* Minneapolis: University of Minnesota Press.

Sher, K. J., & Levenson, R. W. (1982). Risk for alcoholism and individual differences in the stress-response-dampening effect of alcohol. *Journal of Abnormal Psychology, 91,* 350–368.

Tarter, R. E., Alterman, A. I., & Edwards, K. L. (1985). Vulnerability to alcoholism in men: A behavior genetic perspective. *Journal of Studies on Alcohol, 46,* 329–356.

Thomas, A., & Chess, S. (1977). *Temperament and development.* New York: Brunner/Mazel.

Thomas, A., & Chess, S. (1981). The role of temperament in the contributions of individuals to their development. In R. M. Lerner & N. Busch-Rossnagel (Eds.), *Individuals as producers of their development* (pp. 231–255). New York: Academic Press.

Vaillant, G. E. (1983). *The natural history of alcoholism.* Cambridge, MA: Harvard University Press.

Werner, E. E. (1986). Resilient offspring of alcoholics: A longitudinal study from birth to age 18. *Journal of Studies on Alcohol, 47,* 34–40.

Wolin, S. J., Bennett, L. A., & Noonan, D. L. (1979). Family rituals and the recurrence of alcoholism over generations. *American Journal of Psychiatry, 136,* 589–593.

Woodside, M. (1988). Research on children of alcoholics: Past and future. *British Journal of Addiction, 83,* 785–792.

Zucker, R. A. (1976). Parental influences upon drinking patterns of their children. In M. Greenblatt & M. A. Schuckit (Eds.), *Alcoholism problems in women and children* (pp. 211–238). New York: Grune & Stratton.

Zucker, R. A. (1987). The four alcoholisms: A developmental account of the etiologic process. In P. C. Rivers (Ed.), *Nebraska symposium on motivation, 1986: Vol. 34. Alcohol and addictive behaviors* (pp. 27–84). Lincoln: University of Nebraska Press.

Index